Men's Bodies, Men's Gods

Men's Bodies, Men's Gods

Male Identities in a (Post-) Christian Culture

Edited by

BJÖRN KRONDORFER

NEW YORK UNIVERSITY PRESS
New York and London

NEW YORK UNIVERSITY PRESS
New York and London

© 1996 by New York University

Library of Congress Cataloging-in-Publication Data
Men's bodies, men's gods : male identities in a (post-) Christian
   culture / edited by Björn Krondorfer.
      p.   cm.
   Includes bibliographical references and index.
   ISBN 0-8147-4668-3.—ISBN 0-8147-4669-1 (pbk.)
      1. Men (Christian theology)   2. Body, Human—Religious aspects—
Christianity.   3. Men (Christian theology)—History of doctrines.
4. Body, Human—Religious aspects—Christianity—History of
doctrines.   I. Krondorfer, Björn.
   BT703.5.M46   1996
   233'.5'081—dc20   95-32466
                               CIP

New York University Press books are printed on acid-free paper, and their
binding materials are chosen for strength and durability.

Manufactured in the United States of America

10 9 8 7 6 5 4 3 2 1

For my sister in Vienna,
my brother in Berlin,
and others who inhabit
non-traditionally gendered worlds.

Contents

List of Illustrations   *xi*

Acknowledgments   *xiii*

Contributors   *xv*

PART I   Male Gender and Religion

1   Introduction   3
    BJÖRN KRONDORFER

2   Three Arguments for the Elimination of
    Masculinity   27
    SETH MIRSKY

PART II   Male Bodies and the Construction of
        Religious Identity

3   Growing Up Christian and Male: One Man's
    Experience   43
    TOM F. DRIVER

4   Black Bodies, Whose Body? African American
    Men in XODUS   65
    GARTH BAKER-FLETCHER

5   Empowerment: The Construction of Gay
Religious Identities   94
MICHAEL L. STEMMELER

PART III   Male Sexual Identity and the
Religious Body

6   Bringing Good News to the Body: Masturbation
and Male Identity   111
SCOTT HALDEMAN

7   Facing the Body on the Cross: A Gay Man's
Reflections on Passion and Crucifixion   125
ROBIN HAWLEY GORSLINE

PART IV   Male Friendships

8   Men and Christian Friendship   149
PHILIP L. CULBERTSON

9   "The Manly Love of Comrades": Mythico-
Religious Models for an Athletics of Male-
Male Friendship   181
WILLIAM G. DOTY

PART V   Men's Bodies in Contemporary Culture
and Religion

10   The Confines of Male Confessions: On Religion,
Bodies, and Mirrors   205
BJÖRN KRONDORFER

11   Can Men Worship? Reflections on Male Bodies
in Bad Faith and a Theology of Authenticity   235
LEWIS R. GORDON

12   The Masculinity of Jesus in Popular Religious Art   251
DAVID MORGAN

13   Baring the Flesh: Aspects of Contemporary
Male Iconography   267
WILLIAM G. DOTY

PART VI   Concluding Overview

14   Epilogue   311
     JAMES B. NELSON

     Index   319

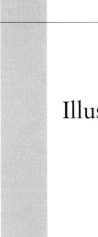

Illustrations

1. Warner Sallman, *Head of Christ*   252
2. Gustave Doré, *Jonathan and David*   254
3. Warner Sallman, *Christ Our Pilot*   256
4. Heinrich Hofmann, *Head of Christ*   262
5. Gianni Versace, advertisement   270
6. 2(x)ist, advertisement   273
7. 2(x)ist, advertisement   277
8. Liberto, Jean advertisement   287

Acknowledgments

Three years ago, I started to solicit manuscripts on the intersection of body, religion, and culture. I looked for scholars in religious studies and cognate areas willing to examine the cultural, religious, and social forces that have shaped male bodies and male identities in the Western tradition(s). Somewhat frustrated with the many new titles on neo-Jungian and archetypal approaches to male spirituality, I asked potential contributors to engage the issue of male gender in non-essentialist categories and to study male identities as part of a complex web of social relations, religious persuasions, spiritual experiences, sexual orientations, and racial differences.

Each contributor helped to define this book, and my special thanks, therefore, go to my colleagues who have taken up the challenge of mapping new terrains and exploring fresh possibilities in the interdisciplinary study of gender, religion, and culture. It was a pleasure to work with them, and I will remember many of our conversations.

I received helpful feedback from the working group on "Images of Masculinity" during the 1994 annual meeting of the *Society for Values in Higher Education* in Atlanta. I especially thank Tom Driver who, as chair of this working group, asked me to present a draft of my chapter on male confessional writings. The annual meetings of the American

Academy of Religion (AAR) became another forum where many of the scholars represented in this volume were able to exchange ideas on an informal basis. Stephen Boyd, co-chair of the "Men's Studies in Religion" group at the AAR, gave some helpful advise in the initial stages of the book.

I am especially indebted to Ruth Ost and Bobby Alexander who, despite other academic commitments, were able to find the time to correct my contributions and make important editorial suggestions. Thanks also to my wife Katharina von Kellenbach, a feminist and scholar in religion, who watched the progress of this book with a critical and supportive eye. Allison Berg directed me to some important resources on autobiography, and William Doty kept me abreast of new publications in men's studies.

Special thanks, too, to Jennifer Hammer, editor at New York University Press, who, from the start, believed in the book's relevance for continuing the discussion on gender.

Last not least, I am thinking of my daughter Zadekia who often imitated me by typing away on her own keyboard. She grew from a baby into a toddler while I completed this book.

BJÖRN KRONDORFER

Contributors

GARTH BAKER-FLETCHER is professor of Christian ethics at the School of Theology in Claremont, California. He is the author of *Somebodyness: Martin Luther King, Jr., and the Theory of Dignity* (Fortress Press, 1993).

PHILIP L. CULBERTSON is director of pastoral studies at St. John's Theological College in Auckland, New Zealand. He is the author of *The Pastor: Readings from the Patristic Period*; *New Adam: The Future of Masculine Spirituality*; *Counseling Men: A Caregiver's Guide to Men in Crisis* (all published by Fortress Press); and *A Word Fitly Spoken: Context, Transmission and Adoption of the Parables of Jesus* (State University of New York Press, 1994). He also has published over forty scholarly articles. He has been active in the men's movement since 1988, regularly leading conferences in America, Europe, and the South Pacific.

WILLIAM G. DOTY is professor of humanities in the department of religious studies at the University of Alabama/Tuscaloosa. He has contributed to many journals and published fifteen books in several fields, including *Myths of Masculinity* (Crossroad, 1993), *Mythical*

Trickster Figures (1993), *Picturing Cultural Values in Postmodern America* (University of Alabama Press, 1994), and a study of interdisciplinary education. He is the editor of *Mythosphere: A Journal for Image, Myth, and Symbol.*

T O M F. D R I V E R is the Paul Tillich professor of Theology and Culture Emeritus at Union Theological Seminary in New York, where he has been a faculty member since 1956. He has held visiting professorships at Fordham University, Vassar College, Barnard College, the University of Otaga in New Zealand, Doshisha University in Japan, and Columbia University. He has published extensively, and his most recent book is *The Magic of Ritual* (Harper Collins, 1991).

L E W I S R. G O R D O N teaches in the philosophy department and the African American Studies and Research Center at Purdue University. He is the author of *Bad Faith and Antiblack Racism* (The Humanities Press, 1995), and *Fanon and the Crisis of European Man* (Routledge, 1995), the editor of *Existence in Black* (Routledge, 1996), and co-editor of *Black Texts and Black Textuality* (forthcoming). He currently is completing *Her Majesty's Other Children,* which is a collection of his own essays and philosophical fiction.

R O B I N H A W L E Y G O R S L I N E is a doctoral candidate in systematic theology at Union Theological Seminary in New York. He identifies himself as a black-positive, white Anglican Unitarian Universalist Radical Faerie. His essay, "Let Us Bless Our Angels: A Pro-Feminist Gay Male Liberation View of Sodom," appears in *Redefining Sexual Ethics.* His research interests include the construction of sex and race in American culture and the relation of male violence and Christian theology.

S C O T T H A L D E M A N is a doctoral student at Union Theological Seminary in New York. He is interested in the social construction of religion, culture, sexuality, gender, race, and class. His chosen method is that of performance and ritual studies. His biggest challenge at present is to live into a world where his daughter will not fear the violence of sexism and heterosexism. His dissertation focuses on the problems and possibilities presented to the worship programs of U.S. churches by the multicultural realities of this nation.

B J Ö R N K R O N D O R F E R is visiting assistant professor of religious studies at St. Mary's College of Maryland. He is the author of *Remembrance and Reconciliation: Encounters Between Young Jews and Germans* (Yale University Press, 1995), and the editor of *Body and Bible: Interpreting and Experiencing Biblical Narratives* (Trinity Press, 1992). He has published in *Journal of Ritual Studies, Journal of Men's Studies, Literature and Theology, Christianity and Crisis, English Education,* among others. He also conducts Bibliodrama workshops and facilitates encounters between groups of (American) Jews and (non-Jewish) Germans. He enjoys parenting his daughter Zadekia.

S E T H M I R S K Y has worked for the past fifteen years on questions of feminism's implications for men. He works as a freelance editor and is a member of the steering committee for the Men's Studies in Religion Group of the American Academy of Religion. He received his B.A. at Wesleyan University and studied at Harvard Divinity School with Carol Christ, Sharon Welch, Katie Cannon, and Mieke Bal. He now lives in a cabin in the North Carolina woods with his partner.

D A V I D M O R G A N is assistant professor of art history and chairman of the Department of Art at Valparaiso University, Indiana. He recently directed a research project funded by the Lilly Endowment on the production and reception of mass-produced popular religious art. He authored and edited *Icons of American Protestantism: The Art of Warner Sallman* (Yale University Press, 1996), and has published articles in *Journal of the History of Ideas, Journal of Aesthetics and Art Criticism, European Romantic Review,* and *Religion and American Culture,* among others. He is currently a post-doctoral fellow in the Pew Program in Religion and American History at Yale and is working on a new book, *Imaging the Faith: Mass-Produced Imagery and American Protestant Piety, 1840–1960.*

J A M E S B . N E L S O N is professor emeritus of Christian ethics at the United Theological Seminary of the Twin Cities. His books include *Body Theology* (1992), *The Intimate Connection: Male Sexuality and Male Spirituality* (1988), *Between Two Gardens: Reflections on Sexuality and Religious Experience* (1983), and *Embodiment* (1978). Most recently, he co-edited with Sandra Longfellow the book *Sexuality and the Sacred*

(1994). He is also the author of numerous book chapters and journal articles, and served as a board member on many committees and task forces on issues of human sexuality, including the *Sex Information and Education Council of the U.S. (SIECUS),* and the State of Minnesota Task Force on AIDS.

MICHAEL L. STEMMELER is associate professor of religion at Central Michigan University. He has published in *Gay-Affirmative Ethics* (Monument Press, 1993) and edited with J. Michael Clark, *Spirituality and Community: Diversity in Lesbian and Gay Experience* (Monument Press, 1994), which includes his chapter on "Family in the Gay Nineties: The Explosion of a Concept." He was the co-chair of the Gay Men's Issues in Religion Group of the American Academy of Religion, and co-produced a video on the experience of gay life and homophobia on the college campus, *In Our Own Words* (Mt. Pleasant, 1992). He is currently working in the areas of gay spiritual identity formation and the ethics of non-traditional relationships.

PART I

Male Gender and Religion

Introduction

B J Ö R N   K R O N D O R F E R

The depiction of man as *homo religiosus* is not simply a semantic accident that excludes women. Rather, it reflects a social practice of Christianity in which male religious institutions, patriarchal authority, and masculine images of God have been dominant. The central Christian doctrines, rituals, and world views were formulated by men for men, and although not all men have enjoyed equal status within the Christian moral and political community, most were assured a privileged position within that universe or, at least, were rewarded if they were willing to conform. We cannot, of course, ignore class, religious, ethnic, or sexual differences among men that have led to numerous forms of repression and persecution of men in Christian history. We only need to recall the oppression of peasants during the feudal system, the persecution of heretics during the Inquisition, the enslavement of Africans during colonization, the antisemitic assault on Jews, and the homophobic retaliation against gender transgressors to realize how many men and women have been marginalized, victimized, and brutalized by the dominant forces of European Christian cultures.

Yet, the fact remains that the dominant traditions have always favored men. Gender-conscious and feminist scholars have repeatedly drawn our attention to the fact that men are normative in theological discourse and enjoy unrestrained access to positions of political, socio-economic, and sacred power. Usually, such patriarchal systems are misogynist in their portrayal of women and negative in their assessment of the body. Women and body, or women as body, are depicted as corrupt and evil. What modern interpretations often overlook, however, is that the male body itself is treated preferentially. After all, men's bodies are like God's body.

The authors of this volume, who are with two exceptions scholars in the field of religious studies, examine different aspects of the male body in the religious and cultural discourse in the history of Western Christianity. How are male bodies constructed in different historical periods and contexts? How is the male body represented in religious and cultural systems? How do race, ethnicity, and sexual preference impact on the intersection of male bodies and religious identity? Does Christianity provide models to cope with the aging and ailing male body? Does it provide models for intimacy between men and women, men and men? Do men see themselves as having a sexual body, a religious body, a social body? How is sexuality linked to spirituality? How do men reflect the carnal dimensions of power, abuse, and justice? These are the kind of questions that the authors of *Men's Bodies, Men's Gods* will raise and discuss.

To provide some context to the book, I will review a few selected themes on the construction and representation of the male gender in the history of Western Christianity.

Ascetics, Celibates, and Preachers

The gospels' proclamation of God becoming flesh through and in his son Jesus Christ is not gender-inclusive. The incarnation occurs in a specifically male body (notwithstanding its claim to universal significance), even if this body is viewed as asexual. To possess male genitalia has validated men's status as sole representative of Christ in the past, and in some churches this remains true to this day. Although theologians, visual artists, and iconoclasts have taken great pains in concealing the savior's pelvic nakedness—with the exception, perhaps, of the *ostentatio genitalium* in Renaissance art (albeit, the genitalia of only the Christ child and the dead Christ were unveiled; see Steinberg 1983)—the ecclesiastical traditions leave little doubt about the centrality of Christ's maleness. Those who have tried to interpret the sex and gender of God's son differently have been punished and marginalized. Whenever women have tried to represent God's son and, hence, move into positions of sacred authority, they were met with fierce resistance. Whether we look at the erasure of women's participation in the leadership of the early church (Fiorenza 1984; Torjesen 1993; Clark 1983), at the mystical visions of medieval women in which they asserted a direct relationship to Christ's body, thus bypassing the restricted access to the eucharist (Bynum 1987), or at contemporary battles over women's ordination, gender has always been a source of conflicts. The recent controversy over a small religious theater company, which cast a female Jesus in a performance during Pope John Paul II's visit to Denver in 1993, reminds us of the anxiety over the "correct" gender representation of Christ. Conservative Catholics called the performance "an assault on a very central doctrine, not only of the Catholic church, but of Christianity," while more liberal voices praised the play, arguing, like Sister Maureen Fiedler, coordinator of Catholics Speak Out, that if one represents "Jesus crucified, I can't think of anyone better in the church than a woman" (Niebuhr 1993).

Early Christian movements experimented with gender-variant behavior and equality of the sexes by manipulating the body. Some groups, such as the Encratites, renounced sexuality. Their practice of sexual continence allowed men and women to talk, travel, and live freely together. But the idea of continence did not gain enough support among the masses of antiquity. To renounce sexuality and live in poverty was a price that only few were willing to pay for a new eschatological vision and gender equality. Other groups, such as the Gnostics, tried to undo the separation of body and matter, man and woman, by developing androgynous images. Gnostic circles, for example, did not assign redemptive power to the continent body itself but, instead, emphasized the need for a spiritual cure with the help of the "feminine" principle of sophia (cf. Brown 1988; Meeks 1974, 1993). This is, perhaps, why the androgynous idealism of Gnosticism, even to this day, has appealed to a few spiritually curious men experimenting with gender variance (Conner 1993; Noble 1992). But it is important to remember that the Gnostics did not celebrate the body. Rather, they strove to become indifferent to it. Ever since Adam, according to the Gnostic myth, human bodies were the work of an inferior creation, a view that resulted in a "moral emptying of the body's significance" (Meeks 1993: 138) and left the body with "little value as a declaratory agent" (Brown 1988: 110). Certainly, Gnosticism did not escape androcentric imagery. The noncanonical, gnostic Gospel of Thomas ends with Simon Peter's demand that women leave the community of disciples, to which Jesus replies, "For every woman who will make herself male will enter the Kingdom of Heaven" (Cameron 1982: 37). The text leaves no room for doubt: redemption lies in the male body, and the androgynous union will only take place in the spiritual realm.

Despite the existence of such groups as the Encratites and the Gnostics, the patriarchal Christian household, which modeled itself after the Roman *pater familias,* became the norm. Gender division was eventually reintroduced into ascetic practices: men's celibacy and women's virginity became models of spirituality that were no longer based on gender equality. This development coincided with the strengthening of a dualistic theology that equated maleness with soul and spirit and femaleness with body and matter (cf. Ruether 1974; Nelson 1978). Such a body-mind dualism, however, does not ignore the male flesh. On the contrary: though it is true that matter, body, and women were perceived as obstacles to men's spiritual liberation from the darkness of sin, Christianity's dualism and misogyny did not render the male body insignificant. Paradoxically, the male body remained men's spiritual battleground.

The issue of asceticism is a case in point. The early male ascetic wanted to free himself from social norms and biological necessities by manipulating the body at its most basic level: food and sexuality. For example, the desert fathers of the third century went into remote areas and refused any natural sustenance to the body. Athanasius reported that St. Antony thought he would blush if he were seen eating by others (Athanasius 1980: 65). Shame prevented those men from swallowing food and spilling semen. Literally and metaphorically, the bodies of the desert fathers dried up as their spirits began to flow—if only in the nightmarish state of *adiaphoria,* in which they experienced the breaking down of boundaries between "man and desert, human and beast" (Brown 1988: 220).

As much as the ascetics worked on effacing the sexual function of the penis, they did not escape phallocentric practices. For male ascetics, the ability to imitate Christ required physical likeness, warranted in the male body. But Christ's body differed from their bodies in regard to spiritual perfection: Christ's body had not been touched by sin and desire while they experienced daily temptations. *Imitatio Christi* meant to live in a male body without masculine desires, a struggle that was impossible to win.

The unruly erectility of the penis constantly reminded men of their weakness. For Augustine, man's lack of control over his vital organ was a sign of humanity's inherent sinfulness. Even renunciation of sexuality did not help man to gain total control over lust. Nocturnal emissions offered conclusive proof. Augustine, like many celibate men before and after him, was bewildered by nocturnally recurring, sensual memories which moved from the realm of dreams straight down to the pelvis. After confessing to involuntary carnal emissions, Augustine, exasperated, prayed to God, "Grieve at my imperfect state . . . and perfect in me your mercies to achieve perfect peace" (1992: 204; see Miles 1992). The ultimate control of male virility was not in man's power but subject to God's mercy.

Despite the projections of male desires onto female bodies and despite men's fantasies about women's seductive power—themes that run through much of Christian literature—men's spiritual struggles were fought within and against their own bodies. The differently bodied woman was excluded from the despair and glory of male-embodied, ascetic practices. The denial of the penis—even in the most radical form of castration, a route Origin, for example, had taken (Brown 1988: 168)—did not remove the spiritual significance of the phallus.

Controlling one's body through asceticism and sexual renunciation, though popular among Christians in the first centuries, was not a model that could ultimately compete with the sexual regulations, gender divisions, and hierarchies of the evolving Christian household and Catholic church. The married Christian householder continued to use the body as sign of his or her moral and political commitments (Meeks 1993), but the more radical forms of bodily practices by which early Christian circles had achieved ritual visibility (e.g., extreme asceticism, celibacy, perpetual virginity, libertine rites) were pushed to the margins and declared heretical.

Ascetic practices, however, survived. They were either adjusted to or separated from the normative codes of the household movement. For example, virginity, as a form of female asceticism, turned into the elaborate cult of the Virgin Mary (Kristeva 1986; Warner 1976) which no longer required perpetual virginity of all daughters of the Christian household. The adoration of the Virgin became compatible with the institution of marriage, thus easing the householder's fear that the practice of continence would disrupt his *oikonomia*. Male asceticism, on the other hand, was channeled into a celibate clergy and monastic orders, while the Christian householder was allowed to engage in a restrained but licit sexual life. As Christianity evolved, the married laity was separated from a celibate clergy—a process that was not completed until the twelfth century, and perhaps not until the sixteenth century, against the bitter complaints of married priests (cf. Barstow 1982; Ranke-Heinemann 1990; Lea 1907).

Yet, a fundamental conflict remained. The theological insistence on the simultaneity of Jesus' maleness and Christ's asexuality seems to have been experienced as a continuous source of frustration, for it produced a paradoxical notion of male spirituality by insisting on phallic power while denying the sexual penis. The only perfect man, Pope Gregory I wrote in the seventh century, is "the one who manages not to burn amidst the fire" (quoted in Ranke-Heinemann 1990: 142). The inevitable psychodynamic tension could only be resolved by entrenching patriarchal power in the ecclesia on the one hand and counterbalancing it with gender-variant imagery, rituals, and symbolizations on the other. This would explain, for example, why, in an all male institution, Christ was time and again represented in highly sensuous and androgynous images. Whether we look at paintings from the fourteenth and fifteenth centuries, the Sacred Heart iconography of the nineteenth century, or the popular portraits of Christ by the American painter Warner Sallman (Morgan 1996), Jesus has feminine facial features, long hair touching his shoulders, and a body wrapped in soft and flowing gowns. His posture on the cross sometimes suggests masochistic self-abandon, and his bleeding wound below the nipple suggests a (spiritual) feeding of humankind, just as Mary's lactating breast fed him (Bynum 1987). Even the fluids (blood, sweat, tears), which Christ's suffering body excretes abundantly, have a "feminine" quality. According to moral theology of the thirteenth century, bodily fluids are more typical of woman's nature. "Woman is less qualified for moral behavior," wrote Albert the Great, the teacher of Aquinas, because she "contains more liquid than the man, and it is a property of liquid to take things up easily and to hold onto them poorly" (quoted in Ranke-Heinemann 1990: 178). Christ's exuding body on the cross betrays a masculine anatomy tainted by "womanish" features.

A peculiarity in the history of Western Christianity is that it does not worship the *linga* directly but rather divinizes the male body by effeminizing it. Those sensuous and androgynous representations are, however, in most cases the product of "male phantasmatics" (Kristeva 1986: 178). Real gender transgressors—gay people, transvestites, men or women pretending to be another gender—have been, and still are, punished by moral and secular law. Though such androgynous imagery suggests the sublimation of the phallic presence in the Christian symbolization of the sacred, it negates neither patriarchal power nor the importance of the biological male sex. This can be seen, for example, in stories about Pope Joan, a female pope, that began to circulate in the thirteenth century. According to medieval sources, Pope Joan, who supposedly reigned briefly between Leo IV and Benedict III in the ninth century, had the misfortune to give birth during a long papal procession through Rome. She and her newborn child were stoned to death on the spot (cf. Pardoe and Pardoe 1988; Gossmann 1994).

Whether we view Pope Joan as a historical figure or as the result of historical fiction, the fact remains that her (real or apocryphal) infiltration into the institution of sacerdotal celibacy required severe punishment. The peculiar dynamic between absent penis and phallic presence—paradoxical, irreconcilable, yet held up to man as a path to spiritual perfection—does not allow the physical presence of a woman. She would be a mockery of the denied penis. Her presence would turn the idealization of celibacy into a sign of impotence and thus threaten to unveil the chimera of phallic power.

In the history of Western Christianity, it did not suffice to subject the clergy alone to the enigma of spiritual perfection (absent penis/phallic presence); moral theology put heavy restrictions also on the sexual pleasures of the laity. Intercourse was permitted on special days and for procreative purposes only, and contraceptive devices, abortion, and intercourse during menstruation were prohibited. Some regulations singled out lay men, such as the notion of *copula sicca* (dry intercourse) or *coitus reservatus,* the withdrawing of the penis after pleasuring the woman "without letting the seed of generation flow forth" (Cardinal Huguccio, quoted in Ranke-Heinemann 1990: 171).

When the Reformation reformulated the Catholic doctrines of venial and mortal sin, men who converted to Protestantism were freed from some of the moral constraints placed upon sexuality. Martin Luther ridiculed sacerdotal celibacy. He regarded sexual instinct as a law of nature that would always override man's vows of chastity. "I am satisfied," Luther once said, "that the saints stick in the mud just like we do" (quoted in Grisar 1971: 514). Although he acknowledged that some men may possess the rare gift of celibacy, he admonished man to "be married [and] have a wife." Calvin, too, wrote that man should "abstain from marriage only so long as he is fit to observe celibacy" (quoted in Douglass 1974: 295–96).

Luther's theology that humans are saved "by faith alone" and that the priesthood extends to all believers opened the door to a more egalitarian understanding of human relationships. Peasants, women, and the radical wing of the Reformation pushed to rectify social injustices, to redefine sacramental authority, and to rethink issues of sexuality and pleasure (Noble 1992: 189; Marshall 1989; Douglass 1974). Today, we know, of course, that these movements were eventually crushed by mainstream Protestantism which insisted on obedience to the state and introduced the idea of individualized piety. The clerical monopoly was replaced by the patriarchal family. Marriage was looked upon in a favorable light, but married couples were, as before, warned of the dangers of uncontrolled lust that polluted matrimony.

Despite the liberating promise of the Protestant spirit, women remained excluded from ordination. When the gates of the women convents and monasteries were opened in Protestant countries, women even lost what little religious autonomy they had retained as nuns (Wiesner 1989). Luther sneered at women saints (Erikson 1962: 71). Women's new place was the home where they could practice their faith as mothers and the wives of pastors. "If a mother of a family wishes to please and serve God," Luther wrote, "let her care for the family, . . . educate and teach her children [and] do her task in the kitchen" (quoted in Douglass 1974: 295). A submissive wife was respected by her husband, but a disobedient wife suspected of sorcery (Barstow 1994: 60; Noble 1992: 188f).

Husbands were also admonished to do their duties in the emerging bourgeois family. "[I]t is of greatest importance for every married man," Luther preached in a sermon on the estate of marriage, "to pay closer, more thorough, and continuous attention to the health of his child's soul than to the body which he has begotten" (reprinted in Lull 1989: 636). Yet, Protestant men, married or not, held onto their leadership positions in the church and continued to determine theological discourse. When the Reformation turned celibate priests into married preachers, it eased the conflict between absent penis and phallic presence but did not change patriarchal dominance. The sexual penis no longer prevented men from offering the sacraments as long as their sexuality was controlled by marriage. Married men were not excluded from power but power remained exclusively among men.

The Reformation freed Protestant men from the psychodynamic tension of having to achieve spiritual perfection through the denial of desire, but it did not challenge phallic power. The Protestant spirit, if viewed as an early expression of modernity, managed to move phallic power from the ecclesia to secular institutions, such as the military, economic, and political elites. As the secular forces of modernity gained strength, men began to seek power, authority, and reputation in the economic, legal, or scientific spheres rather than ecclesiastical circles of male celibates (Noble 1992). Religion, now a matter of private convictions, became a less desirable male domain. Men are public, women are private (Elshtain 1981). With progressive secularization, men lost interest in private and "womanish" religion and withdrew their ambitions from traditional spiritual pathways. The privatization of religion explains, perhaps, why contemporary men feel spiritually impoverished despite the power and privileges they still enjoy. It may also explain why, in the twentieth century, women have been successful in their move into leadership positions in many Protestant churches and why women's ordination is now a fiercely debated issue among Catholics. Once religion is declared a private affair, men leave and women are admitted.

Today, though men may have many good reasons to celebrate the liberation from the religious yoke of celibacy, this comes with losses. A privatized religion has left contemporary men of faith without a medium to talk about their bodies religiously. As convoluted as the moral debates over such issues as *coitus reservatus* may have been, they provided men with a public religious forum to discuss the intimacies of the male body. In modernity, this discourse has become romanticized, sexualized, and medicalized. Like religion itself, the male body is a private affair. The male body excreting liquids is, for example, no longer a spiritual icon but often a pornographic image. In the twentieth century, pornographic language and medical terminology rather than religious imagery seem to dominate the discourse on the male body. Perhaps, the dominant ideal of masculinity in Christian cultures has shifted from denying the penis to oversexing it, albeit never challenging the power and the presence of the phallus.

Wildmen and Mythopoetic Spirituality

In light of this heritage, it is not surprising that many men in contemporary American society feel estranged from religion. Neither Christianity's severe scrutiny of male desires nor modernity's privatization of religion appeals to men in a competitive, consumption-oriented, and pleasure-seeking culture. But in the 1980s, informal groups and gatherings of American men in search for new forms of masculine spirituality gained public visibility. Today, they are known as the mythopoetic men's movement (cf. Kupers 1993: 146–50; Clatterbaugh 1990: 85–103; Nelson 1992: 76–80; Doty 1993). This movement of predominantly white, middle-class men has been able to articulate a sense of spiritual alienation. It also offers a cure: Revitalize the old sources! These sources include Greek mythologies (Bolen 1989; Doty 1993), the biblical traditions (Culbertson 1992; Arnold 1991; Judy 1992), pre-Christian and pagan religions (Rowan 1987; Conner 1993), the masculine wisdom of fairy tales (Bly 1990), and the generative power of male archetypes (Keen 1991; Anderson 1990; Moore and Gillette 1990).

The mythopoetic movement has recently come under serious criticism—though less for its aspiration to find new forms of male religiosity than for its representation of gender. Feminists have been particularly critical of the male mythmakers of the 1980s and 1990s, viewing them as the spiritual expression of the conservative backlash that American society is currently experiencing. Feminist critics have described the work and practice of such men as Robert Bly, Sam Keen, Robert Moore, and Douglas Gillette as a "depolitization" of the concepts of "masculinity" and "sexism" (hooks), a "grotesquely one-dimensional, easily popularized pseudoanalysis" (Randall), as "essentialist" and "dangerous to women" (Brown), an "anti-feminist backlash ... of white men ... reestablish[ing] the traditional male-dominant values of Western patriarchal culture" (Noble), and a "glorification of rapist divinities and sexist fairy tales" (Caputi and MacKenzie; all quoted in Hagan 1992).

Such characterizations unfairly homogenize these groups, glossing over some significant differences among them; yet, considering the numerous veiled and open attacks against feminism in the current literature on masculine spirituality, the women's passionate responses are understandable. Notwithstanding the occasional lip service paid to a woman-friendly agenda by individual authors, the general tone of their argumentation belies the rhetoric. The "wounded man" is the focus of their attention. But little is done to compare the gravity of their wounds to the damaging and painful disenfranchisement of other groups. Thus, the potentially liberating practice of a spiritual men's movement has too often yielded to efforts of consolidating patriarchal power (cf. Bordo 1993; Burant 1988; Nelson 1992: 78; May and Strikwerda 1992: xiv).

Patrick Arnold's book *Wildmen, Warriors, and Kings: Masculine Spirituality and the Bible* exemplifies the extreme end of masculinist religious writings. A "new cultural disease is developing," he claims, "an opportunistic infection so recent that most people neither know its name nor even recognize its existence." Arnold calls this disease "misandry," the hatred of men. "Misandry is an ideological spinoff of extreme feminism. . . . It is often present alongside feminist influence in such major institutions as academia, the church, the arts, business, and law" (1991: 52). In religion, feminists have been especially successful at spreading the disease. "Spirituality is an area where men are probably most vulnerable and where misandrists, in turn, seem to make the most far-reaching and malicious claims. The most virulent sources of this hatred are found in post-Christian feminist religious writings, especially in the burgeoning field of Goddess religion" (1991: 55). The language of more liberal writings may be tamer but the ideas are similar. In *Fire in the Belly*, for example, Sam Keen distinguishes between a prophetic feminism, which is aware of the wounds of both women and men, and an ideological feminism "animated by a spirit of a resentment, the tactic of blame, and the desire for vindictive triumph over men that comes out of the dogmatic assumption that women are the innocent victims of a male conspiracy" (1991: 196).

It is too painful to repeat other flagrantly anti-feminist and misogynist statements; these few examples may suffice to illustrate the emergence of a male-revisionist agenda. The mythopoetic movement is, of course, not monolithic. The spectrum reaches from Patrick Arnold's reactionary views to Sam Keen's liberal androcentrism and the cavernous space hollowed out by Robert Bly's conservative paternalism (see Clatterbaugh 1990). What binds these writings together is their political and religious sentimentalism. By uncritically reappropriating androcentric myths and traditions, they play into the hands of a conservative gender ideology and policy.

Why do so many neo-Jungian writings on male spirituality end up reproaching women for men's lack of religious devotion? Why do mythopoetic men lament their condition of spiritual impoverishment, when, in fact, religious history is filled with books on male-specific, religious practices? It is important to remember that men, unlike women, whose centuries-long marginalization has left them with only a few sources to reconstruct their spirituality, have abundant material to work with. In 1888, for example, de Roskovany produced a bibliography on Christian male celibacy which alone filled seventeen volumes (Barstow 1982: 8). Considering such voluminous archives, are men really "spiritually challenged," or merely threatened by new social, political, and economic realities? Do they attend to their wounds because they wish to rectify the injustices of sexism and racism, or because they seek to regain power over a sphere that they voluntarily gave up when modernity promoted secular notions of progress? Is mythopoesis a spiritual pathway that leads to gender equality and to toleration of gender-variant behavior, or is it a code word for neo-patriarchal values?

The focus on archetypes in the recent literature on male spirituality creates considerable problems. Archetypes easily escape a critical analysis of the economic and political status of men in contemporary society. Archetypes express a nostalgic desire for an untroubled past and are enlisted in the task of envisioning the future of male spirituality—unfortunately, the future does not look so different from the patriarchal past. The "primal spiritual gifts that men can offer to their world," Arnold suggests, are "fighting for what you believe in, loving freedom, and taking responsibility. Masculinity means standing out from the crowd, . . . coming to the rescue when people get in trouble, . . . thinking logically and upholding the law [and] reverencing God as Totally Other" (1991: 50). Such formulations may have the power to reconcile public men with private religion, but they do not transform androcentric structures. They accommodate affluent men in search of a gratifying spirituality without challenging their socially privileged positions.

Toward Gender-Conscious Embodied Spirituality

The contributors to *Men's Bodies, Men's Gods* do not dwell on masculine archetypes as models for a contemporary male spirituality but reflect on the complex and often ambiguous religious forces that shape male bodies and identities, taking into consideration the social, psychological, cultural, and historical dimensions of modern "manhood." The male figures of warriors, wildmen, kings, Iron Johns, lovers, magicians, or shamans may have therapeutic value for a limited group of men, but, more often than not, such archetypal configurations misname the problems, misplace the blame, and simplify the complexity of men's contemporary existence. "For actual men are not timeless symbolic constructs, they are biologically, historically, and experientially embodied beings" (Bordo 1993: 696). Archetypes, on the other hand, are disembodied, ahistorical figures (for a different view, see Wehr 1987). They have more in common with symbolizations of phallic presence—constant, eternal, erect—than the mutable and multiple forms of male bodies—flaccid, aging, excreting.

Particular male bodies continually challenge the transcendent rule of the phallus, religious or secular. Particularity requires that men's diverse cultural and ethnic backgrounds and sexual orientations must be taken into account when moving toward a renewed understanding of male identity and spirituality. Many of the authors of this book not only analyze the problems but are already engaged in reinventing a religious discourse on embodiment, intimacy, and sexuality, a discourse that was lost when religion became a private affair. New theological, spiritual, and ritual pathways for men must take their bodies seriously. For example, in his critique of phallocentric theology, James Nelson admonishes men not to project the "values of *phallos* . . . onto our experienced worlds," but to make the "fully physical, sweating, lubricating, menstruating, ejaculating, urinating, defecating bodies . . . the central vehicles of God's embodiment in our experience" (1992: 94, 31). For men, to become aware of the vulnerability of their bodies is a positive starting point. Rather than building up a muscular, athletic, erect, brave, wise, protective, competitive, iron body, we could try to stay closer to real bodies: itching, aging, flowing, hurting, loving, dying, smelling, praying, masturbating, spilling, adorning, fathering, nurturing, growing fat, getting sick.

Adopting the perspective of a gender-conscious, male religiosity would, moreover, require men to examine the preferential treatment that many of them have enjoyed in Christian traditions and post-Christian cultures. Such a perspective self-critically assesses the wounds that men have inflicted on others and themselves. It leaves behind the models of male celibates, warriors, kings, and wildmen, and investigates differences among men. It searches for spirituality in the unexpected: when men befriend other men, when they explore erotic fantasies, when they change their children's diapers or care for people with AIDS, or when they contemplate the symbolizations of the male flesh.

Men's Bodies, Men's Gods opens with Seth Mirsky's "Three Arguments for the Elimination of Masculinity" because his piece analyzes the academic and political context of the contemporary men's movement and locates the mythopoetic movement within it. Revising Simone de Beauvoir's famous statement to read, "One is not born, but rather becomes a man," Mirsky sets out to investigate the current emphasis on the idea of masculinity. He is skeptical about the renewed interest in masculinity because the latter is too "deeply entrenched in our culture" to become a tool for transformation and liberation. As an essentialist category, masculinity does not distinguish between sex and gender. A masculine (or masculinist) identity, therefore, is a construction that enshrines traditional male gender roles and "precludes the pursuit of a feminist political agenda." The "quasi-religious revaluing of masculine gender identity" advocated by the mythopoetic movement must be criticized for similar reasons. Although Mirsky concedes that the search for male spirituality can be a critique of patriarchal religions, he regards the quest for the "deep masculine" in the archetypal unconscious a "reactionary fiction."

Not every book that carries "masculinity" in its title promotes a conservative agenda, as Mirsky seems to fear. Such works as *Holy Virility: The Social Construction of Masculinity* (Reynaud 1983), *Contemporary Perspectives on Masculinity* (Clatterbaugh 1990), and *Rethinking Masculinity* (May and Strikwerda 1992) are good examples for advancing a progressive discourse (see also Kaufman 1987; Jardine and Smith 1987; Goldstein 1993, 1994). But Mirsky's piece reminds us that the mere existence of a men's movement does not automatically improve the situation. The United States government and General Motors, Mirsky writes, are men's movements, too. Feminist theologian Ruether once remarked that "patriarchy is itself the original men's movement" (1992: 17). Communities of men range from the exclusively male circles of Christian ascetics and celibates to those of modern scientists and stockbrokers, from the military to small groups of white men searching for the archetypal wildman.

Rather than unconditionally praising contemporary male gatherings, it is important to examine the extent to which these men are aware of the consequences of their new rhetoric. Does, for example, the quest for male spirituality produce new fictionalizations of manliness? The strength of Mirsky's piece lies in his questioning of the premises with which contemporary men construct their gender, including those of the mythopoetic movement.

Tom F. Driver's "Growing Up Christian and Male" opens the book's second section on the construction of male religious identity. Driver autobiographically explores the sources which influenced his understanding of Christianity, himself, others, and his body. It is a kind of spiritual archaeology, deliberate in its focus on one man's particular experience, though not exclusive in its ethical and theological considerations. Recalling a "confessional" paper on male identity that he presented in an academic setting in 1978, Driver evaluates the changes he has since undergone. He takes us on a journey from growing up in a "typical" American town that shaped his masculine and Christian identity, through the tumultuous period of the 1960s and 1970s, to the experience of facing death after a heart attack. Male identity, Driver seems to suggest, is a narrative we construct from lived experience—a perspective that leaves room for change and reinterpretation.

The construction of the religious male identity is, of course, different for European American and African American men. Garth Baker-Fletcher's "Black Bodies, Whose Body?" looks at how black bodies were perceived by whites, how blacks imagined themselves, and what role religion played in their identity formation. African American male bodies, Baker-Fletcher writes, are perceived "as sites of labor, instruments of pleasure, or vengeful entertainment." His theological interpretation of the John Henry legend, for example, reveals it as a repressive myth, because it "displays the supernatural physical strength" of African American males, while neglecting the resulting injuries and eventual death. Typically, John Henry is portrayed as a hero. Even in Arthur Mitchell's choreography, performed by the Dance Theatre of Harlem, John Henry's death is redeemed by his heroic resurrection. For Baker-Fletcher, such renditions represent a "subordinationist Christology." Ultimately, the legend of John Henry disempowers African American men, because in the context of American "racist constructions of masculinity" black men are portrayed as "instinct," "unconscious urge," and the "body itself" (Bordo 1993: 701). Baker-Fletcher finds spiritually empowering figures in the trickster-like character of High John de Conquer and the historical figure of Nat Turner: both provide African Americans with political and spiritual pathways to oppose and survive slavery.

Empowerment is also the theme of Michael L. Stemmeler's piece on the construction of gay religious identity. Starting with a brief assessment of the current situation of gay rights in American society, he discusses issues of the "gay self," of "queerness" in the secular and religious community, and of strategies to counter and resist the homophobic fears of the heterosexual majority. Spiritual empowerment for gay people is not simply a private, meditative journey, but a "theopraxis" committed to a just and compassionate society. Anger and rage must be part of a gay spirituality. Reminiscent of Beverly Harrison's (1981) reclamation of the "power of anger in the work of love," Stemmeler argues that "[gay] anger about societal rejection has to be transformed into liberating anger for ourselves and our communities [and] toward social and spiritual change."

The second section of the book thus suggests that the formation of religious identity is intimately linked to societal perceptions of particular bodies, gay and straight, black and white: this is the argument advanced by Tom F. Driver, Garth Baker-Fletcher, and Michael L. Stemmeler. The third section of Men's Bodies, Men's Gods looks at the religious significance of men's sexual identities and erotic bodies. A liberating perspective does not, of course, follow the traditional Christian path of subjecting all sexual activity to moral scrutiny. Rather than rejecting eroticism, it would embrace the sensuality of an embodied spirituality. Scott Haldeman and Robin Hawley Gorsline do exactly that.

Haldeman's "Bringing Good News to the Body" ponders the spiritual and ethical value of masturbation. He depicts modern men as alienated from their bodies and estranged from a concept of love that is simultaneously erotic and caring. Masturbation helps those men to get back "in touch" with themselves. Haldeman concedes that masturbation is an ambiguous gift since it can lead to pornographic activity and a "destructive narcissism." But understood as a "critical praxis," masturbation celebrates "the goodness of one's flesh" created by God, liberates from "the confines of patriarchal images," and raises one's awareness about the connections "between male pleasure and violence against women."

Not every reader may be willing to concede such comprehensive powers to masturbation. Still, Haldeman's essay demands that we pay attention to a socially stigmatized sexual activity. Medieval moral theologians might have had fewer problems in arguing with Haldeman's position (though they would have disagreed with it) than theologians nourished by Puritanism. The nineteenth century medical definition of masturbation as a psychiatric disease and the popular Victorian belief that masturbation can lead to insanity still hold sway over men's repressed relation to autoeroticism (cf. Barker-Benfield 1973; Paige and Paige 1981). James Nelson, for example, found that many denominations in the United States today are "open to the suggestion that divine grace might be powerfully experienced in lovemaking with one's beloved. But when I suggested that masturbation might also be a means of grace, I think I heard gasps. . . . The 'M-word' was a shock" (1992: 96).

As provocative as Haldeman's piece may strike us, the notion that masturbation has sacred import is not altogether new in Christian history. For example, the Phibionites, a libertine Gnostic sect, were accused of gathering the male semen through masturbation and homosexual practices and offering it "in prayer as the body of Christ" (Goehring 1988: 340). The ritual is reported by Epiphanius, a church father who polemicized against the Phibionites. Because of his polemicism, it is difficult to determine the extent of historic accuracy. Our positions may partially depend on our own views of sexuality and spirituality. In *Blossom of Bone*, for example, Randy P. Conner, who belongs to a radical group of California's Gay Spirituality movement, lends credence to the Gnostic practice of ritual masturbation, while others cannot conceive of any Christian sect being involved in such practices (Conner 1993: 130; cf. Benko 1967).

Robin Hawley Gorsline's "Facing the Body on the Cross," which is part confessional writing, part liberation theology, examines how and why the visual representations of Jesus Christ can stir homoeroticized desires. "Many gay men," he writes, "experience Jesus as lover." Adopting Margaret R. Miles's (1985) insight that devotional images in Western Christianity have helped believers to embody religious values, Gorsline articulates an analogous link between the physicality of images and the body-memory of gay people. Though popular images of a blue-eyed Jesus on the cross can be obstacles in a gay man's path toward a liberating spirituality—because Jesus' "whiteness" excludes the experience of men of color, and because the merging of sensuality and violence can lead to sado-masochistic eroticism—less biased images of Jesus encourage men to embody Christian values by developing loving and nurturing relations to other men. "My vision requires that white men must not only remove the body of Jesus from the cross and care for it, but also accept the fact that the body we are loving is not white."

At times, Gorsline's vision of a gay male spirituality is reminiscent of the devotional theology of medieval women mystics. They, too, envisioned a merging of their bodies with the body of Christ, and they embodied their visions in the concrete, spiritual practice of caring for and feeding others (Bynum 1987). The lives of these women were unusual; yet, their hagiographers found ways to integrate their radical theology and devotion into the medieval church. Whether the Christian community today is willing to accept the "queer" theologizing of gay and lesbian Christians is still an open question. "What will the discussion of gay spiritual identity sound like thirty years from now?" Michael L. Stemmeler asks at the end of his piece on gay religious identities. It is too early to make predictions about a society that is still homophobic, he admits, but this does not relieve us from the individual responsibility to create spaces where gay people can explore their differently embodied spiritualities.

In the fourth section of *Men's Bodies, Men's Gods,* Philip L. Culbertson and William G. Doty discuss how modernity's homophobic attitudes have impeded the development of serious male-male friendships. Since friendships are based, among other things, on trust and care, they require emotional and physical closeness. Such intimacy frightens heterosexual men; consequently, they put little effort into deep and lasting male-male friendships— despite their frequent laments of not having friends.

In "Men and Christian Friendship," Culbertson demonstrates that intimate friendships among men were not the exception but the rule in antiquity and early Christianity. Those friendships were celebrated as the highest ideal of human relationships. In his *Confessions,* for example, Augustine reported in great detail about his many intimate male companions. The woman he loved and lived with for thirteen years, however, was barely mentioned; and though she bore his son, we do not even know her name. Indeed, Augustine had no female friends. Culbertson argues that modern men need to restore the sincerity of male-male friendships found in earlier periods of Christianity, but not at the cost of excluding women. "Adult intimate friendship offers men riches other than the riches of marriage," he writes. "The Christian community cannot be healthy until women and men are liberated from the gender-role expectations which imprison them."

Like Culbertson, Doty regrets the current lack of friendship among men, and he proposes to study "traditional religious and mythico-heroic models, not uncritically, but with an eye to the valuable lodes of insight they contain." Men would have "to decide on their own just how their particular contexts and strengths" permit them to use mythological resources for their "new loving male-male relationships."

Of the contributors to *Men's Bodies, Men's Gods,* both Culbertson and Doty are closest to the mythopoetic movement, though they do not readily identify with it. Both have written elsewhere about the wealth and hazards of mythic resources for the experiences of men today. In *New Adam* (1992), Culbertson peruses the biblical tradition for models of male spirituality; and Doty's *Myths of Masculinity* (1993) draws on male heroic figures in Greek, Ancient Near East, and American Southwest mythologies. Their heroes, however, are neither the "muscular Christian" of the nineteenth century, an ideal of manliness Culbertson criticizes, nor the "bodybuilder Americanus" of the 1980s, which Sam Fussell describes as "the muscular Christian . . . turned inward" (1993: 594). Though Doty speaks of an "athletics" of friendship, he does not search for performances of pumped-up bodies but for models of male-male intimacy.

The last section of *Men's Bodies, Men's Gods* examines cultural and religious manifestations of the male body. In "Confines of Male Confessions," I look at how men write about their bodies in autobiographical works. My reflections lead me from antiquity to modernity, from Augustine's austere inspection of every bodily activity to Leiris's trivialization of the male flesh. I ask whether male confessional writings are yet another way of distancing oneself from the immediacy of body experiences—albeit, perhaps, the only way that makes men comfortable to relate to their carnal reality. Pieces of a personal narrative, which are woven into the essay, reveal my search for a more authentic confessional style that eschews the closed male body and rather describes the male body as open, vulnerable, and relational.

Lewis R. Gordon also addresses the question as to whether men can open up and become vulnerable, a precondition, according to Gordon, to receiving God. The male body defines itself as a closed body, and worshiping God requires an open and susceptible body. How, then, can men worship? Gordon approaches this issue through the philosophy of existential phenomenology. According to this perspective, the body is constituted by being seen by others and by one's realization of being seen by others. Hence, in a society marked by anti-black racism, the process of seeing, which constitutes male identity, renders the spiritual experiences of "white" bodies different from "black" bodies.

David Morgan examines visual representations of Jesus in popular religious art of the late nineteenth- and twentieth- century American history. He focuses on responses to Warner Sallman's famous *Head of Christ* and discusses why some people were able to experience the painting as a call to friendship with a tender savior, while others rejected it as an effeminate portrait that would incite feelings of homoerotic intimacy. Did the artist portray Jesus in a sufficiently masculine way or, as one viewer put it, did he mislead the audience by showing only "a woman's face covered by a beard?" Morgan's chapter on "The Masculinity of Jesus in Popular Religious Art" recalls themes already addressed in the section on male friendship and connects them with the final chapter on contemporary iconographies of the male flesh.

William G. Doty's second piece investigates the depiction of men in current advertisements. Similar to the fetishized representation of women, the male body has recently been subjected to idealized beauty standards: young, muscular, hairless. Such a body invites gazing by women and other men. Doty's curiosity about the male body as a visual object is spurred by a cultural perspective, and recalls Lewis R. Gordon's philosophical concern about "bodies being seen." Men are no longer the sole proprietors of objectifying other bodies—female, black, or gay—

but become objects themselves. Do these new iconographies of the male body foster phallic presence because the depictions of muscular, active, and hard flesh displace the penis? Or are they early signs of a post-phallocentric gaze because men themselves become vulnerable to the homo/eroticized stare of others?

Perhaps we do not have enough distance to our own situation to answer these questions. Yet, the fact that today male religious scholars can seriously discuss a non-homophobic and post-phallocentric practice of men's spirituality is a hopeful sign—for it reaches beyond the psycho-dynamic tensions of the traditional Christian model of absent penis/phallic presence, beyond the limitations of modernity's privatized religion and oversexed penis, and beyond the contemporary search for heroic male virility in phallic archetypes.

REFERENCES

Anderson, William. 1990. *Green Man: The Archetype of Our Oneness with the Earth*. San Francisco: Harper.

Arnold, Patrick. 1991. *Wildmen, Warriors, and Kings: Masculine Spirituality and the Bible*. New York: Crossroad.

Athanasius. 1980. *The Life of Antony and the Letter to Marcellus*. Trans. Robert C. Gregg. New York: Paulist Press.

Augustine. 1992. *Confessions*. Trans. Henry Chadwick. Oxford, New York: Oxford University Press.

Barker-Benfield, G. J. 1973. "The Spermatic Economy: A Nineteenth-Century View of Sexuality." In *The American Family in Social-Historical Perspective*, ed. Michael Gordon. New York: St. Martin's Press.

Barstow, Anne. 1982. *Married Priests and the Reforming Papacy*. Lewistown, N.Y.: Edwin Mellen Press.

———. 1994. *Witchcraze: A New History of the European Witch Hunt*. San Francisco: Harper.

Benko, Stephen. 1967. "The Libertine Gnostic Sect of the Phibionites According to Epiphanius." *Vigiliae Christianae* 21:103–19.

Bly, Robert. 1990. *Iron John: A Book about Men*. Reading, Mass.: Addison-Wesley.

Bolen, Jean Shinoda. 1989. *Gods in Everyman: A New Psychology of Men's Lives and Loves*. San Francisco: Harper.

Bordo, Susan. 1993. "Reading the Male Body." *Michigan Quarterly Review* 32 (Fall): 696–737.

Brown, Peter. 1988. *The Body and Society: Men, Women and Sexual Renunciation in Early Christianity*. New York: Columbia University Press.

Burant, Christopher. 1988. "Of Wild Men and Warriors." *Changing Men* 19 (Spring/Summer): 7–9, 46.

Bynum, Caroline Walker. 1987. *Holy Feast and Holy Fast: The Religious Significance of Food to Medieval Women.* Berkeley: University of California Press.

Cameron, Ron, ed. 1982. *The Other Gospels: Non-Canonical Gospel Texts.* Philadelphia: Westminster.

Clark, Elizabeth. 1983. *Women in the Early Church.* Collegeville, Minn.: Liturgical Press.

Clatterbaugh, Kenneth. 1990. *Contemporary Perspectives on Masculinity: Men, Women, and Politics in Modern Society.* Boulder, Colo.: Westview Press.

Conner, Randy P. 1993. *Blossom of Bone: Reclaiming the Connections between Homoeroticism and the Sacred.* San Francisco: Harper.

Culbertson, Philip. 1992. *New Adam: The Future of Male Spirituality.* Minneapolis: Fortress.

Doty, William. 1993. *Myths of Masculinity.* New York: Crossroad.

Douglass, Jane Dempsey. 1974. "Women and the Continental Reformation." In *Religion and Sexism: Images of Woman in the Jewish and Christian Traditions,* ed. Rosemary Radford Ruether. New York: Simon & Schuster.

Elshtain, Jean Bethke. 1981. *Public Man, Private Woman: Women in Social and Political Thought.* Princeton, N.J.: Princeton University Press.

Erikson, Erik. 1962. *Young Man Luther: A Study in Psychoanalysis and History.* New York: W. W. Norton.

Fiorenza, Elisabeth Schüssler. 1984. *In Memory of Her: A Feminist Theological Reconstruction of Christian Origins.* New York: Crossroad.

Fussell, Sam. 1993. "Bodybuilder Americanus." *Michigan Quarterly Review* 32 (Fall): 577–596.

Goehring, James. 1988. "Libertine or Liberated: Women in the So-Called Libertine Gnostic Communities." In *Images of the Feminine in Gnosticism,* ed. Karen King. Philadelphia: Fortress.

Goldstein, Laurence, ed. 1993, 1994. *The Male Body. Michigan Quarterly Review* 32 and 33 (Fall/Winter).

Gossmann, Elisabeth. 1994. *Mulier Papa: Der Skandal eines weiblichen Papstes: Zur Rezeptionsgeschichte der Gestalt der Päpstin Johanna.* Munich, Germany: Iudicium.

Grisar, Hartmann, S. J. 1971. *Martin Luther: His Life and Work.* Adapted from Second German Edition by Frank J. Ebele. New York: AMS Press.

Hagan, Kay Leigh. 1992. *Women Respond to the Men's Movement: A Feminist Collection.* San Francisco: Harper.

Harrison, Beverly. 1981. "The Power of Anger in the Work of Love." *Union Seminary Quarterly Review* 36:41–57.

Jardine, Alice, and Paul Smith, eds. 1987. *Men in Feminism.* New York: Methuen.

Judy, Dwight. 1992. *Healing the Male Soul: Christianity and the Mythic Journey.* New York: Crossroad.

Kaufman, Michael, ed. 1987. *Beyond Patriarchy: Essays by Men on Pleasure, Power, and Change.* New York: Oxford University Press.

Keen, Sam. 1991. *Fire in the Belly: On Being a Man.* New York: Bantam.

Kristeva, Julia. 1986. "Stabat Mater." In *The Kristeva Reader*, ed. Toril Moi. New York: Columbia University Press.

Kupers, Terry A. 1993. *Revisioning Men's Lives: Gender, Intimacy, and Power.* New York: Guilford Publications.

Lea, Henry. 1907. *A History of Sacerdotal Celibacy.* London: Williams and Norgate.

Lull, Timothy F., ed. 1989. *Martin Luther's Basic Theological Writings.* Minneapolis: Fortress.

Marshall, Sherrin, ed. 1989. *Women in Reformation and Counter-Reformation Europe.* Bloomington: Indiana University Press.

May, Larry, and Robert A. Strikwerda, eds. 1992. *Rethinking Masculinity: Philosophical Explorations in Light of Feminism.* Lanham, Md.: Littlefield Adams.

Meeks, Wayne A. 1974. "The Image of the Androgyne: Some Uses of a Symbol in Earliest Christianity." *History of Religions* 13 (February): 165–208.

———. 1993. *The Origins of Christian Morality: The First Two Centuries.* New Haven: Yale University Press.

Miles, Margaret R. 1985. *Image as Insight: Visual Understanding in Western Christianity and Secular Culture.* Boston: Beacon Press.

———. 1992. *Desire and Delight: A New Reading of Augustine's Confessions.* New York: Crossroad.

Moore, Robert, and Douglas Gillette. 1990. *King, Warrior, Magician, Lover: Rediscovering the Archetypes of the Mature Masculine.* San Francisco: Harper.

Morgan, David, ed. 1996. *Icons of American Protestantism: The Art of Warner Sallman.* New Haven: Yale University Press.

Nelson, James B. 1978. *Embodiment: An Approach to Sexuality and Christian Theology.* Minneapolis: Augsburg.

———. 1992. *Body Theology.* Louisville, Ky.: Westminster/John Knox Press.

Niebuhr, Gustav. 1993. "Use of Actress in Jesus Role Stirs Dispute." *Washington Post* (September 11).

Noble, David F. 1992. *A World without Women: The Christian Clerical Culture of Western Science.* New York: Oxford University Press.

Paige, Karen Ericksen, and Jeffrey M. Paige. 1981. *The Politics of Reproductive Ritual.* Berkeley: University of California Press.

Pardoe, Rosemary, and Darroll Pardoe. 1988. *The Female Pope: The Mystery of Pope Joan: The First Complete Documentation of the Facts behind the Legend.* Wellingborough, England: Crucible.

Ranke-Heinemann, Uta. 1990. *Eunuchs for the Kingdom of Heaven: Women, Sexuality, and the Catholic Church.* New York: Doubleday.

Reynaud, Emmanuel. 1983. *Holy Virility: The Social Construction of Masculinity.* Trans. Ros Schwartz. London: Pluto Press.

Rowan, John. 1987. *The Horned God.* New York: Routledge & Kegan Paul.

Ruether, Rosemary Radford. 1974. "Misogynism and Virginal Feminism in the Fathers of the Church." In *Religion and Sexism: Images of Woman in the Jewish and Christian Traditions.* Ed. Rosemary Radford Ruether. New York: Simon & Schuster.

———. 1992. "Patriarchy and the Men's Movement: Part of the Problem or Part of the Solution?" In *Women Respond to the Men's Movement: A Feminist Collection,* ed. Kay Leigh Hagan. San Francisco: Harper.

Steinberg, Leo. 1983. *The Sexuality of Christ in Renaissance Art and in Modern Oblivion.* London: Faber and Faber.

Torjesen, Karen Jo. 1993. *When Women Were Priests: Women's Leadership in the Early Church and the Scandal of Their Subordination in the Rise of Christianity.* San Francisco: Harper.

Warner, Marina. 1976. *Alone of All Her Sex: The Myth and the Cult of the Virgin Mary.* New York: Knopf.

Wehr, Demaris. 1987. *Jung and Feminism: Liberating Archetypes.* Boston: Beacon Press.

Wiesner, Merry. 1989. "Nuns, Wives, and Mothers: Women and the Reformation in Germany." In *Women in Reformation and Counter-Reformation Europe,* ed. Sherrin Marshall. Bloomington: Indiana University Press.

TWO

Three Arguments for the Elimination of Masculinity

SETH MIRSKY

The consideration of masculinity which I undertake here is a response to what I can only describe as the persistence of "masculinity" as a privileged, and maddeningly opaque, term in the overlapping discourses of contemporary men's studies and certain contemporary men's movements.[1] Both the academic field of men's studies and the various politically and spiritually oriented men's groups active today owe their existence, directly or indirectly (and in some cases, I suspect, reluctantly), to feminism, which opened up the whole terrain of gender for exploration, activism, and transformation. If Simone de Beauvoir's famous declaration, "One is not born, but rather becomes, a woman" (1974: 301; cf. Butler 1990), memorably suggested the radical separability of gender from sex in the case of women, then certainly it had similar implications for men: one is not born, but rather becomes, a man. To observe this is to state the obvious, yet men on the whole—with the significant exception of gay men (cf. Kinsman 1987; Kleinberg 1987; Hopkins 1992)— have not been quick to learn from feminist insights, particularly when it comes to that most closely guarded of male mysteries: masculinity.

The title of this chapter is an allusion to cultural critic Jerry Mander's provocative book, *Four Arguments for the Elimination of Television* (1978), calling for the dismantling of a well-established, indeed nearly all-pervasive cultural institution. Mander writes of his own improbable project: "How to achieve the elimination of television? I certainly cannot answer that question. It is obvious, however, that the first step is for all of us to purge from our minds the idea that just because television exists, we cannot get rid of it" (1978: 357). Like television, the notion of masculinity is deeply entrenched in our culture. To even raise the possibility, particularly among men, that the demise of masculinity is devoutly to be wished for, is to place oneself virtually beyond the bounds of civilized—or certainly patriarchal—discourse. Yet, if nothing else, I would like at least to challenge the inevitability of masculinity as a decisive force in men's lives, and its assumed place as the preeminent object of men's studies. The "three arguments" I wish to advance here concern the continuing hold which masculinity exerts on men's imagination in the areas of men's studies, men's movement politics, and men's spirituality.

First, I will provide some background and perspective. The roots of today's men's studies and men's movements lie in the tentative steps taken by some men in the 1970s in response to the emergence of second-wave feminism. Much of that early response is fairly criticized by sociologists Tim Carrigan, Bob Connell, and John Lee, in their overview of men's studies and men's movement literature:

It is not, fundamentally, about uprooting sexism or transforming patriarchy, or even understanding masculinity in its various forms. When it comes to the crunch, what it is about is *modernizing* hegemonic masculinity. It is concerned with finding ways in which the dominant group—the white, educated, heterosexual, affluent males we know and love so well—can adapt to new circumstances without breaking down the social-structural arrangements that actually give them their power. (1987: 164)

At the same time, however, a number of self-identified "anti-sexist men" struggled with some of the deeper implications of feminist critiques and began identifying connections between masculinity and male supremacy, sexual violence, heterosexism/homophobia, and militarism.[2]

Meanwhile, a quarter-century of feminist activism and scholarship has, among other things, expanded upon de Beauvoir's understanding of womanhood as cultural construction rather than natural given. Femininity, as the gender-ideal assigned to women under the terms of patriarchy, has come to be seen as a mark of women's oppression in a system organized around the interests of (putatively masculine) males. As feminist philosopher Mary Daly succinctly puts it, "femininity is a man-made construct, having essentially nothing to do with femaleness" (1978: 68). Not surprisingly, given this sort of analysis, feminist calls for the reform, reconstruction, or recovery of femininity are hard to come by, and I have yet to see women's studies characterized by any of its practitioners as "the study of femininities."

Imagine my surprise, then, to discover the current prominence of the category "masculinity" in the writings of feminist-influenced men across the spectrum of men's studies and men's movement literature. With the proliferation of such titles as *The Making of Masculinities* (Brod 1987b), *Unmasking Masculinity* (Jackson 1990), *Rethinking Masculinity* (May and Strikwerda 1992), *Rediscovering Masculinity* (Seidler 1989), and *To Be a Man: In Search of the Deep Masculine* (Thompson 1991), to name but a few, it is evident that the discourse of masculinity continues to dominate the field, to the near-total exclusion of alternative perspectives. This is in marked contrast to the thoroughly problematized status the discourse of femininity has attained within feminist studies (Butler 1990). So what is it about men and masculinity? Why do so many of us hold on so, when we should know better? Rather than attempting to answer these questions, I suggest that we keep them in mind, for they underlie the specific critiques of the uses of masculinity which follow.

Men's Studies as the Study of Masculinity

In an unusually clear statement of relevant issues for men in light of feminism's critiques, social and political scientist Michael Kaufman lays out some of the ground which the developing academic discipline of men's studies might be expected to cover. "What is actually at stake," he writes, "is not our biological manhood, our sex, but our historically specific, socially constructed, and personally embodied notions of masculinity. We confuse maleness (biological sex) with masculinity (gender) at our peril" (1987a: xiv). Presumably, one of men's studies' central tasks is to elaborate on the distinction between maleness and masculinity, sex and gender, with a view toward diminishing the pervasive confusion which results from patriarchal society's conflation of the two.

Similarly, philosopher and men's studies scholar Harry Brod articulates what is, ideally, the political commitment of men's studies when he declares:

Politically, men's studies is rooted in the profeminist men's movement, analo-
gously to women's studies['] rootedness in feminism. . . . [M]en's studies should
be unabashedly explicit about its roots in the search for progressive, profeminist
change in male roles. (1987a: 45)

Yet, I believe men's studies is hindered in both its descriptive and pre-
scriptive aspirations by the way it constructs its main analytic category
or "problematic," that of masculinity.

To get at the problem, let me raise a simple-sounding question: is it
possible to talk about men and talk about something other than masculinity? In the conceptual framework of much of contemporary men's
studies, it appears to be very difficult indeed, for the study of men has
come practically to be equated with the study of masculinities. Although
broadly social-constructionist in its professed methodological principles
(for example, Kimmel and Messner 1992: 8–9), men's studies seems
somehow determined to reunite what feminist scholarship long ago
constructively rent asunder—namely, sex and gender.

This is accomplished through what I would call the "categorical
assumption of masculinity." By this I mean the tendency of men's studies
analyses to treat the category of masculinity as coextensive with the
category of men's lives. Within such a framework, individual men and
groups of men can always be understood to be exhibiting, expressing,
or struggling with *some* version of masculinity, be it "hegemonic" or
otherwise.[3] While this understanding allows for the study of a proliferation of masculinities seen as specific to various communities, the all-
encompassing character of the category "masculinity" is left unscruti-
nized. That men's lives might be larger than their relationship to a
particular masculinity; that there might be areas or moments in men's
lives in which masculinity is irrelevant; that men might exist without or
beyond masculinity: such possibilities are not comprehended in a men's
studies approach which, against its stated intentions, theorizes masculinity as a necessary attribute of human males.

In criticizing the use of masculinity as the overarching framework
within which men's studies proceeds, I am not suggesting that masculinity is an inappropriate object for investigation and critique. On the
contrary, I am trying to call attention to the theoretical incoherence that
attends its current usage as a universal category. For if all aspects of all
men's lives can be understood as elements in some particular configuration of masculinity, the concept loses its analytical power—not to men-

tion any relevance to feminist politics. Under such circumstances, systematic critique of masculinity is rendered impossible, and all that is left for men's studies is the comparison of a multiplicity of locally defined masculinities. It would appear that men's studies scholars fear that without masculinity, men disappear, or at least become unintelligible as subjects for study.

All of which begs the question, What do we mean when we talk about masculinity? Taking our cue from feminists' general rejection of femininity as an unproblematic descriptive category for women's real lives, we might usefully understand masculinity as a thoroughly contingent category which is politically implicated in the patriarchal structuring of the gender order. For, at a minimum, all masculinities share two central components: the negatively defining characteristic of being *not* feminine, or like women; and the positively defining characteristic of having more power (social, physical, cosmic, and so forth) than that which is feminine, or women. (Note that femininity and women are conflated in this understanding, because that is exactly how the patriarchal structuring of gender functions.)

The challenge for men's studies is to reveal the contingency of masculinity—not only of all particular, local masculinities but of masculinity per se: to write, as it were (in the manner of Michel Foucault), a "history of masculinity," along with a phenomenology of masculinities. Men's studies needs to be able to theorize men as not only embodying or modifying masculinity, but also resisting it.[4] One key to facilitating this line of inquiry lies in achieving some clarity in our use of the gender term "masculinity," insisting upon its distinctness from such terms as "men" or "maleness," which refer more properly to sex.

In a brief but suggestive passage elaborating on her "performative" theory of gender, Judith Butler identifies not two but three dimensions of sex and gender: "anatomical sex, gender identity, and gender performance" (1990: 137). Although the full implications of such a schema remain to be developed, in a men's studies context the corresponding terms for analysis might be "men," "maleness," and "masculinity," respectively. That is, men's studies might explore how (anatomical) men are gendered male within society and perform or do not perform masculinity according to society's norms. This more nuanced, multidimensional approach displaces masculinity as the assumed category for men's studies analysis, and instead recognizes it as always a contested term within the larger context of gendered power relations between men and women.

Perhaps not surprisingly, gay male theorists and others concerned with the relationship of masculinity to heterosexism and homophobia have been quickest to incorporate and develop the insights of feminists and gender theorists in their own work on masculinity. A passage from one such analysis illustrates the potential of a more critical approach to masculinity, and closes my argument against masculinity's prevailing use within men's studies. In an article entitled "Gender Treachery: Homophobia, Masculinity, and Threatened Identities," Patrick D. Hopkins writes:

> The gender category of men constructs its members around at least two conflicting characterizations of the essence of manhood. First, your masculinity (being-a-man) is natural and healthy and innate. But second, you must stay masculine— do not ever let your masculinity falter. So although being a man is seen as a natural and automatic state of affairs for a certain anatomical makeup, masculinity is so valued, so valorized, so prized, and its loss such a terrible thing, that one must always guard against losing it. . . . In fact, although the stable performance of masculinity is presented as an *outcome* of being a man, what arises in looking at heterosexism/homophobia is that being a man, or continuing to be a man, is the *outcome* of performing masculinity. (1992: 123–24)

Men's Movement Politics as the Politics of Masculinity

Not too many months ago, I removed the plain brown wrapper from my newly arrived copy of the *Utne Reader* (May/June 1991), a magazine which bills itself as "the best of the alternative press," and beheld a cover which proclaimed, "Men: It's time to pull together." The subtitle for this cover story was "The Politics of Masculinity." Oh, I thought, here is a welcome men's critique of patriarchy. It turned out the editors had something else in mind, for inside the magazine the special section was titled "The *New* Politics of Masculinity" (emphasis mine), and it contained several proposals for reforming, recovering, or otherwise salvaging masculinity for politically liberal and progressive men. Almost entirely absent was any recognizably critical, profeminist analysis of masculinity.[5] Instead, the prevailing mood was one of regret over the loss of what writer Andrew Kimbrell (1991: 69) called the "long-enduring, rooted masculine role," and of anger over the insufficiently recognized "oppression" of men. For Kimbrell, the solution to these problems lay in the establishment of a "men's movement based on the recovery of masculinity [which] could renew much of the world we have lost" (1991: 74).

Now, before considering which world has been lost and who of us may have lost it, we might keep in mind an observation made by Bob Lamm in his critique of the men's movement back in 1975, published in the profeminist anthology, *For Men against Sexism*: "We live in a world of men's movements. The United States Government is a men's movement. The Soviet Government is a men's movement. Exxon, I.T.T., and General Motors are all men's movements" (1977: 153). Today, we might ask just how the new politics of masculinity differs from the politics of these other men's movements, which also embrace masculinity in their own way. As ethicist Marvin M. Ellison rightly cautions, "It is always wise . . . to ask whose interests are being served by the men's movement and whether feminist agendas are being promoted in any recognizable way" (1993: 103). Unfortunately, for contemporary men's movements an allegiance to the politics of masculinity effectively precludes the pursuit of feminist political agendas.

The problem with advancing a men's politics in the name of masculinity is that it has already been done—for at least several thousand years—and its results have been precisely the patriarchal social and ideological structures which feminism now challenges. The "world we have lost," for which some neo-masculinists now pine, included not only comfortably masculine men secure in their ties to family, community, and land, but also rigidly structured hierarchies of power within both family and wider society, and narrowly defined sexual divisions of labor. Only such a massively sexist infrastructure could establish (some) men securely in their masculinity, at the profound cost of women's aspirations, bodies, and lives.

Contemporary men's movements calling for the reconstruction or reform of masculinity may envision an updated, "sensitive new-age" version of being a "real" man, but they remain premised on unexamined notions of essential gender difference, and therefore fail to make the break with the prevailing gender order that a feminist politics demands. Little seems to have changed from the 1970s-era men's movement, with its primary goal of producing "forms of masculinity able to adapt to new conditions, but sufficiently similar to the old ones to maintain the family, heterosexuality, capitalist work relations, and American national power" (Carrigan, Connell, and Lee 1987: 187). Indeed, it is difficult to conceive of a masculinity-based politics that is anything more than reformist, for such a politics implicitly accepts that which feminism systematically challenges: the assignment of fixed gender identities on the basis of biological sex.

Unless men's movement advocates can show how and why the building of a world without male supremacy demands "new" men still secure in their fundamental difference from women, notions of masculinity ought to have no place in men's movement politics. Rather, our goal should be to get beyond all regimes of compulsory masculinity and femininity,[6] to discover what kind of world becomes possible without them. For, as Kaufman observes:

Masculinity is power. But masculinity is terrifyingly fragile because it does not really exist in the sense we are led to think it exists, that is, as a biological reality—something real that we have inside ourselves. It exists as ideology; it exists as scripted behavior; it exists within "gendered" relationships. But in the end it is just a social institution with a tenuous relationship to that with which it is supposed to be synonymous: our maleness, our biological sex. (1987b: 13)

Whatever else masculinity may be, it is no basis for a profeminist men's politics.

Men's Spirituality as Masculine Spirituality

My final argument concerns the virtual promotion of masculinity to the status of spiritual path in recent years, particularly within the burgeoning "mythopoetic" men's movement.[7] The primary architect of this quasi-religious revaluing of masculine gender identity has been poet Robert Bly (1990), although he has not been alone in his efforts (cf. Harding 1992; Thompson 1991). For Bly and others, contemporary North American men (particularly middle- and upper-class, white, heterosexual men) have successfully escaped the stultifying model of 1950s-style masculinity only to become mired in a debilitating "softness" attributable, at least in part, to feminism (Bly 1990: 1–4). As a remedy for this situation, the mythopoetic men's movement advocates the recovery of something contemporary men sorely lack: a distinctly masculine spirituality.

For these masculinists, however, *authentic* masculine spirituality has nothing to do with the global panorama of male-centered religions, administered by predominantly male priesthoods promulgating male-glorifying doctrines, and worshiping male divinities. Rather, it is the "deep masculine" (Bly 1990: 6–8)—a vaguely defined, murky domain submerged within individual men's psyches and beneath Western industrial society—that is seen to hold the key to contemporary men's spiritual renewal. For the mythopoetic men's movement, the existence of this realm is a primary article of faith, and making contact with it is of crucial importance. Bly, who personifies the deep masculine in the mythic figure of the "wildman," says, "Getting in touch with the wildman means religious life for a man in the broadest sense of the phrase" (Thompson 1987: 180). The religion of the wildman is presented as bringing to men a primal vitality clearly lacking in both contemporary institutionalized religion and secular society: an earthiness, a hairiness, and, of course, a wildness.

The main problem with this approach is that potentially valid critiques of religion and society are being made in the name of a reactionary fiction—namely, deep (which is another way of saying *essential*) masculinity. Once again, gender is assimilated to sex, and men are theorized as both properly and necessarily masculine. In this case, there is an additional wrinkle, for spiritual masculinists use "masculinity" as a term of absolute value, to describe all that is good and true and enduring about men. Where other men's movement advocates might at least concede the occasional necessity of changing certain unpleasant aspects of masculinity—such as a predilection toward emotional numbness or an inclination toward violence—mythopoetic adherents ascribe such failings to the absence of "true" masculinity.

This uncritical use of the concept of masculinity allows spiritual masculinist Forrest Craver to write, apparently without irony: "Throughout human history, male bonding and affiliation has been a crucial dynamic for evoking, sustaining and enlarging masculine energy and directing it with focused and carefully calibrated power into the community" (1991: 5). Masculine energy and power in the form of what? War? Sexual violence? "Monday Night Football"? Ethical distinctions and feminist political analysis vanish in the face of this opaque language, whereby men who commit violence against women become, for archetypal psychologist Thomas Moore, "the weakest, the least masculine, those most lacking in masculine spirit" (1990: 129). Such spiritualizing of masculinity absolves it of its destructive, yet always-contested, history and attempts an impossible escape from the gritty field on which gendered power struggles take place.

But what about the idea of a spirituality for men? At this time when feminism has effectively challenged both mundane and cosmic gender orders, what men do not need is the re-enshrinement of masculinity as a spiritual ideal, be it "deep" or otherwise. I have argued elsewhere (Mirsky forthcoming; cf. Rowan 1987) that men seeking a grounded, embodied, earth-centered spirituality can find much of value in the developing thealogical explorations and ritual practice of contemporary feminist spirituality, and I believe such creative, collaborative work holds considerably more promise than a retreat into a masculinity that never was. Rather than clutching tightly to the mirage of masculinity as it vanishes in the light of sustained feminist scrutiny, men might better endeavor to embrace change and open ourselves to new possibilities heretofore unimagined.[8]

To close, I offer an observation by Patrick D. Hopkins, drawing together much of what I have been arguing: "The logic of masculinity is demanding—protect and maintain what you are intrinsically, or you could lose it, mutate, become something else" (1992: 124). I find the possibility of such change a hopeful and exciting prospect!

NOTES

1. In view of the widely diverging ideological agendas of existing "men's rights," "mythopoetic," and "profeminist" men's groups (to name a few), I believe it is ill-advised and entirely inaccurate to speak of a single "Men's Movement."

2. One of these men, John Stoltenberg (1989, 1993), continues to advance a radical feminist analysis of men and masculinity, and is, unfortunately, virtually ·alone among men in doing so. The essential collection of early anti-sexist men's writings is Snodgrass (1977); also Kokopeli and Lakey (1983).

3. Carrigan, Connell, and Lee develop the idea of "hegemonic masculinity" as "a particular variety of masculinity to which others—among them young and effeminate as well as homosexual men—are subordinated" (1987: 174). I would argue that although "hegemonic masculinity" is useful in describing relations

between groups of men, it tends to obscure the hegemonic nature of *all* masculinities when considered from women's standpoint, in the context of men's domination of women.

4. Foucault's general influence on much of my argument here should be apparent, and I am consciously echoing the title, *The History of Sexuality* (Foucault 1980).

5. The one exception is Dennis Altman's brief, excerpted piece on homophobia (1991).

6. The phrase is suggested by Adrienne Rich's term "compulsory heterosexuality" (1983).

7. For an account of the origin and particular meaning of this term in a men's movement context, see Harding (1992: xx).

8. In this regard, I find particularly suggestive and encouraging the voice of the God invoked by feminist activist and thealogian Starhawk (1992: 36):

> I am not what you expect to see,
> I'll never tell you what to be,
> Look outside every boundary,
> Where there's nothing to hold to, there I'll be.
>
> I'm the word that you can't define,
> I'm the color that runs outside the line,
> I'm the shiver running up your spine,
> Break the pattern, I'll make a new design.

REFERENCES

Altman, Dennis. 1991. "Why Are Gay Men So Feared?" *Utne Reader* 45 (May/June): 75.

Beauvoir, Simone de. 1974. *The Second Sex.* Trans. H. M. Parshley. New York: Vintage.

Bly, Robert. 1990. *Iron John: A Book about Men.* Reading, Mass.: Addison-Wesley.

Brod, Harry. 1987a. "The Case for Men's Studies." In *The Making of Masculinities: The New Men's Studies,* ed. Harry Brod. Boston: Allen and Unwin.

———, ed. 1987b. *The Making of Masculinities: The New Men's Studies.* Boston: Allen and Unwin.

Butler, Judith. 1990. *Gender Trouble: Feminism and the Subversion of Identity.* New York: Routledge.

Carrigan, Tim, Bob Connell, and John Lee. 1987. "Hard and Heavy: Toward a New Sociology of Masculinity." In Kaufman 1987a.

Craver, Forrest. 1991. "Igniting the Masculine Soul." *Edges: New Planetary Patterns* 4(2): 5.

Daly, Mary. 1978. *Gyn/Ecology: The Metaethics of Radical Feminism.* Boston: Beacon Press.

Ellison, Marvin M. 1993. "Holding Up Our Half of the Sky: Male Gender Privilege as Problem and Resource for Liberation Ethics." *Journal of Feminist Studies in Religion* 9 (1–2): 95–113.

Foucault, Michel. 1980. *The History of Sexuality: Volume I, An Introduction.* Trans. Robert Hurley. New York: Vintage.

Harding, Christopher. 1992. "What's All This about a Men's Movement?" In *Wingspan: Inside the Men's Movement,* ed. Christopher Harding. New York: St. Martin's Press.

Hopkins, Patrick D. 1992. "Gender Treachery: Homophobia, Masculinity, and Threatened Identities." In May and Strikwerda 1992.

Jackson, David. 1990. *Unmasking Masculinity: A Critical Autobiography.* London: Unwin Hyman.

Kaufman, Michael, ed. 1987a. *Beyond Patriarchy: Essays by Men on Pleasure, Power, and Change.* Toronto: Oxford University Press.

———. 1987b. "The Construction of Masculinity and the Triad of Men's Violence." In Kaufman 1987a.

Kimbrell, Andrew. 1991. "A Time for Men to Pull Together: A Manifesto for the New Politics of Masculinity." *Utne Reader* 45 (May/June): 66–74.

Kimmel, Michael S., and Michael A. Messner, ed. 1992. *Men's Lives.* Second Edition. New York: Macmillan.

Kinsman, Gary. 1987. "Men Loving Men: The Challenge of Gay Liberation." In Kaufman 1987a.

Kleinberg, Seymour. 1987. "The New Masculinity of Gay Men, and Beyond." In Kaufman 1987a.

Kokopeli, Bruce, and George Lakey. 1983. "More Power Than We Want: Masculine Sexuality and Violence." In *Off Their Backs . . . and on Our Own Two Feet.* Philadelphia: New Society Publishers.

Lamm, Bob. 1977. "Men's Movement Hype." In *For Men against Sexism: A Book of Readings,* ed. Jon Snodgrass. Albion, Calif.: Times Change Press.

Mander, Jerry. 1978. *Four Arguments for the Elimination of Television.* New York: William Morrow.

May, Larry, and Robert A. Strikwerda, ed., with the assistance of Patrick D. Hopkins. 1992. *Rethinking Masculinity: Philosophical Explorations in Light of Feminism.* Lanham, Md.: Rowman and Littlefield.

Mirsky, Seth. Forthcoming. "Men and the Promise of Goddess Spirituality: Reflections along the Way." In *Redeeming Men: Essays on Men, Masculinities, and Religion,* ed. Stephen B. Boyd, Merle Longwood, and Mark W. Muesse. Louisville, Ky.: Westminster/John Knox.

Moore, Thomas. 1990. "Eros and the Male Spirit." In *Men and Intimacy: Personal Accounts Exploring the Dilemmas of Modern Male Sexuality,* ed. Franklin Abbott. Freedom, Calif.: Crossing Press.

Rich, Adrienne. 1983. "Compulsory Heterosexuality and Lesbian Existence." In *Powers of Desire: The Politics of Sexuality,* ed. Ann Snitow, Christine Stansell, and Sharon Thompson. New York: Monthly Review Press.

Rowan, John. 1987. *The Horned God: Feminism and Men as Wounding and Healing*. London: Routledge and Kegan Paul.

Seidler, Victor J. 1989. *Rediscovering Masculinity: Reason, Language and Sexuality*. London: Routledge.

Snodgrass, Jon, ed. 1977. *For Men against Sexism: A Book of Readings*. Albion, Calif.: Times Change Press.

Starhawk. 1992. "A Men's Movement I Can Trust." In *Women Respond to the Men's Movement: A Feminist Collection*, ed. Kay Leigh Hagan. San Francisco: HarperSanFrancisco.

Stoltenberg, John. 1989. *Refusing to Be a Man: Essays on Sex and Justice*. Portland, Oreg.: Breitenbush Books.

———. 1993. *The End of Manhood: A Book for Men of Conscience*. New York: Dutton.

Thompson, Keith. 1987. "What Men Really Want: An Interview with Robert Bly." In *New Men, New Minds: Breaking Male Tradition*, ed. Franklin Abbott. Freedom, Calif.: Crossing Press.

———, ed. 1991. *To Be a Man: In Search of the Deep Masculine*. Los Angeles: Jeremy P. Tarcher.

PART II

Male Bodies and the Construction of Religious Identity

Growing Up Christian and Male: One Man's Experience

TOM F. DRIVER

Introduction (1993)

To speak honestly of men's bodies and men's gods requires awareness of plurality and change. We need to ask: What men? At what time of life? Where, and when?

We need also to recognize that the gods themselves are not immutable. Although they endure from generation to generation, they change as time passes, little by little adjusting (as how could they not?) to the transformations their devotees undergo in the course of personal and historical experience. "All things change—some faster than others" (Driver 1990 [1977]: xxii).

In 1978, I wrote an autobiographical paper for a panel on the study of men's religious experience that was arranged by the Women's Caucus of the American Academy of Religion in New Orleans. I was invited to this task by my friend Carol Christ, then a professor of religion at San Jose State University in California and formerly my junior colleague at Union Theological Seminary and Columbia University in New York. Her letter was dated January 24, 1978:

> We feel it is time men came out of the closet and started reflecting on the male experiences (body, culture, or whatever) which give rise to specific themes in theologies written by men.

43

I took the invitation as an opportunity to reflect upon the childhood origins of my self-understanding as both a male and a Christian. The resulting paper was delivered in November 1978 but has never been published until now, when an inquiry from the editor of the present volume, asking for thoughts about men's bodies and men's gods, has prompted me to bring it to light.

Under these circumstances, the current assignment has turned into a kind of archaeology of my changing experiences of being both male and Christian, and my gradually shifting visions of God. The paper itself makes reference to several layers of time. To it I will add a few more layers, partly as brief notes inserted into the text in brackets, and partly in the form of a concluding commentary written in 1993, after an interval of fifteen years.

Confessions of a Male-Centered Christian (1978)

Male Renown

Self-evident to me as I grew up was the pre-eminence of men. To think of this as "male supremacy" or "male chauvinism" did not occur to me until the women's movement became newly vocal a few years ago *[that is, in the early 1970s]*, but the fact of males at the head of everything important was obvious.

There was one exception in our town.

[A place of about 25,000 people in the border South—the Appalachian foothills of east Tennessee, to be more precise. My childhood memories refer mostly to the 1930s, the time of the Great Depression.]

The postmaster, as almost everyone called her, was a woman. However, the job seemed to give her no noticeable power, and the main talk about her that I remember was some wonderment about why she wanted the job in the first place.

The best phrase I have ever heard to describe the sexism of our town is the title of an anthropological book about Papua New Guinea and the Trobriand Islands—*Women of Value, Men of Renown* (Weiner 1983 [1976]). I think the phrase comes from an expression used by certain New Guinea people themselves.

[Of course, I didn't hear these words in childhood but only about two years before writing the paper, after I had visited New Guinea. Recollection is not necessarily invented but is surely shaped by important experiences near the time of writing. The past cannot be known "as it was," but only as it now seems that it was, given the rememberer's present knowledge and point of view.]

Women in our town were certainly valuable, but if they became re-nowned it could only mean they had done, or were about to do, something bad.

[My mother often said that it was most unfortunate for a woman's name to appear anywhere in a newspaper except on the "Society Page," where engagements, weddings, and other social events were chronicled. The obituaries were another, partial exception: a woman's obituary should not be too long.]

Men, by contrast, were expected to be renowned, and it was unfortunate for them if they failed to achieve it.

From this milieu, which now seems as typically American as almost everything else in our town, I absorbed a clear understanding of masculinity, closely linked to a certain view of the world that I also took in. To be masculine was to have public recognition combined with direct influence on communal events. If you had influence without recognition, you didn't quite make it. I am thinking of a certain wealthy man who, as I learned from my banker father, wielded a lot of power but was reclusive, barely known by sight, or even by name, to most of the citizens. I did not think of him as very masculine.

[It also happened that this man's physical stature was very small, a fact which, added to his reclusiveness, made him appear wraithlike. To me as a child he appeared to possess no weight or substance, which made it hard for me to understand my father's stories of his economic success and influence. That I left this point out of the original paper seems strange until one notices that the entire paper was cast in such a way as to minimize the importance of men's bodies, their physical activities (as in sports, for example) and their sexuality. Why? I think because when I grew up I did not identify my masculine self with these things, and do so only partially today.]

We also had a few men who gained notoriety by feats of derring-do but otherwise had no influence. They were thought of more as boys than as men. The status which a real man attained was that of influential renown.

Masculinity went hand and glove with both personal and public self-esteem. Personal self-esteem, for a male, required public performance. It was not something you could have without an audience. Thus, it interlocked with the self-esteem of the community. The town thought of itself as masculine. It wanted regional and national recognition. It wanted political influence. It was proud of its initiative and autonomy. Masculinity was identical with its idea of the good. That does not mean that femininity in women was bad. It was simply irrelevant. At the most, it was decorative of the public good. Fine sermons on Mothers' Day, active PTA, DAR, and Blue Stocking Club did not counteract but reinforced this assumption in my mind.

[*Today, in retirement, I spend about half my time in another small town, in New England. Here, more than fifty years later, the situation seems not entirely different. The town I know today is like two towns in one. One of these lives by a code strikingly similar to the one I am describing. The other has come to appreciate the many women in town who are prominent in business and public affairs, which has meant a changed self-understanding on the part of men. These two towns occupy the same space, often the same household. Many individuals experience themselves as citizens of both.*]

Life in our town provided the social substance for what I mean when I describe myself as male-centered. I must add to the picture a psychological component which I know by introspection. How many men in our town shared it I have often wondered. Most of them, I am inclined to imagine; but I cannot be sure.

The identification of masculinity with renown and influence meant that masculinity was not ostensibly a matter of sex. About sex there was a lot of squeamishness, certainly in all public communication and in the circles in which my own family moved. One did not become masculine by having women, getting married, or fathering children. Hence, while being masculine required male gender (in the sense of having a male body), it did not require sexual activity, which was either taken for granted or viewed with suspicion. Sex was as private as masculinity was public.

[These generalizations seem very specific to my own social class, which the paper identifies only obliquely. I belonged, then as now, to the educated upper middle class. In the South in those days this meant being brought up in a tradition of gentility, boys taught to become "gentlemen," a tradition reflected here in several ways, especially the discreet separation between masculinity and sex.]

It followed, at least in my mind, that masculinity had nothing to do with women. It was not a complementary quality. Thinking back on it, I am hard put to explain why this was so. Every man was more or less expected to be married, most social gatherings were of mixed company, and the value of women, as I have said, was clearly recognized. My own parents formed a very clear team whose love for each other I never doubted and whose division of labor was both clear and harmonious.

[As far as I could then see. Today I am inclined to think that, although it was a solid and loving marriage, there was more disharmony than met the child's eye, some of which had to do with my mother's frustration in a gendered role that she did not outwardly question in my hearing. To recount why I think so would make a long story, of which I was only beginning to be aware when I wrote the paper.]

Nevertheless, masculinity, as I perceived it, was not the complement of femininity. The latter was a pejorative term. While there might be feminine virtues, femininity as such had no standing. It was simply the negation of masculinity, which was a virtue in itself.

[Since 1978, feminism has taught me a great suspicion of the words masculine, feminine, masculinity, and femininity. I've become aware that these terms point to ideas and values socially constructed by patriarchy. The paper implies this but does not say it, because at the time, although I knew of "the social construction of reality" (Berger and Luckmann, 1966), I had read little or nothing about the social construction of gender.]

Insofar as masculinity depended on renown, it was narcissistic. Insofar as it depended on influence, it was a one-way street. It had an indepen-

dent status in being. Masculinity was thus an object of desire and
adoration, for it stood at the pinnacle of real value. This attitude, as I
later learned [in college, right after World War II], was that of the
classical Greek writers, especially Plato. Still later [1976] I saw it in what
I fancy is pristine form in the highlands of New Guinea, where the self-
importance of men is virtually unrestrained. Having learned something
about male mystique in those exotic societies, I do not think I am
reading it backward into the small town of my boyhood, because I
vividly remember sitting on the front steps of my house each afternoon
at the age of four or five waiting for the bigger boys to come down the
street from school and the fathers to come up the street from work. My
mother and sister inside the house were not as real, because not as
enviable, as the boys and men who had been out doing their thing. My
desire was to be around them, belong to them, be one of them. What
could be more natural, we may ask. And what could do more to inform
one's sense of the world?

[This is one of the most formative of all my memories. It is a scene
which returns to me frequently at every stage of my life—as a
youth, a young man, a soldier, a scholar, a husband, a parent, a
teacher, and now a senior citizen. Neither time, place, nor circumstance dulls the image.]

Women of Strength

A few women were of great importance to my development through
high school, after which I went away from our town. My mother was
the most important. Of her I will say here only that she dominated our
household by the totality of her dedication to it, and in this she appeared
to have had the complete consent of my father. They had three sons and
a daughter.

Looking back, I am amazed that in a family of four males and two
females the males formed no strong bonding among them. We liked each
other (well, I liked my brothers part of the time) but we did not bond. I
ascribe this to the sense we had that the family really belonged to my
mother. My father took pride in his work at the bank, his leadership in
civic organizations, his work at home, and his children; but he always
referred to the home as belonging to Sarah. In this I believe he imitated

the relation between his own parents, and my mother did the same for her part. After going through college she had returned to her parents' house, doing nothing in particular until she got married. She did do some rather good paintings and some even better charcoal drawings, but after marriage she did them no more.

Almost all my school teachers were women. Only the high school principal and two or three of his faculty were men. Women taught me to read, write, do figures, dream, and think. Their eyes were not fastened on our town but on the great world of culture to be known in books, art, and travel. Learning of all this from them, I developed mixed feelings concerning masculinity. It meant having influence on public things right in your own sphere in a directly visible way. It did not usually mean having imagination about the world at large. This was another way in which masculinity was self-referential. Those who seemed to dream of a larger, more exciting world, a world of Shakespeare, Shelley, and Thomas Kepler, of Athens, Rome, and London, were women who taught in school. I was deeply torn between the parochial glory of men and the imaginative reach of my women teachers. There were well-to-do men in our town who had lots of books and went off on long trips, but whatever they knew of foreign culture they kept secret. They did not use it to enhance their influence and renown.

[I note today that the "larger, more exciting world" my women teachers taught me to dream of was entirely Eurocentric. There was no dreaming about Africa or Latin America, and almost none of Asia. In other words, the exciting world was the one in which colonialist power was concentrated, not the regions over which that power reigned. By the same token, my imagination was not turned toward the Black, Hispanic, or Native American peoples of my own land. One name for this type of education is elitist. A more informative name is patriarchal: I was taught, even by my women teachers in school, to identify with, and dream of, the achievements of a patriarchal Euro-American culture.]

The woman, apart from my mother, who influenced me the most was Director of Christian Education at our church. I think if my parents had known what she was doing to me they would not have admired her as much as they did, but they approved on principle everything connected with the Methodist Church, especially the State Street Methodist

Church. Virginia Stafford could be found at the church any afternoon after school, and that's were I went more days than not.

[On the other days, I was likely to be at the movies with my friends. The influence that the movies of the 1930s and 1940s had upon my gender formation must have been quite strong, but that's a topic I have not yet thought through.]

She would give me the keys to the organ console and let me teach myself to play it in the empty sanctuary. Enticing me with such pleasures, she set about to improve upon my education. Wanting to make a liberal out of me—theologically, politically, and racially—she fed me books to read and discussed them with me. She also took me and some of my peers to conferences far and wide. At these I remember my first experiences of social equality with black people—"colored," as we said then. Virginia Stafford was not married, as most of my school teachers were. She dressed, moved, spoke, and worked as if she did not care what people thought. I had never seen that before in a woman, and was drawn to it as to a magnet.

Church of Men

As for the church, it was masculine. I come now to matters that are full of ambiguity and strong feeling. How was the church masculine?

Being Protestants, we did not often refer to Mother Church. Nonetheless, the church nurtured me, perhaps even more than the school, and my mother viewed it as an extension of her own family. Most boys went to it as seldom as possible, and my going there so often, even on weekdays, did nothing to enhance my reputation as a real guy. Indeed, it was part of what was called the sissy in me, like playing music and going into the kitchen to make cookies. But I knew that I was drawn to the church because it was masculine.

There comes to mind a remembered scene. Sunday church is going on. The preacher's head is bowed as he prays a long prayer, and the congregation's heads are down, too. I am a little boy who can't keep his eyes shut. I look around. At the back of the church several men are standing. Their eyes are not closed, and their heads are not bowed. They are looking all around, and some are even talking softly together. I am astonished. It occurs to me that this is their place and they can do what they please in it. I see no women or girls not bowed in prayer.

The motif here is submission. The church was feminine insofar as its behavior was submissive. All the women in it, except Virginia Stafford, were there, it seemed, to submit; and so were some of the men. They surrendered to church in a mixture of duty and comfort. The church in its piety was feminine.

But some people, I realized, do not submit. They run the place. They are the greeters at the door, the ushers, the deacons, the elders. They are all men, and the masculinity here is the same as elsewhere in our town: visibility and influence. These qualities also belong to the church itself. Few organizations, and fewer buildings, in our town have more visibility and influence than the churches. They carry weight. The big ones form a fraternity with the town's secular institutions. Even a child could sense this.

As a growing boy, I knew there was power in the church, and I wanted it. I did not want to be one of those deacons or elders, but I wanted influence and I wanted recognition for it, as I did also at school; and I got it. My life being what it has been, my sense of my own masculinity is tied in with that of the church. It has always been hard for me to think of them separately.

At the center of the church somehow (the how was rather vague to the young boy) there was Jesus. In Sallman's portrait, which hung prominently in the church office opposite the face of John Wesley, Jesus did not look very masculine; but you knew that he had visibility and influence—and that he was male. Jesus was the most renowned person of all time, and his influence was everywhere. Only God had more. God was the biggest man of all.

[*My then recent visit to Papua New Guinea has once again left its mark on the paper. This sentence echoes the New Guinea highland expression "Big Man," which means a self-made man, a local wheeler-dealer who has gained renown, wealth, and clout.*]

Everything referred to God, and his influence was said to be all-powerful. It did not even seem to me, although I heard it often enough, that God was invisible. How could someone be invisible if you had their picture clearly in your mind? The image of God as an old man with a white beard sitting on a throne held no interest for me. Having heard it ridiculed in sermons, I regarded it as both false and unappealing. The God I saw was large, robust, full-faced and in the prime of adult life. I saw only his face and curly dark hair, so I never could tell what clothes he wore or if he was naked. The ultimate masculine was God.

> [Note that I imagined the masculinity of the God, like that of boys and men, as having little or nothing to do with sex or women. The maleness of God had rather to do with renown and power. Note also that the power, since it was omnipotent, ran in one direction only—from God outward. No outside power could affect God. Note again that the renown of God required an audience full of praise and awe. God's essence, then, was self-referential. Later, when studying theology, I saw this expressed as God's eternity, aseity, and ability to create from nothing. It is a masculinity that requires to be beheld but is not beholden—a divine narcissism. In the late 1960s and early 1970s, when I began to question Western imperialism and the divine right of patriarchy, I came to believe that the idea of divine self-sufficiency is a theological mistake. Yet it remains characteristic of too much theology, which holds out, at some point, for a non-relational quality deemed essential if God is to be God. I no longer think so.]

Male God, Male Minister

The masculinity of the Christian minister is a strange topic. I felt this acutely as a youth, for I was attracted to the ministry at a very young age, and in high school I received a ministerial "call"; yet I resisted this in great agony, fearing the loss of my autonomous manhood. *[I have since described this experience. See Driver 1991: 70]*

On the one hand, since I was religious and a good public speaker, the ministry offered me a clear road to renown and influence. At the age of six, I used to come home from church, rig up a pulpit in the backyard while waiting for my mother's Sunday dinner, and harangue the birds and bees with the good news of the gospel. Oh, what a fine preacher was I!

On the other hand, the ministry threatened to set me apart from other men in a stereotyped role that would take away my autonomy in the same measure in which it gave it to me. Ministers were of necessity men (the only exception I heard of as a child was the notorious Aimee Semple McPherson), but ministers were not real men. It was not only that they couldn't cuss and tell dirty jokes. It was that they were servants. Conspicuous as they were, renowned as some became, influential as they might be, they had to submit to elders, deacons, bishops, and God. They couldn't even get mad and quit, as men in business could do. When I received my "call" I told none of my friends about it, for I knew they would feel sorry for me.

What I actually did was say *yes* to the "call" and later go into theological teaching, which is a much more independent vocation. For some years during high school, the army, college, and seminary, I intended to be a pastoral minister. Contrary to what a psychoanalyst might think, I believe that these years were decisive in the evolution of my male-centered Christianity. In any case, they were the years of my sexual maturation, unless the latter is what is occurring to me now in middle age.

Be that as it may, I devoted myself to God and sex at the same time. In both respects, I must explain, my imagination far out-ran my activity. My first sexual experiences were with boys. I dreamed of naked women (whom I had hardly ever seen) and clung to boys my age for what little sexual contact there was. I graduated from high school during World War II and went straight into the army. I hated everything about it except being constantly in the company of men, which I enjoyed even when I did not like all of the men. I refer to this in order to indicate in myself an eroticized view of masculinity that is linked to my experience of the Christian church.

[There's an unexplained shift in the paper here, from a picture of masculinity as having nothing to do with sex to "an eroticized view of masculinity." This reflects mainly, I suppose, a shift from boyhood into adolescence and young adulthood. The main theme of this section in the paper is the confluence of maleness, eroticism, God, and the church that began when I was a teenager.]

If you want to think in the usual psychological way, you can say that I had such a view [of masculinity eroticized] from early childhood and would have attached it to any institution I took seriously. I don't deny that and could even cite my life-long interest in theater, where similar dynamics were at play. My point, however, is that the theater and other institutions lack the church's ultimate rationale for preoccupation with masculine identity. Worship of a self-contained male God extends to male narcissism the quality of something religious. Of this I have no doubt. In fact, I believe that the homophobia of the church, its categorical condemnation of homosexuality as sinful, is a defense against its own homosexual latency.

Going on from Here

Skip now to the year 1972, when I am forty-seven years old. I have married long ago, have three teen-age children, and am a seminary teacher. My wife and many other women I know are in feminist consciousness-raising groups. Several of us husbands decide to form a men's group. We have no trouble getting participants, and the group, as it turns out, meets weekly for four years before finally disbanding.

Membership in that group provided the first occasion of my life for regular association with men in a context that was not competitive. It is hard for me to describe how important that experience was to me, and apparently to most of the others.

That men have to relate to each other primarily by competition was something I had believed all my life. It was the way my two brothers and I had related. The boys I knew at school and around town were forever competing in sports, and those of us who were less athletic competed for grades. The army had more camaraderie at times, but everyone's motive had been to get promoted, get out, or both. In my professional life competitiveness was rampant. Academics seemed constantly to score points against each other. All this seemed to me simply natural. Boys will be boys, after all, and so will men. For a long time I knew how to play that game with excitement. It is, you see, a concomitant of the identification of masculinity with renown and influence.

I may not say that our men's group was entirely free from competition. Two or three of us brought very competitive life-styles with us, and we vied with each other for attention and dominance. But the group as a whole was not interested in this, so the basic ethos in our meetings provided no supporting context to encourage or justify competitive behavior. As this gradually dawned on me, years of burden seemed to fall from my shoulders. I was at last among men who took manhood for granted and did not feel the need to prove it. The anxiety associated with renown and influence was absent.

As a result of the men's group, I know more clearly what I am looking for today. I call it a non-chauvinistic fraternity. We usually think of male chauvinism as an attitude of superiority toward women, but that is only part of what I mean by the word. Primarily, I think of chauvinism as an attitude men have toward each other, leading toward competition for renown and influence, so that their associations almost always result in a pecking order. Where one stands in the pecking order indicates one's degree of masculinity. In such a condition, masculinity is always a performance, something put on like a theatrical role or a priest's vestments. Its purpose is to attract attention, and masculinity turns out to exist in the eye of the beholder. *[I shall have more to say about performance below.]*

When I speak of a non-chauvinist fraternity, I mean a mutual understanding among men obviating the necessity of demonstrating their manhood. The latter, instead of being self-referential, can then be released to look and move outward toward other people and the world in ways more truly loving and ethical.

[Recently, John Stoltenberg (1990 [1989]; 1993) has taken a different, no doubt better tack. Instead of looking for a redeemed and redeeming form of manhood, he argues that manhood must be repudiated for the sake of "loving justice."]

I experience this very seldom. Our economic system is antithetical to it, I hardly need say. And so is most of the Christian religion, for reasons I have already indicated. We need a theological revolution that can enable us to take a new look at monotheism. To insist, as we have done, that God is one, or even a self-contained "economy" of *three-in-one*, does not simply go hand in hand with God's maleness; it is the very same thing.

[The unity of God in our Western tradition has not been the unity of things that are different, each having a rightful place in the sun, but has been the unity of that which is like unto itself. Such a unity must be called self-referential, narcissistic, or chauvinistic, for its aim must necessarily be to call attention to itself and seek to be imitated. See Driver 1981.]

I do not know whether men in large numbers can lay their anxiety about masculinity to rest. I know they can sometimes do it in small numbers. I find myself looking today for such leaven. I believe that until men discover how to love each other without competitive narcissism they are not very good at loving women, children, and all manner of folk who are quite different from themselves.

In much writing today, it is fashionable to speak of the narcissism in our society and to blame it on a so-called "inward turn" of the 1970s. I read the phenomenon differently. The roots of narcissism in American culture go back, I think, to the ethos of the self-made man, which we Americans did not invent but did raise to a high pitch. Religiously, these roots go further back. They lie in doctrines of a self-made God, who ultimately requires of men only one thing: that they should worship him absolutely. I am wanting to suggest a necessary connection between narcissism and the idea of an absolute God.

[It's not entirely clear what I meant by this "necessary connection." Among the ancient Greeks, for example, there was plenty of male narcissism without the monotheistic idea of an absolute God. But if we turn the matter around, we can see what I had in mind: the absoluteness of God, with its corollary of self-sufficiency, must necessarily connect with a kind of worship or adoration of the self. Or else it issues in a sense of the human self as absolutely worthless, a kind of inverted narcissism.]

I would like also to suggest that if people turn inward that does not prove they have given up on society—although there is other evidence in this decade which does point to such a despair. One motive for turning inward is to get such a clear view of one's self as will enable a clearer view of others. Where this is the case, self-knowledge and becoming a responsible self can go hand in hand with belonging to a communitarian world.

Addendum—Fifteen Years Later (1993)

The author of the paper—who was (is?) myself at a different "layer" of time—was a married man, 53 years old, a professor of theology and culture at a liberal, ecumenical, theological seminary. He had two daughters and a son who were in their twenties. He was, although he did not say this to himself, undergoing a mid-life crisis. In other words, he was struggling with self-recognition, not as a youth of untested potential but as a man with more than half his life behind him. He had achieved, he thought, a modicum of renown. The question now was his value.

Carol Christ knew that for about seven years, since 1971, I had been teaching theology from the vantage point of life experience. That is, I had been encouraging my students (and myself) to examine the connections between our experienced lives, our theological perspectives, and the academic materials we encountered in a seminary curriculum. My book growing out of that teaching, *Patterns of Grace: Human Experience as Word of God* had been published in 1977, but it gave no attention to experiences that might be said to belong specifically or exclusively to men.

When the book had come out, it was the subject of a public discussion one evening at Union Seminary, in the course of which several women pressed me to account for the fact that all references to God in the book were to a male figure: I had referred to God only as father and as "he." The only answer I could give was the truthful one that a male God was the only deity of which I had had any experience.

I use the word "experience" to point to the intersection between cultural, historical, personal, and psychological factors. I do not think that these several aspects of experience can be separated, even though we may distinguish them for analytic purposes. The following story about the gender of God may illustrate their interconnection.

Seven years before starting to write *Patterns of Grace,* and about thirteen before writing the "Confessions" paper, I had spent a summer with Anne Barstow, my wife, in the Middle East, one of the highlights of which was a journey we made to an important archaeological dig on the Anatolian plain in Turkey, a site known as Çatal Hüyuk. The neolithic city that was being unearthed there was devoted to the worship of a goddess, a deity depicted in no uncertain terms as female, most strikingly as a mother in the act of giving birth to a child. Our encounter with this mother-goddess imagery at Çatal Hüyuk turned out to be transformative for Anne, who was not yet a feminist because there was in 1965 no movement to give her that name and that self-understanding, but who was, without knowing it, waiting for that movement to happen. Still and all, her life experiences had prepared her to have a powerful reaction to the mother/female religious imagery at Çatal Hüyuk. A few years later she wrote an article about it that is often cited (Barstow 1978; 1983 [1978]).

As for me at Çatal Hüyuk, I was not then ready to take in what I was seeing, at which I looked with a professionally detached, albeit appreciative, eye. I was by then a trained scholar of literature and a frequent commentator on theology and culture. But I was not yet aware of the reality of patriarchy, of its limits and injuries. I was too immersed within patriarchy to let my identity and my theological convictions be unsettled by religious images that, however striking, had for me neither a cultural nor a personal frame of reference. The unsettling was to come in 1972.

When I visited Çatal Hüyuk I was 40. The year was 1965, when public attention was directed toward the civil rights struggle and the war in Vietnam. Gender questions had not yet arisen for me in any *public* sense. I stumbled upon them daily, as husband, father, and teacher, without any way to recognize them, for lack of a relevant language. Feminism was to create the language through much struggle and pain during the 1970s.

By the time I wrote the paper, gender issues had become part of public discussion, and I had been challenged, as I've said, about the unchastened male imagery in my own published work. Prompted by women who were tired of being left out of the language, the history, the religious imagery, and most of the halls of renown, tired of being used and left anonymous—prompted by such women and the new gender discourse they were inventing, I could begin to think out loud about the correlation between myself as male and the male God I worshiped.

Although the 1978 paper was my first public venture into the discussion of gender, the seismic upheaval that feminist thought created for me had come six years earlier. In the summer of 1971 I read *Sexual Politics*, by Kate Millett (1990 [1970]), and was never the same again. It was a feminist reading of Western literature from the Greeks to the moderns, and it was a battle cry. It so happened that Millett's study was done in the course of her doctoral program in English and Comparative Literature in the very same department at the same university (Columbia) where I had earned my own Ph.D. I had read most of the works she discussed, and I had a pretty good idea what they were about. And I knew they did not mean what she was saying they meant. If they did, I would have seen it, wouldn't I? I would read a page or two of Millett, throw the book down, fume about it, cool off a little, and read more in spite of myself. When I finished the book I was ill. I went to bed for two days.

This was crisis and turning point. Not that the book did this all by itself. A lot of changes connected with feminism had been going on in my family, among my colleagues and students, and in the society. Millett's book precipitated a crisis I was sure to have had sooner or later. I tell the story because it dramatizes the fact that I was converted to feminism kicking and screaming. Two decades later, I still backslide frequently. Once you become addicted to the myth of male renown, recovery is painful, slow, never complete.

There is a final observation to be made about the paper, one that concerns my marriage and my sexuality. Anne Barstow and I had married when I was twenty-seven, and our marriage has lasted, miraculously I often think, to the present day—more than forty years. Yet this sturdy marriage, notable when considered in light of the nation's divorce rate, not to mention our deep (and often deeply troubled) love for each other, makes no appearance in the paper. Although when I wrote the paper I had already been married for twenty-six years (almost half of my lifetime then), I gave the reader no clue to this aspect of my situation. But that's not all.

Truth to tell, I did not even notice the absence of my married life from the paper and my commentary upon it until Anne, after looking at a draft of the present document, asked whether I had ever thought my way through to a theology of heterosexuality, a question that brought me up rather short. The paper is clear in its critique of a male-centered and strictly monotheistic theology, which it views as the reflection of male narcissism. But the paper says nothing about what kind of heterosexual theology could be written, nor what ideas concerning gender and sexuality it might include. Reflection now indicates that heterosexuality has never quite come into focus for me. Let me explain, hoping thereby to cast a small light on something that pertains not only to myself but also, I think, to many men.

The paper makes clear that I had given a great deal of thought to that portion of me that is *not* heterosexual. I had thought about everything in me that draws me toward other men, including emotions that are certainly erotic. These have never been hidden from my consciousness, nor have they been frightening to me, as it seems they are to many men, giving rise to much homophobic behavior. And yet these feelings have constituted a *problem*, since they represent something forbidden to boys and men brought up as I was—not only forbidden but unspeakable.

Awareness of something problematic in my own gendering enabled me, once I got over my initial shock reaction to feminist thought, to appreciate its critique of patriarchy, including patriarchy's insistence upon what has come to be called "compulsory heterosexuality." In brief, my upbringing and my individual psychology prepared me to think long and hard about masculinity, including what is wrong with it. But this formation did not prepare me to think long and hard about men in their positive relation to women, our attraction to them, our love of them, our partnership with them, our sexual connection with them, our parenting with them, and yes, our fear and mistrust of them. Convert to feminism though I was, or hoped I was, I had never learned to take women seriously in their sexual relation to men (or ours to them) since I was still taking this relation for granted. It remained "natural." It was a part of my life I had never put to a Socratic examination.

Anne's question about a theology of heterosexuality reminded me that I had indeed once taken a run at it, in a chapter called "Woman, Man, and Christ" in a book subtitled "Toward an Ethical Christology" (Driver 1981). Prompted by her question, I now reread the chapter and found it both promising and disappointing. The promising part lies in the theology of relationship and co-creation, which I had first worked on in *Patterns of Grace*, where it had to do with the relationship between God and humanity, and which here is brought to bear upon connections between and among human beings. This theological insight, plus my involvement with feminism, led me in the chapter to stress most of all the need for equality between men and women:

In my mind's eye . . . there is a vision of relations between women and women, women and men, men and men. The vision is hardest to bring to focus when the partners are women and men. . . . The vision itself was memorably stated by Marlo Thomas in a newspaper article (*New York Times*, April 19, 1978). She wrote of herself and other women learning "to look directly into the eyes of men from whom you want nothing—except a serious conversation." This "innocent" vision has everything to do with sexuality, as I hope may be clear. It does not envision the denial of sex for the sake of a "better" transaction but the affirmation of equality for the sake of a more wholehearted sexuality. To want "nothing except conversation" is not necessarily to exclude sex but to be free of the partner's sexual demand, including the projection of that demand onto oneself as a seductress and a sex object.

The chapter continues by noting that the mutual recognition of equality between persons leads toward ecstasy and holiness:

The awesomeness of the experience of looking deeply into the eyes of another person and recognizing there a self equal in power and need to one's own is the awareness that our mutual recognition is a constellation of energy within a relational field of infinite power and meaning. It is holy. . . . Sexism is the fear of equality, and fear of equality is dread of the holy infinite, which beats its wings around us ever more audibly as we give ourselves the more fully to those who are with us in the world. (Driver 1981: 144)

This passage offers, I still think, a promising lead toward a theology of sexuality. It is disappointing in that it fails to bring heterosexual relations into focus. I said, correctly, that it is hardest to bring the vision of equality into focus when the partners are women and men. I did not quite succeed in doing it. Most of the chapter is devoted to an attack upon dualistic thinking, which tends to fix a gulf between male and female. The chapter is also concerned, rightly, with showing that heterosexuality should be neither compulsory nor the necessary norm of sexual relationships. But what the chapter does not do is to address the problematic of heterosexual relationships, the way that they constitute a severe challenge in patriarchal culture (or perhaps in any imaginable culture) and therefore need our sustained attention. If I knew enough not to regard heterosexuality as the necessary norm, I was not wise enough to lift it out of the fog of "normality." I was still, in the last analysis, taking it for granted.

So the task of working out a theology of heterosexuality lies still ahead. Much help is to be found in the writings of James Nelson (1978, 1983, 1988, 1992) and others, but I think no feminist theologian, male or female, has yet done anything like the serious work on heterosexuality that conservative and sexist theologians have, alas, written so much about.

When I look in the mirror to see myself during the decade and a half since I wrote the "Confessions" paper, I see a process of very gradual change, in which the principal ethical and theological motif is a shift from renown to value. It is surely no accident that this has been occurring while the male body that is me has been passing from the middle to the senior time of life and has suffered a certain measure of illness and pain.

As we age, gender differences diminish. Our physical bodies tend to grow more rather than less alike. Society places upon us less demanding gender expectations. While the younger man with my kind of social origins was constantly urged to seek a name for himself, the senior one such as I am now is relieved of that injunction.

About the middle of March 1991, I then being in what an earlier generation would have called my sixty-seventh year, I lay in a bed at St. Luke's/Roosevelt Hospital in New York City awaiting coronary bypass surgery the next day. Two weeks before, I had survived my third heart attack, the first having been ten years earlier, the second just seven months prior to the third. From these experiences I had learned to accept the fact of my own mortality. When younger, I had the same thought as William Saroyan when he wrote on a piece of paper found in his desk after he died: "I know that all men are mortal, but I have always believed that in my case an exception would be made."

The first heart attack, not to mention the second and third, had taken away that illusion, and because of it I felt not only saner but somehow less morbid. Refusal to look death in the face is, paradoxical as it may seem, far more morbid than to gaze into its eyes. Illusions are, in their way, more deadly than heart attacks. I feel entitled to say this, because I have known more than once the instinctive and ghastly fear, I call it the animal fear, the terror that accompanies, and even signals, a myocardial crisis.

My friend Roger, not much younger than I, fell unexpectedly ill not long ago and called me with a question as soon as he was home from hospital. "Tom," he said, "what's the matter with these bodies of ours?" I heard myself answer: "Roger, the warranties have run out."

I live now with no guarantees, proceeding at my own risk. This is me here, not anybody else. Least of all is it the man of renown I was once supposed to be, or might have been, the mythical man whose reality needed confirmation in the eyes of beholders, the man who, like the God of his youth, wanted nothing so much as praise.

One of my visitors the afternoon before surgery was my niece, a young woman who, loving me very much, came to see how I was doing and to wish me well. But it soon became apparent that she was in great distress over my ordeal, was quaking with fear that something would go wrong, and had come, in fact, as much to be comforted as to comfort. I felt her need weighing upon me, knew that the only way to lift it off was to be honest with her.

"Betty Ann," I said, "let me tell you what I have come to realize, lying here thinking about how they are going to put me to sleep in the morning, and cut me open right down the middle of my chest, spread me apart like a clamshell [the image my cardiologist had used], and take my insides out, and work me over, try to jump-start my heart again, and if that works, sew me up and send me to Recovery and hope I make it through the night."

She shuddered and held back tears.

"I've come to realize two things," I went on. "One is that what happens tomorrow is entirely out of my control. It's like getting on a commercial airplane. Once you decide to get on board, you have to let somebody else do the flying, whether they crash it or not. And the other thing is, I know that I am in good hands."

"You trust the surgeon that much?"

"I've been told he's as good as they come, and I like him. So that's part of what I mean."

"What do you mean?"

"I mean that even if he louses up. Even if he gets in there and something goes wrong. No matter what. I know that I am in good hands. . . ."

Silence. She looked at me long and hard, and then for the first time she took a deep breath. There was a sigh. We sat wordless for a time, until at last she stood up, and I got out of bed and walked her to the door, and she kissed me and touched my cheek and went home.

It is not renown on which I rely today. Not my own, and not God's. By the same token, it is not God's omnipotence, for which HE (emphatically HE) was famous, but which was always chimerical. For me and countless others the omnipotence of God did not survive the Holocaust. The hands of God are good, but they cannot do everything. Today, it is enough for me if they just do something.

They hold me. They caress me. They bear me up. They wipe away tears—my own and God's own and those of the dead and dying in Haiti, whom I love.

In workshops I have often asked a roomful of people to close their eyes, mill about, and find someone's right hand to hold. Then I ask them, their eyes still closed, whether they know whose hand it is. If not, I ask whether they know the hand to be that of a man or a woman. In most cases, they cannot tell. When I bid them to open their eyes, they look in wonderment.

The hands of God are fully gendered, because they are as real to me as human hands. But I cannot tell what gender they are. I can only tell how expressive they feel, and how I long, every now and again, for them to touch me.

REFERENCES

Barstow, Anne L. 1978. "The Uses of Archaeology for Women's History: James Mellaart's Work on a Neolithic Goddess Cult at Catal Huyuk." *Feminist Studies* 4 (October).
———. 1983 [1978]. "Early Goddess Religions." In *An Introduction to the Religion of the Goddess*, ed. Carl Olson. New York: Crossroad.
Berger, Peter L., and Thomas Luckmann. 1966. *The Social Construction of Reality*. New York: Doubleday.
Driver, Tom F. 1981. *Christ in a Changing World: Toward an Ethical Christology*. New York: Crossroad.
———. 1990 [1977]. *Patterns of Grace: The Word of God as Human Experience*. Reprint, New York: Union Theological Seminary. Original edition, San Francisco: Harper & Row.
———. 1991. *The Magic of Ritual: Our Need for Liberating Rites That Transform Our Lives and Our Communities*. San Francisco: HarperCollins.
Millett, Kate. 1990 [1970]. *Sexual Politics*. New York: Simon & Schuster.
Nelson, James B. 1978. *Embodiment: An Approach to Sexuality and Christian Theology*. New York: Pilgrim Press.
———. 1983. *Between Two Gardens: Reflections on Sexuality and Religious Experience*. New York: Pilgrim Press.
———. 1988. *The Intimate Connection: Male Sexuality and Masculine Spirituality*. Philadelphia: Westminster Press.
———. 1992. *Body Theology*. Louisville, Ky.: Westminster/John Knox Press.
Stoltenberg, John. 1990 [1989]. *Refusing to Be a Man: Essays on Sex and Justice*. New York: Meridian.
———. 1993. *The End of Manhood: A Book for Men of Conscience*. New York: Dutton.
Weiner, Annette B. 1983 [1976]. *Women of Value, Men of Renown: New Perspectives in Trobriand Exchange*. Austin: University of Texas Press.

FOUR

Black Bodies, Whose Body?
African American Men
in XODUS

GARTH BAKER-FLETCHER

History sometimes flows in violent eddies and swirling cur-
rents. The historical stream of time that created a "New World" for
European immigrants swept African American men and women into
places of profound exploitation, sacrifice, and yet unquenchable love.
While Europeans were fleeing from religious tyranny and oppression,
they set themselves as masters and mistresses of dark-skinned slaves.
Former peasants, outcasts, and even prisoners could become the rulers
and dominators of black-skinned bodies in the "New World" of
America. The domination that was achieved over the minds and bodies
of enslaved Africans was never as complete as slavers imagined, but it
was systemic, pervasive, and effective in perpetuating itself from 1619 to
1865.

In order to understand how African American male bodies are perceived in the contemporary post-modern world as sites of labor, instruments of pleasure, or vengeful entertainment, we must look at the interaction of three factors: (1) how black bodies were understood by whites,
(2) how blacks imaged ourselves, and (3) the role religion played, both
positively and negatively. It is important to excavate the social discourse

of institutionalized slavery from which negative images of the black body were constructed and exploited. On the other hand, one must also understand how African American persons extracted meaning from those exploitative practices, sometimes even wresting positive body-valuations from the degraded and stereotyped bodiliness of white construction. The role that religion, particularly Christianity, played in constructing both the negative discourse of exploitation by the exploiters and a positive reaction to that exploitation by the exploited cannot be over-emphasized. I shall examine in detail representative documents for their theological, Christological, and ethical implications. Part of the analysis will be to show how certain myths of black manhood (Sambo and John Henry) have functioned in an ambiguous way for African American male body-self imaging. Part of the re-constructive and corrective task these ambiguous legends require is a grounding in the positive power of the High John de Conquer legend and the historic revolutionary Nat Turner. In conclusion, I shall present a way in which African American males may move toward body-self affirmation. Such an affirmation is already part of the current Africentric movement in intellectual, educational, and church circles. Africentricity is really a cultural and spiritual "XODUS" (the "X" honoring the spiritual-cultural journey of Malcolm X) away from European-dominated space. African American males must join the XODUS journey, which requires a reinvigorated sense of body-selfhood as we construct a space suitable for the flourishing of the bodies, souls, minds, and spirits of all African peoples.

Do They Have Souls?

Notions of converting "heathen" Africans to the "superior" religion of Christianity animated the missionary justification for slavery. Noted historian Albert J. Raboteau discovered that even as early as the late fifteenth century, a Portugese historian named Gomes Eannes de Azurara was providing a theological justification for the enslavement of Africans (Raboteau 1978). Azurara noted that the enslavement of Africans was for their "greater benefit . . . for though their bodies were now brought into some subjection, that was a small matter in comparison of their souls, which would now possess true freedom for evermore" (Raboteau 1978: 96). Notice that Azurara implies that bringing bodies under subjection entails taking away someone's bodily freedom, but that such denial of bodily freedom is to be considered secondary to the primary value ("greater benefit") of possessing "true freedom for evermore" by converting to Christianity. Such a theological construct assumes three things that were to become fundamental to Christian justification for the enslavement of Africans:

1. The soul is eternal. The soul in its natural state is sinful, separated from God, threatened by eternal damnation, and requires salvation. Such salvation is the release of the soul from the bounds of sin, setting it free. Therefore Christian salvation is a salvation of the soul and not of the body.

2. The body is a container for the soul. It may be detained or brought under the subjection of whip, chain, and slavery. The body is not as important as the soul, since it is the soul that is saved from damnation and judgment.

3. Slavery is theologically justified because it brings the bodies and souls of heathen Africans to Christians for the purpose of converting them.

Azurara's text is representative of how both the souls and bodies of Africans were assessed in a purely Eurocentric value system. In another passage Azurara constructed an implied hierarchy of culture in which African bodies were placed at the level of beasts:

And so their lot was now quite the contrary of what it had been; since before they had lived in perdition of soul and body; of their souls, in that they were yet pagans, without the clearness and the light of the holy faith; and of their bodies, in that they lived like beasts, without any custom of reasonable beings—for they had no knowledge of bread and wine, and they were without the covering of clothes, or the lodgement of houses; and worse than all, they had no understanding of good, but only knew how to live in bestial sloth. (Raboteau 1978: 97)

It is apparent in the above quotation that Azurara placed African bodies and souls on a lower level of value than Europeans. The judgmental notions that Africans had "no knowledge of bread and wine" and were without covering of clothes or lodgement of houses can easily be translated to mean that they did not adhere to European ideals of proper food, clothing, and shelter.

Notions of bestiality that connected Africans with having no understanding of "the good," however, require a nuanced reading of what the good was understood to be at this time. Azurara's language suggests that at least part of his meaning of the good is to be neither bestial nor slothful. What is unclear is whether Azurara meant to say positively that working hard and behaving as a "reasonable being" (knowing how to feed, clothe, and shelter oneself) is what the good really is! While we would now generally concede that this was a racist understanding of Africans, I assert that such notions still have currency in the marketplace of contemporary social values. A belief in the degradation of African customs, clothing, food, and relaxed attitudes toward work ("laziness") still infects the body politic of contemporary white Americans. So while most Americans might disapprove of the kind of rash religious judgments Azurara made, they practice in their everyday lives the same social-customary condemnations of the descendants of Africans. The site whereby such condemnations are projected is the African American (read "black") bodies.

White Americans throughout the period of enslavement in the United States struggled over whether it was proper to Christianize Africans. Azurara disconnected the subjection of African bodies from the question of whether Africans had souls, for he apparently held that Africans did possess souls. Americans seemed to sense that both proselytizing and baptizing Africans implied that they possessed souls worthy and equal to white souls, a socially dangerous proposition. It was dangerous because it implied that by possessing souls equal to whites, Africans might deserve the physical (read "bodily") freedom of whites. Americans connected spiritual freedom to bodily freedom in a way that Azurara did not.

Arguing that Africans possessed both souls and bodies, Anglican bishop Edmund Gibson instructed his slave-owner charges of the American "colonies" to:

Encourage and Promote the Instruction of their Negroes in the Christian faith ... to consider Them, not merely as Slaves, and upon the same level with Labouring Beasts, but as Men-Slaves and Women-Slaves, who have the same Frame and Faculties with yourselves, and have Souls capable of being eternally happy, and Reason and Understanding to receive Instruction in order to it. (Raboteau 1978: 101)

Such an imperative must be understood as set against the prevailing opinion about the state of Africans as persons. For many in the early American frontier, the only Africans who were not considered beastly, crude, possessing no soul, and having no rational capacity, were those native-born in America! So-called imported Africans were considered unreachable. Native-born Africans, however, were often raised as Christians. Accordingly, Christianity itself had to be modified to accommodate the egalitarian evangelical nature of Christianity, which implied that all persons had souls and bodies of equal merit. Such a view of Christianity contradicted the view institutional slavery held, that black bodies were beastly property, and that black souls were not worthy of serious theological consideration.

By the mid-eighteenth century, with the swelling tide of the Great Awakening arousing both black and white souls, Christianity had accommodated itself to the socioeconomic realities of slavery by insisting that religion made slaves better slaves. Such a stance effectively separated the spiritual salvation and freedom of blacks from the release of the black bodies from physical bondage. By the mid-eighteenth century, Americans had finally formulated the theological justification necessary to ensure the institutional longevity of slavery by separating soul-freedom from physical bondage. The Portugese had settled for the same thing comfortably in the late fifteenth!

African Americans in slavery, however, understood the function of Christianity as "the release of the yoke," and "setting the captives free." Former slave Henry Bibb's critical 1852 letters from Canada to his former master, Albert Sibley, demonstrated a sophistication in theological reasoning unexpected by whites. Bibb based his criticism of Sibley on the latter's avowed high standing in the Methodist Church as a teacher of the Bible. Bibb held up a radically different understanding of Scripture than did Sibley, and in so doing, stood the contradictory propositions of "slaveholding religion" on their head. Speaking about how both he and his brothers had run away from physical and mental bondage after serving for over twenty years "without compensation," Bibb asked:

Is this incompatible with the character of a Bible christian? And yet I suppose that you, with your man robbing possee, have chased them [the brothers] with your dogs and guns, as if they were sheep-killing wolves upon the huge mountain's brow, for the purpose of re-capturing and dragging them back to a mental graveyard, in the name of law and slaveholding religion. (Blassingame 1977: 50)

In this quotation, Bibb reversed the perception of slaves as beasts implied in the phrase "sheep-killing wolves." Instead, white males with dogs and guns were morally reproved as being evil hunters in the phrase "man-robbing possee." The evil of these hunters, for Bibb, was their acting on behalf of the accepted law and slaveholding religion of the United States. Bibb attacked the Methodist Church with his own biblical exegesis in the following:

Oh! what harmony there seems to be between these twin sisters; the Fugitive Slave Law and the Methodist E. Church. —Listen to the language of inspiration: "Feed the hungry, and clothe the naked: "Break every yoke and let the *oppressed go free:*" "All things, whatsoever ye would that men should do unto you, do ye even so unto them, for this is the law and the prophets." (Blassingame 1977: 50)

Notice how Bibb used a combination of prophetic injunctions with the Golden Rule to make his point. He identified slaves as being the same as the oppressed of biblical injunction. With this analogy drawn, Bibb demonstrated how even the central moral teaching of Christianity—The Golden Rule—could be applied to condemn the institution of slavery. He went on to present his most devastating critique of the Methodist Church:

While on the other hand your church sanctions the buying and selling of men, women, and children: the robbing men of their wives, and parents of their off-spring—the violation of the whole of the decalogue, by permitting the profanation of the Sabbath; committing of theft, murder, incest, and adultery, which is constantly done by church members holding slaves and form the very essence of slavery. Now, Sir, allow me with the greatest deference to your intelligence to inform you that you are miserably deceiving yourself, if you believe that you are in the straight and narrow path to heaven, whilst you are practising such abominable violations of the plainest precepts of religion. (Blassingame 1977: 50–51)

What is particularly striking about these passages was Bibb's ability to self-consciously contrast the perceptions of beastliness projected upon African descendants with his jeremiad against the moral repugnancy of slaveholders. Bibb's use of the biblical phrase "break every yoke, and let the oppressed go free" [1] reveals a profound understanding of the connection between physical bondage and the yoking of the mind. He insisted that slavery was a "mental graveyard," a willful destruction of "social happiness" (Blassingame 1977: 55), as well as a cruel institution that had broken the physical constitution of his mother. Bibb built a kind of legal case against Sibley, and in so doing, wove a mantle of accusation against the abusiveness of slavery: mental, emotional, physical, and spiritual. Finally, Bibb demonstrated how there was a connection be-

tween the tenets of slaveholding religion and the psychic-physical abuse
of black bodies.

Sambo the Entertainer

The peculiar exploitative twist of African American male bodies may be
revealed in the three-hundred-year career of the entertainer figure of
Sambo. While black female bodies were often forced to submit to the
desires for sexual "entertainment" of white males in violent rape, black
male bodies entertained through self-ridicule, jokes, tom-foolery, and
dancing. The degradation of both genders was related in a profound
way to social constructs of maleness and femaleness. The reputed virginity, sexual "purity," and "true womanhood" attributed to white women
were degraded in black women by systematic rape, involuntary concubi-
nage, and the loss of sexual control over their own bodies. The qualities
of power, control, reason, and social poise attributed to white male
slaveholders (remembering that even poor white males were exempted
from this dignity) were denied black males, as in the childish, emotional,
and silly behavior of the Sambo character.

Even the naming of a black clown character was a process of systematic humiliation of African maleness. Sambo was the name in the eighteenth and nineteenth centuries for male slaves who danced and clowned
for the entertainment of whites. Several other names were regional
favorites: "John," "George," "Pompey," "Sam," "Uncle Tom," "Uncle
Remus," and "Rastus." For female slaves certain names became "fashionable," such as "Diana," "Mandy," "Dark Mear," Brown Sugar,"
"Auntie," and "Aunt Jemima." The familial title "Uncle" or "Aunt"
was given to slaves who had a hierarchical relationship to the masters.
The name "Sambo" itself apparently has some West African roots,
having a neutral meaning for the Hausa people ("second son," "Name
given to anyone called Muhammadu," and "name of a spirit"), a name
of disgrace and shame for the Mende and Vai peoples, and even a name
of "one in power." Evidently the derogatory naming of Sambo arose
from both English culture where "Sam" was a name used often for a
comic, and "zambo" in Spanish. Zambo refers to "a person who is
bowlegged or knock-kneed," or "a type of monkey" (Boskin 1986: 34–
38). The reference connecting black male bodies and enforced comical

behavior to that of a monkey—animal-like—was intentional. Europeans had called Congolese Africans "macaques," or rhesus monkeys, as a way of deriding their humanity. Such naming questioned whether Africans could be considered fully human and misperceived their bodily movements as less than human.

Was Sambo a real flesh and blood character? Through a strange mixture of contempt and admiration—since whites enjoyed seeing their slaves dance, sing, and make merriment—the Sambo character became a perverse socio-cultural product. Even in the early 1700s the dancing of slaves "made us pastime" according to the captain of a slave-ship (Boskin 1986: 44). Viewing the obvious joy of the dancing captives, several captors noted with delight that these slaves demonstrated pleasure, satisfaction, and a good nature—suitable qualities for slaves! Sambo was a blend of actual bodily gyrations, mimicking sounds, and rollicking laughter, observed by white captors and attributed to a stereotyped African behavior.

Whites were strangely drawn and repulsed at the same time by the ecstasy of the dances, the fervor of the humor, and high volume of African laughter. Even into the eighteenth and nineteenth centuries, the "passionate guffaw" of blacks puzzled, delighted, and offended whites. For whites accustomed to puritanical notions of moderation, seriousness, and restraint, "the black laugh appeared . . . too vigorous, too unrestrained, and connoted frivolity and immediacy" (Boskin 1986: 66).

The stereotype of the African male as a clown, performer, a figure whose sole purpose in life was to entertain whites "took root in white consciousness in the pre-Revolutionary period" (Boskin 1986: 67). Those blacks who seemed to have a talent for provoking the humor of whites were carefully cultivated and feverishly employed as part of the popular shows of that time. Legendary figures such as "Old King Charlie" and "Reverend Jonathan Todd" were known to entertain white adults and children for hours at a time.

Sambo did not become a permanent part of North American culture until the character was written into the structure of traveling shows, light operas, and comedies. From the late eighteenth century into the mid-twentieth century, Sambo was in fact a black-faced caricature of African males performed mostly by whites. While Southern whites had slaves to entertain them, the black-faced white male was introduced in the North first (Boskin 1986: 69). Dressed in extremely outlandish costumes, speaking in exaggerated dialect taken to be that of a "Negro," the minstrel became a permanent fixture in American entertainment. Often minstrel shows would ridicule black illiteracy by giving the character the name "professor," and denigrate black intelligence with long discourses, such as the following:

> I hab come, as you all know, from 'way down in ole Warginna, whar I studded edicashun and siance all for myself, to gib a corse of lectures on siance gineraly, an events promiscously, as dey time to time occur. De letter ob invite I receibed from de komitee from dis unlitened city, was full ob flattery as a gemman ob my great discernment, edication, definement, and research could wish. [2]

Eric Lott (1993) believes that Sambo minstrelsy owed much more to the Punch-and-Judy and British clown tradition than to the animal tales and trickster traditions of African origin. Lott claims that the two most highly recognizable figures on stages—the plantation rustic (Jim Crow) and the urban dandy (Zip Coon)—owe much of their bluster, exaggeration, and bravado to popular Southwestern mythological figures such as Davy Crockett and Mike Fink performed with an exaggerated Negro dialect. This ridiculing of black males, according to Lott, allowed whites a "black mask . . . to play with collective fears of a degraded and threatening—and male—Other while at the same time maintaining some symbolic control over them" (1993: 22).

Lott provocatively suggests that the exaggerated bodiliness of the Sambo minstrel—especially dressed in a long, loudlycolored tailcoat, implied white male's obsession with a "rampageous black penis" (1993: 25). In language colored by a cultural anthropologist's sensitivity to symbolism, Lott says:

> As Ellison puts it, "The Mask was the thing (the 'thing' in more ways than one)." Bold swagger, irrepressible desire, sheer bodily display: in a real sense the minstrel man was the penis, that organ returning in a variety of contexts, at times ludicrous, at others rather less so. (1993: 26)

If Lott is moving in the right direction, then it would be fair to say that the black man represented by white men playing black men was a "man on display." This male, on display for public consumption and amusement, provided a kind of ultimate symbol of the black male body and of black sexuality. It was a sexuality that was bold and threatening on the one hand, and laughably ridiculous on the other. The clowning and dancing dimension of performance took the fearful threat away, removing dignity and authenticity at the same time.

Black-faced comedy was met in the black community with greatly ambiguous feelings. Joseph Boskin has noted that during the period of slavery humor was an acceptable way for whites and blacks to lessen the tremendous social chasm between them. Using Sigmund Freud's concept of humor as "wholly a social process wherein the shared experiences of the participants enable them to aggress and/or regress together," Boskin claims that humorous interchanges acknowledged whites as possessing a superior social location while at the same time "blacks were able to develop a repertoire of retaliatory humor to partially offset their situation" (Boskin 1986: 58–59). If blacks were allowed a "safe space" through clever forms of retaliatory humor, then we are still left with the question of whether Sambo could articulate that kind of humor or not. For this author it is apparent that Sambo's antics and humor were designed specifically for white amusement by his long articulations of exaggerated self-deprecation. Further, the figure Sambo, created with greasepaint and burnt cork, provided too small of a space for a satisfactory retaliation against white racism, even if some blacks were played out African trickster tales which were then symbolized as tales of Sambo.

Black ambiguity toward Sambo, Jim Crow, Zip Coon, and the host of clowns became more complex from the late nineteenth century into the twentieth century. On the one hand, by the turn of the century the minstrel shows opened up opportunities for blacks to compose original ragtime music. On the other hand, because the black-faced style—with its exaggerated facial painting of white and red set against a charcoal black—was hegemonic, black troupes were forced to wear the black make-up! (Boskin 1986: 85) So a strange phenomenon developed where authentically black performers had to imitate white males in black-faced imitations of black life. The celebratory physicality of African dancing, and its enormous creative energy could be subtly introduced into the dancing of clown minstrelsy by black performers. In fact, blacks refined clown performance with the adding of "splits, jumps, and cabrioles" (Boskin 1986: 84). Black minstrels wove such current innovations as the "jog, buck-and-wing, Virginia 'essence,' soft shoe, and stop-time dance" (85) into their shows.

Even if we examine popular shows of the 1950s, such as "Amos-n-

Andy," the 1970s antics of Jimmy Walker in television's "Good Times," and more recently the swagger of Martin Lawrence in "Martin," or the antics of "Urkel" in "Family Matters," [3] we see the Sambo character still very much alive and well. While minstrel shows were labeled as racist and eliminated in the 1960s, it is apparent that the residue of a centuries-old caricature remains firmly planted in the American mind. When white Americans are drawn to a black male entertainer (or female for that matter!), most often it is their self-deprecating, exaggerated dialect, bright mismatched clothes, and swaggering bodily movements that keep them popular. Such characteristics are the archetypal qualities of Sambo, who lives on as a living symbol in the entertainment world.

Moving beyond analyzing the entertainment world, there is a surprising retention of Sambo's threatening/ridiculous sexuality in whites' perceptions of black males, which deserves our attention. We must dig beneath the appearance of "integration" at jobsites and examine the fabric of white-black relationships. Contemporary black males are stereotyped into two possible roles in our relationships with whites. We are perceived as either threatening because our language, gestures, bodily movement, and demeanor are not submissive and entertaining, or funny because we continue the bodily movements and humor of Sambo. Both of these perceptions are strangely attractive and repulsive to most whites, mixed together at the same time. The underlying truth is that blacks, male or female, are perceived as threatening to whites because we perceive ourselves as genuinely equal, whether we act in a threatening manner or not.

The Sambo figure, if we take Lott seriously, was a penis walking around on stage who yet symbolized reassuring control of that penis. If we examine the stereotypical reactions most African American males receive from whites, then it is not an exaggeration to claim that even now we are perceived to be Threatening Penises Who Need White Control. African American males who are outspoken and not funny are ostracized from white society and "proper" black middle-class society as being too radical (read "threatening"). The purported sexual prowess of black males, more fiction than truth, becomes the invisible "spook sitting at the door" of every encounter with whites.

If Sambo is indeed a permanent fixture in white America's social mind, then it is up to African Americans to reconfigure that image in ways that are helpful to us. We must put together the shattered pieces of humanity that make up the traditional Sambo in a new fashion. Surely, we must eliminate most of those pieces! We would have to eliminate his servile, self-deprecating, self-ridiculing speech and mannerisms. Our deconstruction would have to challenge both white Americans and black Americans to debunk, unmask, and disentangle[4] the web of manipulative cultural production that has kept Sambo alive as a funny man. After deconstructing the traditional Sambo, a positive reconstruction of Sambo could use his qualities of humor as a way of blunting the threatening power of outspoken black male presence. A new Sambo construction would hide allegedly threatening qualities behind swagger, outlandishness, and outrageous bravado. Sambo as a genuine psychological mask seems necessary for most whites who grasp at the idea that the United States is no longer racist. A mask, or masking behavior, seems appropriate if there is no other means for getting at the truth of racism's persistence. To possess a sharp social rhetoric and critique of racism that is also humorous may provide a significant contribution toward a new view of African American maleness. Such qualities have surfaced momentarily in many of the comedians who came to the fore in the 1960s such as Richard Pryor, Redd Foxx, and Bill Cosby. The ribald, hit-and-miss, exaggerated comedy of the controversial program *In Living Color* reveals that African Americans may yet be finding ways to reconstruct Sambo in a way that addresses white racism. If Sambo is a permanent fixture in American consciousness, for good and for ill, then intelligent African Americans will have to wrest some hidden positive potential meaning out of the archetype.

John Henry the Worker

The legend of John Henry has actual historic roots in the late nineteenth century. Briefly retold, John Henry was a miracle baby who was born with "a hammer in his hand." Able to do a "man's day of work" at an early age, he astonished his parents and community with outstanding feats of strength. Leaving home, John Henry's feats of strength and endurance multiplied. Once he single-handedly turned the paddle-wheel of a steam-boat that had broken, bringing the passengers safely to shore after turning the wheel through a long, foggy night. Another time, John Henry laid more track than any other worker in a day's stretch. The climax of the legend, of course, is the competition between John Henry and a steam-drill in seeing which one would tunnel through a mountain first. The rapid blows of John Henry's hammer proved more powerful than that of the machine's, but in the end, "He laid down his hammer and he died," as the concluding lyric of the folksong reports.

There are profoundly Christological overtones in the John Henry legend that cannot be ignored. Positively, John Henry was a kind of Black Suffering Servant whose work was aided by supernatural strength. Born with miraculous power in his body, John Henry used his hammer as an instrument of creativity. In the paddleboat incident, John Henry's physical power became a force of deliverance, saving the lives of those who needed his assistance.

There are negative Christological overtones as well. Instead of Christ as a Conquering Hero riding on a white horse (as in the Book of Revelation), John Henry yielded a hammer. John Henry's hammer, however, did not strike blows for the freedom and justice of his people. Instead, John Henry's power was subjugated and made into an instrumentality of American industrial progress. The train was a primary symbol of nineteenth-century progress in the legend of John Henry, requiring the absolute, unswerving power and devotion of all of the man's life energies. As Christ died for our sins so that we might live, John Henry died opening up a way through mountainous obstacles so that the railroad could move forward. John Henry's supernatural energies are controlled, tamed, and channeled by the greater unseen Power of American Might which required that he become the sacrificial Lamb in this legend.

Unlike the passion of Christ, John Henry's sweat, life-blood, and body did not regenerate after a period of time. John Henry did not rise again. His power, his talents, and his contribution are used up in one final glorious display, tunneling through a mountain. His "great heart" is mentioned near the end of the legend as being broken. Yet the rending of John Henry's heart did not result in a cosmic release of resurrective energy. John Henry simply laid down his hammer and died.

John Henry is a repressive myth, a legend of a Curbed Passion with his black physical powers safely corralled into a final moment of servitude, and then thrown away. John Henry as Black Suffering Servant dies for the Almighty White Man/Master whose invisible presence and will demands the ultimate sacrifice without uttering a word. The will of this Master God is enacted at the price of a supernaturally powerful black male who gives up his life in order to do "the Master's will" (a favorite phrase in black Gospel songs).

John Henry as Suffering Servant suggests a perverse social interpretation of what theologians call "subordinationist Christology" where Christ submits his life to the overwhelming will and plan of God the Father. In the legend of John Henry, the will and plan of the White Master/God is to go by any means and to any length necessary for the railroad trains to have transcontinental access. John Henry is but a tool in the hands of this Master, a means whereby the grace of industrial progress might move everlastingly toward the *eschaton* of universal profit. There can be no hope for John Henry's life, for his life does not belong to him, just as Christ's life did not belong to Him, but to God (in a subordinationist Christology). Such a vision of Christ tends to turn God into a cosmic Tyrant, demanding the sacrifice of His only son. It instrumentalizes Christ's life, turning all of the choices of Jesus of Nazareth into the pre-planned moves of a holy automaton. Similarly, John Henry's choices for serving and saving other lives while ultimately giving up his own are never called into question, since they appear to be following faithfully some great hidden plan. However, John Henry's self-sacrifice does not lead to a glorious resurrection: he just dies. It is a tragedy. The subordinationist Christ does rise again, and there is a sense of God's ultimate justice. Where is God's justice, power, and vindication for John Henry?

In our contemporary world we are given mighty examples of African American males who display amazing physical strength. From the high leaps of "Air" Michael Jordan in basketball to the rocket-like speed of runner Carl Lewis, African American males are given much encouragement to develop their physical prowess for the purpose of athletic fame. One popular TV commercial proclaims that "Bo knows." The character referred to, Bo Jackson, has played professional baseball and football. He is also a leading track athlete, and has skill in several other areas. Bo was severely injured in the hip during a football game, and all of the authorities predicted that his sports career was finished. He had given his mind, body, skill, and style to several different arenas of athletic prowess, and had become a symbol of excellence. Yet with this injury, and the resulting artificial hip implant operation, he was condemned to the ignominy of a great "has been." However, unlike John Henry, Bo did not stay dead, but pushed himself beyond the normal limits of human endurance, pain, and exertion to come back as a designated-hitter for baseball's White Sox team. Bo hit a home run the first time he returned to bat! So the legend of Bo Jackson is ongoing. Will his resurrection be an inspiration for other injured persons who have been cast away as useless, or will he give up his life tragically, as the John Henry legend grimly proclaims? Will he break the self-sacrificial model of black male achievement glorified in John Henry and become a new, more satisfying myth?

Deeper questions are suggested beyond the current resurrection of the highly marketable "Bo." Even if "Bo doesn't know" everything, why is it that he, like John Henry, has been required to be a sacrificial hero? What inner compulsions, fears, and needs drove Bo to arise from the "tomb" of anonymity, or was it just that there was too much money to be gained if he tried? If Bo had tried and failed, or if his current try turns into a failure, will it not reinforce the power of the John Henry legend, especially for African American males? These questions can lead us into a deeper need for a critical deconstructive strategy whose aim is to destroy the strongholds of the White Master's financial will in order for African American bodies to be given respect and esteem outside of their instrumentality. African American males cannot wait for the White Master to deliver our bodies to us, for when "He" is finished, it's always after our energies, strength, and productivity have been exhausted. Our bodies must be reclaimed as sacred space belonging to none other than, God, ourselves, and our communities.

In order for a reconstructive effort to begin, a few examples from African American male history may be chosen to provide a sturdy foundation. This particular foundation will be built on the imaginative trickster legend of High John de Conquer, and the visionary, revolutionary leader Nat Turner.

High John de Conquer

High John de Conquer is a uniquely African American mythological figure. Although his legend was conveyed originally in black oral culture, the preeminent cultural anthropologist and folklorist Zora Neale Hurston took down several tales attributed to High John as narrated to her by "Aunt Shady Anne Sutton." Hurston believed that the figure High

John de Conquer provided an enduring gift of laughter and "source of courage" to the United States (Hughes and Bontemps 1959: 102).

High John de Conquer had a supernatural beginning, arising from the sorrows, pain, and enslavement of his African children in America. Hurston writes about High John's origins this way:

> High John came to be a man, and a mighty man at that. But he was not a natural man in the beginning. First off, he was a whisper, a *will to hope, a wish to find something worthy of laughter and song. Then the whisper put on flesh.* His footsteps sounded across the world in a low but musical rhythm as if the world he walked on was a singing-drum High John de Conquer was a man in full, and had come *to live and work on the plantations, and all the slave folks know him in the flesh.* (Hughes and Bontemps 1959: 93; emphasis mine)

The invisible/visible incarnational element of High John has obvious Christlike resonances. High John's power was enfleshed for the slaves, who recognized him as a "man" who worked and lived with them on the plantations. They recognized the presence of High John through his sign which was "a laugh, and his singing-symbol was a drumbeat." The two signs, a laugh and a drum-beat, were taken as symbols of the irrepressibility and unquenchable qualities of High John by the slaves. White slavemasters misunderstood both signs, however. For them, the laughter of slaves was a sign of their happy-go-lucky, good-natured, and childish character, while the drumbeat was a sign of impending insurrection, unrest, and trouble. High John symbolized a quality of character that could "beat the unbeatable," that was "top-superior to the whole mess of sorrow" in the slaves lives (Hughes and Bontemps 1959: 93–94). The laughter and the drumbeat were but signs of the presence of these courageous qualities which the slaves took to be the spirit of High John.

High John was a spirit within the slaves which arose from Africa. In Hurston's account, "Distance and the impossible had no power over High John de Conquer." Thus High John responded to the cries of oppressed Africans. Like the Jesus of the Gospels, "He came walking on the waves of sound. Then he took on flesh after he got there [America]." High John rode the "waves of sound" of African pain and hope, following the slave ships by flying over them "like the albatross" riding the winds. Further, High John's presence was meant to be hidden from the ears and eyes of whites. After all, "They were not looking for any hope in those days, and it was not much of a strain for them to find something to laugh over" (Hughes and Bontemps 1959: 94–95).

One of Aunt Shady Anne's stories of High John had him acting in the trickster tradition of the Br'er Rabbit tales. In the tale High John stole some of the master's favorite young pigs to eat for himself. Even after the master caught him preparing the pig, High John pleaded that the cooking pig was really an "old weasly possum" too sickly for the master! After the master insisted on eating with him, High John slyly responded, "Well Massa, I put this thing in here a possum, but if it comes out a pig, it ain't no fault of mine." The master was taken with High John's humor, and laughed in spite of himself! In the end, the master repented of his selfish use of pigmeat, and occasionally served all the slaves "at the big house after that" (Hughes and Bontemps 1959: 97–98). John's courageous action of stealing the master's favorite food—note that stealing from a master is not morally condemned—opened up an opportunity for a change of heart in the way that the master acted toward the entire slave community. John was not a liberator here; he cajoled the master, and through his mastery of sly humor enabled the slave community to survive with a higher quality of life ("higher" for the slaves who evidently enjoyed tender pigmeat!). In this tale, High John did not alter the structure of slavery, but changed the heart of the oppressor.

In another tale, High John took the slaves who were scared of running away on what we would today call an out-of-body experience. High John reassured them saying, "Just leave your work-tired bodies around for him [the master] to look at, and he'll never realize youse way off somewhere, going about your business" (Hughes and Bontemps 1959: 99). Finally, with "Old Massa and Old Miss" sitting on the veranda of the "big house," High John told the slaves to "reach inside" themselves for the fine spiritual clothing they would need for their journey:

Just reach inside yourselves and get out all those fine raiments you been toting around with you for the last longest. They is in there, all right. I know. Get 'em out, and put 'em on. (Hughes and Bontemps 1959: 99)

To their delighted surprise the slaves reached inside of themselves and found not only "fine clothes," but the "musical instruments" they would need to play on their journey. High John proceeded to take them on their journey riding on a gigantic black crow so large that "one wing rested on the morning, while the other dusted off the evening star" (Hughes and Bontemps 1959: 99).

High John took them across oceans, into Hell, and finally up to Heaven before they returned. In search of their freedom "song," the mythic scope of their journey Hurston compared to that of Jason in search of the golden fleece. Finally escaping from Hell they rode the Devil's two fastest horses, "Hallowed-Be-Thy-Name," and "Thy-Kingdom-Come" up the Mountain into Heaven! In Heaven, they found the spiritual refreshment and glorious melodies of the "song" for which they had been searching. In Heaven, promenading between "Amen Avenue" and "Hallelujah Street," they encountered the rich harmonies of divinity sung and played on glorious golden instruments. The journey to Heaven came to a beatific climax when they were called before "Old Maker," who in front of "His great Workbench,"

made them a tune and put it in their mouths. It had no words. It was a tune that you could bend and shape in most any way you wanted to fit the words and feelings four had. (Hughes and Bontemps 1959: 100)

Upon their return, which was rudely initiated by the harsh call of "Old Massa" hollering, the slaves began to immediately return to their former depressed state of mind. High John, however, reminded them of their transcendent journey, their supernatural enjoyment and refreshment, and of how the master was not to be told:

Us got all that, and he [the master] don't know nothing at all about it. Don't tell him nothing. Nobody don't have to know where us gets our pleasure from. (Hughes and Bontemps 1959: 101)

After hearing these words, the slaves rejoiced in their secret, and in finding out how to access inner joy and strength despite the harshness of slavery. Breaking out into singing, they noticed how even the day seemed shorter and the heat less hot after this experience.

In this tale, we see that High John enabled the African slaves to own their interior spiritual resources in order to survive the harsh oppression of slavery. The oppressor was not changed, the system of slavery was not altered, but the slaves were transformed.

The most interesting thing about High John according to Aunt Shady Anne, however, was in the way that she attributed the emancipation of the slaves to his power. Aunt Shady Anne said that High John had told black people "one hundred years ahead of time" that freedom would one day arrive (Hughes and Bontemps 1959: 96). She laughed at young blacks attributing emancipation to the Civil War because according to what her mother had told her, "John de Conquer had done put it into the white folks to give us our freedom, that's what" (97). Although "old Massa fought against it," the inevitability of freedom was assured for all those who believed in High John's word. For Aunt Shady Anne, "the war was just a sign and symbol of the thing" (97). The "thing," of course, being High John's accurate foretelling of freedom's coming one hundred years before it actually occurred. Hurston reports that with freedom's coming, High John "could retire with his secret smile into the soil of the South and wait" (101). Those who reverence High John's power, living in the secret dwelling of a special root, remember and honor his contributions.

It is important to notice that unlike the first two tales, this spiritual teaching or knowing attributed to High John implied that while High John the Trickster could change the hearts of individual masters, or enable the slaves to access powerful inner resources to survive slavery's cruelties, his final intention was to free the descendants of Africans from their bondage. In this way High John was a powerful Liberator figure. He is a figure that requires theological analysis, and an appreciation of the fact that he is a genuinely positive, African American Liberator Christ-figure. Moving in ways that were invisible to oppressive masters, High John lived as Jesus did, incarnated as a living, breathing member of a suffering segment of humanity. High John retires into the earth waiting for a time when he might be needed again. Is such a moment now?

Nat Turner

While there are many historical figures that could be used as notable examples of the interaction of religion in the souls and bodies of African American males, the story of Nat Turner is quite provocative. By his interpretation of dramatic visions and portents, Turner believed himself to be an apocalyptic prophet wreaking a just verdict on slaveholders. He led an insurrection in which fifty-seven whites were killed and more than one hundred slaves were killed in response. His life's mission was consummated by his reluctant following of what he took to be heavenly signs of the impending doom of slaveholders, in which he and a small band of followers slaughtered white men, women, and children. While such an account might seem the height of violent religious fanaticism, it is worth looking at the deeply religious response of one black man to the horrors of enslavement.

Turner, according to Gayraud Wilmore, had discovered the revolutionary empowerment of the biblical God who demanded justice. To "know him and his Son Jesus Christ was to be set free from every power that dehumanizes and oppresses" (Wilmore 1983: 64). In relationship to the denied manhood of all male slaves, Wilmore suggests that Turner's violent turn provided a radical solution which by its bloodshed seemed to match the fanatical denial of slaveholders in maintaining the systematic denial of what has been taken as "authentic manhood." If slaveholders projected an image of manhood that conveyed the impression that authentic masculinity meant violently dominating the will, body, and soul of whoever one wished to dominate, then Turner's insurrection was an act of tragic vengeance. Turner believed himself to be a prophet. If Turner's insurrection was not merely an act of vengeance in order to authenticate white norms of maleness, but of a religiously inspired prophet of Divine Wrath and Justice, then we ought to examine the ways in which Turner's religious consciousness eventuated in armed insurrection.

In Nat Turner's confession to Thomas R. Gray in 1831, Turner indicated that his mother perceived him to be a person "intended for a great purpose" (Sernett 1985: 89). The practice of discerning God's will through signs was part of his mother's religious practice and that of the slave community. As Turner told it, as a child of "three or four years old" he was overheard telling other children of an event that had occurred before his birth. This occasion was taken to be a confirming sign of Nat's prophetic calling, a calling that the slave community had been alerted to in his infancy by observing "certain marks on my head and breast" (Sernett 1985: 89). While the white confessor Gray insultingly denounces such discernment as "a parcel of excrescences," it is important to note that the African slave community carefully observed and interpreted marks on one's body as signs of one's spiritual life purpose. Such observation and interpretation were considered something unworthy of serious attention by whites, but were taken (and in some quarters are still taken) quite seriously by blacks. While it is beyond the scope of this chapter to reveal the detailed links between these practices and traditional West African religious beliefs, such a connection is distinctly implied. There is a profound reverence for the connection between bodily marks, blemishes, and the shapes of these marks with spiritual knowledge, prophecy, and direction in several West African traditional religions. Theologically, the basis for such practices is in the claim that the presence and influence of spirits make physical changes apparent to those *who have eyes to see.*

Turner was considered a precocious child, and was taught to read and write by an indulgent master. His ease at mastering intellectual matters, lively imagination, and restless energy made him something of a legend within the slave community. Through it all he maintained a strong self-discipline of prayer and fasting, withdrawing from the crowd to meditate on things that he had read in the Bible and elsewhere. During his periods of withdrawal, he began to manifest a visionary capacity which he called "communion with the Spirit," sharing insights gathered during these times with both slaves and whites who believed that his "wisdom came from God" (Sernett 1985: 90). The sense of a divine promise and purpose in his life increased, and he "began to prepare them [other slaves] for my purpose" (91). Although he tried to run away from both his purpose and an overseer, a vision directed him to return to the plantation. This caused quite a controversy among the slaves, who murmured against him and questioned his sense. The struggle about his visionary capacity and the spiritual destiny of leadership was a tremendous source of inner conflict for Turner, and found its resolution in a famous vision.

The climactic vision became the impetus driving Turner out of the indecisiveness of inner turmoil toward insurrectionary action. The vision was of warring white and black spirits engaged in a battle accompanied by dramatic cosmic events:

and I saw white spirits and black spirits engaged in a battle, and the sun was darkened—the thunder rolled in the Heavens, and blood flowed in streams— and I heard a voice saying, "Such is your luck, such you are called to see, and let it come rough or smooth, you must surely bare it." (Sernett 1985: 91)

The intensity of this vision caused Turner to withdraw even more from daily living with other servants. It suggested that he was to become a leader of a violent occurrence involving bloodshed between blacks and whites. It also suggested that it was his destiny to face this battle, come what may.

Turner's second vision was of lights in the sky which had been misnamed by "the children of darkness." These lights were revealed to Turner, in his own words, by the "Holy Ghost" standing in the heavens:

"Behold me as I stand in the Heavens"—and I looked and saw the forms of men in different attitudes—and there were lights in the sky to which the children of darkness gave other names than what they really were—for they were the lights of the Savior's hands, stretched forth from east to west, even as they were extended on the cross of Calvary for the redemption of sinners. (Sernett 1985: 91)

This vision suggests a conflation of the redemptive outreach of Christ on Calvary's cross with the redemption of the enslaved. The hands of the Savior, instead of being pinned down on a cross and subjected to bodily torture, are reaching out from one end of humanity to another, "from east to west." [5] Yet this vision caused Turner such confusion that he prayed for further interpretive guidance and understanding. The guidance came from dramatic natural signs which he found in the field and woods of his plantation. The first sign was of drops of blood "on the corn as though it were dew from heaven." The second sign was more enigmatic, of "hieroglyphic characters, and numbers, with the forms of men in different attitudes, portrayed in blood, and representing the figures I had seen before in the heavens" (Sernett 1985: 91). After the two visions and the two signs Turner finally had a third vision which revealed the meaning of these miracles to him:

For as the blood of Christ had been shed in this earth, and had ascended to heaven for the salvation of sinners, and was now returning to earth again in the form of dew—and as the leaves on the trees bore the impression of the figures I had seen in the heavens, it was plain to me that the Savior was about to lay down the yoke he had borne for the sins of men, and the great day of judgment was at hand. (Sernett 1985: 91–92)

The impression this revelation had on Turner caused him to proclaim it to white and black alike. It even had a transformative effect on a white man whom Turner had told, causing him to pray, fast, and bleed for nine days before ceasing. The previous cruelty and insensitivity this white man had displayed he now forsook.

While apocalyptic imagery was a standard part of some preaching, it is also apparent that Turner believed himself to be the one called to proclaim the imminent End. Further, this End was intimately connected to a war between white and black in which blood was to be shed in great profusion. It ought to also be noted that the powerful imagery of the Book of Revelation in the Bible has always been attractive to black preachers since slavery. Notice, as well, how the visceral imagery of blood and dew is tangibly connected to the redemptive activity of a coming Christ. The Christ who had "borne the yoke of sins" for all persons was now about to return in blood-judgment. Yet Turner did not act, waiting for other signs.

Three years later Turner had a profoundly apocalyptic vision in which the Serpent was loosed and social relationships were reversed:

On May 12th, 1828, I heard a loud noise in the heavens, and the Spirit instantly appeared to me and said the Serpent was loosened, and Christ had laid down the yoke he had borne for the sins of men, and that I should take it on and fight against the Serpent for the time was fast approaching when the first should be last and the last should be first. (Sernett 1985: 92)

This was the moment when the visions became connected to what Turner knew that he must engage himself to do. The calling to "fight against the Serpent" became a symbolic representation of Turner violently confronting the entire white system of slavery. The purpose of this fight was not bloodshed, but in order for the roles of first and last to be reversed. The struggle was against bodily enslavement, and for freedom. Turner's Serpent, an image in Christianity of evil or even the Devil himself, symbolized white slaveholders. The Serpent also symbolized what must be defeated in order for freedom to be attained. This final vision became a way of gathering together the meaning of all the previous ones, galvanizing Turner to realize that now he had been summoned to physical combat in order to attain liberation. Further, that the liberation he sought was a part of an apocalypse, that the Great Judgment was going to be bodily combat with those who enslaved black bodies. It brought together biblical eschatological imagery with a perceived calling to physical combat in order to attain liberation.

Turner waited another three years before an eclipse of the sun (August 1831) was taken to be the sign calling for action. Calling his closest "disciples" together, they partook of a "last supper" in which Turner re-called the purpose of all the visions and of their great calling to "strike a blow for freedom." [6] That midnight the Judgment Day began.

While it would be much easier to simply dismiss all of the previous visions, signs, and interpretations as indicative of the rantings of a dangerous fanatic (and that is what most people, especially whites, have done historically), there is more here than meets the eye. Nat Turner's plot failed to free the slaves, and even caused a wave of repressive legislation to be enacted across all Southern slaveholding states. Turner's name became associated with all that the slaveholders feared, because his acts made it clear that there were at least some blacks who would rather die fighting for their freedom than live enslaved, their bodies in subjection. Turner's uncompromising struggle to follow his spiritual destiny deserves to be recognized as a prophetic sign even now. It suggests that the One who made the Universe, all creatures, and all human beings has inspired some brave souls to fight for their freedom against injustice. For these kinds of courageous persons, the violent and confrontational aspects of religious inspiration become embodied in action. Their visions become the impetus for bodily striving against subjection. They will not shirk using their bodies in the struggle. They will fight with their bodily strength even unto death rather than live under a system of bodily subjection. So doing, such prophets as Nat Turner re-fashion vision away from privatized experiences into inspirational calls for an embodied, liberating struggle. While others preach words describing the glories of a disembodied Heaven, prophets of the order of Turner march, burn, and, if needs be, take lives in accordance with their heavenly visions of freedom. Such prophets own their bodies fully, for in the physical confrontation with oppressive force the power of physical subjection is broken.

XODUS Journeying

It is some one hundred and thirty years after the official ending of slavery. We live almost three decades removed from the agitation, bloodshed, inspiration, and dreaming of the civil rights revolution in our own century. There is a gigantic historic leap we are required to take between

Nat Turner, High John, and ourselves. Yet most in the various African American communities of the United States are still suffering from the continuing effects of racial discrimination, class exploitation, and gender discrimination that have affected our existence since the Middle Passage. There is a sameness to black existence that transcends the specific historical differences between slavery and our time. In the midst of conflicting voices—some calling for accommodation and socio-political retreat, others calling for a separate nation, and many others demanding economic and political empowerment—the movement of Africentricity is a call to XODUS. We might call it XODUS to honor the X of the followers of the Nation of Islam, the most famous being Malcolm X. Malcolm X, newly rediscovered hero of our nihilistic age, speaks the words of black rage in a voice strangely relevant for one slain now for so many years. Yet the thundering confidence and searing social critique of Malcolm X's speeches have enthralled a new generation of young African Americans.

Africentricity is a pan-African struggle to remove European and American cultural imperialism from its ideological centrality. Cain Hope Felder (1993) has accurately named "Afrocentricity" (which some of us prefer to call Africentricity since we are speaking of "Africa" not "Afroca") as corrective historiographic recovery of the pieces of African history that have been misnamed, neglected, stolen, or white-washed. Felder questions whether there is a common African cultural heritage to be appealed to, and condemns as outright racist those whose black nationalism casts Africans as superior in some fashion. Africentricity, when understood to be a move toward correction of historical errors, is a firm basis upon which future creative work may be done. It is proactive without vilifying any other race or group of individuals, and is a movement toward creating a space of our own outside of the dominance of Eurocentrism. This space of our own must include a new vision of African American masculinity and embodiment.

What will be the constitutive elements of an Africentric vision of maleness and embodiment?

This essay names four principles based on a careful deconstruction and re-construction of both legendary figures and one historic African American male. The four principles are just the beginning of future work:

1. Our Bodies for Our Communities
(John Henry Reconsidered)

The physical power and seemingly supernatural strength of our bodies are not to be degraded into an instrument for entertainment or the economic gain of other peoples. Primarily, African American male bodies ought to be committed to the rebuilding of broken humanity, for recapturing inspiring models of manliness for a lost generation of young black males, and the creation of flourishing enterprises for the economic uplift of African American communities.

2. Humor Is Only One Means of Creatively Expressing
Rage (Sambo New Revised Standard Version Absorbed in
High John)

Humorous gestures and banter are but one means toward the greater goal of creatively expressing the rage that is tearing up African American communities. This rage is pervasive, for affluent or poor, because the racist culture which is still operative in North American culture denies African Americans ways of directly expressing disapproval, frustration, or especially outrage. Outrage denied becomes dangerous rage, whereas outrage expressed can become healing. Black male bodies which have internalized rage suffer disproportionately from high blood pressure, heart disease, ulcers, and other stress-related physical disorders.[7] African American males on the average do not live to see their seventieth birthday, but are often dead by the age of sixty-two. Too young even to collect Social Security! The internalization of rage has a long-term deleterious effect on the longevity of black male bodies. The traditional Sambo's antics might be viewed as a way to alleviate such bodily tension, but the cost to African American male dignity was too high. Yet Sambo's usage of humor should be given a second look. Perhaps we may yet find ways to use humor in such a way that rage be expressed. Humor could be a way for racism to be criticized without suffering racist punishment—meant here in the sense Michel Foucault spoke of as a means for disciplining errant members of an oppressive regime. The tales of High John de Conquer's exploits, tricking Old Massa and then making him laugh, are legendary examples of such humor. This kind of humor, which we could call subversive humor, provides African American males with a way of articulating rage safely. In fact, subversive humor has always been the way that African Americans have entertained ourselves. Now we are called to discover new ways to articulate subversive humor as a means of changing oppressive social structures.

Finally, humor ought not be the only permissible means for us to express our rage. Black rage is as deep as the ocean where slaveships brought our chained bodies, as wide as the vast African motherland from which we were stolen, and as rich as the chocolate-cinnamon-mocha-yellow colors that comprise our varied skincoloring. Rage will act, and it is up to us to define how it will act. It can be self-destructive or creative, transformative or genocidal. African American males must decide for ourselves, with the women and men we love, for the sake of the children we nurture, how our rage will be expressed. Such expression of rage cannot wait for a time "acceptable" to whites, but must flow through our poetry, our singing voices, our rap and hip-hop rhythms, our sermons, and our plans to build banks, corporations, and malls. Humor is but one means for releasing the kind of rage which must be ultimately viewed as an impetus for the transformation of African American communities.

3. Accessing Vision from Within
(High John Conquering Power)

The ability to affirm one's dreams, hopes, plans, and visions cannot be found outside of ourselves, but must be accessed from within. Yet our souls, minds, and emotions are not divorced from our bodies. We are body-selves, joined together, fused in a fashion that in many ways defies words. To access our inner "fine clothes" and "music," as High John taught the slaves to do, is a matter of re-claiming something that many have forgotten in African American communities. Yet it is not so far away in time that it cannot be remembered. The spiritual clothes and music are still resonating in our churches, mosques, and associations of uplift. The visions are still present, however muted they sometimes have become, or lost in mediocrity.

Part of accessing African American body-self vision is to renounce all sexist attitudes, behaviors, and traditions. African American males do not need to imitate any other "model" of masculinity, including many of the highly patriarchal African models. Instead, we must live into this new age with the women and the children we love. We ought to sort through all African models of manhood and take what we can use, discarding what we know to be harmful to the bodies and souls of women and men. We must come to a place of realization that accessing our body-self power is affirming the body-self power of women as well. The liberation of African American communities must be inclusive of men and women, or it will fail.

4. Body-Selves Must Unite to Fight Oppression (Nat Turner for the Streets)

Part of reconstructive African American manhood must be the realization that being a "man" does not involve violent demonstrations as a show of "manly" force. Force, however, cannot be avoided if we are to realistically face the horrors of life in a world where we are still not considered human. Our body-selves must learn that the real power of physical force is not in its careless and promiscuous demonstration, but in its ability to restrain destructive violence. Our body-selves, united to stand with force restraining intracommunal violence, will be a power to be reckoned with. Such force will be impressive to ourselves and other communities because it will reveal the kind of self-love and self-determination that all peoples must have in order to be free. That is the kind of self-love Malcolm X spoke about, and not a violence that is suicidal. Our body-selves fight oppression with all that is in us. Our minds, our hearts, our emotions, and whatever technological skills we possess ought to struggle for liberation. That is how the spirit of Nat Turner may be resurrected today. Such body-self power has always been perceived as a threat by oppressors. We must not be deterred, for the stakes are too high, and the gain too precious.

NOTES

1. Bibb repeated this phrase in two of the five letters now extant to his former master.
2. Boskin 1986: 79. This was a section of a minstrel's speech from an 1855 show entitled "Black Diamonds, or, Humour, Satire and Sentiment, Treated Scientifically by Professor Julius Caesar Hanibal in a Series of Burlesque Lectures Darkly Colored."

3. Urkel is a "new Sambo, a new accent, and a slightly different shuffle," according to the Reverend George Lakes, Jr., in a conversation with the author.

4. The three steps of Katie Cannon's (1988) womanist deconstruction used as social-critical tools for reconstructing the African American community.

5. Much of this interpretation arose in conversation with a colleague, Professor Lori Anne Ferrell (October 8, 1993).

6. Wilmore (1983: 69–70) describes this last meal as a "supper of barbecue and brandy" which took on overtones of a passover Last Supper.

7. Data cited from 1990 U.S. census in *Report on the State of African American Males,* Commission on the African American Male (Indianapolis: Mayor's Office, 1993).

REFERENCES

Blassingame, John, ed. 1977. *Slave Testimony: Two Centuries of Letters, Speeches, Interviews, and Autobiographies.* Baton Rouge: Louisiana State University Press.
Boskin, Joseph. 1986. *Sambo: The Rise and Demise of an American Jester.* New York: Oxford University Press.
Cannon, Katie Geneva. 1988. *Black Womanist Ethics.* Atlanta: Scholars Press.
Felder, Cain Hope. 1993. "The Imperative for a Multicultural Christian Education Curriculum." *The BISC (Biblical Institute for Social Change) Quarterly* 4:2.
Hughes, Langston, and Arna Bontemps. 1959. "High John de Conquer," by Zora Neale Hurston. In *Book of Negro Folklore.* New York: Dodd, Mead & Co.
Lott, Eric. 1993. *Love and Theft: Blackface Minstrelsy and the Working Class.* New York: Oxford University Press.
Raboteau, Albert J. 1978. *Slave Religion: The "Invisible Institution" in the Antebellum South.* Oxford, England: Oxford University Press.
Sernett, Milton C. 1985. "Excerpts for the Confessions of Nat Turner." In *Afro-American Religious History: A Documentary Witness.* Durham, N.C.: Duke University Press.
Wilmore, Gayraud. 1983. *Black Religion and Black Radicalism.* Maryknoll, N.Y.: Orbis.

FIVE

Empowerment: The Construction of Gay Religious Identities

MICHAEL L. STEMMELER

This chapter attempts to talk about gay religious identities as they were developed by some lesbian and gay American authors. The title uses the word "gay" in a sense not known thirty years ago. When I use the term I refer to men and women who have arrived at an acceptance of their same-sex sexual orientation and have integrated this orientation and preference of physical sexual expression into the whole of their lives. Compared to the identity of nations and peoples, like Jews, Americans, or Australians, the self-identity of gays and lesbians is relatively new. Because it is so relatively new, a few notes about the political context for gay people in the United States is in order before I proceed to the main issue of the construction of gay religious identities.

The Situation in 1993

Joint efforts of gay people in the past twenty-four years since the 1969 Stonewall uprising in New York City have resulted in the establishment of significant freedoms for people whose sexual orientation differs from mainstream assumptions. Rights were claimed against opposition from religiously and politically conservative circles. Social responsibilities were assumed by gay people with particular respect to People Living with AIDS (PLWA). Of course, not everything that happened in the past two decades can be described as a bed of roses. There was the infamous 1986 U.S. Supreme Court decision in *Bowers* v. *Hardwick* which upheld the State of Georgia's sodomy law. The U.S. Supreme Court, in fact, allowed states to continue to criminalize all kinds of same-sex behavior or encouraged others to think about legal proscriptions of same-sex behavior. One always has to remember that in the last decade of the twentieth century nearly half of the fifty states of the United States still have sodomy laws on their books. The District of Columbia most recently repealed its version of the sodomy law and recent ballot initiatives in Oregon, Florida, and Colorado aim at reversing affirmative state legislation or municipal ordinances of the past. Despite the fact that the state referendum in Oregon failed in the 1992 and 1994 general elections, and in Idaho in the 1994 election, some counties and municipalities were successful in placing rewritten versions of the statewide anti-gay constitutional amendment onto local ballots and won electoral support. In Colorado, the anti-gay constitutional Amendment 2 was passed in the general elections, was subsequently challenged, and placed under an injunction by a state judge. The case is currently being played out in the Colorado courts. Politically conservative and religiously fundamentalist groups have jointly and vigorously tried to undo what small gains have been made against sexual-orientation-based discrimination.

A handful of states and a number of local administrative units, however, have to be pointed out for their recent affirmative legislative stand against discrimination based on sexual orientation. Eight states and thirty-five counties and municipalities, among them Wisconsin, Massachusetts, Hawaii, and New Jersey, have voted to include sexual-orientation discrimination into their civil rights bills. In Rhode Island and in many other states, lesbian, gay, and bi civil rights activists are busy trying to write an end to sexual-orientation discrimination into their legislative agendas. But as any lesbian and gay person in the United States knows, we still have a long way to go.

Parallel to the fight for gay rights in state legislatures and courts, but not radically disassociated from it, is the movement carried by individual lesbians, gays, and bi-sexuals and by collective units to reflect on our beings and our lives in ways different from that of the citizen, the *civil persona,* who is actively engaged in the making and shaping of her or his own socio-political destiny. There are interesting and powerful manifestations of a search for gay-specific religious and spiritual identities. Available patterns of religious identity were perceived as being rooted in heterosexual and heterosexist culture and popular religiosity. They were identified as oppressive and manipulatory manifestations of religion. Rejection of these patterns became an ethical necessity, construction of appropriate gay religious identities a challenge.

Who are we, as gay people, in addition to being socially conscious and politically active citizens and denizens in our various biological and local communities? To answer this question, gay people must first answer other questions of their life-experiences: How do we experience ourselves? Where and when do we experience the limits of our selves? In what way does the experience of our selfhood transcend our sociopolitical identities and move toward the formation of gay-specific religious identities?

In the following I will relate some basic reflections of lesbian and gay writers on their own experiences. Incidentally, most of the authors I am relying on in my work have had some religious training in the past or have been closely associated with organized religion.

The Experience of the Gay Self in Society

As gay people wrestle with their specific gay identity, they are also struggling with experiences of inclusion and exclusion in the social and religious environments in which they move. Of course, we are citizens, permanent residents, or temporary sojourners of a particular country and are, therefore, constantly reminded about what our duties as citizens are. We are held responsible for our actions just as non-gay people are in their social and legal environments. At the same time we experience exclusiveness. When it comes to constitutional protection, we become aware that certain rights do not exist for us and that not all of the constitutional rights apply to us. In the United States there is no constitutionally protected right to privacy for two people of the same sex who want to engage in consensual sexual activity. We cannot marry our life partners—notwithstanding recent challenges to this discriminatory legal practice in Hawaii and in Washington, D.C.—and we have a hard time persuading courts that we make as good foster parents as heterosexuals, that, in fact, the capacity for successful parenting is completely independent from our and any person's sexual orientation. Although many of our relationships may last statistically longer than the average heterosexual marriage, public recognition of our loving and sharing, caring and constructive relationships is radically denied.

For many gay people it can only sound ironic that mainstream society speaks and behaves in ways that ignore our presence and denies our participation in society in a meaningful manner. "Silence equals Death," the anti-AIDS button says. It also expresses the silencing of our existence by mainstream society. It reflects society's often vaguely concealed desire to make us disappear, never to become a "problem" for its middle-class self-sufficiency. However, ten percent of the general population (here, I am citing the contested 1948 Kinsey statistic) is not a number that can be easily disregarded. Gay people are already here and there, they have been here and there in the past, and it appears that they are not going to go away either. Gay people are the only minority that crosses all boundaries of race, class, gender, and religious and political orientations.

Gay people are integral parts of human societies in their socio-political and religio-spiritual manifestations. As the battle cry of the radical gay action group "Queer Nation" goes: "We're here! We're queer! Get used to it." The slogan points out that it is nothing new for a society to have homosexual members. Radical newness may only be discovered by the heterosexual majority as they listen to the third part of the battle cry. Societies have to come to realize that gay people have been, are, and will be a part of their constituency. They are involved in shaping their social and political environments. Religious communities, too, cannot avoid to realize this basic fact about their memberships.

Gay people experience exclusion in all areas in which their rights to full participation in the shaping of a community's destiny are denied. Secular and religious societies break the bonds of community with their gay members by stigmatizing them as outcasts, by strictly controlling their lives and by demanding strong legal restrictions for their sexual expressions. Religious communities add pastoral care and a moral and theological paternalization to such stigmatization. Gay people are perceived and portrayed as weak or sick, deviant or sinister, criminal or psychologically arrested, or all of the above. Such characterizations provide the social and religious communities with a welcome excuse to affirm their assumed moral superiority.

Nonconformity as a Place to Start

One of the earliest experiences—if not *the* earliest experience—for gay people is that we do not seem to belong into the micro- and macro-societies into which we are born, raised, and where we try to make a living. We sense a difference between our being as such and the ways in which we want to be a part of society. Instead of discovering a harmonious environment in which every human being can live in peace, develop her or his particular potentials, and work for the social and spiritual benefit of all, we experience a hostile social structure which runs, for the most part, along the lines of a capitalist, market-oriented, highly competitive, and exploitative system.

Writings by lesbian and gay authors, who address the issue of nonconformity with respect to its religious and ethical implications, reveal that the development of gay peoples' spiritual-religious identities is fundamentally shaped by experiences of alienation from the heterosexual majority, a society which pervasively and invidiously attempts to marginalize, exclude, and sometimes even annihilate its lesbian or gay "elements."

Experiencing oneself fundamentally different from the ways and values of the heterosexual majority society can cause two reactions. On the one hand, it can throw the individual back upon her- or himself. Difference is experienced as exclusion, separation, prohibition, and persecution, and can lead to such resigned expressions as, "Am I the only one like that in this world?" or, "How can I survive when being shut out and shut off of all the relations and institutions that others enjoy and value so much?" The most desperate attitude is suicical: "If this is my destiny, wouldn't it be better to be dead?" The appalling statistics on suicide among gay teenagers tell their own story (see Maguen 1991).

On the other hand, the experience of separation and marginalization can also lead to opportunities that are, *prima facie,* hidden by such negative experiences. Such opportunities need to be discovered by the individual gay person and made fruitful in an attempt to "find" oneself. Carter Heyward, lesbian episcopal priest and theology professor at Episcopal Divinity School at Harvard, wrote that the coming out of a lesbian or gay person has to be understood as an act of resistance to the status quo (1989: 28). It is an act designed to disrupt the existing orders. The act of resistance changes everything for the gay person. Nothing in the world will remain the same. "Coming out-as-resistance" to whatever is experienced as oppressive results in a restructuring of priorities in a gay person's world.

The act of coming out does not only reject the ways and values of a heterosexist culture and society, but is also a radical affirmation of the gay self. It turns the experience of separation and exclusion into a creative process with previously unimagined potentialities.

In an article entitled "Hiding Is Unhealthy for the Soul," Rachel Wahba (1989) regards nonconformity as a starting point for the development of a lesbian- and gay-specific religio-spiritual identity. She compared coming out in a hetero-dominated society to the experience of a Jewish person in a non-Jewish, Christian-dominated society.

As you all know, hiding is very unhealthy for the soul. We don't hide as Jews when we wear our Magen Davids, form an anti-defamation league, support Israel, fail to assimilate and remain proud to be Jews. We never stop "coming out" as Jews every time we speak up and refuse to disappear. As Jews we all know how important it is to have a voice and to be openly visible. And when you are gay in a heterosexual society, it's the same: you never stop "coming out." (1989: 56)

In her own commentary on this passage, Wahba compares the coming-out process as the soul's healthy alternative to "passing through life in various shades of invisibility" (1989: 56).

The experience of nonconformity is at the beginning of a gay person's journey from invisibility to self-affirming visibility in the secular and religious environments in which he or she moves. Despite the fact that the experience of difference and separation may in the end bear very positive results, arriving at this point is arduous psychological and emotional work. How can we come to terms with our experiences of difference and separation? How can these phenomena be integrated into the whole of one's life? Oftentimes, gay people have no name for the difference they discover. For socio-cultural reasons, terms that are available for our self-description seem unacceptable, if not repulsive. They range from the scientific "gemixtepickle" term *homosexual*[1] to such prejudicial terms as faggots, dykes, and fairies.

Not knowing how to name oneself, or not having an appropriate name available to express one's being, is a significant obstacle in the process of leaving the various shades of invisibility behind.[2] Felice Yeskel, a working-class lesbian Jew, writes about the initial inarticulability of her experience of difference and separation:

> One of my primary experiences of growing up is that of being different, or at least of feeling different. While the "reason" that I felt different changed from year to year, my experience of alienation remained the same. Being a Jew, a lesbian, and not being middle class were three of the biggest reasons. —My sense that I was not like other girls grew into the knowledge that I was a lesbian. . . . Again, I found myself in the position of being different and not having a name for my difference. (1989: 41)

As soon as one is able to express one's experience of difference, the situation changes dramatically. Once a word becomes available, the human voice can learn to speak it, learn to describe with its help a person's innermost existence, and can assist the gay person to embark on a qualitatively different life's journey. The possibility of appropriate self-description enables the actualization of liberating powers in the human being, powers which call for an engagement to change the world, rooted in a position of radical knowledge about the self.

The realization of our nonconformity as gay people in our multiple experiences of difference, separation, rejection, alienation, and persecution energizes us—far more so than members of the heterosexual majority society. It assists us to concentrate on actions leading to self-affirmation (Boyd 1987: 78–87). It energizes us to do so because we have to. Psychologically, it is a survival strategy. But it is more than mere survival, for nonconformity also carries a strong element of pride, as is manifest in such actions as rallies on Gay Pride Day, Christopher Street Festival, or Halstead Street Day.

In our affirmation of "queerness" we affirm our difference and separation as a creative chance toward change. Malcolm Boyd, a gay episcopal priest and member of the Los Angeles AIDS Task Force, said that being queer and different "is a part of our God-given creation and gifts" (1987: 84). I think that both our God/dess-given creation and the gifts with which we have been endowed by the creating power have to be put to appropriate use. For gay people, this means to name ourselves, to celebrate our communities, and to develop into guiding lights and corrective agents for the surrounding heterosexual society with its exploitative warrior mentality. Gay people have the chance and the obligation to develop into what Craig Pilant has termed "wounded healers" (1993:

61–79). Our own experiences will serve as catalysts in the healing process of ourselves and, subsequently, in the healing of the homophobic society in which we live. One may also draw on the biblical image of the suffering servant to illustrate the powerful spiritual role gay people have to play in the correction of society at large.

The images of the wounded healer and the suffering servant have both negative and positive connotations. The notion of suffering and woundedness is negative insofar as it limits human beings in their full actualization, degrades people, and belongs to the dark side of human nature. On the other hand, being a servant and healer highlights the gratification and wholeness which are gained when gay people and their communities get involved in helping to mend a broken society.

Empowerment and Divine Presence

Gay people who have accepted their particular sexuality often complain that they are unable to find a place for themselves within organized religious communities. We experience ourselves as located on the margins. Even if we decide to remain closely affiliated with organized religion, either professionally or privately, we develop an existence for ourselves which is essentially shaped by the experience of who we are and how we see ourselves in the environments that surround us. In the process, we realize that for gay people theology and theopraxis fall together (Clark 1989: 121). Our talk about God/dess as compassionate, just, and merciful demands actualization of exactly these divine qualities in the world in which we live.

The prerogative of gay theology is the call for the actualization of these qualities. The creation of justice and liberation becomes *the* task for gay people. Out of the experience of separation and rejection, we develop a desire to become "handmaids" in the realization of the divine imperative, calling for the creation of a just and free society for all human beings. With J. Michael Clark, a former minister of the United Methodist Church, gay people can say that they themselves are ultimately

responsible for seeking, demanding, and creating justice and liberation. Conversely, our failures to assume responsibility, our fearful refusals to claim and to use our power to effect liberation, not only function to forestall our liberation; such failures and refusals may actually undercut our very humanity. (1989: 121)

Rage and anger which we may feel or have felt at the experience of rejection and ridicule by the dominant heterosexual society cannot be left untransformed. Our anger about societal rejection has to be transformed into liberating anger for ourselves and our communities. Our rage about mainstream cultural imperialism has to be transformed into rage toward social and spiritual change. Liberating and grace-filled anger empowers us both to abandon our oppressive past and look toward the future with our demands and actions for liberation (Clark 1989: 126).[3] In manifestations of liberating and transformative anger and rage we discover divine empowerment, because "we realize the righteousness of our anger and the consequent need for prophetic, corrective activity in the face of oppression" (Clark 1989: 126; also 1987: 67).

Liberating anger reveals compassion for all creation. The experiences of gay people endow us with a sensitivity for all creation and creation's need for liberation. Here is where gay people can and do assume prophetic leadership. Our concerns for the world and our compassion for the suffering creation empower us to step forward in a liberating and re-creating manner. It is the discovery of genuine divine presence in our beings, our lives, and our actions (Clark 1989: 126–27).

As we transform our anger into compassion and empathy, gay people experience their collective spiritual power which separates them from the "power-over" ideology of the patriarchal and heterosexist society. Genuinely concerned about the fellow lesbian sister and gay brother, gay people realize their spiritual power and express it by focusing on their relationships with each other and the world. The divine is present in the concern for equality and mutuality in our relationships. Carter Heyward describes the interdependence of equality and mutuality, two concepts so dear to scholars and activists who are engaged in liberating work:

As a description of how we experience relational power, mutuality does not necessarily imply equality, nor does equality assure mutuality. Equality denotes a sameness of position or status, while mutuality describes a dynamic relational movement into a vision of ourselves together. (1989: 34)

Heyward accurately describes the horizontal presence of the divine in empowerment toward mutuality. Gay people discover the relational power of the divine *in* their anti-oppressive activities and *as* their engagement for liberation.

As individuals and as members of communities, gay people realize that they create themselves and their community in each instance in which they actualize the divine relational power of mutuality and justice. They create themselves, each other, and the community by letting themselves be guided by the divine relational spirit which exhorts them to "speak the truth" (Heyward 1989: 29) and to refuse "passive victimization" (Clark 1989: 129). Gay people can thus become corrective instruments to the victimizations and untruths of the majority culture which defines itself through "power-over" relationships. With the lesbian activist and poet Judy Grahn one can say that "gay people have social purpose" (1987: 5).

Gay-specific spiritual consciousness of empowerment, actualized in the struggle toward ending oppression, affirms and secures religious purpose for lesbians and gays as critically corrective elements in society. John J. McNeill's book *Taking a Chance on God* (1988: 200–206) argues, for example, for a gay-specific spirituality that offers the human community at large the values of relational ethics. A liberating spirituality which has its roots in concrete gay experiences is subversive of the domination-dependent relationships of a heterosexist ethics.

Manifestations of Empowerment

1. In Faith and Hope

Genuine divine presence experienced as empowerment becomes public in the radical expressions of faith and hope. Gay people have some intuitive sense that the societies in which they live lack genuine humanness toward them, mainly because they oppress everyone who does not play by their rules. A system of lies perpetuates such victimization, and gay people can experience the oppressive weight of those lies in themselves as internalized homophobia and self-hatred (McNeill 1988: 203). Gay people also know intuitively that the physical space they inhabit on earth is in need of rest and recovery, because it too has been subjected to oppression and exploitation by a profit-oriented, patriarchal society. Gay people believe that the world, including themselves, needs healing.

In order to truly evolve as a "gentle, loving people," gay people must be energized by their faith to participate in actualizing the possibilities of healing victimized individuals and a destroyed nature. Harry Hay, the founder of the Radical Faery Movement in the United States, developed a "creedal" statement focusing on what gay people are not.

- They are *not*, by nature, territorially aggressive and do not impose their political claims on others.
- They are *not*, by nature, competitive but are passionately interested in sharing with others.
- They are *not* interested in conquering nature but are interested in harmonious living with all of nature.
- They are *not* interested in denying bodiliness and carnality but are passionately involved in celebrating all aspects of human sexuality and value both bodiliness and carnality as "the gateway to the growth of spirit and mind" (Hay 1987: 280).[4]

Possessing intuitive faith-knowledge of the divine as relational power, gay people engage in work toward peace among themselves and all human beings, and toward justice, equality, and mutuality in all their relations.

The Pattern of the Sacred in our life together is justice. The shape of God is justice. The movement of the Holy in our common life is toward justice. The justice of God is both with us now and coming. . . . In this realm, justice is right relation, and right relation is mutual relation. (Heyward 1989: 22–23)

Here, the principle of hope is at work. Similar to philosopher Ernst Bloch's idea of "concrete utopia" and Gutiérrez's notion of the centrality of hope in the various strands of liberation theology (Gutiérrez 1983), gay people are led by hope as the guiding principle in their activity toward a radical and healing change. Prayer and contemplation, which are significant parts of gay religious communities, seamlessly connect with the practical work of generating peace, justice, and mutuality.

2. *In Love and Charity*

As indicated in Harry Hay's "negative creedal statement" quoted above, gay people celebrate the sexual contents of their relationships in a way unknown to members of the heterosexual community. Gays give their expression of sexuality a central place in their lives. It is important to remember that gay people have to articulate a fundamental human need (sexuality) that is taken for granted by the majority culture. The non-gay world often misunderstands the importance of sexuality in the lives of gays and lesbians by trying to reduce their entire being to sexuality and sexual expressions. It only shows, however, that large parts of the non-gay world have yet to come to terms with their own sexuality (see Heyward 1989: 28).

As they physically express their love, gay people make the relational power of the divine blossom. Our physical relationships are "sexual Godding," to use one of Heyward's expressions (1989: 34). They make the sacred palpable at the moment of a loving, physical interaction and create it anew in each instance of sexual physicality. J. Michael Clark expresses the same sentiment more dramatically, though filled with undeniable joy and pleasure:

[W]e must affirm that God was as present in the ooze and smells of the baths before AIDS as he/she is today in the stickiness of non-oxynol-nine lubricants and the snap-tightness of condoms. God is invoked in the flesh on/in flesh of our sexual loving, in the rituals of S/m, and in the archetypal manifestations enhanced by alcohol or drugs. —God comforts the lonely while also permeating all the networks of relationships which exist *outside* the ghettoes and bars as well. (1991: 41–42)

Perhaps, the spiritual dimensions of empowerment become most visible to the public in the charitable work done by many lesbians and gays. Our experiences of marginalization, rejection, and separation have sensitized us to the special obligation we have toward the suffering members of our community. In the last sixteen years our brothers and sisters living with AIDS have attracted much of our philanthropic and charitable attention. Beginning with the foundation of the Gay Men's Health Crisis network in New York City, involvement in all types of AIDS ministries and services has become our special mission. Gay people have counseled those of us who are HIV-antibody-positive and those who are People Living with AIDS (PLWA), educated our communities about "safer sex" practices, and tended to the physical and emotional needs of PLWAs through the "buddy system." Despite the hard physical work and emotional frustrations, gay people involved in AIDS ministries and services have experienced a spiritual power in their activities, strengthening their mutual bonds.

In their charitable labor, gay people learn to appreciate even more who we are and what social purposes we can claim. The AIDS Quilt project is a good example. It came into existence in San Francisco during the last decade, at a time when our knowledge about AIDS was still in its infancy and the syndrome exuded an air replete with fatalism, mor-bidity, and mortality. But the healing work by thousands of gay people had a definite impact on the way the country as a whole has improved its ways in dealing with the health crisis and in coping with the monumental amount of grief.

Charitable work also needs to be done for the environment and earth. Gay men participating in the Radical Faery Movement and lesbians and gays active in Greenpeace, Sierra Club, or Robin Wood do so because they are driven by a desire to extend justice, harmony, and "right relation" to all of creation (see Hunt 1991: 87–114). The divine is experienced not only as relational power between gay sisters and broth-ers but also in their relationships with nature. The healing of wounded nature is a part of the spiritually rooted activity toward the creation of a "whole" world. Creation of "whole" selves and creation of a "whole" world are intrinsically linked in gay spirituality.

In conclusion, I would like to raise a question: What will the discus-sion of gay spiritual identity sound like thirty years from now? I admit, it is a somewhat rhetorical question. But it points to the fact that regardless of what ideas we have as scholars and what intuitions we may follow as religious people, in every new generation individuals must discover their sexual orientation anew and must connect this discovery to their spiritual identity and commitment to a liberating practice.

NOTES

1. For his explanation of the "gemixtepickle" term *homosexual,* see Harry Hay (1987: 279–91).

2. See especially Malcolm Boyd's introduction to his book *Gay Priest* (1986: 1–3).

3. J. Michael Clark integrates into his thinking Rosemary Radford Ruether's line of argumentation in her book *Sexism and God-Talk* (1983).

4. For the entire "negative creedal statement," see Hay (1987: 279–91).

REFERENCES

Boyd, Malcolm. 1986. *Gay Priest: An Inner Journey.* New York: St. Martin's Press.

———. 1987. "Telling a Lie for Christ." In *Gay Spirit: Myth and Meaning,* ed. Mark Thompson. New York: St. Martin's Press.

Clark, J. Michael. 1987. *Gay Being: Divine Presence: Essays in Gay Spirituality.* Las Colinas, Tex.: Tangelwüld Press.

———. 1989. *A Place to Start: Toward an Unapologetic Gay Liberation Theology.* Dallas, Tex.: Monument Press.

———. 1991. "Prophecy, Subjectivity, and Theodicy in Gay Theology: Developing a Constructive Methodology." In *Constructing Gay Theology,* ed. Michael L. Stemmeler and J. Michael Clark. Las Colinas, Tex.: Monument Press.

Grahn, Judy. 1987. "Flaming without Burning: Some of the Roles of Gay People in Society." In *Gay Spirit: Myth and Meaning,* ed. Mark Thompson. New York: St. Martin's Press.

Gutiérrez, Gustavo. 1983. *The Power of the Poor in History: Selected Writings.* Trans. Robert R. Barr. Maryknoll, N.Y.: Orbis Books.

Hay, Harry. 1987. "A Separate People Whose Time Has Come." In *Gay Spirit: Myth and Meaning,* ed. Mark Thompson. New York: St. Martin's Press.

Heyward, Carter. 1989. *Touching Our Strength: The Erotic as Power and the Love of God.* San Francisco: Harper and Row.

Hunt, Mary. 1991. *Fierce Tenderness: A Feminist Theology of Friendship.* New York: Crossroad.

Maguen, Shira. 1991. "Teen Suicide: The Government's Cover-up and America's Lost Children." *The Advocate* 586 (September 24, 1991): 40–47.

McNeill, John J. 1988. *Taking a Chance on God: Liberating Theology for Gays, Lesbians, and Their Lovers, Families, and Friends.* Boston: Beacon Press.

Pilant, Craig W. 1993. " 'We Shine a Ferocious Light': The Gay Community as Wounded Healers." In *Gay Affirmative Ethics,* ed. Michael L. Stemmeler and J. Michael Clark. Las Colinas, Tex.: Monument Press.

Ruether, Rosemary Radford. 1983. *Sexism and God-Talk: Toward a Feminist Theology of Liberation.* Boston: Beacon Press.

Wahba, Rachel. 1989. "Hiding Is Unhealthy for the Soul." In *Twice Blessed: On Being Lesbian or Gay and Jewish,* ed. Christie Balka and Andy Rose. Boston: Beacon Press.

Yeskel, Felice. 1989. "You Didn't Talk about These Things: Growing Up Jewish, Lesbian, and Working Class." In *Twice Blessed: On Being Lesbian or Gay and Jewish,* ed. Christie Balka and Andy Rose. Boston: Beacon Press.

PART III

Male Sexual Identity and the Religious Body

Bringing Good News to the Body: Masturbation and Male Identity

SCOTT HALDEMAN

I masturbate. I do it often and in a variety of ways. I do it most often in the shower. As water flows over my body, rinsing away the grime of New York City and awakening me to another day, I feel refreshed and renewed. I touch my body, all of it, to wash, yes, but also simply to touch. Sometimes I linger. Sometimes my touch takes on an urgency that corresponds with a feeling of excitement inside that manifests itself in an erection. Then, I touch myself quite a bit. My penis catches my attention but I feel pleasure all over from the water, from the soap, and from my wandering hands.

Sometimes I rush to orgasm, frustrating myself with too quick a climax. Sometimes I pound away until my skin is raw. Sometimes, fantasies are not enough and I ache for the touch of another. At those times I am lucky if my wife is home because sometimes she will join me in the shower or just reach in to touch or kiss me. Sometimes, though, when she is home, I feel like I have to be secretive and spend more energy worrying about being caught than enjoying myself. Sometimes I build up slowly and then stop to relax before building again. Sometimes I find just the right rhythm.

Then, my body tenses. My pelvis begins to rock. The muscles in my arms and legs contract. Blood comes to the surface of my body; my chest and face redden. And I come. Release. Endorphins. I stagger a bit, feeling flushed. The fluids that my body creates come out; my life-force overflowing. Then, I am calm, at peace, happy, ready for the day. I am my body. My body is me. I am one and I am connected to the life force that let me rest and that awakens me now for my work.

Masturbation, for me, is a means: to relax when I am tense, to calm down when I am agitated, to energize me when I nodding off while trying to work, to satisfy an urge when my wife isn't in the mood or too tired, and to allow me to feel lovable when I feel unattractive. Sometimes it's an escape. Sometimes it's a way to deal with tension by not dealing. Sometimes it's a way to avoid the hard work of being in a relationship. But also sometimes it's a way back into relation—it's a means of self-affirmation which makes me feel worthy of asking for, even fighting for, what I need. It can also be a time for letting go of my self-control; of falling into freedom where I find myself and tap my creative energy. Masturbation is a spiritual practice for me, a way to express my yearning for love and life, even though my desire is rarely satisfied and even when it is, the satisfaction is temporary, ambiguous, and fragile.

Masturbation influences many aspects of my life, always with the potential to move me toward more mutual and responsible relationships with myself, others, and my God, or of allowing me to slip further into isolation and self-centeredness. My experience reveals the richness of masturbation as a means to investigate men's lives but also the ambiguity of its practice. It is no wonder that many cultures are skeptical of this practice that I would like to call "self-loving" but which is more commonly known as "self-abuse."

Mark Twain, in an 1879 essay entitled "Science of Onanism," illustrates the ambivalent attitude toward masturbation that still exists today. He begins,

I will continue [my predecessor's] good work in the cause of morality by cautioning you against that species of recreation called self-abuse, to which I perceive you are too much addicted. (Neider 1987: 58)

After quoting short lines from many sources both praising and criticizing masturbation, Twain concludes:

As an amusement it is too fleeting. As an occupation it is too wearing. As a public exhibition there is no money in it. It is unsuited to the drawing room. And in the most cultured society it has long since been banished from the social board. It has at last, in our day of progress and improvement, been degraded to brotherhood with flatulence. Among the best bred these two arts are now indulged only in private. . . .

My illustrious predecessor has taught you that all forms of "social evil" are bad. I would teach you that some of those forms are more to be avoided than others. So in concluding I say, "if you must gamble away your lives sexually, don't play a Lone Hand too much." (Neider 1987: 59–60)

I share Twain's ambivalence about masturbation but not for the reasons he gives. I am concerned with the relation of male masturbation to the construction of masculine identity in and by our society. Masturbation, depending on the critical awareness and choices of practice of its performers, both reinforces and challenges the hegemonic definition of male identity given to and reproduced by U.S. men.

But here I need to make a few caveats. First, my sources are, almost exclusively, white, privileged, well-educated U.S. men (although, both gay and straight), and some women. My research indicates that masturbation is not a topic that has generated much public discussion outside this group. Perhaps practice and meanings would be different for men from other racial/ethnic or socio-economic categories, perhaps not. At this point, I cannot be sure. In addition, the subject, as it is related to leisure activity (no matter how necessary I may want to argue masturbation is for a healthy identity), may not be a priority in the day to day survival struggles which occupy men from so-called minority or poor communities.

Second, I will not review the history of moral teachings about masturbation; that has been done by many—a good summary of Judeo-Christian teachings is provided by James Nelson in his work, *Embodiment* (1978). The etymology of the word may suffice here. "Masturbation" is derived from the Latin words for "hand" and "defilement" (Allworthy in Woods 1981: 7). The history of repression is significant in its effect on the construction of our experience of separation of our minds from our body, with the former being valued as superior. Traditional teachings also magnify our sense of guilt and shame in giving ourselves pleasure and "wasting the male seed." Fortunately, notions of the psychological or physical harm resulting from masturbation are being dissipated by new, and less biased, research (cf. Dodson 1987; Woods 1981; Zilbergeld 1978).

But what is this "male identity" that I claim masturbation influences

and challenges? No monolithic "male identity" exists; many masculinities are identifiable within any given culture. For men of different racial,
economic, educational, and sexual orientation classes, the options of
how to act as a man are variously open or confined, supportive or
defiant of the social structure, and conducive or destructive to their
struggle to develop a healthy sense of self-esteem and relational identity.

I do believe that, although the identity of a given man would result in
different interpretations of the same phenomenon, there are certain
facets of men's self-understanding that are influenced by their decisions
about masturbation. These are the relationship of a man: to his physicality, to his sexuality, to his spirituality, to those with whom a man finds
himself in intimate relationship, and, finally, to women in general. It is
not easy to draw distinctions between these areas; overlap is evident.
However, the delineation of this structure allows us to identify some of
the problems and gifts of the practice of masturbation.

Physicality

Men like the strength of their muscles. They like to play sports and do
"man-ual" tasks that push them to new limits of endurance. Men like to
punish their bodies, to conform them to their control, to "whip them
into shape." But I don't know if men like their bodies. James Nelson,
commenting on professional football, addresses the ambivalence toward
the body of male acculturation. He writes, "For all its celebration of
bodily toughness, it depends upon dissociation from the body—not
listening to its feelings of tiredness or pain or tenderness" (1988: 68–9).
The body in this culture is less than the mind and so our attitude toward
the body is one of instrumentality. In other words, we ask how can we
use our body to the greater goals of the mind, such as victorious competition, economic success, or emotional imperviousness.

I believe, on the whole, men are alienated from their bodies. Most
men are—to use Dodson's phrasing—"out of touch" with their own
needs for touch, receptivity, and a realistic understanding of their physical limits and vulnerability. This cuts men off from their own true
strength, the reality of their inter-dependence with other people and the
world (Nelson 1988: 101–5). In turn, this out-of-touchness shuts off
access to their feelings (Lowen 1990: 70ff) and, therefore, to empathy
with others. Marvin Ellison writes:

Disassociation from the body and from the emotions is at the root of this absence of moral sensitivity to the suffering men inflict on ourselves and on others. Since we are connected to ourselves and to the world only in and through our bodies, when we no longer feel and experience our bodily connectedness, we literally lose touch with reality. As men who batter others give ample testimony, those not able to feel their own pain are more likely to inflict pain on others. (1991: 192)

Masturbation can, at least, serve to put men back "in touch" with themselves. Men cannot jerk off without some physical contact with their bodies. Unfortunately, masturbation often reinforces, rather than addresses, the alienation of men from their bodies when it is focused solely on genital stimulation and release. Zilbergeld writes:

Because of these feelings [guilt and shame], and also because men have had little permission and practice in being sensual, many men do not derive as much pleasure as they could from masturbating. It is usually done very quickly, the whole object being to achieve orgasm and to get it over with. Masturbating this way presents some problems. It develops a habit of coming quickly, which may carry over to sex with a partner. And it also reinforces our tendency to ignore bodily sensations more subtle than orgasm and reinforces our inability to linger over and prolong pleasure. (1978: 168)

Orgasms, sometimes without pleasure, are the focus of attention and not the variety of physical sensations, fantasies, and feelings that accompany the basic act of touching oneself.

On the other hand, masturbation can be an attempt to move beyond simple gratification towards self-knowledge and the reintegration of the body, mind, and heart. Dodson writes of the power of masturbation to break through addictions, conditions which, I think, are related to the shutting off of feeling, low self-esteem, and insecurity. She writes: "We can all heal ourselves with massive doses of selflove and orgasms by designing and practicing our own individual rituals of pleasure" (1987: 129). If one can pause to let the feelings come as well as the ejaculate, the deadened parts of our physical and emotional selves may come forth.

Sexuality

The renewal of a man's relationship with his body is related to, and a part of, a man's image of his sexuality. Men think of their penis as the definitive sign of their identity as men. And, of course, it is not just their penis but their erect penis—hard and straight and ready for action (Monick 1987). But such a definition is one of exclusion. We are also our larger selves and the rest of our bodies. To define ourselves as those people with penises is to equate women with those who don't have penises, clearly an identification few women are willing to accept. Dworkin writes:

> Men renounce whatever they have in common with women so as to experience no commonality with women; and so what is left, according to men, is one piece of flesh a few inches long, the penis. The penis is sensate; the penis is the man; the penis is human; the penis signifies humanity. (1989: 53–54)

Men's sexuality is formed by this in-group and out-group mentality (cf. Stoltenberg 1991). Their sexuality is tied up with violence against those who are not men, or not "real men."

> [T]he continuing urge to masturbate must mean that the boy is attracted to the male body—his own. Thus the psychic anxieties of defending himself against homosexuality are attached to masturbation and become another source of resentment projected outward. However, in this instance the projection is aimed not only at homosexual males, who symbolize what the boy fears in himself, but also at women, who represent bodiliness itself. (Nelson 1988: 77)

Within this complex social construction of gender, the penis is separated from the rest of the body as an independent entity whose desires excuse men from the brutality of rape. The dynamics of sex become those of dominance and submission rather than mutual pleasure. Maleness is identified with having power over, and fear that this power is not real leads to acts of violence against women and gay men. Men are alienated from their sexuality, running from their homophobia, unable to escape from the deadly equation of sex with violence.

Masturbation, again, can reinforce or challenge these aspects of male identity. Masturbation can be the worship of phallus as weapon: a ritual of witness to its power, the equation of its pleasure with domination, and practice for coming quickly and hard without regard for another's feelings. When connected to pornography, masturbation can reinforce the objectification of others for one's own pleasure.

But masturbation can also move us toward less destructive ways of being. Nelson writes:

> To experience the heights of sexual pleasure I must let loose of my need to control. I must let go, giving myself over to the delicious moment. It is a paradox

known in other ways in the gospel but applicable here as well: losing the self means finding the self. Sexual pleasure nurtures the reunion of the self with the self. My body so often alien and disconnected becomes me again. I not only experience myself, I experience love for myself and recover a sense of the goodness of being alive. (1988: 59)

Masturbation can expand our sexual vocabulary, reawaken our erotic imaginations, help us recognize our enjoyment of our penises and reevaluate our understandings of our sexual orientation beyond homophobia and towards acceptance of the variety of bodies and body parts we find exciting. It may even help us participate in creative social change.

Our cultural denial of masturbation sustains sexual repression. From childhood through adulthood, we feel guilt and shame over masturbation. Deprived of a sexual relationship with ourselves, we are easier to manipulate and more accepting of the status quo. I believe masturbation holds the key to reversing sexual repression. (Dodson 1987: 4)

Experiencing pleasure in our bodies awakens a desire for pleasure with others, a desire that moves us beyond a lust for dominance and towards more just relations with all.

Spirituality

The spirituality of our Christian culture is commonly believed to deny the power of the body to tell us about God. It denies that our desire for pleasure, for touch, for connection with human skin is as important as connection to an invisible god. It condemns sexual pleasuring, by ourselves or with others, for purposes other than pro-creation as "unnatural."

However, it is also true that the body and its senses are the only means of connection between ourselves and all reality beyond us, whether sacred or profane. Some Christian theologians argue for a spirituality based in bodily experience. Driver writes:

[The theologian] knew enough to know that the gospel was not an idea but a deliverance. It was therefore an act. No act, not even an act of the mind, was conceivable bodiless. The gospel would bring good news to his body or it would liberate nothing. (1977: 4)

Spirituality, our living out of our sense of connectedness to all life, is mediated by the body. In keeping with this latter sense of spirituality, male masturbation focuses on two particularly significant phenomena: phallus and orgasm.

Men of every time and place have known a religious quality to their phallic experience. To adapt Rudolph Otto's words, it is the *mysterium tremendum*. Such encounters with the numinous produces responses of fascination, awe, energy, and a sense of the "wholly other." Through phallus, men sense a resurrection, the capacity of the male member to return to life again and again after depletion. An erection makes a boy feel like a man and makes a man feel alive. It brings the assurance and substantiation of masculine strength.

Yet, as with other experiences of the holy, males feel ambivalent about the phallus. Erections must be hidden from general view. They are an embarrassment when they occur publicly. Men joke about erections with each other but cannot speak seriously. The secret is exposed only with another person in intimacy or when a male permits himself to experience his potency alone. (Nelson 1988: 92; cf. Monick 1987)

Monick writes: "Phallic worship today, as a man's personal and tangible homage to his inner life force, takes the form of masturbation" (1987: 113). The phallus is a *mysterium tremendum*, appearing as it wills, not when we will it to (and sometimes not appearing when we will it to come). It grabs our attention, often embarrassing us and sometimes calling us to action. Erections come and go—perhaps being the one male connection to the cycles of life. And, in orgasm, as we let ourselves go, life-giving fluid is released into the world.

In addition to the potentially spiritual dimension of a man's relationship to his erect penis, orgasms can be numinous occasions. Orgasm is an experience of unification of self (mind, body, and spirit) and of unification (some might use the word "transcendence") of self with world/cosmos/god. "Meditative sex [is] using sexual energy to bring my body, mind, and spirit into perfect alignment with orgasm—a cosmic moment of joy" (Dodson 1987: 120). I know that immediately following orgasm, I feel fully alive, fully male, centered and grounded.

The orgasmic sexual experience brings its own revelation. The hard and explosive phallic achievement becomes in an instant the soft, vulnerable tears of the penis. Both are fully male. Both are deeply grounded in men's bodily reality. (Nelson 1988: 111)

Masturbation can be relationship-denying, frustrating, self-centered. It can also be centering, creative of creative energy, an expression of our desire to touch the life-force inside and see it manifest. On the connection between masturbation and creative energy, Woods writes: "love for the self can be translated into a means of achieving energy relief, spiritual growth, and a method of plumbing new artistry in thinking, feeling, writing, and growing" (1981: 10).

Masturbation can be a cursory exercise of tension release or an intentional ritual of worship of the goodness of flesh and of our desire to be whole. A ritual of self-love can be an entry into the land of the erotic, the deep power of our sensual life. Audre Lorde writes:

> that deep and irreplaceable knowledge of my capacity for joy comes to demand from all of my life that it be lived within the knowledge that such satisfaction is possible, and does not have to be called marriage, nor god, nor an afterlife.
>
> This is one reason why the erotic is so feared, and so often relegated to the bedroom alone, when it is recognized at all. For once we begin to feel deeply all the aspects of our lives, we begin to demand from ourselves and from our life-pursuits that they feel in accordance with that joy which we know ourselves to be capable of. Our erotic knowledge empowers us, becomes a lens through which we scrutinize all aspects of our existence, forcing us to evaluate those aspects honestly in terms of their relative meaning within our lives. (1984: 57) [1]

Men will masturbate and the practice will shape the men. Masturbation can serve as devoted and uncritical worship of a god of war or a god of peace. Masturbation can be an exercise in self-glorification or a ritual of self-pleasure that can lead to a renewed awareness of one's sacred embodiment, one's inter-dependence with others and one's commitment to the betterment of all life.

Relationality

No matter if he has one partner or many, or if the partners are men or women, a man may have trouble sharing intimacy. In his discussion of the relation between gender roles and various conceptions of power, Nelson describes the incompatibility of the "male role" with relationality.

> The "masculine" has been under attack because it suggests the urge to dominate others without being at the same time influenced by them. . . . The "feminine" fears self-dependence, while the "masculine" fears inter-dependence. Such fear is born out of insecurity. It is the absence of authentic power. (Nelson 1988: 102)

Masturbation can dissipate or exaggerate these fears. Nelson writes elsewhere: "[Masturbation] can be pleasurable, comforting, vicariously adventuresome, and entertaining—or it can be a neurotic escape from a relationship and a frustrating solution to inner problems" (1978: 170).

On the one hand, masturbation can be an isolated and isolating practice, done to fulfill a man's desires beyond what his current partner can agree to and serving as a wall of secrecy between himself and the other. "Many adults are only vaguely (if at all) aware that they *like* to feel naughty when they masturbate. The idea that masturbation can be openly enjoyed without guilt may be unwelcome and, at least initially, anti-erotic" (Morin 1980: 96).

On the other hand, masturbation can function as one more expression of a mutual sexual vocabulary: a vehicle for learning new sexual skills, a way of reducing pressures to get one another off or whatever. Dodson relates the sense of freedom and deepening intimacy that occurred in a relationship once she and her partner began to perform masturbation in each other's company. They found they were then able to be more honest with each other about their desires in the area of sexual play and subsequently in other aspects of their relationship.

Becoming responsible for our own orgasms was a basic statement about individuality and equality. It established us as people who had a choice when it came to lovemaking. We were moving away from romantic sex toward the infinite delights of erotic loving. (Dodson 1987: 24)

Masturbation can help a man find his authentic power, which is based on a robust love of self that is not incompatible with inter-dependence on others. Through self-touch one builds self-esteem and increases the capacity to feel both pleasure and pain, reversing the cycles of isolation and repression that separate us from one another. Experiencing pleasure alone makes it possible to share pleasure with someone else and shared pleasure, while certainly not the only way, does allow intimacy to be continually deepened.

Gender Equality

Finally, masturbation influences the larger question of the relationship between men and women. Masturbation meets misogyny at the intersection known as pornography. Men use pornography regularly when they masturbate. Pornographic images come to define what men think is sexually stimulating, which includes images of the degradation of women.

Porn is a complex subject not only because of the numerous levels which need to be addressed by an analysis: the portrayal of women; the lived experience of these women; the production, sale, and consumption of these images; the use by men and its impact on their behavior toward women; the relation of gay and straight porn, etc. Even if we could come to some consensus about a definition of pornography and its meaning for this culture, we would still have to argue about what strategy to adopt in order to respond to this pervasive phenomenon.[2]

Porn may be the most accessible source of information about sexuality for men. For gay men, the role of porn in helping to come to a sense of comfort with one's identity cannot be underestimated (cf. Tucker 1990). For straight men, and in some gay material, however, porn's educational function might be better thought of as a perpetuation of the ideology of gender domination. Here, porn and the masturbation that is associated with it reinforces the lessons men get about associating sexual pleasure with the subjugation and violent treatment of women. Stoltenberg writes:

Pay your money and jerk off. That kind of sex helps the lie a lot. It helps support an industry committed to making people with penises believe that people without penises are sluts who just want to be ravished and reviled—an industry dedicated to maintaining a sex-class system in which men believe themselves sex machines and men believe women are mindless fuck tubes. (Stoltenberg 1991: 153)

While agreeing that most porn supports patriarchal cultural norms, I do not think porn can be equated simply with that which teaches sexual domination. There is "feminist" porn now and growing numbers of women are buying and using porn themselves. Additionally, the tendency to call what you like "erotica" and what someone else likes "porn" reveals the subjectivity and often the class bias of such distinctions.

However, I would prefer to encourage masturbation without porn. I would like people to challenge themselves to imagine their own exciting erotic encounters and to develop an expanding sexual vocabulary, instead of uncritically consuming the images presented to them by the multi-national conglomerates which today have the power to mold even our most intimate thoughts.

Masturbation is a door into the world of fantasies and desires that each of us has within and that leads us to life and life abundant if we will simply turn off the old tapes and free our bodies to speak. Even the most insensitive person, I believe, yearns for some sort of better way — some escape from the deadness of violent existence, a space where touch is truly felt and feelings truly known. We can begin to learn of this place by following the wisdom of our body, which we begin to know as we touch it. Here, we return again to the possibility for self-knowledge, self-integration, and healthy self-esteem which can benefit from practicing masturbation.

A critical praxis of masturbation brings good news to men's bodies. The good news, the central message of the Christian religion, in my interpretation, is not an uncritical celebration of the way we live our lives. Rather, it is a call into mutuality and community where one has a sense of self and honors the integrity of the other.

If masturbation is practiced as a conscious ritual of celebration of the goodness of one's flesh as a gift from God, one can regain the sense of bodily connectedness which leads to a renewed sensitivity to one's own feelings and the feelings of others.

If masturbation is practiced with an open awareness of one's sexual desires and fantasies so that they do not encourage further repression but serve as a door into greater self-knowledge, it can serve as a liberating tool from the confines of patriarchal images of maleness and the falsity of dualistic gender role models — and thereby into more just relations with others who cannot make themselves conform to such destructive identities.

If masturbation is practiced as a conscious ritual that celebrates the unpredictable and miraculous force of life within our bodies, it can free us (through, and not outside of, direct bodily experience) into oneness with ourselves, our human lovers, and our goddesses/gods.

If masturbation is practiced as one of many erotic pathways in a relationship, it can serve to bolster one's own responsibility for pleasure, which can free everyone to relate in equal and mutually pleasuring ways.

If masturbation is practiced with awareness of the power of pornography to legitimate relations of social domination of men over women, it can serve as a way to free us from erotic addictions and help us to fall into the freedom of pleasuring for aliveness instead of as an escape from deadness. It can be empowering in raising our consciousness about the connections between male pleasure and violence against women. It can be the basis for pleasure through life-giving touch—one's own and that of others—which can free us from the need to objectify and violate in order to feel alive.

Masturbation is ambiguous. It can result in the deadening of senses and the destructive narcissism of the worship of the self. Or it can put us back in touch with our bodily reality, through which all truth is known and which is the basic location of the extent of our justice, the concreteness of our love and the mutuality of our relationships. Touch brings life. And so I say, returning to Twain's words, "if you must gamble away your lives sexually," play the "Lone Hand," play it knowingly. Unless your play brings good news to your own body, it will not bring good news to those with whom you are in relationship. In, or rather, on the other hand, good news to you means liberation and that can only be contagious.

NOTES

1. I quote Lorde tentatively. In this work, she considers this capacity for deep feeling, the erotic, a special possession of women. But I know the deep yearning for, and fleeting experiences of, better ways of relating to others and the world; and I can find no better language than what she has provided with which to name it.

2. The pornography debate within feminist circles and between feminists and others is raging. I follow Mariana Valverde who does not concentrate on defining pornography narrowly enough to create legal standards for censorship, as do Dworkin and others. Instead, she seeks to identify cultural norms which are degrading to women and then to empower women to mobilize for more sweeping and less government-dependent reforms. She defines porn as a "complex cultural process." She writes: "Pornography is not an aberration in an otherwise civilized and egalitarian culture. It is part and parcel of the cultural industry that gives us sexist advertising, racist war movies, and classist soap operas. My contention here is that its specific role in this cultural industry is to eroticize social domination, and most notably gender domination. . . . If the main problem with porn is that it eroticizes male sexual domination and other forms of social domination, then the only real solution is to empower women and other oppressed groups so that we can begin to redefine what is erotic and what is not" (1985: 125, 132, 144).

REFERENCES

Davies, Susan E. and Eleanor H. Haney, eds. 1991. *Redefining Sexual Ethics: A Sourcebook of Essays, Stories and Poems*. Cleveland: Pilgrim Press.
Dodson, Betty. 1987. *Sex for One: The Joy of Selfloving*. New York: Crown Trade Paperbacks.
Driver, Tom. 1977. *Patterns of Grace: Human Experience as Word of God*. Lanham, Md: University Press of America.
Dworkin, Andrea. 1989. *Pornography: Men Possessing Women*. New York: E. P. Dutton.
Ellison, Marvin. 1991. "Refusing to Be a Good Soldier." In Davies and Haney 1991.
Kimmel, Michael S., ed. 1990. *Men Confront Pornography*. New York: Crown Publishers.
Lorde, Audre. 1984. *Sister Outsider: Essays and Speeches*. Trumansburg, N.Y.: Crossing Press.
Lowen, Alexander. 1990. *The Spirituality of the Body*. New York: Macmillan.
Monick, Eugene. 1987. *Phallos: Sacred Image of the Masculine*. Toronto: Inner City Books.
Morin, Jack. 1980. *Men Loving Themselves: Images of Male Self-sexuality*. Burlingame, Calif.: Down There Press.
Neider, Charles, ed. 1987. *The Outrageous Mark Twain: Some Lesser Known but Extraordinary Works*. New York: Doubleday.
Nelson, James. 1978. *Embodiment: An Approach to Sexuality and Christian Theology*. Minneapolis: Augsburg Press.
———. 1988. *The Intimate Connection: Male Sexuality, Masculine Spirituality*. Philadelphia: Westminster Press.
Stoltenberg, John. 1991. "How Men Have (a) Sex." In Davies and Haney 1991.
Tucker, Scott. 1990. "Radical Feminism and Gay Male Porn." In Kimmel 1990.
Valverde, Mariana. 1985. *Sex, Power, and Pleasure*. Toronto: Women's Press.
Woods, Margo. 1981. *Masturbation, Tantra, and Self-Love*. San Diego: Mho and Mho Works.
Zilbergeld, Bernie. 1978. *Male Sexuality*. New York: Bantam Books.

SEVEN

Facing the Body on the Cross: A Gay Man's Reflections on Passion and Crucifixion

ROBIN HAWLEY GORSLINE

He stretched out his arms upon the cross, and offered himself, in obedience to your will, a perfect sacrifice for the whole world.
— *The Book of Common Prayer*

The death that Jesus suffered on the cross was of his body.
— Arthur Evans,
The God of Ecstasy

The body in the mirror forces me to turn and face it. And I look at my body, which is under sentence of death. It is lean, hard and cold, the incarnation of a mystery.
— James Baldwin,
Giovanni's Room

We are what we look upon and what we desire.
— Plotinus,
Ennead

I have a complicated history of bodily relatedness with Jesus which informs my gaze upon the man Jesus from the foot of the cross where his naked, dead body hangs. My relation with Jesus—body to body—is a curious mixture of desire and violation, of friendship and exclusion, of worship and fear. These ambivalences also are central components of my relationships—body to body—with other gay, bisexual, and transgender men. I want to explore some ways in which the very complicated relations between the bodies of men and the body of Jesus are reflections of the equally complicated relations among us here and now, and I will do so by reflecting upon enactments and structurings of desire by some men toward Jesus. I share Audre Lorde's view that "The erotic is a measure between the beginnings of our sense of self and the chaos of our strongest feelings" (1984: 54). My reflections upon this embodied desire is a homoeroticized gaze toward, and response to, visual images of Jesus, using those images as mirrors of our desire. I hope that one result of this work will be a greater appreciation of visual images as sources for theological reflection, especially for men working for fundamental social change.

By focusing on the body and thus the maleness of Jesus I intend to contribute to the unmasking of the theological construction of masculinity in Jesus' day and our own. Some feminist theologians are deconstructing and decentering the maleness of Jesus by developing Christologies which expand the meaning of Christ to be more inclusive of the wider community, of which women are the majority. Others have advocated a greater focus on Jesus' doing rather than his male being. My own work as a profeminist man owes much to lesbian feminist theologian Carter Heyward (1982, 1984, 1989a, 1989b), womanist theologian Delores S. Williams (1993), feminist theologians Joanne Carlson Brown and Rebecca Parker (1989), and Rita Nakashima Brock (1989, 1991), as well as the ethical explorations in Christology of Tom F. Driver (1981). The work of profeminist and prowomanist men is, it seems to me, to extend this deconstruction and decentering by bringing the maleness of Jesus into proper scale, i.e. removing it from the realm of the divine and placing it in the realm of the mundane. My focus on desire by some men for Jesus is intended to facilitate this move toward the mundane.

I hope that the reappreciation of images of the embodied Jesus can help end violence among men. One of the most culturally central enactments of male-over-male violence is the crucifixion of Jesus, and this essay may be understood as a reflection upon and critique of the traditional Christian doctrine of the atonement, the belief that "sinful humankind has been redeemed because Jesus died on the cross in the place of humans, thereby taking human sin upon himself" (Williams 1993:

161–62). My focus on male-over-male violence is not intended to elide violence against women and children, but rather to put accountability to the well-being of women and children and other marginalized persons (e.g., men of color in a white-supremacist world) at the very center of our lives as men. In some way, then, this is a Christo/anthropo-logical exploration—a meditation on the body of Jesus on the cross as it serves as a mirror of other bodies on other crosses.

One of the primary components of male-over-male violence in our culture is white supremacy, the belief that whiteness is preferable to blackness, and that it reigns supreme over blackness. Of course, blackness is not the only color over which whiteness claims to rule. But in the United States, white supremacy is structured historically and foundationally in anti-blackness. White supremacy is not only a matter of prejudicial feelings white people have against black people, but also, as bell hooks says, "a system that promotes domination and subjugation" (1992: 15). White supremacy is domination structured by color, and white men, even the well-meaning liberals and liberationists among us, routinely resort to it as a way to exert social control over men and women of color. White gay/bi/transgender men are not automatically excluded from our shared white supremacy.

Violence among men is grounded in competition among men for control of and power over women and children. Violence among men also is grounded in structured racism which, in the United States, sustains an economic system of neo-colonialism at home and abroad. Thus, engaging in critical analysis of our relations as men is to bring feminist and womanist critiques right into the center of the white supremacist, patriarchal "beast" where, as men, we live. The inter-structuring of oppressions is not only visible among those affected but also among those whose social locations gives them greater opportunity to oppress— but only if men who possess birthright privileges are willing to unmask themselves and their privileges.

My Desires, My Identities

My particular standpoint is that of a mature, white man who earlier as a devoutly Episcopalian, sexually repressed adolescent developed a highly spiritualized and eroticized relation with the images of a handsome, yet eventually violated, Jesus. At one time married to a woman, I am a gay-identified, bisexual father of three intelligent, sensitive, and beautiful daughters. While retaining considerable emotional and theological connection with the Episcopal Church, I also find a denominational home in Unitarian Universalism. The Radical Faeries, a far-flung, intentionally decentralized network of politically radical, counter-cultural (almost exclusively white) gay men and a few lesbians, comprise my community of spiritual activism. I now position myself as an Anglican Unitarian Universalist Radical Faerie and companion of Jesus.

Although I remain white in color and thus retain considerable white privilege, my research and writing about the liberating theological resources in the lives and works of James Baldwin and Audre Lorde lead me into an increasingly active "in the life" collaboration with black brothers and sisters. "Men of difference" are my primary spiritual community: men of all colors who are gay/bi/transgender or "queer" and who value both our commonalities and our differences as sources of the holy. The criteria by which I choose male companions is the strength of their commitment to the well-being of women, children, and marginalized men, who usually are the least valued in any group. They are my primary community of accountability.

I choose Jesus as a companion for two reasons: he was a "man of difference" and he was committed to the well-being of women, children and marginalized men. However, my relationship with Jesus is complicated. Queer performance artist Tim Miller speaks for me when he writes:

The first man I was ever in love with was Jesus. He was sweet. He was strong. He didn't play football or scream at me and he wore great clothes. This feeling I had for him from a very early age is part of my love for other men. I imagine him as a generous and sensitive lover, ready to give and receive pleasure. I see him there for the other person. Rubbing tired muscles with all those sweet-smelling balms and ointments that they keep talking about in the New Testament. My relationship with Jesus is in a direct heartbeat to my gay identity. (1991: 63–64)

I can recall adolescent fantasies about Jesus when thinking about a classroom in my parish church which I used as a place to study and ponder theological issues. That classroom had a picture of the blue-eyed Jesus looking quite sensual in his agony on the cross. I am not accustomed to thinking of myself as interested in sado-masochistic eroticism, yet the merging of sensuality and violence in that picture is hauntingly clear to me.

Moreover, when I was a married homosexual man, struggling to fit the heterosexist mold, I felt connected not only to the beautiful Jesus but also the suffering Jesus on the cross. The dying/dead Jesus felt more real to me because I was dying, too—emotionally and relationally, but dying nonetheless. Feeling the agony of the cross, wallowing in it, was a way to mask the pain of my deeply conflicted existence. While still closeted as a layperson in a parish and later as an Episcopal seminarian, I found preaching Christ crucified a satisfactory outlet for my internalized pain and anger.

Erotic Desire and the Visual Representation of Jesus

Many gay men experience Jesus as lover, not just the cosmic lover of humanity, but real, embodied, sweaty, sexy, passionate lover between the sheets, or on the beach, perhaps even on the cross. When I was a newly-come-out seminarian in the Boston area, I spent many a long evening in gay bars listening to Irish Catholic men who had wanted to be priests, confessing their love for Jesus and their hurt and anger at the church's rejection of them. One evening, a man, quite sober, broke down in sobs, relating to me how he had always been "faithful" to Jesus, his first and still only true love. In hushed tones, punctuated by furtive glances to reassure himself no one else was listening, he told me how he masturbated frequently to his favorite picture of Jesus—the blonde, blue-eyed, soft-skinned boy-man staring "longingly" from the cross.

Another experience of desire, that of a young black male for a white Jesus, is recorded in Guy-Mark Foster's short story, "The Book of Luke" (1991). The twelve-year-old African American boy lives with his mother, a "full-time prayer woman," who has left his father after a violent quarrel. The boy misses his father, who has been harshly judged by his mother, much as he thinks Jesus was harshly judged and abandoned by his "father." The central action of the story occurs in the shower room of a public swimming pool where the protagonist is viewing the naked body of a slightly older, white boy reminding him of the picture of the white Jesus on his mother's wall. Watching this boy, and others like him, with shoulder-length, wavy hair brings the picture of Jesus to life. Ordinarily, the white boys, whose bodies he stares at with open desire, beat him up and call him names, but this time the white boy responds positively. In the heat of their shared desire, the protagonist wonders

Can it be possible that I've pulled Him down from the wall of one religion, stolen his unclad body into the room of another . . . and bolted the door? I cannot tell where I am, or if the date of my daddy's birth has passed and it's another day, a brand new year, or whether I am older than my age now, or younger. All I know is that Son of God is smiling upon me and I am jacking Him off with my huge smile of a body. This has to make my mother happy, too, I think: this sudden conversion to a worshiping faith. And if it doesn't, so what. I'm happy enough for the both of us. I am so happy I might let myself explode into a zillion particles of blinding white light . . . Oh, *Jeee*sus! (Foster 1991: 27)

Margaret Miles observes that visual images "are primarily addressed to comprehending physical existence, the great, lonely, yet universal preverbal experiences of birth, growth, maturation, pain, illness, ecstasy, weakness, age, sex, death." Historically, she says, visual images record "the ways by which the nonprivileged understood and coped with physical existence" (1985: 36). For some contemporary gay men, in a society where male-male love is prohibited from achieving full and free expression, various visual images of Jesus function in nontextual, nonverbal ways to assist our comprehension of and integration into physical and erotic existence.

Feminist literary critic Eve Kosofsky Sedgwick argues against the usual assumption that the main impact of Christianity on men's desire for the male body is prohibitive. Instead, she contends that prohibition serves to stimulate desire (desire for that which is forbidden), and that many Christian practices serve directly to articulate and promote male-male desire.

Catholicism in particular is famous for giving countless gay and proto-gay children the shock of the possibility of adults who don't marry, of men in dresses, of passionate theater, of introspective investment, of lives filled with what could, ideally without diminution, be called the work of the fetish. Even for the many whose own achieved identity may at last include none of these features or may be defined against them, the encounter with them is likely to have a more or other than prohibitive impact. *And presiding over all are the images of Jesus.* These have, indeed, a unique position in modern culture as images of the unclothed or unclothable male body, often in extremis and/or in ecstasy, prescriptively meant to be gazed at and adored. The scandal of such a figure within a homophobic economy of the male gaze doesn't seem to abate: efforts to disembody his body, for instance by attenuating, Europeanizing, or feminizing it, only entangle it the more compromisingly among various modern figurations of the homosexual. (Sedgwick 1990: 140, emphasis mine)

Images of Jesus re-present an actual man, allowing the men to whom he is thus presented to enter into a relationship with Jesus as lover. The relation of these lovers to Jesus' images may be unlike their relation to other images of sexually alluring men (such as erotic pictures of men in overtly sexual poses or even milder pictures of movie idols) in that the men who gaze lovingly, adoringly, lustily apprehend the images of Jesus from a place grounded in a faith relation with one who saves them from sin/death and gives them new life. The images, of course, cannot be understood apart from theological texts and ecclesiastical teachings. However, visual images are, as Miles contends, "representational rather than discursive and as inherently multivalent, can offer formulation and expression simultaneously to a wide variety of persons with different perspectives" (1985: 37–38). This means that the relation of the lovers of Jesus to his images also can be erotic or "pornographic," that is, overtly sexual and orgasm-producing. Different men respond to these images differently, and their responses are conditioned not only by faith but also by desire.

Miles also suggests that unlike women who experience physical existence as constituted bodily in irreversible change and discontinuity, "the implicit model of the history of ideas and the predictable continuity of male physical existence have permitted and encouraged male intellectuals to ignore the absolute dependence of human beings on the body, its exigencies, and its natural environment" (1985: 36–37). I seek to overcome the neglect of male physicality by focusing attention on the particularities of men's bodily experience, especially those experiences which contradict the usual views of Jesus and men's relationships with him. The activity of surfacing contradictions is, as Jonathan Dollimore writes, "enabled by and contributes to transgressive or dissident knowledge." Transgression, in Dollimore's view, does not lead automatically to social change, but it may subvert established thought patterns by way of "the dangerous knowledge it brings with it, or produces, or which is produced *in and by* its containment in the cultural sphere" (1991: 88–89).

Many gay men, and certainly some white gay male theologians, appear to believe homosexuality (or gay identity) constitutes, *prima facie,* an oppositional stance toward white supremacist, patriarchal constructions of masculinity. The reality is considerably more complex. Dollimore and Sedgwick, among others, have pointed to the centrality of male homosexuality in the construction of social meaning in the twentieth century, a centrality which is maintained within a compulsorily heterosexual culture which obsessively denounces homosexuality and— when necessary to maintain heterosexist domination—silences or kills those who act or appear to act homosexually. Clearly, many cultural activities in contemporary Western culture, especially advertising, film, and theater, are heavily laden with gay and homoerotic content and style which contribute much to the marketability of products in a consumer-oriented society. Thus, homosexuality, gay identity, and homoeroticism do not necessarily constitute transgressive knowledge.

One of the ways in which gay male culture does not produce transgressive knowledge is the exclusion and invisibility of men of color, going hand in hand with the invisibility of women. By and large, the homosexuality at the center of constructions of social meaning is supremely white, and thus can hardly contribute to the deconstruction and elimination of structures of white domination. I agree with the assessment of many black men that the adjective "gay" largely connotes "white gay." The picture of Jesus on the wall in that classroom in my parish church years ago is a false and racist image of Jesus; it is unlikely any Palestinian Jew ever looked so Aryan. Nonetheless, this image helped me stay in touch with some measure of my desire, keeping it alive until I could acknowledge and act upon it in relation to other men.

Desire for Liberation and the Image of the Black Christ

That image hardly serves me well today, and I rather recall the image of a black, beautiful, sensual Jesus crowned by a ring of thorns in a funeral home on 131st Street in Harlem. As I attended a wake for the brother of a seminary friend, I gazed on that Jesus and prayed deeply and earnestly for my mourning friend and her family, for her dead brother and for our brother Jesus. In that moment I accepted existentially for the first time what I had come to understand intellectually, namely the reality and power of the "Black Christ" whom James H. Cone had begun to articulate more than twenty-five years ago. I was face to face with the Black Christ not only because the image on the wall was that of a man with African features, but also because that black Jesus stood watch with us and over us at the wake for an African American man killed in his prime by an unknown person. In the funeral home I was in a space of mourning unlike any other I had ever encountered. Death was as palpable in the peeling paint, rickety chairs, and cramped, tiny room as it was in the body lying in state; and yet life was more palpable than in many living rooms in which I have lived. Cone writes:

Christ's blackness is both literal and symbolic. His blackness is literal in the sense that he truly becomes One with the oppressed blacks, taking their suffering as his suffering and revealing that he is found in the history of our struggle, the story of our pain, and the rhythm of our bodies. . . . Christ is black, therefore, not because of some cultural or psychological need of black people, but because and only because Christ *really* enters into our world where the poor, the despised, and the black are, disclosing that he is with them, enduring their humiliation and pain and transforming oppressed slaves into liberated servants. Indeed, if Christ is not *truly* black, then the historical Jesus lied. (1975: 136)

For Cone, the importance of the Black Christ is that "it expresses the *concreteness* of Jesus' continued presence today." Jesus stands before us, beside us, behind us today as a fully embodied black man who is engaged in the struggle to overcome the suffering of the poor and the oppressed. Cone indicates that the skin color of Jesus is irrelevant in one sense, but goes on to say that "*Jesus was not white* in any sense of the word, literally or theologically." Recognizing that most white people (and some black people, too) become quite distraught at the thought of a Black Christ or the non-white Jesus, Cone asks: "Is it possible to talk about suffering in America without talking about the meaning of blackness? Can we really believe that Christ is the Suffering Servant par excellence if he is not black?" (1990: 123). Cone asks white men and women to become black, not by changing their skin color but changing the "color of your heart, soul, and mind. To be black means that your heart, your soul, your mind, and your body are where the dispossessed are" (1989: 151). Cone is asking white Americans, including white gay/bisexual/transgender men, to remove from our churches and our hearts the image of Jesus as white, replacing it with a man of color. Few white-dominated churches and white people have been willing to take this latter step.

Black theology challenges us to choose our objects of desire with great care because they can keep us bound in relations of domination and oppression: but they equally can help us to move toward a more egalitarian social order.

> The appearance of Jesus as the black Christ also means that the black revolution is God's kingdom becoming a reality in America. . . . The kingdom is not an attainment of material security, nor is it mystical communion with the divine. It has to do with the *quality* of one's existence in which a person realizes that *persons* are more important than property. (Cone 1990: 124)

Jesus can be fully transgressive for white gay men only if his person, the body in which we desire him, transgresses the white supremacist racial codes which still govern America. However, I have experienced a personal struggle between a willingness to re-image Jesus as black and a fear that in doing so I am objectifying black men. The white supremacist gaze, the gaze of a tourist on the prowl among "exotic" men of color for a cheap thrill, is deeply ingrained in many gay white U.S. men (cf. hooks 1992: 17ff). Sensitivity to that gaze is one step toward overcoming it, but overcoming white supremacy requires breaking the white theological silence about blackness. And that means taking sides by crossing the socio-political color line while remaining in one's own skin. Crossing and re-crossing the color line constitutes a new situation for many white people, even as it is an everyday occurrence for most people of color. I have experienced internal conflict about taking sides as "disloyalty" to white people, and these feelings help me understand the power of structured white supremacy, which reaches into the most intimate areas of life.

I have begun to speak of my struggle to challenge white supremacy to black friends. None of them has let me off my own white supremacist hook and each has helped me clarify how I wish to embody that challenge. One of my friends has helped me envision desire which opposes domination by telling me about the picture of a black Jesus beside his bed, a sensual, bare-chested, dreadlocked, brown-skinned man with a rope around his neck and his hands bound by ropes. Around the center are smaller images of this black Jesus in various stages of his life and death: Jesus in the manger, at the Garden of Gethsemane, being beaten by Roman soldiers, hanging on the cross, and, finally, "risen," standing and bathed in light. My friend told me that in many years of theological training and spiritual seeking he had never felt, in his body, drawn toward any images of the white Jesus. His most enfleshed experience of God came when he held his lover in his arms. When his lover died from AIDS-related complications he felt God had died. The picture of this black Jesus, however, enabled him to see the face of his lover as Jesus and the face of Jesus as his lover.

During our conversation I decided to get a picture of a black Jesus for myself. I went for a walk among the street vendors on 125th Street in Harlem and found the very picture my friend had described. I was amazed by how much the image of Jesus resembled my friend. As I write this, that Jesus and I gaze at each other with fondness and love. My friend and I are joined through this Jesus. Speaking of our respective desires (for Jesus and other men), and thus also of our fears, has helped us forge a new alliance for deeper inter-personal love and social change. To speak of desire for Jesus, then, is always a matter of embodiment, and it matters which body of Jesus we desire. However, I am not suggesting that sexual desire or the desire for liberation is dependent upon skin color. Rather, the key issue is how Jesus serves as an element of dangerous or politically transgressive embodied knowledge. To desire the Jesus who is not white, the Jesus who is black, is to place desire in the service of overcoming domination.

Embodied Desire and the "Queer" Jesus

Embodied desire for Jesus forms a kernel of transgressive knowledge which can contribute to destabilizing dominant views of Jesus, because it is one form of relation the church has been at great pains to deny. Denial of the desire for Jesus is predicated on the church's denial of Jesus' own embodied desire. The biblical silence about Jesus' sexuality may or may not reflect his actual life situation. Whether he was celibate or sexually active, the celibate priesthood eventually enshrined a historical "picture" of Jesus' non-erotic existence while emphasizing his maleness and insisting that his priests be male. Even Protestant objections to clerical celibacy have never overcome the underlying view that Jesus was asexual. Insisting that Jesus was both sexually male and sexually inactive contributes to erasing desire as a category of experience shared between him and the people who follow him. Relating to Jesus as lover, as beloved body, as object of desire, may alter one's view of Christian teachings, including those about the crucifixion.

Some years ago, when still fairly new to my identity as an "out" gay man, I referred to the "gay Christ." A friend asked me how the gay Christ differed from the regular one (whatever *that* is). I described a man on the cross completely naked with a cute face, well-developed "pecs" and large penis, wearing an earring in his left ear, which was a custom for gay men back then. The image was of a sexy man still in the throes of death: Christ crucified with the earring in the correct ear. Clearly a mixed message.

What is clear to me today is that there is no gay Christ but a queer Jesus—that is, a man who liked men and women sensually and who acted contrary to the gender, racial, and religious norms of his day. Robert Goss's (1993) impassioned argument for a queer Jesus follows my own view in some ways, although I am less certain than Goss that seeing Jesus as queer is really a sufficiently radical response to the current situation of lesbian/gay/bisexual/transgender people or other oppressed people.

The definition of "queer" is fluid. Gay men and lesbians contest not only the appropriateness of "queer" but also what it means. Many would argue that a queer man is a gay or bisexual man who is political, works for the liberation of all people, and flouts genderized and racialized conventions. Since I cannot assert that Jesus liked men sexually or that he enjoyed genital sex with anyone male or female, it seems unwarranted to call him gay (just as it is unwarranted to call him "straight"). However, he appears to have lived in a high degree of intimacy with members of both sexes. He appreciated sensuality and he continually confounded the gender, racial/ethnic, and religious conventions of his day. In Jesus' context, such attitudes and behaviors seem to have been as out of the ordinary, i.e., strange or "queer," as it is in our own. When ACT UP invaded St. Patrick's Cathedral several years ago to protest the homophobia of Cardinal O'Connor and the Roman Catholic hierarchy, I realized they were doing as Jesus had done when he angrily overturned the tables of the money changers in the temple. That was the moment I began to see how queer Jesus had been. Goss correctly draws a connection between Jesus' "Stop the Temple" action and ACT UP's "Stop the Church" actions (1993: 147–56).

We who are white must not lose sight of the central importance of which Jesus we desire. Who, then, is the "queer Jesus?" In our contemporary white supremacist social order, it is not queer to image Jesus as white. Jesus is "queer" in our society, in part, because he was not white. For white men, queerness requires an awareness that the men most likely to be crucified in our culture are men of color, and it requires an active commitment to ending the violence against them. For white gay male theologians, queerness demands that we cease the invisibility of lesbian/gay/bisexual/transgender people of color.

I agree with Elias Farajajé-Jones who advocates an "in-the-life" theology. He asserts that "in-the-life" is an historically accurate term to describe black theology which includes lesbian/gay/bisexual/transgender or queer people because

it has been used in our African-American tradition for generations to connote a broad spectrum of identities and behaviors, and because of the rich spiritual connotations of the word "life," especially for people continually confronted with suffering and death. "In-the-life" also shows inclusivity, shows that we are all included *in-the-life*. Therefore, an in-the-life theology of liberation would be one that grows out of the experiences, lives and struggles against oppression and dehumanization of those *in-the-life*. (1993: 140)

Imaging Jesus as one who was in-the-life acknowledges the wideness of his ministry, the diversity of the people he served, and the fact of his non-whiteness. An emphasis on "life" is consonant with Jesus' repeated focus on bringing about life in abundance for all. While it is inappropriate for those of us who are white to claim to be "in-the-life," we may be followers, or companions, of Jesus who was.

Re-Imaging the Crucifixion

"Bodily integrity is central to the liberation struggle." When I wrote those words some years ago, I was referring to rape and attempted rape in the Hebrew Scripture, especially in the story of the destruction of Sodom. I also wrote then that "We must insist that the authority of scripture be viewed critically and that the numerous acts that undermine bodily integrity be unmasked and disentangled in order to overcome their gruesome effects" (Gorsline 1991: 48–49). Unexamined anti-Semitism surely played a role in my thinking when I proposed to search only the Hebrew Scriptures for the many instances of bodily violations. Today, I see that the pivotal point of traditional Christian belief, Jesus' death on the cross, is based upon bodily violation as well. We cannot, nor should we, deny the reality of his crucifixion, but solidarity with the queer Jesus and all the others whose bodily integrity has been and is being violated every day, requires saying no to the idea of glorifying suffering and death, saying no to the violation of bodily integrity as a means to achieve a godly or a human way to salvation.

Interpretations of the crucifixion depend on the context. For example, among the suffering masses in Latin America, Christ crucified on the cross is a highly liberating and redemptive symbol. For many African Americans, the suffering Jesus is profoundly redemptive. However, to raise critical questions about doctrines, symbols, and images which have been problematic with respect to liberation for a particular community is as much the work of liberation as affirming doctrines or symbols which sustain the liberating work for another community. If our current social and political context is analogous to those who erected the cross on Calgary—the ruling class, including the religious and political authorities—we need to divest ourselves from overidentifying with the victim on the cross. Writing about religious images, Margaret Miles contends that whether they are experienced "as dangerous or emancipatory will be a function of the interest of the viewer. . . . The viewer of a historical religious image can ignore the [intended] message and substitute a meaning quite different in accordance with his interest" (1985: 30). Their plasticity may be precisely the value of visual images. In contrast to a traditional Christian theological system which is built upon the ideas and precise theological systems of a few great thinkers and church councils,

attitudes, values and concepts can also be based on physical existence; Christianity, understood not primarily as a nexus of ideas but as concrete participation in a body—the "body of Christ"—provides a strong formulation of the centrality and significance of physical existence, in which human life itself is understood as given in physical existence—creation—and fulfilled only in physical existence—resurrection of the body. (Miles 1985: 36)

Miles is not suggesting that we abandon the study of religious texts or great theologians but that we improve our skills in "reading" and interpreting images in order to bring them into dialogue with our written language.

I would like to move beyond Miles's historical project and propose we conceive new images which can alter our old views. The crucifixion image is one of those images we can re-read and re-imagine. Such re-reading requires a willingness to move beyond the narratives as they are recorded in the synoptic gospels to an imaginative re-telling and re-seeing of the crucifixion story based on values of caring and justice, values which are present in Jesus' life and which we also embody, in our better moments, in our own lives today.

Miles is right to stress the physicality of images and their primary task to reflect our physical existence. Our re-imaging and our re-reading of these images should be centered in our physical existence, in our embodiment. More specifically, for queer men, the re-imaging begins in our erotic desire, for it is here that many of us have been most drawn to Jesus and at the same time most repulsed by the church. We have much work to do to reclaim the Jesus who loved and still loves us into self-love and love of other men. That work requires that we leave behind the ecclesiastical Jesus who only loves us without our bodies and our desires. But we must also be attentive to the bodies which we shun, the bodies we claim not to desire because of some physical characteristic, like skin color, which we define as alien or less than fully human.

We must dig deeply into what feminist liturgist Janet Walton calls our body-memory. For gay/bisexual/transgender men, our body-memory includes our bodies which have been beaten on the "playgrounds" of our childhoods and bashed by homophobic brothers, fathers, uncles, strangers, and (male) bishops. Our ever-present memory includes self-hating homosexual bodies which have bashed queer bodies in fear and loathing, and those for whom H.I.V. is the latest (and for many, the last) form of male-over-male violence—a way of killing women, children, and men by the willful neglect of the men who run the governments, scientific laboratories, and medical-industrial complex. But our bodies also may have been soothed by a male friend's gentle touch or vigorous kneading of our tired muscles (as Tim Miller's Jesus does). We can go deeply into our body-memory for the ecstasy of sex with another man (or woman, or men, or both), the soothing of massage, the delight of dancing, and the life-giving of casual touch and elaborate rituals of connection. We can remember the pleasure of heavy gazes while cruising and being cruised. We can dig deeply into our body-memory of the "high" of physical exertion and the contentment and aches which follow. We can relive the embodied pleasure of life with our children.

The purpose of digging into our individual and corporate body memories is to allow our bodies to inform our images as much as images inform our bodies. If we are fortunate, body-memory brings joy and pleasure. Just as often, body-memory touches deep places of sadness and anger. At other moments, body-memory brings repentance. As a gay-identified bisexual man, as a queer, as a white man of considerable privilege, I can remember Jesus, and other righteous brothers killed to make the world safe for erotophobic patriarchy, with affection and esteem and tears, and even call on their names for sustenance and power in my ever-present need for both. But this is not sufficient ground on which to glorify their sufferings and deaths. Latina theologian Teresa Delgado told me once that anger, finely honed and transformed into a passion for justice, is a healthy, embodied response to the murder of Jesus. I agree.

Anger can be directed, first, at the Roman civil authorities whose system of state-sanctioned violence ended his life. Moreover, we are angry at those religious authorities who did not intervene in an attempt to stop the execution. However, anger also is righteously due toward church and secular authorities who, for centuries, scapegoated the Jewish leaders and thus perpetuated the crucifixion of the one Jew, Jesus, in pogroms, crusades, inquisitions, and a Holocaust which murdered millions of his people, just as the Inquisition scapegoated, tortured, and murdered women and free-thinking and differently acting men. Anger is due toward church and secular authorities who helped sustain the brutally attempted extinction of Native Americans and the forced enslavement and wholesale butchery of millions of Africans. And it is justly directed at those who have portrayed Jesus as white, blonde, and blue-eyed. These authorities are among the men who are complicit in the actual and repeated ritualized murder of Jesus as well as the murders of millions of his brothers and sisters in death. They have helped to create a culture of death, indeed a cult of male killing and dying. We may recognize ourselves among those who have helped to sustain this cult, either by active complicity or the complicity of silence in the face of evil.

Let us look at the scene of the cross at Calvary. Who is there? The women. Who is not there? The men, with the exception of the disciple whom Jesus loved (John 19:25–27). We commonly say "the disciples" were afraid and confused, but we mean the men around Jesus were absent. Who would not be afraid and confused in the face of state-sanctioned murder? But when our friend dies, should we not at least offer some comfort and visit the widow, the parents, and the children? When our friend is dying, do we not keep vigil, do we not, as Bonhoeffer says, "throw ourselves completely into the arms of God, taking seriously, not our own sufferings, but those of God in the world—watching with Christ in Gethsemane" (1972: 370)? Do we not hold our friend's hand and wipe his fevered brow and sing softly to soothe his fevered brain? Do we not pray, weep, and rail against God for "allowing" our friend to die and simultaneously praise God for our friend's goodness, asking God for forgiveness for all who are dying, dead, and living?

Some men do these things. They may be saviors in our world, saving us one person at a time. Joseph of Arimathea insisted on burying Jesus in his own tomb in accord with rabbinic tradition that a dead body should not remain unburied after the day of death. Scholars debate, as the gospel accounts disagree, about Joseph's motive: Was he a secret sympathizer with Jesus and his disciples? Was he a disciple himself? Or was he an observant Jew? The point may be not so much his motive as his action. He cared for the dead body, treating it with respect. He did not forsake Jesus, who was hanging on a cross as a criminal.

Today, few queer men in the United States have avoided vigils at the bedsides of friends and lovers dying of AIDS. Young and youngish men learn about death through their own dying, and old men comfort them and those they leave behind. Men with H.I.V. who retain their visible health are supported in whatever processes they require to sustain and extend life. Men dance with the "well-sick" and they share in sexual pleasures. Dying men are read to, fed, taken to the hospital and hospice, bathed, held up, carried, prayed for. Dead men are buried with respect and affection, the mourners weeping and laughing, sometimes simultaneously. Marchers, poster-makers, chanters, and activists resist the silence which threatens to envelope all persons living with H.I.V./AIDS in death. In the face of a society which has yet to weep for the dying and dead, yet to rise up to demand and obtain the necessary focus on a cure, and which still harbors in many places the belief that these men have caused their own death by loving one another, these men (and women, to be sure) stand at the foot of the contemporary crosses caring for the bodies with a tenderness and toughness which can move us to tears and to action. Their actions, their lives of caring and resisting, tell us who and what is missing from the gospel accounts of Jesus' death: his male friends responding to his dying with tender affection and tough action. Our aching, sorrow-laden, angry body-memories remind us what his friends might have done.

Our new vision requires that his friends at least stand vigil, that they bring his body down from the cross to wipe his brow, give him drink, tell him of their love, and spread healing balm on his awful wounds. The soldiers might hurt or kill them, the crowds might stone them. But what we need are men who dare to say no to patriarchs, and who embody resistance at the point of greatest tension with patriarchal domination. Jesus' male friends have left to us the task of relieving his body, of caring for his wounds, of giving him the kiss of peace which signals resistance and liberation and which intends to disturb the peace of those in power. To care for the despised is not only an act of love but also an act of political resistance.

Traditionally, the period between the Last Supper and the crucifixion of Jesus is referred to as his passion. As Carter Heyward says, it was "a time during which Jesus bore the passion of his time, his culture, his religious heritage . . . [and his] passion was a challenge, a threat, to those around him who were willing to settle for less than passion" (1984: 20). I am suggesting that men, queer and non-queer, create new images in which the passion of Jesus be matched by our own passion, a passion that there be an end to violence among men and, therefore, against women and children. Such passion is grounded in a passionate desire for men—which can be sexual or not, but through it we must be willing to see men as embodied friends rather than disembodied enemies.

My vision requires that white men must not only remove the body of Jesus from the cross and care for it but also accept the fact that the body we are loving is not white. Jesus was not white, just like most of those bodies which have hung and are hanging from crosses today. White gay male theology, queer theologizing by white men, if it truly means to overcome the violation of men's bodies, must repent and lead the way in recognizing that dominant European and American theological traditions have falsified our images of Jesus. These traditions have resisted the claims of Black Theology for the Black Christ because a man of color on the cross would force us to face all the other bodies of men (and women) of color on the crosses erected by white supremacist patriarchy.

To remove the black Jesus, our brother who was in-the-life, from the cross means refusing to nail any more black, Latino, Asian, and Native American bodies to crosses today. He who was/is in-the-life shall die no more forever.

Seeking to free us from a Christocentrism which devalues humanity, Gary David Comstock urges us to acknowledge Jesus as a dead friend with whom we are in a relationship of autonomy. Comstock also argues that we do not need to image Jesus at all because doing so makes a hero out of one man "at the expense of the particular experiences and lives of the many in our midst—the very lives Jesus himself attended to in his own time" (1993: 97). Comstock is both right and wrong.

Conclusion

The effect of imaging Jesus as Lord and Savior who died in a burst of bloody glory to save us all from sin serves the interests of patriarchs and their church to the exclusion of, and damage to, the lives of ordinary people, especially those who are oppressed by sex, race, or class. The problem of images, however, is not having them but insisting that they be limited. To cease imaging our friends, to cease allowing our images of them to be reflected in us, and to cease imaging ourselves through images others reflect back to us, is to cease living relationally. Developing images of new friends expands our circle of friends, companions, and comrades, including those different from ourselves, who might love us if we show signs of loving them. "We are what we look upon and what we desire," Plotinus remarked, and that includes the images shaped by our gaze upon our own and other bodies. For many of us, our gaze remains focused on Jesus' body because it mirrors our own and those we desire, as it also mirrors those whom we fear and refuse to see.

James Baldwin's *Giovanni's Room* is, for queer men, one of the important novels of this century. At the conclusion of the novel, the protagonist David, who has tried to deny his homosexuality, is alone in a rented house in a French village. He has abandoned his former lover Giovanni who is, that very day, being guillotined for petty theft and trumped-up charges of sexual advances toward an aging bar owner. Giovanni is being executed on a cross of denied desire—the rejection of his own desire for David and the rejection of the desire of the aging bar owner for Giovanni. David imagines Giovanni's execution, the buckling legs, the jellying thighs, the quivering buttocks, the secret hammering inside, the shame of uncontrolled urination, the sweat, the tears. He then removes his clothes and sees in the mirror the reflection of his naked body which is the source of his own troubles and also the key to his salvation. Both his salvation, ultimately unable to save his body, and his corruption, which began the day he was born, are hidden in his flesh which is reflected back to him in the mirror. In that sense, David's naked body in the mirror also is on a cross: the cross from which he has failed to free Giovanni is now his own.

The image Baldwin draws of Giovanni's execution floats in and out of my images of Jesus on the cross. When David looks in the mirror, he does what each of us must do: face the body at Calvary and other crucified bodies. Facing our own crucifixion and our participation in the crucifixion of others, we can stop nailing the bodies of women, children, and men on the crosses, where we know none belong, and begin to bring them down.

REFERENCES

Baldwin, James. 1956. *Giovanni's Room.* New York: Dell Publishing.
Bonhoeffer, Dietrich. 1972. *Letters and Papers from Prison.* Ed. Eberhard Bethge. New York: Macmillan.
Brock, Rita Nakashima. 1989. "And a Little Child Will Lead Us." In *Christianity, Patriarchy, and Abuse: A Feminist Critique,* ed. Joanne Carlson Brown and Carole R. Bohn. New York: Pilgrim Press.
———. 1991. *Journeys by Heart: A Christology of Erotic Power.* New York: Crossroad.
Brown, Joanne Carlson, and Rebecca Parker. 1989. "For God So Loved the World?" In *Christianity, Patriarchy, and Abuse: A Feminist Critique,* ed. Joanne Carlson Brown and Carole R. Bohn. New York: Pilgrim Press.
Comstock, Gary David. 1993. *Gay Theology without Apology.* Cleveland: Pilgrim Press.
Cone, James H. 1975. *God of the Oppressed.* New York: Seabury Press.
———. 1989. *Black Theology and Black Power: Twentieth Anniversary Edition.* San Francisco: Harper.
———. 1990. *Black Theology of Liberation: Twentieth Anniversary Edition.* Maryknoll, N.Y.: Orbis Books.
Dollimore, Jonathan. 1991. *Sexual Dissidence: Augustine to Wilde, Freud to Foucault.* Oxford, England: Oxford University Press.
Driver, Tom F. 1981. *Christ in a Changing World: Toward an Ethical Christology.* New York: Crossroad.

Evans, Arthur. 1988. *The God of Ecstasy: Sex-Roles and the Madness of Dionysius*. New York: St. Martin's Press.

Farajajé-Jones, Elias. 1993. "Breaking Silence: Toward an In-the-Life Theology." In *Black Theology: A Documentary History, 1980–1992*, vol. 2, ed. James H. Cone and Gayraud S. Wilmore. Maryknoll, N.Y.: Orbis Books.

Foster, Guy-Mark. 1991. "The Book of Luke." In *Brother to Brother: New Writings by Black Gay Men*, ed. Essex Hemphill. Boston: Alyson Publications.

Gorsline, Robin. 1991. "Let Us Bless Our Angels: A Feminist-Gay-Male-Liberation View of Sodom." In *Redefining Sexual Ethics: A Sourcebook of Essays, Stories, and Poems*, ed. Susan E. Davies and Eleanor H. Haney. Cleveland: Pilgrim Press.

Goss, Robert. 1993. *Jesus Acted Up: A Gay and Lesbian Manifesto*. San Francisco: Harper.

Heyward, Carter. 1982. *The Redemption of God: A Theology of Mutual Relation*. Washington, D.C.: University Press of America.

———. 1984. *Our Passion for Justice: Images of Power, Sexuality, and Liberation*. New York: Pilgrim Press.

———. 1989a. *Touching Our Strength: The Erotic as Power and the Love of God*. San Francisco: Harper & Row.

———. 1989b. *Speaking of Christ: A Lesbian Feminist Voice*. Ed. Ellen C. Davis. New York: Pilgrim Press.

hooks, bell. 1992. *Black Looks: Race and Representation*. Boston: South End Press.

Lorde, Audre. 1984. *Sister Outsider: Essays and Speeches*. Trumansburg, N.Y.: Crossing Press.

Miles, Margaret R. 1985. *Image as Insight: Visual Understanding in Western Christianity and Secular Culture*. Boston: Beacon Press.

Miller, Tim. 1991. "Jesus and the Queer Performance Artist." In *Amazing Grace: Stories of Lesbian and Gay Faith*, ed. Malcolm Boyd and Nancy L. Wilson. Freedom, Calif.: Crossing Press.

Sedgwick, Eve Kosofsky. 1990. *Epistemology of the Closet*. Berkeley: University of California Press.

Williams, Delores S. 1993. *Sisters in the Wilderness: The Challenge of Womanist God-Talk*. Maryknoll, N.Y.: Orbis Books.

PART IV

Male Friendships

EIGHT

Men and Christian Friendship

PHILIP L. CULBERTSON

Now if Eve was not made for Adam to be his helper in begetting children, what good was she to him? She was not to till the earth with him, for there was not yet any toil to make help necessary. If there were any such need, a male helper would be better, and the same could be said of the comfort of another's presence if Adam were perhaps weary of solitude. How much more agreeably could two male friends, rather than a man and a woman, enjoy companionship and conversation in a life shared together.

—St. Augustine,
The Literal Meaning of Genesis

We live in complex societies, interweavings of blood relationships, marital relationships, extended family relationships, business and professional relationships, formalized fraternal relationships, and a whole host of informal relationships loosely referred to under the heading of "friendships" (cf. Cicero 1913: 57). Julian Pitt-Rivers (1968; cf. Herman 1987: 32) has attempted to systematize a portion of this complex spectrum of relationships within which we live and work, understanding social relationships such as kinship and friendship to be expressions of the common principle of "amity." In Pitt-Rivers's schema, godparents would be one example of "ritual kinship"; college fraternity

TABLE I

"Real" Kinship	Kinship Adoptive Kinship	"Amiable Relations" Ritual Kinship	Friendship Ritualized Friendship	Unritualized Friendship

brothers and fellow Rotarians would be an example of "ritualized friendship." "Unritualized friendship" is such a broad category that it defies schematization, ranging from those with whom we carpool, to those we meet regularly in the pub, to most of those whom men would term "my best buddy."

While the contemporary literature on "unritualized friendship" seems plentiful, most of the research has been done within the fields of sociology, psychology, or cultural anthropology. Much less has been written on friendship within the Christian or Jewish traditions. For example, in neither the *Encyclopedia of Early Christianity* nor the recent encyclopedic *Anchor Bible Dictionary* will one find any entry under the headings of "Friend" or "Friendship." In the *Encyclopedia Judaica*, "friendship" merits only one half of one column. My task in this chapter is to track selectively the subject of friendship in Christian literature from the patristic period (roughly the first six hundred years of church history), particularly as it echoes classical Greek and Roman writers on the subject; to point to the possibility that friendship between men is considered to be homosexually dangerous by many, all the while masking a homosocial attraction between heterosexual men; and to set forth a hypothesis about certain influences of Christian theology which continue to keep friendship between some men a near-impossibility, even with the increasing influence of the men's movement. [1]

Analyzing Male Intimacy

As I explained in my book *New Adam* (1992), I understand the relationship between Jonathan and David (1 Samuel 13 to 2 Samuel 1) to be an intimate friendship unjustly doomed to end because of external suspicion about whether it was homosexual in character. Patristic writers struggled with the same issue: how could two adult men develop an intimate friendship that was beyond all taint of suspicion, all the while enjoying, in early Christian thought, a relationship far superior in virtue to the marital relationship between a man and a woman. Though the Scriptures contain no examples of such friendship beyond that of Jonathan and David, male friends were expected by the early Christian writers to be so intimate that they could think each other's thoughts, to turn down career advancements in order to stay together, and to exemplify the ancient saying that "two friends have one soul," for each is the alter ego of the other.

Quickly severed from its Jewish origins, early Christianity in the Greek and Roman world was ripe for the shaping of its intellectual and theological tradition by the classical literature of the great pagan writers. As it was nearly *de rigueur* for the classical writers to produce an essay or two on friendship between men, the intellectual shapers of Christian tradition produced derivative essays on friendship between men as the highest expression of God's love acted out in public. A certain number of Biblical texts were appropriated and interpreted as equivalent to the classical proverbs concerning friendship. Various stylistic formulations of male friendship-values even find their way into the New Testament epistles. Reciprocally, classical proverbs about male friendship seem occasionally to have been accorded the authority usually due a Biblical text. For example, in the fifth century St. Augustine of Hippo reverenced Cicero's definition of friendship as being both correct and spiritually inspired. Augustine's admiration of classical insights is so great that he even claims Cicero's elegant literary style as being superior to Scripture's cruder expression (*Confessions* I.5.9 in Augustine 1955: 66).

Three classical proverbs in particular are repeated again and again in patristic literature, as though these proverbs were divinely inspired extensions of the foundational principle to "love one's neighbor as one's self" (Lev. 19:18). The three are "Friends are one soul in two bodies," "A friend is a second self," and "Friends hold all things in common." The lack of concern by the patristic writers over whether the three proverbs originated in classical or Biblical thought can be illustrated by a survey of some of the sources quoting the three:

TABLE 2
"Friends Are One Soul in Two Bodies"

Classical Sources	Biblical and Patristic Sources	Subsequent Sources
• Cicero, *De officiis* I.xvi (1913: 59; 1947: 850). • Cicero, "Laelius," xxi.81, xxv.92 (1946: 189, 199). • Plutarch, "Of the Plurality of Friends," *Moralia* (1911: 313). • Horace, Ode I, 3:8 (1967: 4). • Aristotle, *Nicomachean Ethics* IX.8, 1168a33 (1925: 234). • Diogenes Laertius, *Lives of the Eminent Philosophers* V.19 (1925: I.463).	• Psalm 55:13. • Acts 4:32. • 1 Corinthians 5:3. • Philippians 1:27. • Colossians 2:5. • 1 Thessalonians 2:17. • Ambrose, "On the Duties of the Clergy," III.22.133 (1990: 149). • Synesius, Epistles 140 and 152 (1926: 233, 249). • Augustine, *Confessions* IV.6.11 (1955: 82). • Minucius Felix, *The Octavius* 1:3 (1974: 51). • Gregory of Nazianzus, Oration 43.20 (1968: VII.402). • Gregory of Nazianzus, Epistle 53 (1968: VII.477). • Gregory of Nazianzus, *De vita sua,* lines 223–31 (1987: 83). • Gregory the Great, Homily 27 on John 15:12–16 (1990: 215). • Paulinus of Nola, Epistles 11.4–5, 13.3 (1966: I.92–94, 119). • Cassian, Conference XVI.3 (1968: XI.451).	• ibn Zabara, *Sefer HaSha'ashuim* XII (1914: 138; 1932: 156). • ibn Ezra, *Sefer HaIyyunim vehaDiyyunim* 97a (1975: 183). • Shakespeare, Polonius to Laertes in "Hamlet," Act I, Scene III. • Ralph Waldo Emerson, "Friendship," (1990: 119).

The origin of these three proverbs is obscure. Cicero (1913: 61) attributes the idea that friends form one soul to Pythagoras (sixth century B.C.E.), as does Diogenes Laertius (1925: II.329). Also to Pythagoras was attributed the proverb, "friends have all things in common" *(koina ta ton philon),* perhaps growing out of the practice of the Pythagorean community in which everything was apparently shared (White 1992: 19). The classical source of the friend as another self is Zeno, according to Diogenes Laertius (1925: II.135), though Philo attributes it

TABLE 3
"A Friend Is a Second Self"

Classical Sources	Biblical and Patristic Sources	Subsequent Sources
• Cicero, *De officiis* I.xvii (1913: 59; 1947: 850). • Cicero, "Laelius," xxi.80 (1946: 189). • Aristotle, *Nicomachean Ethics* IX.7, 1169b3 (1925: 228). • Plutarch, "Of the Plurality of Friends," *Moralia* (1911: 306). • Diogenes Laertius, *Lives of the Eminent Philosophers* VIII.23 (1925: II.135). • Philo, *Questions and Answers on Genesis* 1.17 (1961, 11).	• Deuteronomy 13:6. • 1 Samuel 18. • Proverbs 18:24. • Ben Sira 6:11 and 17. • Ambrose, "On the Duties of the Clergy," III.22.133 (1990: 149). • Augustine, *Confessions* IV.6.11 (1955: 82). • John Chrysostom, Second Homily on Thessalonians 2 (1968: XIII.380–81). • Synesius, Epistle 100 (1926: 187). • Jerome, Epistle 130.12 (1968: VI.267). • Paulinus of Nola, Epistle 11.6 (1966: I.94). • Cassian, Conference XVI.6 (1968: XI.452).	• Maimonides, *Avot* 1.6 (1961: 14). • ibn Aqnin, *Sefer ha-Mussar* (1967: 11). • ibn Zabara, *Sefer Ha-sha'ashuim* XII (1914: 138; 1932: 155). • Shimon b. Zemach Duran, *Magen Avot* I.6 (1961: 22). • Ralph Waldo Emerson, "Friendship," (1990: 122).

TABLE 4
"Friends Hold All Things in Common"

Classical Sources	Biblical and Patristic Sources
• Cicero, *De officiis* I.xvii (1913: 59; 1947: 849). • Cicero, "Laelius," xxvii.103 (1946: 211). • Euripides, *Orestes,* 735 (1958: 51). • Aristotle, *Nicomachean Ethics* IX.8, 1168a33 (1925: 235). • Diogenes Laertius, *Lives of the Eminent Philosophers* VII.24 (1925: II.229; but see X.11, II.539).	• Acts 2:44. • Acts 4:32. • Galatians 6:2. • Clement of Alexandria, "Stromateis" 2:19. • Valerius Maximus, "De amicitia," (1888: 201–10). • Gregory of Nazianzus, Oration 43.20 (1968: VII.402). • Gregory of Nazianzus, *De vita sua,* lines 223–31 (1987: 83). • Jerome, Epistle 130.12 (1968: VI.267). • Maximus the Confessor, "Four Centuries on Charity" III.79 and IV.93 (1955: 188, 207).

to Pythagoras (1961: 11). Gregory of Nazianzus (1968) uses the term *homopsychoi* to indicate the "second self" which unites two male friends; the Latin is *alter idem* or *alter ego*. St. Augustine (1982b) uses the Latin *ex pluribus unum facere* to indicate the "one soul"; the similarity to the American national motto is obvious.

Friendship and the Ultimate Good

With this sort of historical weight, it is no wonder that adult male friendship was considered the primary crucible within which were born the moral foundations of any society. Indeed, Aristotle wrote that without friendship, life was worthless, and "no one would choose to live" (1925: 192). Gregory of Nazianzus observed that friendship between adult males was "More to be desired than gold, even much fine gold; sweeter also than honey, and drippings of the honeycomb" (Psalm 19:10; quoted in White 1992: 51). For Gregory's intimate friend Basil, the bonds of divinely endowed friendship between men was the basis for ecclesiology: communities of the faithful were formed by interlocking networks of men who were generous and loyal to each other. The shapers of early Christianity would agree with Euripides, who observed in his drama *Orestes* that "One loyal friend is worth ten thousand relatives" (line 804, 1958: 59; cf. Cicero, "Laelius," v. 20, 1946: 129). The concurrence between classical and patristic writers, that male friendship is the crucible in which a society's morals are born, can also be charted:

TABLE 5

Classical Sources	Biblical and Patristic Sources
• Xenophon, *Memorabilia* II.4 and 6 (1903: 100, 105).	• Ambrose, "On the Duties of the Clergy," III.22.132 (1990: 148).
• Cicero, *De officiis* I.xvii, par. 55–56 (1913: 59).	• Augustine, *Confessions* IV.8.13 (1955: 83).
• Aristotle, *Nicomachean Ethics* VIII.1, 1155 (1925: 192–93).	• Basil, Epistle 2.2 (1968: VIII.110).
	• Gregory of Nazianzus, Oration 8.1 (1968: VII.238).

For the early Christian writers, God was the source of all good. Society was presumed to be good, including its ordering into hierarchical structures of power and privilege. If these structures were the expression of God's good will, then how much more so were the friendship networks upon which society was constructed. Friends were understood as gifts of God, and indeed God directed specific people's paths to cross in life so that they might have the opportunity to develop an intimate friendship. Carolinne White (1992: 122) points to two New Testament verses often cited in support of these beliefs:

John 15:14 is of course one text which is often referred to by Christian writers on friendship, pointing as it does to a correlation between love of God and our duty to love our neighbor; men are joined with others in friendship and are thereby also friends of Christ. This is not something emphasized by Ambrose. Instead he makes the interesting observation that God gave us the pattern of friendship for us to follow so that we might do our friend's will, reveal all our innermost thoughts to our friend and learn his secrets too. He supports this prescription by a reference to John 15:15.

Other patristic writers who developed the thought that our friends are God's intentional gifts include Augustine, in *Confessions* IV.10.15 (1955: 85) and *On Christian Doctrine* I.xxvii-xxix (1982a: 23–25); John Cassian, Conference XVI.13 (1968: XI.454, citing John 4:16); and Paulinus of Nola, Epistles 3.1, 11.1, 11.5 (1966: I.44, 90). The same thought is echoed much later in Ralph Waldo Emerson's 1841 essay entitled "Friendship" (1990: 112–13).

The Dark Side of Friendship

According to Ben Sira 6:7, "When you gain friends, gain them through testing, and do not trust them hastily." Classical and patristic writers were also not unaware that friendship can have its dark side. Certain caveats were noted throughout the literature, cautioning one not to have too many friends, for the human capacity to love is limited; to make friends selectively and slowly, testing possible friends before making weighty commitments to them; and to work to prove one's love for another person through deeds. Words were not enough to try friendship; it must be shown repeatedly through acts of generosity and loyalty. According to Arthur Adkins (1963: 34, 41), male friendship in the

TABLE 6
Friendships Should Be Limited in Number and Developed Slowly

Classical Sources	Biblical, Patristic, and Later Sources
• Hesiod, *Works and Days,* lines 713–14 (1959: 103). • Aristotle, *Nicomachean Ethics* VIII.6, 1158a (1925: 201). • Plutarch, "Of the Plurality of Friends," *Moralia* (1911: 306–8). • Theognis, "Maxims," lines 31–128 (1914: 219–24). • Xenophon, *Memorabilia* II.6 (1903: 105). • Cicero, *De officiis* I.xvi, par. 60 (1913: 61). • Cicero, "Laelius," v.18, xxi.79, xxii.85 (1946: 129, 187, 193).	• Ben Sira 6:7 • Ben Sira 9:10. • Shakespeare, Polonius to Laertes in Hamlet," Act I, Scene III.

classical literature (and to a large degree continuing into the patristic literature) "is an *act* which creates or maintains a co-operative relationship and *it need not be accompanied by any friendly feeling at all:* it is the action which is all important." Loyalty often was expected to take

TABLE 7
Friends Prove Their Loyalty through Deeds and by Remaining Together

Classical Sources	Biblical and Patristic Sources
• Aristotle, *Nicomachean Ethics.* IX.12, 1172 (1925: 246). • Xenophon, *Memorabilia* II.6, line 73 (1903: 110). • Cicero, *De officiis* III.x, par. 43 (1913: 311). • Cicero, "Laelius," xvii.65 (1946: 175). • Plutarch, "Of the Plurality of Friends," *Moralia* (1911: 309 • Solon, I.60 in Diogenes Laertius, *Lives of the Eminent Philosophers* (1925: I.61)	• Ruth 1:16–17. • Psalm 68:7. • Psalm 133:1. • Proverbs 17:17. • Proverbs 27:10. • Qohelet 4:9–10. • Ben Sira 29:10. • Galatians 6:2. • Valerius Maximus, "De amicitia," (Kempf 1888: 201–210). • Gregory of Nazianzus, Epistle 6 (1968: VI.447–48). • Gregory of Nazianzus, *De vita sua,* lines 223–31 (1987: 83). • Basil, Epistle 71 (1968: VIII.167). • Cassian, Conference XVI.3 (1968: XI.451).

the dutiful form of turning down opportunities for professional advancement, in order to stay in the same location as one's best friend. In fact, when possible, it was best that friends live together, maximizing their intimacy through the frequency of shared daily contact.[2]

Of course, it was not always possible for friends to decline advancements, or neglect the need to move in order better to support their families. Letter writing became the way that friends stayed in touch with each other while separated. The formulae used in such letters between intimate friends became quite stylized, but even through the formality, the words expressed an intimacy which was judged to be a "mirror of the soul." Through letters, friends were united as though they were still together in one place, two bodies sharing one soul. These formulae had a particular impact on the New Testament epistles, employed by the authors as proof of their extreme affection for the congregations to which they were writing.[3]

An Example of Patristic Intimate Male Friendship

One of the most celebrated such friendships in patristic history is that during the fourth century between St. Basil, who became bishop of Caesarea, and St. Gregory of Nazianzus, later patriarch of Constantinople. The primary sources are their letters to each other, Gregory's autobiographical poem *De vita sua,* and his Oration 43, the funeral speech which he wrote for his friend after Basil's death in 379 (cf. Basil of Caesarea 1962, 1968; Gregory of Nazianzus 1968, 1987).[4] Nazianzus in particular wrote several essays on the subject of male friendship. He was heavily influenced by Greek and Roman philosophers, but claimed such relationships as logical extensions of a true faith in Christ. In their younger years, Gregory and Basil lived together as intimate roommates, shared everything, and each considered himself the alter ego of the other. In Epistle 58 (1968: VI.454), Gregory writes to Basil, "The greatest benefit which life has brought me is your friendship and my intimacy with you." In Epistle 53 (1968: VI.477), Gregory cries out that he has always loved Basil more than himself. In his oration at Basil's funeral, Gregory expresses his sense of being but half-alive, cut in two, haunted by thoughts of his dead friend. Yet, there is a dark side to the friendship between the two men as well. When Basil became bishop of Caesarea, he not only abandoned his friend for a distant city, but he did not even draw his intimate Gregory into consideration of whether to accept the election. Essentially, Gregory never forgave Basil for having left him. Among the many expressions of his yearning for Basil, Gregory also writes vitriolicly of his betrayal, his loss, his incredulity at being so summarily dropped by Basil. The break in their friendship was perhaps Gregory's most bitter blow, even in a life full of theological and political controversy (cf. "Laelius" x.34, Cicero 1946: 147).

The problem between them may be understood as a differing philosophy about the ultimate purpose of friendship. Gregory and Basil seem to recapitulate the differences between Plato and Aristotle over the philosophy of friendship. At question is whether friendship should move from particular to universal, or universal to particular. Gilbert Meilaender (1981: 8) summarizes the two differing points of view:

Plato and Aristotle offer us representative expressions of what may be the two most important competing theories of friendship. For Plato, friendship is a universal love which grows out of more particular, affective attachments. For Aristotle (and for the majority of classical thinkers who, on this point, follow him rather than Plato) it is a narrowing down of the many toward whom we have good will to a few friends whom we especially choose. Plato's theory begins with a particular attachment, which then grows toward a more universal love. Aristotle's moves in precisely the opposite direction. Plato grounds friendship in sentiment; Aristotle in choice.

Basil's philosophy, particularly as revealed in his "Rule," seems to mimic Plato's, whereas Gregory's mimics Aristotle's. To Basil, in his Aescetic Sermon I citing Matthew 5:45, perfect love must be impartial in its imitation of God's love for humanity. Gregory seems to have wanted a particular friendship with Basil, but Basil refused, and so embittered Gregory.

The Particularity of Homosociality

For approximately one thousand years from 500 B.C.E. to 500 C.E., and well beyond in more isolated instances, intimate friendship between adult males was valued as the ultimate expression of human relationship. But at the same time, there has been a sense of competition between friendship and marriage, the other commitment expected of adult men. This competition too has a Biblical basis: according to Ben Sira 40:23,

"A friend or companion is always welcome, but a sensible wife is better than either." Only once in the Bible is a wife referred to as a friend— Malachi 2:14—and much subsequent Christian and Jewish literature takes pains to contradict that claim (see, e.g., ibn Zabara 1914: 138). The competition between friendship and marriage finds clear expression in the patristic literature. Meilaender (1981: 2) points out the powerful attraction of marriage:

the erotic relationship between a man and a woman—crowned at one time, if no longer, in Christian marriage—became the bond of love in which people invested themselves most deeply. . . . If the bond of friendship lost its pride of place it is partly because the roots of Christian culture go very deep into a man who is reported to have said: "If you love those who love you, what reward have you? . . . And if you salute only your brethren, what more are you doing than others?" (Matt. 5:46f).

Peter Brown (1985), Rosemary Radford Ruether (1983), James A. Brundage (1987), and others have traced the process by which marriage came to replace male friendship as the higher good within Christian thought. Each raises the issue of how much this reversal of valuation was the result of the increasing hold upon emergent-European society of powerful white males, for whom marriage functioned as a malleable form of social control and barter.

Anthropologists Claude Levi-Strauss (1969) and Gayle Rubin (1975) have defined this social control and barter even more sharply, as "the male traffic in women." According to their theory, each adult male has a limited number of powers, but wishes to accrue more power or greater powers. He can do this only by entering into overt or covert agreements with other men who also wish to trade or improve their limited numbers of power. The tradeable commodity in the improvement of one's own power is women. Women thus serve to mask the fact that power remains a man's game, in which unequally powered men seek more power by entering into (usually unconscious) agreements with other men. Men "court" each other by hiding their need for each other behind women's skirts (Tiger 1984).

Recent literary criticism, including the work of Mary Jacobus (1982–83) and Eve Kosofsky Sedgwick (1985), has examined how this process is reflected in the history of English literature. Sedgwick, for example, describes the process whereby men attempt to establish some intimacy with each other, usually in a triangulated relationship with a woman who functions to disguise the gestures between the men, as "homosociality":

"Homosocial" is a word occasionally used in history and the social sciences, where it describes social bonds between persons of the same sex; it is a neologism, obviously formed by analogy with "homosexual," and just as obviously meant to be distinguished from "homosexual." (Sedgwick 1985: 1)

Sedgwick's theory is directly related to family systems theory, presuming that human beings relate to each other within triangular structures (see Bowen 1985; Friedman 1985). In the triangle of two men and a woman, the attraction between the two men must be taken at least as seriously as the attraction between each man and the woman. The attraction is heightened when either man realizes that he can gain inflated power and influence by forming an alliance with another of the two members of the triangle. Since women rarely have power, the obvious choice with whom to form the alliance is the other man. The alliance may take the form of cooperation or competition or even aggression. Whatever its form, the alliance's power cannot be denied. This desire to unite powers with another man is one possible non-genital form of eros, this desire and attraction creating the exaggerated impulse to homosociality. In John Cassian's Conference XVI, for example, Abba Joseph describes certain male friendships as follows:

In the case of others some bargain or agreement to give and take something has joined them in the bonds of love. Others a similarity and union of business or science or art or study has united in the chain of friendship, by which even fierce souls become kindly disposed to each other, so that those, who in forests and mountains delight in robbery and revel in human bloodshed, embrace and cherish the partners of their crime. (1968: XI.450)

This patristic source reflects on the theory of homosociality: The "something" bargained can well be a woman, however covertly, while the description of rival robbers captures succinctly the erotic bonding within overt competition. Sedgwick (1985: 21) describes the homosocial attraction as "intense and potent." Most men operate this way on occasion, though few are aware of it.

Sedgwick writes: "for a man to be a man's man is separated only by an invisible, carefully blurred, always-already-crossed line from being 'interested in men' " (1985: 89). Crossing the line is controlled by ideological homophobia, which allows two men to relax in their intimate bartering of power, since neither of them has to worry that their intimacy will be misunderstood, issuing in a confusing act of sexual aggression by the other. Alan Bray (1982) dates the rise of this form of ideological homophobia to the Restoration period of the late-seventeenth century. Until that point, social power rested within the church, which had interpreted Scripture and tradition as the sufficient controls to prevent homogenital activity. When power began to shift to the secular world, such as the state and the sciences of medicine and individual psychology, this transfer of assignment entailed an increasingly stressed and invasive homophobic division of the male homosocial spectrum. As homosociality and homophobia moved out of the church into the secular world, they brought with them their predictable attendant baggage of gynephobia and anti-feminism.

Theological Controls on Male Intimacy

Little analysis has been done on the role of Christian theology in promoting the married heterosexual paradigm as a disguise for men's conflicted feelings over their innate homosocial character. Men desire to spend time with other men. They know they need it for emotional and spiritual health. But men today also seem confused when they are abandoned by their wives. Often these men feel that they have undertaken painful personal changes in response to women's demand for justice and equality, and yet they cannot keep their wives happy enough to stay. What remains insufficiently examined is men's complicity in homosociality, particularly when homosociality masquerades as friendship. Women continue to feel that they are being bartered by homosocial men when men use their marital status as an excuse to feel secure about participating in the men's movement. Until men can learn to form intimate friendships with other men in a manner which does not use women as a proof of their masculinity, the line between friendship and women-bartering homosociality will remain destructively blurred. While today homosociality operates largely in secular society, its historical source is within the church, as is the source of its attendant baggage: homophobia, gynephobia, and the reification of women as commodity.

Because men have been taught to be uncomfortable with male friendship, men mask their fear by making sure their heterosexual status is clearly proven in public, by reaffirming marriage as more important than friendship, and even by justifying the covert bartering of women as a prerequisite for men's retention of personal power. Christian thought and theology have contributed to this masking in at least four ways:

1. *Making Friendship Look Dangerous and Untrustworthy*

The Biblical tradition takes adult male friendship seriously, offering supportive maxims and aphorisms in the books Proverbs and Ben Sira; extended friendship stories, such as David and Jonathan, Ruth and Naomi, or the friends of Job; and a handful of New Testament parables structured around the interaction between friends. But paradoxically, the Bible also makes friendship look dangerous by reflecting upon the bitterness of betrayal by friends or the dangers of being swayed in the wrong direction through peer pressure. The corrective to these dangers is to spread friendship thinner. Eugene Borowitz (1971: 195) writes, "The Bible seems to emphasize proper concern for one's neighbor as a means for the creation of a sacred society, rather than intense person-to-person relationships. This may be a safeguard against homosexuality, which was so much a part of the Greek conception of friendship." While Borowitz is correct that the Greek idea of friendship did approve of what we would now call pederasty among the upper classes,[5] it did not approve of what we today call homosexuality, nor does the Bible much concern itself with the subject at all.

Among the Biblical passages which caution that friends may betray or wound us, and thus are not to be easily trusted, are Psalms 41:9; Proverbs 14:20, 19:6, 27:6; Micah 7:5; Ben Sira 6:8–13, 12:8–9, 13:21, 22:26, 37:1–5; Matthew 5:46; and Luke 14:12. Rabbinic tradition is equally cautious about friendship. The friendship of Jonathan and David is held up as the supreme example of self-sacrificing love at Mishnah Avot 5:19, and BT Taanit 23a cries out "Friendship or Death!"[6] Contrarily, when the sage Rav praised Job's friends for visiting him in his distress, the sage Rabbah replied sarcastically, "Either a friend like the friends of Job or death" (BT Baba Batra 16b). Even more interesting is the way Biblical passages get interpreted to show caution about friendship. For example, when Deuteronomy 13:6 speaks of one's most intimate friend as "your friend who is like your own soul," the *Sifre Devarim*, Piska 87 (Hammer 1986: 138) re-interprets "your friend" as meaning one's consanguine brother, and "your own soul" as meaning one's biological father. The text thus reveals a significant discomfort with intimate adult male friendship, erasing the Biblical approval by arguing an alternative reading.

2. *Raising the Specter of Homosexuality within*
Intimate Friendship

In general, the patristic literature praises intimate adult male friendship without worrying about its homosexual possibilities. St. Basil, in his "Long Rules" (1962: 220), is one of the few who cautions against *prospatheia* (feelings of partiality) within a monastic community on the grounds that they might tempt men to be genitally intimate with each other. The word "homosexuality" was coined by K. M. Benkert in 1869 (Money 1988: 9). Alan Bray's excellent study *Homosexuality in Renaissance England* reveals that legal circles in England did not distinguish homosexual behavior from the catch-all crime of "buggery" (involving either men or women) until the 1860s (1982: 134). Careful reading of the patristic literature reveals that the early writers' real concern was with any lack of discipline, rather than singling out homosexuality as a particular danger, for indiscipline suggested a lack of proper focus on God. For example, in his Epistle 366, Basil writes: "We should not look upon continence as of only one kind, in regard to sexual things, for example, but also in relation to all the other things which the soul wrongly desires, not being satisfied with the bare necessities for it" (Culbertson and Shippee 1990: 122). Continence and discipline were expected in every aspect of a person's life, so that human energy would be maximized and then directed Godward. In relation to homosexuality, we must question whether a culture really fears something for which it does not even have a name.

Recent studies in cultural anthropology suggest that homophobia is part of the inheritance carried to the ends of the earth by Christian missionaries in the eighteenth and nineteenth centuries. Today most non-Christian societies continue to accept "institutionalized bisexuality"—that certain types of homosexual activity are a part of the requisite maturation process for males—as the norm, failure to engage in occasional same-sex genital activity indicating an arrested social development (Money 1988: 9). This was also the case prior to the arrival of Christian missionaries among the Native Americans, the Hawaiians, and the Maori of Aotearoa/New Zealand. Defining homosexuality as either a crime or a sin is, then, at least culture-specific or ethnocentric, and is probably Christocentric. The moral judgment of homosexual behavior has little to do with Scripture or the early patristic tradition. According to John Boswell (1980: 124, 172), the first person put to death on the demand of the church for an act related to homosexuality was killed in 390 for selling males into prostitution; the first person put to death for homosexual genital acts was Bishop Alexander of Diospolis in Thrace, c. 550, who died by castration. The classification of homosexuality as a mortal sin becomes a Christian obsession due to the later complicated interaction between forces in European society and the needs of power and control in institutionalized Christianity. The seeds of homophobia may have lain in the patristic theology of friendship, but it took the subsequent development of ecclesiastical power and authority for those seeds to overwhelm the positive evaluation of intimate male friendship as the highest expression of Christian love.

The point is that since most men are socially conditioned to behave heterosexually, same-sex genital activity is of little "danger" in intimate friendship between adult males anyway. To attach the specter of homosexuality to male friendship says more about those who do the attaching than it does about behavior between friends. C. S. Lewis remarks, "Those who cannot conceive Friendship as a substantive love but only as a disguise or elaboration of Eros betray the fact that they have never had a Friend" (1960: 91). Christianity's obsession with homosexuality (perhaps more exaggerated today than ever before in history) serves to inflate the importance of heterosexual marriage by making men fear male friendship. Since same-sex genital activity holds little attraction for the majority of men with a Western enculturation, to persist in promoting this fear suggests that a different agenda is at work.

3. Spiritualizing Men's Friendship, Thereby Disassociating It from Their Bodies

Echoing their classical heritage, the early patristic writers spoke of friendship in very physical terms. Living together, as male friends were expected to do unless married, is a very physical process. The phrase "one soul in two bodies" suggests the importance of the body as that which allows men to bind themselves to each other. But Christianity also bought into a body-soul dualism which argued for the disassociation of higher goods from the confines of mortal limitation. This disassociation became even more exaggerated with the development of the doctrine that the human body was by nature sinful. The human body needed not only disciplining. Even mortification of the flesh implies a certain attention to and awareness of biological needs. The ultimate goal in Christian thought became ignoring the body altogether, concentrating on the disembodied immortal soul, which could then unite with a disembodied risen Christ.

Augustine developed this doctrine systematically in relationship to male friendship. To love someone as a "second self" was not only the appropriate living-out of Leviticus 19:18 ("you shall love your neighbor as yourself"), but it also expressed the Divine economy, in that Christ was a "second self" of God the Father (see also Cassian [1968], Conference XVI.6, XI.452, citing John 6:38). To love another man was a Christian act, and as such, must be free from all taint of sin, including any appreciation of another's physical body. Friendship as two souls knit together in one disembodied whole was not unlike Jesus' command concerning heterosexual marriage, "the two shall become one flesh" (Matthew 19:5, Mark 10:8). The ironic reversal of friendship as "one soul in two bodies" with marriage as "two souls in one flesh" seems to have escaped Augustine's careful theological gaze. In this way, Augustine and others spiritualized friendship by disassociating it from human particulars and partiality, making friendship a Christian responsibility to be extended to all. When one can overlook the vicissitudes of the human body, almost anyone becomes loveable, just as God's love knows no partiality. Once friendship was spiritualized, it was easily universalized. Once universalized, it was essentially emasculated.

Augustine and others could argue their doctrine only by making sharp and innovative distinctions among *agape, philos,* and *eros,* three common Greek terms for love. The distinctions seem not to be as sharp in the original Greek as more recent interpreters wish to suggest.[7] In a recent essay, New Testament scholar Robin Scroggs corrects this mistaken differentiation: "The distinction we should make . . . is not between agape and eros but between a dehumanized eros, driven by a sad lack of self-acceptance of the self, and an eros that is able to live out of fullness because it lives out of a self-accepting self" (1993: 154). Citing the work of Brown and Marcuse on eros, Scroggs (1993: 163) shows that eros and agape, particularly as discussed in the Pauline epistles, have three qualities in common: (a) the presence of non-aggressive characteristics; (b) enjoyment and appreciation of others; and (c) the mutuality of loving. What distinguishes "good" eros from "bad" eros is that the eros/agape interchange contains no need for anyone to dominate or possess another. But this distinction was not useful for Christian thought as it sought to separate itself from a "perverse" world. To emphasize the Christian disdain for debauchery, eros was relegated to the physical world and agape to the spiritual, thereby constructing an artificial distinction which not only violated Scriptural tradition, but served the church's purposes of maintaining control and conformity.

4. Developing Muscular Christianity

The late Victorian era (the mid-1800s) saw the rise of a movement known as Muscular Christianity. This movement too had its roots in patristic Christian thought. Synesius of Cyrene ends his Epistle 140 with a farewell, calling his friend Herculian to behavior befitting a manly man—one whose emotions are carefully shut down:

May you continue in good health—may philosophy keep you in calm cheerfulness, O admirable master! If philosophy knows how to give the first place to absence of emotion itself, and if the intermediary states consist in the moderate experience of passion, where on earth shall we place the extreme of passion and the extreme of humiliation? Shall we not place them outside of philosophy, of which we prayed earnestly that you might be the priest? Not that, at all events, most dear to me of all men! Show yourself *a more manly friend* to us. (Synesius 1926: 235, emphasis added)

The stage was next set for Muscular Christianity in the writings of Samuel Taylor Coleridge (1772–1834). Coleridge equated manliness with charity, virtue, and good-will, all of which would lead a right-living man to the fulfillment of his potential in a better and more useful life. Coleridge's philosophy is well-illustrated in a section of his *Aids to Reflection* (the full title, according to some sources, adds *in the Formation of a Manly Character*):

Let it not, however, be forgotten, that the powers of the understanding and the intellectual graces are precious gifts of God; and that every Christian, according to the opportunities vouchsafed to him, is bound to cultivate the one and to acquire the other. Indeed, he is scarcely a Christian who wilfully neglects so to do. What says the apostle? Add to your faith *knowledge,* and to knowledge *manly energy* (2 Pet. 1,5); for this is the proper rendering of , and not *virtue* at least in the present and ordinary acceptation of the word (Comment to Aphorism XIIc, 1905: 6–7, emphasis original).

Virtue was manly energy for Coleridge. This manly energy was to be applied to the intellectual pursuits. In the generation next after Coleridge, it was an easy shift from intellectual pursuits to even more manly ones on the athletic field.

In 1876, Thomas Hughes gave a series of lectures, published three years later under the title *The Manliness of Christ.* The term Muscular Christianity is usually attributed to T. S. Sandards (Newsome 1961: 198). Christianity was interpreted as synonymous with robust energy, spirited courage, and physical vitality. Hughes and his followers, particularly Charles Kingsley, George Selwyn, and Thomas Arnold, channeled their new theological insights into reforms affecting school education, competitive sports, and overseas missionary activities. Whereas Coleridge had regarded manliness as a description of maturity, Kingsley and Hughes stressed the gender and muscular connotations of the word manliness, emphasizing these qualities by identifying the converse of manliness as "effeminacy" (Newsome 1961: 197). Hughes wedded the virtues of manliness, godliness, and strenuous physical exertion in his writings, the most famous of which is *Tom Brown's Schooldays.*

Christian Manliness was the antidote to "effeminacy" (by which Hughes and Kingsley meant homosexuality, not "an obsession with women," though as well every Christian young man should hold himself pure for the virgin he would marry and impregnate).[8] In 1861, Hughes wrote in his sequel *Tom Brown at Oxford,* "Sir, you belong to a body whose creed is to fear God, and walk 1,000 miles in 1,000 hours."[9] In the same period, but across the ocean, Ralph Waldo Emerson wrote in his essay entitled "Friendship":

I hate the prostitution of the name of friendship to signify modish and worldly alliances. I much prefer the company of ploughboys and tin-peddlers, to the silken and perfumed amity which celebrates its days of encounter by a frivolous display, by rides in a curricle, and dinners at the best taverns (Emerson 1990: 118).

Interestingly, Emerson's essay combines the three classical proverbs "one soul in two bodies," "a second self," and "friends hold all things in common"—with an emphasis on an exaggerated virility, thereby suggesting that true friendship could exist only between two pious Christian athletes.

Muscular Christianity was premised on the physical superiority of males; if God made them physically superior to women, that extra advantage must be developed to the maximum in order to be faithful stewards of God's gifts: to fight in His service, to protect the weak, to conquer nature. No less important to Kingsley, it was a man's duty to fulfill his sexual function by the procreation of children in that bliss which is the marital state (Newsome 1961: 209). Healthy competition was worked out on the rugby field, and "impure" thoughts were kept under control by cold showers and sleeping in the winter with all the windows open.[10] Boys were encouraged to become rugged men in keeping with an eccentric mis-quotation of Psalm 147:10 as "The Lord delighteth in a pair of sturdy legs." Muscular Christianity was worked out not only on the rugby field, but in the mission field as well. New Zealand author Jock Phillips summarizes the philosophy of Muscular Christianity as "the duty of patriotism; the moral and physical beauty of athleticism; the salutary effects of Spartan habits and discipline; the cultivation of all that is masculine and the expulsion of all that is effeminate, un-English and excessively intellectual," all combined with a simple and unquestioning Christian faith (1987: 216). The impact of Muscular Christianity was pervasive and international; a hundred years later, its residue continues to influence Christian suspicion of intimate male friendship.

Defining Friendship

The efforts of Christianity to regulate and finally discourage male friendship are necessary because males are by nature homosocial. To a degree, contemporary American society tolerates male packs as long as they are ritualized, institutionalized, and controlled. Boy Scouts, Rotary Clubs, college social fraternities, amateur athletic teams, and men's prayer breakfasts are acceptable because they are public and predictable. Other associations are not yet fully acceptable to society or to the church, including both men's movement groups and intimate adult male friendships in which the company of another man is preferred over the company of a (preferably fertile) woman. To a degree, these efforts at control and discouragement explain why we are having such a hard time with friendship, even after the men's movement. The men's movement is trying to push the limits, to see how far society's toleration can stretch before breaking, by analyzing and sometimes rejecting society's reasons why men should not love each other as much as they love women, in spite of that love being different.

What is this friendship that we so yearn for and yet so fear? Eisenstadt and Roniger (1984: 290) observe that friendship is as impossible to define well, as is love. Cora Du Bois has attempted to schematize friendship, distinguishing between exclusive, close, and casual friendships, and remarking on whether each is expressive or instrumental, dyadic or polyadic, as well as the degree of intimacy, mutability, and duration (Eisenstadt and Roniger 1984: 7). Du Bois omits what other studies suggest is men's most common form of friendship, the utilitarian—those whom we befriend because we sense that they will be useful to us in some capacity. But these, however common, are not the relationships that trouble and ultimately elude us. Rather, we seek but fear some friendship which is "close" in that it is "expressive-instrumental" but feels "exclusive"—we want our friendships to be inclusively intimate and we hope that they are permanent (since most men are married, the purely dyadic/exclusive friendship is out of the question). Epicurus highlighted the role of utility even in exclusive friendships. In one of his letters, he wrote that the wise man will need friends, "that there may be someone to sit by him when he is ill, to help him when he is in prison or in want" (1964: 67). We want our friends to remain our friends forever, with us in sickness and in health wherever we are, as opposed to the distant memory of someone who was our best friend when we were younger. Thus, religious ethicist Gilbert Meilaender, citing Proverbs 17:17—"A friend loves at all times"—can observe that the three basic components of friendship are benevolence, the desire to enjoy the other person in a reciprocal union of the affections, and undying loyalty (1981: 49, 54).

In surveying the philosophy and goals of adult male friendship in the patristic literature, Carolinne White (1992: 55) comes to a remarkably similar set of characteristics:

What might be said to be the distinctive characteristics of the traditional view of friendship? A fundamental belief in reciprocity as a *sine qua non* of friendship, a high degree of intimacy between two or at most a few persons which made it possible to think of a friend as a second self; the idea that a friend ought to possess some reason for being loved, which in the case of good men would be their virtue, and that friends should share material things and have interests in common.

Social psychologists come up with a similar definition of friendship. According to Secord and Backman (1964: 247),

a person is likely to choose the following individuals: (1) those with whom he has a greater opportunity to interact, (2) those who have characteristics most desirable in terms of the norms and values of the group, (3) those who are most similar to him in attitudes, values, and social-background characteristics, and (4) those whom he perceives as choosing him or assigning favorable characteristics to him, (5) those who see him as he sees himself, and (6) those whose company leads to gratification of his needs.

We see then that the qualities which adult males seek in intimate friendship are consistently: mutual attraction and admiration, similarity of attitudes and values, parity of social status, loyalty even in the face of idiosyncrasy, and reciprocal gratification in each other's close company. The company we keep, and the quality of our friendships experienced in the above characteristics, are the school in which we learn what it means to love anyone. Most schools of psychology agree that if we have not mastered these intimacy skills with someone of our own gender, we are not equipped truly to love someone of the opposite gender. The classical and patristic writers would agree with such a claim, that homosocial love must not only precede heterosexual love, but must continue alongside it, in order for heterosexual love to survive. Perhaps this explains why they valued same-gender friendship so highly. Without the school of love, society would have no hope for the future.

Friendship, Privacy, and Institutionalism

Why hasn't the men's movement been more successful in facilitating adult male intimate friendship? The easiest explanation is that too many activities associated with the men's movement remain self-serving. Shared activities premised on self-discovery, such as "finding the wild man within," focus us away from others rather than toward others, leaving us further paralyzed in the male self-sufficiency paradigm, "one soul in one body." Until the men's movement addresses more actively the issue of other-oriented relationships, most men will continue to rely on the "male traffic in women" to be able to form relationships with other men. But as feminism empowers more and more women to refuse to be bartered, men feel even more lost.

The mistakenly self-centered focus in the men's movement is not the only continuing discouragement to male friendship. As well, friendship looks scary when it is private, when it is deemed anti-social or anti-institutional, and when it is devalued for not making a contribution to the progress of broadly accepted but unexamined social goals. In other words, friendship always runs the risk of appearing to be a useless or even a dangerous luxury.

Friendship is by nature private. We have few friends, even in the best of circumstances, and we tend therefore to protect our friendships from too much public scrutiny to avoid undue interference from others. Perhaps we recognize that the bonds of friendship, particularly between men, are still too fragile. Perhaps we are afraid that if the intimacy yearnings of our few friendships were known, in a sex-sick world the specter of homosexuality would be raised, no matter how unfounded, as in the Biblical story of Jonathan and David. At any rate, our friendships are private, whereas for most men their marriages are quite public. On our desks at work, we place pictures of our wives and children, but rarely pictures of our best friend. When single men are invited to a work-related social function, they are encouraged to come alone, or to find an "acceptable" date, but never to bring their best friend. Relationships conducted in public are scrutinizable, regulable, controllable, manipulable; relationships conducted in private make others nervous, because we have been taught to fear both male behavior and male sexuality, as though either might spin out of control at any moment unless open to external controls. The private nature of friendship makes it inherently anti-social. We are not to have too many friends, say the classical, Biblical, and patristic sources, because there isn't enough of any person to go around to all those other men who need friends. But exclusivity means that others will be deprived, and thus friendship is anti-social. As C. S. Lewis observes, "To say 'These are my friends' implies 'Those are not' "(1960: 90). For human beings, exclusion is more comfortable when we are the excluders than when we are the excluded.

Friendship is also anti-institutional. Businesses attempt to make regulations about who can be friends under what circumstances. Friendship means that trust has been placed outside the institution, and institutions hear in that an implicit judgment. The institution loses its grip on its members when trust is placed elsewhere. Power is lost when one says, "I'd rather be spending my energies on my best friend than on furthering the power and financial security of the company."

As well, friendship does not produce a product which is an acceptable and visible contribution to the economic welfare of society. Children, the most visible product of marriage, contribute to the progressive good of any society, for they are its measurable future. An attractive home, a stable and successful career, a multi-generational or extended family, and public modeling of happiness and tradition are values which please institutions. Adult male intimate friendship offers none of these things readily. Because of these three reasons—privacy, anti-institutionalism, and unmeasurable productivity—friendship is deemed useless by most institutions, or in the extreme, dangerous.

Re-Thinking Christian Friendship

Throughout most of the world, Christianity understands itself as institutional and public. Since the character of friendship is anti-institutional and private, it will be difficult to move Christianity back to any appreciation of the value of adult male friendship, in spite of its indisputable importance in early Christian sources. C. S. Lewis literally sets the description of friendship as "one soul in bodies twain" side by side with the Christian understanding of marriage as a "one flesh" union (two souls in one body): "Lovers are normally face to face, absorbed in each other; Friends, side by side, absorbed in some common interest" (1960: 91). His phrasing echoes not only the contrast between "two bodies" (side by side) and "one flesh" (face to face), but his description of friends echoes nicely the classical proverb that friends create one soul in two bodies (as does Martin Buber's dialogic model in his 1958 *I and Thou*). The Church seems to have opted for the loss of uniqueness and individuality, the indistinguishability of the many within the one, the pinioning of the two in one, as opposed to the liberation of a soul set free into more than one body.

Male friendship re-considered should not be spiritual in the sense of disembodied, for God's presence in the world is premised upon human physical agency. Rather, Christian friendship should be spiritual in the sense that it deals in realms of beauty, tenderness, and loyalty—so foreign to society's self-preserving utilitarian values. Meilaender has observed that perhaps friendship is too "spiritual" to be entirely safe (1981: 104–5). However, beauty, tenderness, and loyalty imply that men's physical bodies are also involved in this spirituality. The Christian faith was considered dangerous by the classical cultures within which it emerged because it did not support the empowered establishment or the exploitation of women, the poor, or the aged. In this sense, adult male intimate friendship is the perfect expression of a kind of patristic liberation theology in its confrontation of power and authority.

Friendship as a type of radical liberation spirituality will by nature be liminal, not only in the sight of economic institutions, but even within the church, at least for the present time. Victor Turner has defined liminal phenomena as "phenomena at the boundaries of institutional life, with potential antinomian tendencies, often also exhibiting a strong emphasis on the attempt to build *communitas,* unrestricted by the social division of labour and of power" (Eisenstadt and Roniger 1984: 18). Gregory's intimate friend Basil claimed that the bonds of divinely endowed friendship between men were the basis for ecclesiology: communities of the faithful were formed by interlocking networks of men who were generous and loyal to each other. In the 1990s, we cannot agree with Basil that male friendship alone is the appropriate basis for understanding Christianity as a spiritually based community, particularly given such friendship's liminality. We can, however, hold up male adult intimate friendship as an appropriate component for the continuing constitution of ecclesial communities, particularly now that the nuclear family, so widely assumed as the primary crucible in which Christian faith is nurtured and modeled, is in such a state of irreversible decline.

In his "Conference XVI on Friendship," John Cassian (c. 360–435) laid down six steps by which Christian men could build bonds of intimate friendship among their male peers, a model still valuable for Christians today:

1. The first step on this road is to understand that nothing in life is more valuable than quality relationships. These relationships of necessity include our marital partners and our children, but since no single person can meet all the needs of another, men's needs for intimacy, affirmation, and object-generosity should be spread out to male friends as well as life partners. Friendship needs to be understood within a Christian community as complementary to, rather than competitive with, marriage.

2. The second step is to choose to value the virtues, the knowledge and skills, and the wisdom of our friends above our own. Self-pride is not conducive to healthy friendships, and has long been considered in Christianity as an expression of the most human tendency to put ourselves first, others second, and God last.

3. The third step is an environmentally sensitive one, to realize that all our choices, including the values expressed by our choice of intimate friends, must embody the ultimate Christian values of love and peace.

4. The fourth step is to control our own angers and frustrations in such a way that they do not interfere with the building of intimacy within our friendships.

5. The fifth step is to seek our friends' happiness and security above our own, including being the first to apologize for unintended offense.

6. The sixth and final step—and certainly the most radical—is to live out the conduct of our friendships as though this day were our last day. Such an attitude not only puts our daily irritations and misunderstandings into perspective, it also underlines the basic human need to tell another on a regular basis that we love him and value him as though he were our second self.

Ultimately, adult intimate friendship offers men riches other than the riches of marriage. It offers us the chance to express the values of unconditional love, of beauty, tenderness, and loyalty, and as marriage remains so transient, offers us a different possibility of permanence. The Christian community cannot be healthy until women and men are liberated from the gender-role expectations which imprison them. Christ the Liberator has called the church to be a faithful community in service to the oppressed, affirming equality and justice for all people as mature beings in God's image, and modeling God's all encompassing love for the human community. Men's fear of intimate male friendship is one of the most critical forms of oppression under which they live. As men struggle toward a profeminist, less-abusive masculinity, uncowed by the abuses of other men, our first step must be reclaiming our right to be intimate friends with other men. It is a bold step, but a necessary one if men are to learn again to love, whether to love women well, or to love men at all. When we can take this bold new step, however haltingly, we will see a new health emerging within the church, a realization of God's long-promised reign which is opened first to the powerless, the self-emptying, and the humble.

The final word belongs to Gregory of Nazianzus (1968). In about the year 360, he wrote a letter to his intimate friend Basil, with whom he had shared a home and a life before Basil was elevated to the episcopacy:

I beg you to come be here with me, to grow with me in virtue, to share with me, and to help me by your prayers to hold tight to the good life we used to have together, that I may not perish little by little, like a shadow as the day draws to a close. I would rather breathe you than the air. I am alive only when I am with you, preferably in your presence, but at the very least, in my memories of you while you are absent. (Epistle 6)

NOTES

1. Special thanks for research assistance to Helen Greenwood, Erice Carley, and Judith Bright of Kinder Library, and to the students in my Human Relations class at St. John's College, Auckland, for critiquing the final draft of this essay.

2. See Rashi to BT Shabbat 31a (Steinsaltz 1985: 127) and to Proverbs 27:10. In both places, Rashi bases his remarks on the Proverbs passage, "your friend who is also your father's friend, do not abandon." Accordingly (and perhaps defending Aqiba), when we refer to our friends and neighbors, God is included, for God is not only our neighbor but also our *habib* who loved our parents, and therefore must love us too (cf. Isaiah 41:8 and II Chronicles 20:7). In the same vein, the first five commandments and the second five are yoked, to show the inseparable character of the responsibility to God and to neighbor, and the responsibility of the individual and of the community (see Jacobson 1956: 97–98 and Soloveitchik 1974: 35).

3. Such expressions are found at 1 Corinthians 10:15; 2 Corinthians 1:16 and 5:3, and possibly 10:1–2; Philippians 1:7–8 and 2:17–18; Colossians 2:5; 1 Thessalonians 2:17 and 3:6–10; Philemon 22; 2 John 12; and 3 John 14. This general philosophy can be found with frequency in patristic writings, including Augustine, Epistle 205 (1956: 8–9); Synesius, Epistle 138 (1926: 231); and Paulinus of Nola, Epistles 11.4, 13.2 (1966: I.92–93, 118).

4. The poem *Concerning His Own Life* is the earliest piece of Christian autobiography we possess, c. 381(?); see White 1992: 20.

5. See, e.g., Callimachus (d.240 BCE), Epigram LVI: "The beautifully swarthy Theocritus, if indeed he hates me, you would hate four times as much: if he loves me, you would love him. Yea! by the fair-tressed Ganymede, O heavenly Jove, thou too wast once in love. I will not speak more at length" (1914: 211).

6. Another interesting friendship developed in rabbinic thought is that between David and Ahitophel. A variety of sources for exploring this complicated and ill-fated relationship can be found in Ginsberg 1968: IV.94ff, VI.256–58, and VII.23.

7. For instance, Nygren (1932–39) erroneously argued that *eros* is to be

associated with the "dirty" body, while *agape* is the expression of the pure, disembodied soul-love upon which Christian faith is founded. The Greek Septuagint uses the word *agape* to describe Amnon's lust for his sister Tamar at 2 Samuel 13:4 and 15, and Shechem's lust for Dinah at Genesis 34:3 (cf. also the Septuagint to Genesis 24:67; 29:18, 20, 32; 34:3; Judges 16:4; 16:15; Ruth 4:15; 1 Samuel 1:5, 18:20; 2 Samuel 13:1, 4, 15; Tobit 6:19 [S]; Qohelet 9:9; Song of Songs 1:3, 4, 7; 3:1–4 for similar usage; and see Scroggs 1993: 154, note 2). On *philia* as sexual passion, see Adkins (1963: 36), and Graves citing Xenophon (Xenophon, 1875: 630).

8. During the Renaissance, "effeminate" meant "obsessed with women," an exaggerated Don Juanism. But as we shall see, by the late Victorian era, effeminacy had been pre-empted by Christian theology and its meaning changed, to indicate the opposite of "true" Christianity, which was to be aggressively "manly."

9. In 1879, Hughes emigrated from England to America, where he established an experimental community on the Cumberland Plateau, northeast of Nashville, Tennessee. The colony, aptly named Rugby, was intended as a utopian colony founded on Christian Socialist principles (Hughes had been much influenced by F. D. Maurice), where "Tom Browns without vocation could go to learn the lessons of cooperation in an atmosphere of pioneering endeavor, free from the degrading demands of modern competition" (Newsome 1961: 214–15). By the turn of the century, the experiment had failed. The town was only recently revived and restored as a tourist attraction.

10. Kingsley was severely beaten as a child by his father, leaving him with a life-long stutter. One cannot help wondering how this shaped his later philosophy of manliness. He also believed that "a man has only to take a cold bath every morning to become morally good, a conviction for which generations of English public schoolboys have had reason to curse him" (Chitty 1974: 221). Apparently his own obsessive washing of both body and clothes was connected with an exaggerated aversion to sex.

REFERENCES

Adkins, Arthur W. H. 1963. "Friendship and Self-Sufficiency in Homer and Aristotle." *Classical Quarterly* 13:30–45.
Ambrose. 1990. "On the Duties of the Clergy." In Culbertson and Shippee 1990: 138–48.
Aristotle. 1925. *The Nicomachean Ethics of Aristotle*. Trans. David Ross. London: Oxford University Press.
Augustine. 1955. *Confessions and Enchiridion*. Trans. Albert C. Outler. Philadelphia: Westminster.
———. 1956. *Letters, Vol. V:207–270*. Trans. Wilfred Parsons. Washington, D.C.: Catholic University of America Press.
———. 1982a. *On Christian Doctrine*. Trans. J. F. Shaw. Edinburgh: T. & T. Clark.

———. 1982b. *The Literal Meaning of Genesis.* Trans. John Hammond Taylor. New York: Newman Press.

Basil of Caesarea. 1962. "The Long Rules." In *Moralia, Ascetical Treatises.* Trans. M. Wagner. Washington, D.C.: Fathers of the Church.

———. 1968. "The Letters." In ed. Philip Schaff and Henry Wace. *Nicene and Post-Nicene Fathers,* Second Series. Vol. VIII. Grand Rapids, Mich.: Eerdmans.

Borowitz, Eugene. 1971. "Friendship." In *Encyclopaedia Judaica* VII, ed. Cecil Roth. New York: Macmillan.

Boswell, John. 1980. *Christianity, Social Tolerance, and Homosexuality.* Chicago: University of Chicago Press.

Bowen, Murray. 1985. *Family Therapy in Clinical Practice.* Northvale, N.J.: Jason Aronson.

Bray, Alan. 1982. *Homosexuality in Renaissance England.* London: Gay Men's Press.

Brown, Peter. 1985. *The Body and Society: Men, Women, and Sexual Renunciation in Early Christianity.* New York: Columbia University Press.

Brundage, James A. 1987. *Law, Sex, and Christian Society in Medieval Europe.* Chicago: University of Chicago Press.

Buber, Martin. 1958. *I and Thou.* New York: Charles Scribner.

Callimachus. 1914. *The Works of Hesiod, Callimachus, and Theognis.* Trans. J. Banks. London: G. Bell and Sons.

Cassian, John. 1968. "The Conferences." In *Nicene and Post-Nicene Fathers,* ed. Philip Schaff and Henry Wace. Second Series. Vol. XI. Grand Rapids, Mich.: Eerdmans.

Chitty, Susan. 1974. *The Beast and the Monk: A Life of Charles Kingsley.* London: Hodder and Stoughton.

Cicero, Marcus Tullius. 1913. *De officiis.* Trans. Walter Miller. London: Heinemann.

———. 1946. "Laelius on Friendship." In *De Senectute, De Amicitia, De Divinatione.* Trans. William Armistead Falconer. London: Heinemann.

———. 1947. "The Moral Duties of Mankind." Trans. Cyrus Edmonds. In *Greek and Roman Classics in Translation,* ed. Charles Theophilus Murphy, Kevin Guinagh, and Whitney Jennings Oates. New York: Longmans, Green.

Clement of Alexandria. 1982. "The Rich Man's Salvation" (Quis Dives Salvetur). In *Clement of Alexandria.* Trans. G. W. Butterworth. Cambridge: Harvard University Press.

Coleridge, Samuel Taylor. 1905. *Aids to Reflection.* Edinburgh: John Grant.

Culbertson, Philip. 1992. *New Adam: The Future of Male Spirituality.* Minneapolis: Fortress.

Culbertson, Philip, and Arthur Shippee. 1990. *The Pastor: Readings from the Patristic Period.* Minneapolis: Fortress.

Diogenes Laertius. 1925. *Lives of the Eminent Philosophers.* 2 vols. Trans. R. D. Hicks. Cambridge, England: Harvard University Press.

Duran, R. Shimon b. Zemach. 1961. *Magen Avot.* Jerusalem.

Eisenstadt, Shmuel N. and L. Roniger. 1984. *Patrons, Clients and Friends:*

Interpersonal Relations and the Structure of Trust in Society. Cambridge: Cambridge University Press.

Emerson, Ralph Waldo. 1990. *Essays: First and Second Series*. New York: Vintage Books.

Epicurus. 1964. *Letters, Principal Doctrines, and Vatican Sayings*. Trans. Russel M. Geer. Indianapolis: Bobbs-Merrill.

Euripides. 1958. *Orestes*. Ed. by David Grene and Richmond Lattimore. New York: Modern Library.

Friedman, Edwin. 1985. *Generation to Generation: Family Process in Church and Synagogue*. New York: Guilford Press.

Ginsberg, Louis. 1968. *The Legends of the Jews*. 7 vol. Philadelphia: Jewish Publication Society.

Gregory of Nazianzus. 1968. "Oration 8," "Oration 43, The Panegyric on S. Basil" and "The Letters." In *Nicene and Post-Nicene Fathers*, ed. Philip Schaff and Henry Wace. Second Series. Vol. VII. Grand Rapids, Mich.: Eerdmans.

———. 1987. *Three Poems: Concerning His Own Affairs, Concerning Himself and the Bishops, Concerning His Own Life*. Trans. Denis Molaise Meehan. Washington, D.C.: Catholic University of America Press.

Gregory the Great. 1990. *Forty Gospel Homilies*. Trans. Dom David Hurst. Kalamazoo, Mich.: Cistercian Publications.

Hammer, Reuven. 1986. *Sifre: A Tannaitic Commentary on the Book of Deuteronomy*. New Haven: Yale University Press.

Herman, Gabriel. 1987. *Ritualised Friendship and the Greek City*. Cambridge, England: Cambridge University Press.

Hesiod. 1959. *The Works and Days*. Trans. Richmond Lattimore. Ann Arbor: University of Michigan Press.

Horace. 1967. *Q. Horatii Flacci, Carminum Libri IV: Epodon Liber*. Trans. M. Page. London: Macmillan.

Hudson, Patricia L. 1988. "Revival in Rugby." *Americana* (April): 28–32.

Hughes, Thomas. n.d. *Tom Brown at Oxford*. The Nelson Classics. London: T. Nelson.

ibn Aqnin, Yoseph b. R. Yehuda. 1967. *Sefer ha-Mussar*. Ed. W. Bacher. Jerusalem: Meqitze Nirdamim. Originally published 1911 in Berlin.

ibn Ezra, Moshe. 1975. *Sefer HaIyyunim vehaDiyyunim*. Ed. Abraham Halkin. Jerusalem: Meqitze Nirdamim.

ibn Zabara, Joseph ben Meir. 1914. *Sefer HaSha'ashuim: The Book of Delight*. Ed. Israel Davidson. New York: Rabbinical Council of America.

———. 1932. *Sefer HaSha'ashuim: The Book of Delight*. Trans. Moses Hadas. New York: Columbia University Press.

Jacobson, B. S. 1956. *Meditations on the Torah*. Trans. Zev Gotthold. Tel Aviv: Sinai Publications.

Jacobus, Mary. 1982–83. "Is There a Woman in This Text?" *New Literary History* 14:117–41.

Jerome. 1968. "The Letters." In *Nicene and Post-Nicene Fathers*, ed. Philip

Schaff and Henry Wace. Second Series. Vol. VI. Grand Rapids, Mich.: Eerdmans.

John Chrysostom. 1968. "Homily II on 2 Thessalonians 1.I,2." In *Nicene and Post-Nicene Fathers*, ed. Philip Schaff and Henry Wace. Second Series. Vol. XIII. Grand Rapids, Mich.: Eerdmans.

Levi-Strauss, Claude. 1969. *The Elementary Structures of Kinship*. Boston: Beacon.

Lewis, C. S. 1960. *Four Loves*. New York: Harcourt Brace Jovanovich.

Maimonides. 1961. *Peirush LeMasekhet Avot*. Ed. Mordecai Dov Rabinowicz. Jerusalem: Mossad HaRav Kook.

Maximus the Confessor. 1955. *The Ascetic Life, The Four Centuries on Charity*. Trans. Polycarp Sherwood. New York: Newman Press.

Meilaender, Gilbert. 1981. *Friendship: A Study in Theological Ethics*. Notre Dame, Ind.: University of Notre Dame Press.

Miller, Stuart. 1983. *Men and Friendship*. Los Angeles: Jeremy P. Tarcher Inc.

Minucius Felix, Marcus. 1974. *The Octavius*. Trans. G. W. Clarke. New York: Newman Press.

Money, John. 1988. *Gay, Straight, and In-Between: The Sexology of Erotic Orientation*. New York: Oxford University Press.

Newsome, David. 1961. *Godliness and Good Learning: Four Studies on a Victorian Ideal*. London: John Murray.

Nygren, Anders. 1932–39. *Agape and Eros: A Study of the Christian Idea of Love*. Trans. A. G. Hebert and Philip S. Watson. 2 vols. New York: Macmillan.

Paulinus of Nola. 1966. *Letters of Paulinus of Nola*. Trans. P G. Walsh. Westminster, Md.: Newman Press.

Phillips, Jock. 1987. *A Man's Country? The Image of the Pakeha Male—A History*. Auckland: Penguin Books.

Philo. 1961. *Questions and Answers on Genesis*. Trans. Ralph Marcus. 2 vols. Cambridge: Harvard University Press.

Pitt-Rivers, Julian. 1968. "Kinship, III: Pseudo-Kinship." In *International Encyclopedia of the Social Sciences* VIII:408–13. New York: Macmillan and Free Press.

Plato. 1956. *The Great Dialogues of Plato*. Trans. W. H. D. Rouse. New York: New American Library.

Plutarch. 1911. *Plutarch's* Moralia: *Twenty Essays*. Trans. Philemon Holland. London: J. M. Dent.

Rubin, Gayle. 1975. "The Traffic in Women: Notes on the Political Economy of Sex." In *Toward an Anthropology of Women*, ed. Rayna R. Reiter. New York: Monthly Review Press.

Ruether, Rosemary Radford. 1983. "An Unrealized Revolution: Searching Scripture for a Model of the Family." *Christianity and Crisis* (October 31): 399–404.

Scroggs, Robin. 1993. *The Text and the Times: New Testament Essays for Today*. Minneapolis: Fortress.

Secord, Paul F., and Carl W. Backman. 1964. *Social Psychology*. New York: McGraw-Hill.

Sedgwick, Eve Kosofsky. 1985. *Between Men: English Literature and Male Homosocial Desire*. New York: Columbia University Press.

Soloveitchik, Joseph. 1974. *Shiurei HaRav: A Conspectus of the Public Lectures of Rabbi Joseph B. Soloveitchik*. Ed. Joseph Epstein. New York: HaMevasser.

Steinsaltz, Adin, ed. 1984–91. *Talmud Bavli*. 23 vols. Jerusalem: Israel Institute for Talmudic Publications.

Stowers, Stanley K. 1986. *Letter Writing in Greco-Roman Antiquity*. Philadelphia: Westminster.

Synesius of Cyrene. 1926. *The Letters of Synesius of Cyrene*. Trans. Augustine Fitzgerald. London: Oxford University Press.

Theognis. 1914. "Maxims." In *The Works of Hesiod, Callimachus, and Theognis*. Trans. J. Banks. London: G. Bell and Sons.

Tiger, Lionel. 1984. *Men in Groups*. 2d ed. New York: Marion Boyars.

Valerius Maximus. 1888. "De amicitia." In *Factorum et dictorum memorabilium libri novem*, ed. Carolus Kempf. Lipsiae.

White, Carolinne. 1992. *Christian Friendship in the Fourth Century*. Cambridge, England: Cambridge University Press.

Xenophon. 1875. "Hiero: On the Condition of the Royalty." *The Complete Works of Xenophon*. Trans. Robert Graves. London: Chatto and Windus.

———. 1903. *Memorabilia*. Ed. Josiah Renick Smith. Boston: Ginn & Company.

NINE

"The Manly Love of Comrades": Mythico-Religious Models for an Athletics of Male-Male Friendship

WILLIAM G. DOTY

I should wish our Courtier to have one special and cordial friend [and] that he should love, honor, and respect all others according to their worth and merits, and seek always to associate more with those who enjoy high esteem, are noble, and known to be good men, than with the ignoble and those of little worth; in such a way that he too may be loved and esteemed by such men. And he will succeed in this if he is courteous, humane, generous, affable, and gentle in his association with others, active and diligent in serving and caring for the welfare and honor of his friends, whether they be absent or present, tolerating their natural and bearable defects, without breaking with them for some trivial reason, and correcting in himself such defects as are in kindness pointed out to him.

—Baldesar Castiglione,
The Book of the Courtier

I will plant companionship thick as trees along all the rivers of America, and along the shores of the great lakes, and all over the prairies,

A longer form of this chapter, entitled " 'Companionship Thick as Trees': Our Myths of Friendship," is © 1993 by the Men's Studies Press. All rights reserved. Revision of this essay is by permission.

I will make inseparable cities with their arms about each other's
necks,
By the love of comrades,
By the manly love of comrades.   —Walt Whitman,
                                        "For You O Democracy"

That we are living in a time of crisis with respect to masculinity is affirmed repeatedly. A corresponding crisis with respect to male-
male friendship may not be as obvious, but it is real and pervasive—I
am following Karl Kerényi (1983: 9) in defining "crisis" as "a situation
in which no values are of uncontested validity, no behavior indisputably
correct." Both crisis and critical are derived from the Greek *krinein* (to
separate, choose, judge), so perhaps the problem of values can provide a
turning point (another meaning of "crisis") and lead to new criteria
(also from *krinein*).

In the midst of this crisis with respect to masculine values, nearly
every man with whom I discuss male-male friendship with considers it to
be his own personal problem. Identifying the problem not as something
primarily personal but as part of our present social situation leads me to
propose that we develop disciplined reflections, even an "athletics," that
would include attention to mythological models. I anticipate a method
of using mythological resources, and develop an initial access-to-tools
approach appropriate to several varieties of mythology that reflect what
was developed in *Myths of Masculinity* (Doty 1993).

Initially, I look at the social and individual aspects, blaming the
latter for much of our crisis of male friendship, and argue the need for
developing a better erotics of relationship. Next, I address the benefits
of an articulated history and discipline ("athletics") of friendship and
list positive and negative elements that foster or hinder friendship. Then,
I turn to ways of reintegrating the social and individual aspects by
means of ethnographic-comparative-archetypal, historical, and mythical
models. In the following section, I urge care in selecting and refining
mythographic methodologies, naming some pratfalls and recognizing the
importance of not only such classical models as the traditional Hero, but
also their contemporary transformations. In the concluding section, I

glance beyond dysfunctioning mythico-heroic images to suggest that new options are models that foster generativity within a creative athletics of friendship.[1]

The Problematic Faces of Male-Male Friendship Today

Many groups within the contemporary men's movements arose as responses to perceived crises in the nature of masculinity today, some as reactions to what feminists brought to public awareness as malfunctional gender roles in our society, and some as attempts to reclaim a heritage of masculinity now threatened (for good or bad) by a postmodern society in which almost every traditional model quavers before an endless variety of (seemingly equally valid) choices.[2] Much of our self-confidence about received masculine gender models shatters when we own up to the negative sides of "patriarchy" and its attendant values, or when we recognize that modern masculinity and rationalistic scientism have gone hand in hand, leaving us with brilliant technicians whose ethical values provide little guidance in making decisions that may affect millions of human lives (see Easlea 1983).

I am not so much responding retrospectively to feminist attacks on patriarchy or to male domination in the past as recognizing that the points of those attacks need to be taken seriously as we look ahead, prospectively. The issues are too crucial for vituperative recalling what might have been; unless all of us are committed to reconceiving and reenacting gender modeling in our society, we simply will not have the vital flexibility that will be demanded in the onrushing millenium:

If our society is to survive, when traditional family patterns are evolving and geographical mobility strains the limits of intergenerational connections, it is up to innovative individuals to search new forms for intimate relationships beyond sexual partnerships. We need to analyze and nurture our long-term close friendship networks as the best possible base on which to build an emotionally satisfying future. (Williams 1992: 199)

A similar admonition is expressed by Sherrod, but in the context of his argument that men need to work on male-male friendships because in the two-career household now prevalent, their lives and those of their wives or companions are increasingly separate from their own:

If men are to offer each other the kind of emotional support they have previously obtained from their wives, I believe males will have to adopt more direct avenues to emotional intimacy. To do so, men will have to learn skills that their culture has not necessarily provided but that still exist in many of the world's traditional cultures. (1987: 237)

There are many aspects of male-male friendship that I cannot engage; others will have to address the question of friendships in sports (see especially Pronger 1990 and Messner 1992), in commercial, fraternal, and professional associations; in recent media representations and in literature, and so forth. My focus is individual male-male friendships.

Remembering some of the painful aspects of male friendship, I recall the feeling of failure I have often had when I have initiated friendship with another man, only to have the sense that I did something wrong or he didn't like me or he thought I was coming on sexually to him or _____ (most men can fill in the blank with their own reasons, because they have been there as well). Although I have been studying materials about masculinity for years, it took a recent reading of Stuart Miller's brave book, *Men and Friendship* (1983), to help me realize that my feelings of failure might have been more appropriately feelings of anger toward a society that dropped male friendship out of the "approved relationships" column almost entirely, largely because modern society vastly expanded the expectations of the marriage or couple relationship to the extent that such a relationship is conceived now as the only appropriate sphere for loving or friendly relationships of great depth and significance.

One indication of the arbitrary nature of such expectations is noted by Walter Williams (1992: 190) in his observation that in the majority of Native American societies, marriage has been primarily an economic arrangement; males expected to find their primary psychological needs satisfied by long-term childhood male friends outside the home. Yet in a 1990 professional survey abstracted in *Men's Life* (Arrington 1990: 65), ninety percent (plus or minus four percent) of the American men queried answered "wives" to the question, "Who is a man's best friend?" It is easy (and sad) to recognize how such a narrowing of relational energies has led to so many behavioral dilemmas in marriages and families, as couples expect to satisfy within the primary bond many interests and needs that can be adjuncts of male-male friendships as satisfactorily.

How little such friendships seem viable or important is reflected in the narrow range of behaviors the commercial world finds profitable to model seductively. Lance Strate's "Beer Commercials: A Manual on Masculinity" (in Craig 1992: 78–92) concludes: "for the most part, beer commercials present traditional, stereotypical images of men, and uphold the myths of masculinity and femininity." In advertisements, male friends drink scotch as they ogle a woman walking by; quaff beer together to celebrate a job promotion; share tips about stocks while playing the golf course; and lift weights side by side as one tells another about the best remedy for jock itch or smelly feet. The commodification of our lives, even friendship, is pervasive, but I don't often find my own values with respect to friendship represented in such commercials, or in the entertainment media, where anything other than compulsively heterosexual friendships becomes a target of a comedian's ridicule, if mentioned at all.

Other aspects of our social environment also screen out powerful friendships between men, and are emphasized in Miller's reflections on the two-year period in which he attempted self-consciously to develop close friendships with other males. Repeatedly he experienced an initial positive attraction—apparently mutual—and then a subsequent slackening of intimacy until the friendship clearly aborted. I've had the same experience a number of times: an initial lunch or informal conversation when another man and I seemed to hit it off; arranging for a meal or a concert; then making the arrangements again, until I realized I was always the initiator. And repeatedly finding that the other man felt too pressured—by business, scholarship, his marriage, or whatever—to expend the time needed to nurture our friendship. Hence, like most other men today, I had many casual friendships, but few that fed my needs for close male companionship, and I believe that the scarcity of close friendship led me to get involved in activities and relationships that (in hindsight) I think of as primarily compensatory.

Miller's book helps me to understand how the issues are not primarily personal but social. The issues reflect the values we enforce when we value productivity, competition, and aggressiveness—what our society usually identifies as typical "male" qualities—over against receptiveness, intimacy, and cooperation. Given our social context wherein competition and achievement are praised above all else, no wonder male friendships are tainted by the suspicion that the person making the initial overtures must be seeking to gain something or to take some advantage.

As Perry Garfinkel puts it (1985: 1–2), "this dominant competitive theme in men's relationships is clearly the reason that men fear and avoid intimacy with each other. After all, men reason, what fool would open up to one's potential rival?" Garfinkel's book revolves around problems caused for men in fathering, mentoring, sibling relations, friendship, and groups by our emphasis upon power, control, competition, and jealousy.

Ethnographic materials portray a very different picture of male friendship elsewhere (see Brain 1976; Strathern 1988; and Gilmore 1990). Hammond and Jablow (1987) provide a useful bibliography for other comparative studies of friendship, but it is striking how few collections of essays on men's issues, or compilations of male-related literature, select "friendship" as one of the classifications used to organize the materials. Robert Brain's comparative study of friendship (1976) is especially helpful because it shows both how unique contemporary American patterns are, and how all-encompassing aspects of male friendship are within most societies: they involve such matters as the blood brother relationship and other fraternal networks, commerce, inlaw relationships, godparentage, patronage, group bonding, and so forth. And although aggressivity and competition are certainly not lacking in other cultures, they are not frequently allowed to regulate male friendships; in fact, they are the opposite of the qualities that do so. One of the underlying themes of Brain's book is that "love and friendship—or cooperation and reciprocity, exchange and alliance—are as important, if not more important, for personal well-being and the survival of culture as aggression" (207).

Cooperation and alliance: the image contrasts with recent American images of *machismo:* the solitary town marshal expelling the forces of evil on the frontier; the clever entrepreneur making his millions by isolating and dominating a small window of the market; the Rambo warrior single-handedly revenging slurs to the national pride; Ross Perot's David against the Republican and Democratic Goliaths; and so forth (Hamill 1978 delineates the elements of American *machismo* long operative in our fiction and public life). Media representations of the American masculine, the context of contemporary male friendships, derive from the capitalist ideology of the individual doing his own thing in isolation from or in opposition to society. Aligning with such models, students often find it almost impossible to collaborate on class research projects, and committees reviewing materials submitted for professional advancement are so suspicious of interdisciplinary team work that they demand to know exactly how much each team member contributed in specific numbers of pages of each report published, rather than how cooperatively the person participated with and nurtured others.

In such contexts, putting friends and friendships near the top of one's set of priorities is increasingly difficult, and competitive values regulate against feeling comfortable within a friendship, that is, within an atmosphere of relaxation, easiness, and safety; against softness and peaceful interaction instead of roughness; against sharing sentimental feelings and a complete freedom for one another. This summary is from Miller (1983: 10–11), who amplifies: "These are some of the special aspects of close male friendship: a willingness to take a dangerous stand for another; a special relaxation and safety; an end to competitiveness, alienation, and self-alienation; a pleasure in doing masculine justice to others, an enhancement of men's own vitality and being. Above all, *a holding in the heart*" (15, my emphasis), which is certainly a manifestation of eros.

In his lively interviews about friendship with a number of men in the San Francisco Bay area, James Maas (1985) found similar characteristics named frequently: feeling safe to disagree; facing one's anger at and fear of the other; being committed to honesty; having a range of friends from different spheres of life and different age groups; recognizing that friendships vary in needs for intimacy, self-revelation, and caring for one another. We could augment either list easily, or consider the opposite qualities that actually structure most of our daily relationships. These include striving for success; eagerness to come out on top; achieving more (status, money, sex) than anyone else; always being the one to criticize others from a superior position; and maintaining a stiff upper lip as just the tip of the well-defended body—the sort of commodified model observable in a sidebar to the "Cooling Down" page of a 1992 issue of the slick magazine, *The Best of Men's Workout:* "A truly confident man has the muscle to back up any challenge. Physical power can strengthen the mind, creating an air of invincibility. Strive to become a total package." A step away from selling a machine to commodify the body, such advice "to become a total package" can only indicate getting wrapped up in one's own privately competitive muscular shell, not a position in which one is open to mutual sharing with another.

At this point, we might analyze the blatant physical eroticism of the muscle mags, but when I speak of "erotic energy" in such a connection I am anticipating discussing a more central issue that works strongly against male friendship today, the fear that any really deep friendship will either be, or be seen as, homosexual. Not only capitalist teachings but pop-psychological interpretations of Freud are at fault, with their easy assumptions that we are always either moving into a sexual relationship or spending the capital of our precious energies pretending that we don't want to. The leap from friendship to homosexuality gets founded in the assumption that any intimate relationship between males that isn't competitive will be the polar opposite of competitive heterosexuality—an assumption that builds competition *into* a putatively normal masculinity, and simultaneously plays into the hands of those who define regulative heterosexuality in terms of aggression and dominance. In such a framework, the contrary cannot be a measured intimacy, but as the ideologue sees it, a full-blown "descent" into genital homosexual coupling. Or models of restrained expression of feelings are based on the assumption that only women, and by extension, gay, "women-like" men, can express intimacy and emotions other than hating the enemy or competitor. Hence one must kick ass or be considered a fairy.

Nonsensical logic such as I've just presented surrounds us and leads to needless awkwardness. Several male teachers have told me that they are now wary of taking a small crying male child in their arms or patting an adolescent boy's shoulder for fear of being accused of homosexual abuse; even all the bear-hugging at men's gatherings portrays the awkward A-frame embrace that assures that only the arms and shoulders touch, and not, god forbid, anything else. No wonder that with respect to male friendship "most people find the subject *unutterable*" (Miller 1983: xv, my emphasis) and that "in fact, deep friendship between adult men is quite rare in our society" (4, referring to the well-known long-term study of males by Levinson and others, 1978).

The similarly unutterable decimation of AIDS has brought its own burden to the question of male friendships, and the changes in homosexual social life that avoidance of the HIV virus has necessitated have been examined with much agonizing in the gay press. It has also contributed some very moving accounts of friendship at its extreme, as surviving lovers recount the demoralizing extended illnesses and deaths of their beloveds (see for instance Monette 1988a, with its elegiac companion piece, Monette 1988b). Among the reasons for the growth of gay schol-

arship, particularly in literary studies, have been the search for models
of positive and healthy long-term male-male friendships or monogamies
in literature, as opposed to an earlier gay liberation model of many serial
sexual encounters, and the need to turn linguistic usage inside out as
repeatedly metaphoric images such as "the plague," or the equation
"silence = death," are coined to express the unutterable but real facts of
the disease and its impacts upon long- and short-term friendships (see
Edelman 1989).

I have looked primarily at some of the painful and awkward aspects
in our cultural treatment of the erotic, and I will have to leave development of the more positive aspects to the athletics I want to propose
subsequently. Overall, we lack sophistication in speaking about non-
genital sexual connections, the "erotic" that looks to the quality of the
loving relationship rather than which parts of the bodies connect. But
who can deny that the call of the other to which one responds as friend
possesses connective power, has indeed an energy lacking in casual daily
contacts? We need to devise a language and a discipline for naming and
nurturing that energetic power, and *friendship* is an important arena
within which men can recover loving relationships with other men,
relationships that may or may not include a genital component, but for
the majority of men probably won't.

Seeking an Athletics of Friendship

Observation of other cultures discloses that frequently they have provided extensive guidance and discipline with respect to relationships,
even an aesthetics of friendship. I would like to reclaim the term "athletics" in its early Greek connection not only with physical training, but
with art, music, and medicine (Wright 1949: 116), in order to argue
the importance of regarding the historically-dated, specific, and varying
contexts of friendship as a type of social practice, and of friendly emotions—which likewise are not universals but are expressed through
particular historical shapings. Humans seem always to take the present
as the norm or "the natural," but examination of historical and cross-
cultural perspectives usually discloses how recent and how limited contemporary practices are, particularly when we confront the sense that
one ought to know *intuitively* how to be a friend—an instance of

American naivete about relationships not peculiar to the sphere of male-male friendships.

In this instance we learn that several pre-American cultures have promulgated standards for ideal relationships in court politics (the classic from the Renaissance is Castiglione 1959 [1516]: 126; see my first epigraph), friendship, amours, and other aspects of daily life. In cultures other than our own, not only do manuals of noble behavior normally guide specific types of relationship, but explicit rituals and careful pedagogy stipulate how friends ought to treat one another, and indeed the relationship is often more openly demonstrative. Williams (1986: 187) notes that "American mainstream masculinity is rather unique in its suppression of displays of affection, and of close and intimate friendships, between adult men." In observing how seldom we attend to anything like a formal discipline with respect to friendship, Brain (1976: 83) remarks that "it would appear that our society is the exception in a world where friendship is a social and psychological need cemented by formal behavior and ceremony."

We suffer from recent anti-ritualistic attitudes, and hence a repugnance toward anything repeated more than once—assigning to ritual, a vastly important element of human cultural experience, a negative value for one of the first times in history.[3] Add our distrust of regularizing or ritualizing behavior to what Miller (1983: 34) identifies as "a taboo on anything [having] to do with friendship that smacks of deliberation," and we begin to see how hard we will have to struggle to communicate a need to devise a contemporary discipline of friendship. Yet the same author argues that we must address the "necessity for an art of male friendship," even though much in our culture resists it. Miller proposes a list of "bold acts of consciousness" that might belong in his handbook to the art, including "inwardly accepting the necessity to give friendship one's closest attention and recalling the social obstacles to friendship"; "being willing to acknowledge the hurt of your own loneliness"; making room for male friendship in one's life; "being willing to be hurt, repeatedly, by people you befriend"; "being persistent"; and "acting forthrightly with your friend and with the courage of your own delicate needs and desires by living the openness, generosity, and commitment you want from him" (195–96).[4]

We lost much of the sense of common bonding-together that friendship connoted earlier and elsewhere when the relational and "love" aspects got so reduced to the genital-erotic. Mostly that reduction is a consequence of the Western anti-body, anti-material bias that continued to haunt our thinking and speaking even as it was replaced by a materialistic, mercantile orienting of the culture, with the curious result that *in effect* if not in ideal, we recompense the thinker whose work is precisely the most abstract and non-embodied (and who ought by the traditional bias to be at the top of the heap), namely the philosopher or theorist, much less than we pay the merchants or engineers whose careers are indeed very materialistic, embodied in the tangibles of our lives. But relationships are part of the matter (material) of our lives as well, and perhaps it's time for us to cease assuming that the *maters* (mothers, the feminine, women in general) constitute the only gender appropriate to do the emotional work of connecting and loving and feeling.

Surely it is time for men to grow emotional muscles through a disciplined athletics of friendship, so that our souls' relational biceps pump up just as much as those of our arms. Those muscles might be pumped up by communal sharing and caring for one another in a rediscovery of the loving nature of friendship.

Hence what might initially be seen as defensive against society—two buddies linked against the crowd, as in many war and espionage movies—comes into view now as the preamble to the rediscovery of community that seems crucial to the revivification of Western culture. It returns us once again to the need to develop a discipline of friendship, now not only for two individuals at a time, but for the polis, the collective.

Attitudes toward Myth and History

Mythic figures and images as well as their many contemporary literary transformations can provide models in an imaginal, psychological, and interrelationally based discipline by which we decide to configure masculinities and friendship patterns appropriate to our own politics and histories. However, it is important to think critically about some of the methodologies and attitudes with which we approach literary and mythological materials as we construct our toolkits. Such hermeneutical reflection is crucial insofar as influential decisions about appropriation are made daily and usually unself-consciously or ideologically: by advertisers, who select from cultural images those considered most likely to sell a particular deodorant; by the media, who spectacularly isolated and trivialized the imagery and behavior surrounding Robert Bly and the "mythopoetic" spectrum within the men's movements; by religious groups, whose presses are rushing to publish "men and spirituality" materials, some of which are misogynistically reactionary (Arnold 1991), if not blatantly co-optative and colonialist (Dittes 1991); by individuals who have had as heroic models only shallow and often inhumane versions of masculinity displayed across the news and entertainment media and in politics and sports.

Reflection on attitudes for approaching mythic resources involves evaluating how there may or may not be appropriate connections between their originating cultures and our own; hence ethical reflections ought to precede conscious choices of particular models we would replicate today. We must learn to recollect and to reevaluate our history, a lesson from feminist scholarship that has transformed intellectual inquiry in the contemporary world by asking long-ignored questions: Where are materials situated politically, economically, and religiously in the cultures in which they were produced? (see Doty 1986 and 1995). Are they materials produced by the dominating class or a subordinate/ subaltern group? Do they replicate systems of oppression or liberation or do they provide for them (the question pressed relentlessly by deconstructionist criticism)? Are they available for appropriation variously by different groups in the culture, or are they monolithically enforced by means of authoritative canons, communications media, and governmental structures?[5]

The contemporary understanding of the functioning of ideological systems embedded already unself-consciously in our language and worldview, adds the understanding that masculinity has been an unrecognized construct (like "nature") that must be acknowledged for its below-the-boards influence. Lynne Segal's *Slow Motion: Changing Masculinities, Changing Men* emphasizes some of our cultural trouble spots, such as the linking between misogyny and homophobia (1990: 16) and the policing of gay men as a component of the reactionary and self-defensive responses to the sexual liberation that have marked this century (98–99). These responses function efficiently precisely because they are mostly unexamined and implicit. Segal particularly understands the subtly encompassing power of the symbolic: a master category such as masculinity, for instance, "does not operate in splendid isolation from other social forces" (91); rather, myths and symbols are so thoroughly integrated ideologically and psychologically into our traditional worldview that they reinforce the notion that masculinity is a single, monolithic pattern, an undivided, seamless construction that one merely manifests "naturally" or "physically."

Traditional and Generative Mythic Heroes

Such perspectives as those I have been reviewing are part of the homework that ought to be completed before looking at specific mythological materials in terms of how they might contribute to an athletics of friendship. Just as I suggested that we must learn to see beyond the personal in order to understand the problematics of masculinities or patterns of friendship today, so we learn to approach specific stories and figures with the transpersonal, the mythico-archetypal and the sociopolitical simultaneously in view. Otherwise, we don't see the forest for the trees, we risk misinterpreting any particular local myth because we are not aware of how it functions cybernetically within the capacious storehouses of cultural wisdom in the mythologies of the world; just as any mythico-heroic figure appears within a family system, so myths themselves are constrained by the cultural networks in which they appear. One learns quickly enough that a mythic tradition has not yet died even when the majority of people in the culture no longer remembers the precise plot of its story or its cast of characters. Mythic materials are reappearing materials, they reach down deep into cultural models and up high, latching onto contemporary scenes every time a child tries to figure out an appropriate role model, every time a demagogue seeks the most efficient way to exert control, every time a professional advertising campaign spotlights its product.

Myths of friendship abound in mythological and religious materials. Itemizing those from antiquity and from other cultural traditions would be rewarding, but I suggest that before we utilize the data of such a catalogue in a contemporary athletics of friendship, we need to be aware that the results can function both negatively and positively. Negatively, they can merely reinforce certain stereotypes that we encounter daily when someone disagrees with us: "Oh that's just a myth!" is one of the most frequent rhetorical ploys used to dump on someone. Positively, mythical materials are significant because they represent age-old experiences in situations similar to those we face today, and we can learn from their contents to view our own situation in deeper detail and longer-range perspective.

With such a broad schooling, one then can explore quite possibly the oldest myth our culture has, that splendid account of the friendship between Gilgamesh and Enkidu, and see what it does—and does not—provide as guidance for male relationships.[6] Do we begin by discussing the homosexual relationship between the two principal males? Then we haven't learned to ask the questions about the appropriateness of contemporary sexual behavior patterns when approaching materials from antiquity. In this case, they're not much use, since the canons of the intervening centuries filtered out such aspects anyhow; the situation is the same with respect to the lovers Achilles and Patroklos in the *Iliad*. Before we can learn from the relationship in either mythic instance, we need to know rather a lot about sexuality in antiquity, so that we do not find mere reflections of our own behaviors and values (see the path-breaking studies of Winkler 1990 and Halperin 1990). Biblical friendships have been surveyed repeatedly, but never in rewarding comparative depth.

Other mythic figures can be explored in terms of what sorts of friends they would be, how they might help to model friendships, and whether they model dysfunctional or healthy friendship relations. For instance, what about the stories concerning militaristic Ares (the Roman Mars), whom "all the gods hated"?—many American men certainly *did not* hate George Bush for his role as a dictator in declaring and administering war on Iraq! (On Ares, see chapter 8 in Doty, 1993). Or poor old lame Hephaistos (Vulcan)—he cleverly catches his adulterous wife, Aphrodite, in the arms of his brother Ares by making an invisible metal net that falls upon the careless lovers as they approach orgasm. To what extent do our friendships include possible sexual connections between primary partners? Or Narkissos (Narcissus), whose very name is a component of "narcotic," and who fades away because he refuses to respond to the call to love from *both* boys and girls? Is his "narcissism" the same as the twentieth-century personality disorder, or might it not have something more positive to contribute to our notions of self-regard? How might one bring a Narkissos-friend into the self-conscious mainstream of complex relationships today? (See chapter 6 in Doty 1993.)

Subsequently, the many modern transformations of mythic images must be charted: what are the religious prototypes of the Marlboro Man and Arnold Schwarzenegger's public roles? Do contemporary transformations function in the same ways as their archetypes, or does the postmodern context alter the influences of prototypes inescapably, in its revisionist reprocessing of the traditional? What aspects of contemporary and future friendship are already present in classical and traditional myths and models of friendship? It will be obvious that such questions as I have raised with respect to a few of the many mythical examples (and I have not even begun working with myths specific to the theme of male-male friends here) lead me back to questions of our own day, and how so many of our problematic experiences of masculinity are grounded in cultural, mythical, and ideological histories.

Providing specific mythic examples here would expand this essay inordinately, but I can at least begin to note some revisionist views in the instance of the mythic hero. Certainly we have had to recognize that many of the standard models of heroic masculinity have become problematic as we have come to grips with our ignominious defeat in Vietnam and the unavoidable lesson that neither America's "carry a big stick" expansionist foreign policy nor a post-World War II anti-Communist "containment policy" is any longer tenable. And we question not only the militaristic models behind such a policy but also the traditional figures of success: the John Wayne isolationists and the aggressive territorializing frontiersmen (seldom, one notes, models famous for their friendships). The colonial baron and even the capitalist chairman of the board seem not only useless, but outright dangerous as we now move into a period of a genuine multiculturalism and internationalism that cannot afford such premodern relics.

We have to learn to look beyond the traditional models of heroic aspiration that drive men to type-A-personality heart failures and a manifest rate of physical breakdown that is simply astonishing and entirely out of balance with women's health statistics. While completing a recent exploration of contemporary critiques and revisionings of the hero/ine (Doty forthcoming), I learned a great deal about the social production of Western heroes from Mark Gerzon's *A Choice of Heroes: The Changing Face of American Manhood* (1992 [1982]), and it is on my short list of recommendations for works that help us to see through the problematic models that have come to seem "natural" in our society. Gerzon documents the dangerous connection between heroism and militarism, showing for instance just how the characteristics that nearly every man who has ever worked through problems in psychotherapy has to struggle to get beyond—invulnerability, insensitivity, lack of compassion, toughness, aggressiveness, and an armored and sealed off inner self—are precisely the appropriate traits of the soldier, who must learn to repress his fears of and compassion toward an enemy. Indeed, courage has to be redefined, suggests Gerzon: "it no longer hinges on how much violence a man can inflict, but on how much he can prevent" (1992 [1982]: 246). Surely we are ready to move beyond dysfunctional machismo when such redefinitions appear in highly successful books that remain in print and are worthy of revision ten years later.

New heroic symbols stress generativity and nurturance of others, and Gerzon notes how such models have begun to appear in the images of the healer, companion, mediator, colleague, and nurturer. I find it strik-ing that these are largely roles fulfilled *within friendships!* The healer, for instance, is the environmentalist who will readily recognize the im-portance of friendships in organizing others to generate and broadcast concern for the planet, and who cooperates with ecofeminists. Or, the healer is the inspiring leader of groups working collaboratively against violence against women, children, and other men.

The companion celebrates friendship in marriage or another primary bond and shares parenting and mentoring as he reshapes the old image of the patriarchal breadwinner. The mediator sees beyond competitive and violent relationships, greediness, and often beyond warfare, as in the nuclear-containment movement. The colleague is the interdisciplinar-ian who recognizes the significance of moral choices and personal affecti-vity in the shared project, the new business leader who recognizes the importance of worker teams sharing decision-making, and the politician who knows that affirmative action programs succeed in the long run only when adequate bases of trust can be established on other than purely legal foundations.

And finally, the nurturer replaces the power-wielder as one who fosters generativity (Erickson's term to characterize the person whose self-concept is strong enough to enable aiding others: see Doty 1994)—an emerging hero-model, as males learn to take on many supportive roles previously dumped in the laps of women, and as they learn to foster relationships in which neither partner is necessarily dominant.

Were I to add another characteristic of the new hero/ine friendship model, it would be that s/he is a sharer, a person willing to open up to others and to grant them the affirmative space they need to develop fully. Such a characteristic does not seem particularly "heroic" in terms of the old models, but it is precisely the characteristic named repeatedly in surveys asking about the impact of effective men's groups upon their members (documented by Stein 1989). Part of the athletics of friendship obviously involves how individual men and men's groups discipline themselves and how they learn to be mutually supportive—not something that comes naturally in the competitive social history of Western masculinity, but something that can indeed be learned.

Conclusion

Never one to denigrate the contemporary, I remain simultaneously a partisan of the mythico-traditional and religious where it enables us to see beyond the limitations of our own immediate horizons. To die inwardly for want of a true friend is no less a tragedy today than it has ever been, yet we pay little heed to the cultivation of the arts of friendship that may yet save us from such a dead end.

A truly heroic endeavor today might entail not slaughtering dragons so much as taking the first step, then the second and third steps, toward the friendships that may become for us truly mythical and sustaining. I have proposed here that a first step may be study of traditional religious and mythico-heroic models, not uncritically, but with an eye to the valuable lodes of insight they contain.

In evaluating the resources of traditional materials that may configure the myths of friendship to embody our new loving male-male relationships, readers will have to decide on their own just how their particular contexts and strengths will or will not connect with loving male-male relationships of their own kenning, brought alongside traditional prototypes. As feminists affirm, the personal is the political. As males revisioning traditional models of friendship might affirm, the personal-political only begins to tap into the long-term mythico-relational paradigms that enable us to imagine and subsequently and consciously to instantiate the friendships that distinguish our species.

To be sure, historical and mythological instances of friendship denote only some of the highway markers guiding where we may go. Situations in which our hearts connect with others outside the traditional couple bond begin to appear not as threatening, but as enriching possibilities.

Something of Castiglione's sixteenth-century idealism then begins to be conceivable anew: demanding that we might be *courteous, humane, generous, affable, and gentle in our associations with others.* Reminding us that we must be *active and diligent in serving and caring for the welfare and honor of our friends.* Tolerating their defects yet joining them in the birthing of relational significances that just may enable us to recover anew those sacred bonds of friendship that will reawaken our perceptions of the handsome inner qualities of one another. And, as a modern-day courtier might put it: *revitalizing the ancient joys of having friends 'til death do us part.*

NOTES

1. More friends than I can acknowledge have shared long, passionate responses to earlier versions of this essay, and I am grateful to them for their challenges, criticisms, and contributions. With its new title, the essay represents a considerable reduction of its original contours in the *Journal of Men's Studies* 1/4 (1993): 359–82, from which the surviving portions I have selected are reproduced by permission.

2. The literature about the contemporary postmodernist climate is now vast; as an example of the lack of ethical clarity, I can refer to a collection of essays reflecting on the Persian Gulf War in the light of traditional "just war" theory (Decosse 1992). The authors in that volume demonstrate that even in the long-established field of ethics, values choices are now almost undecidable. Traditional just war theories stipulate that no matter how ruinous actual warfare may be, a war is just so long as civilian supplies are not hindered and civilians are not attacked. But today, because of international dependence upon non-native foods and materiel, a prolonged blockade of nearly any city or country is equally as destructive as outright war, so does one change the concept of the just war, or junk it?

3. I've discussed some of the problematics in Doty (1986) and (1992b). My friend Hank Lazer remarked to me the persistence of ritualizations in Greek organizations on campuses, and one might reflect upon the fact that religious liturgies are still performed—but I would argue that the Greeks often feel awkward precisely when the ritualistic aspect of fraternity/sorority life comes up, and that the largest growth in American institutional religion has been among the less-liturgical branches of Protestantism.

4. There are positive elements to be sought in group friendships as well as in the individual relationships I am discussing here, and they usually require just as much discipline and commitment to develop adequately: patience, hearing one another accurately and thoroughly, sharing emotional concern and love for one another, facing disagreements and differences honestly, creating a safe space for

exploring change and sharing criticism of one another, balancing centrifugal needs of members with centripetal goals of service to a community, and so forth. The men's movement literature now includes several guides to effective and supportive group dynamics in men's groups.

5. One work that makes inescapable several awkward historical questions about the nature of sexuality or masculinity is the essay by Tim Carrigan and others, "Hard and Heavy: Toward a New Sociology of Masculinity" (1987), which essentially is a metastudy on masculinity that critiques underlying issues and politics while recounting some of the ways in which masculinity has come to be constructed in our own time. The authors pull no critical punches in their judging the bulk of most recent social science analysis of masculinity as trivial or irrelevant. Only space restraints keep me from praising and discussing the historical essays that E. Anthony Rotundo has been developing from his doctoral research at Brandeis (Ph.D., 1982); he notes that early nineteenth-century customs surrounding appropriate male behavior—such as nonsexual sharing of a bed, arduously expressing one's romantic love for a male friend, and physical kissing and touching—are almost as foreign to (heterosexual) contemporaries as customs from foreign lands.

6. I prefer Mason's (1970) free-verse translation, although there are several more recent technical text editions available. I devote a chapter to the loving friendship between Gilgamesh and Enkidu in Doty (1993).

REFERENCES

Arnold, Patrick W. 1991. *Wildmen, Warriors, and Kings: Masculine Spirituality and the Bible.* New York: Crossroad.
Arrington, Carl. 1990. "A Generation of Men Grows up: Survey of American Males, 1990." *Men's Life* 1/1: 64–70.
Brain, Robert. 1976. *Friends and Lovers: Approaches to Anthropology.* London: Hart-Davis, MacGibbon.
Carrigan, Tim, Bob Connell, and John Lee. 1987. "Hard and Heavy: Toward a New Sociology of Masculinity." In *Beyond Patriarchy: Essays by Men on Pleasure, Power, and Change,* ed. Michael Kaufman. New York: Oxford University Press.
Castiglione, Baldesar. 1959 [1516]. *The Book of the Courtier.* Trans. C. S. Singleton. Garden City, N.Y.: Doubleday.
Craig, S., ed. 1992. *Men, Masculinity, and the Media.* Research on Men and Masculinities, 2. Newbury Park, Calif.: Sage.
Decosse, D. E., ed. 1992. *But Was It Just? Reflections on the Morality of the Persian Gulf War.* New York: Doubleday.
Dittes, James. 1991. "A Men's Movement for the Church?" *The Christian Century* (29 May–5 June): 588–90.
Doty, William G. 1986. *Mythography: The Study of Myths and Rituals.* Tuscaloosa: University of Alabama Press.

Doty, William G. 1992a. "Returns to Fathers and Other Archetypes." *Continuum: A Journal of History, Hermeneutics, and Social Concern* 2/1: 30–42.

———. 1992b. "Wild Transgressions and Tame Celebrations: Contemporary Construals of Ritualization." *The Journal of Ritual Studies* 6/2: 115–30.

———. 1993. *Myths of Masculinity.* New York: Crossroad.

———. 1994. "Evolving Beyond the Adolescent Warrior: Postheroic Masculinist Generativity." *Journal of Men's Studies* 2/4: 353–73.

———. 1995. "Silent Myths Singing in the Blood: The Sites of Production and Consumption of Myths in a 'Mythless' Society." In *Picturing Cultural Values in Postmodern America,* ed. Doty. Tuscaloosa: University of Alabama Press.

———. Forthcoming. "From the Traditional Monomythic Hero to the Contemporary Polymythic Hero/ine." In *Foundations and Facets Forum* (Robert W. Funk Festschrift), eds. Bernard Scott and John L. White.

Easlea, Brian. 1983. *Fathering the Unthinkable: Masculinity, Scientists, and the Nuclear Arms Race.* London: Pluto Press.

Edelman, L. 1989. "The Plague of Discourse: Politics, Literary Theory, and AIDS." In *Displacing Homophobia: Gay Male Perspectives in Literature and Culture,* eds. R. R. Butters, J. M. Clum, and M. Moon. Durham, N.C.: Duke University Press.

Garfinkel, Perry. 1985. *In a Man's World: Father, Son, Brother, Friend, and Other Roles Men Play.* New York: New American Library.

Gerzon, Mark. 1992 [1982]. *A Choice of Heroes: The Changing Face of American Manhood.* Boston: Houghton Mifflin.

Gilmore, David D. 1990. *Manhood in the Making: Cultural Concepts of Masculinity.* New Haven: Yale University Press.

Halperin, David M. 1990. *One Hundred Years of Homosexuality and Other Essays on Greek Love.* The New Ancient World. New York: Routledge.

Hamill, Pete. 1978. "A Farewell to Machismo." In *The Myth of American Manhood,* ed. L. Kriegel. New York: Dell.

Hammond, D., and A. Jablow. 1987. "Gilgamesh and the Sundance Kid: The Myth of Male Friendship." In *The Making of Masculinities: The New Men's Studies,* ed. Harry Brod. Boston: Allen and Unwin.

Kerényi, Karl. 1983. *Apollo: The Wind, the Spirit, and the God. Four Studies.* Trans. Jon Solomon. Dunquin Ser., 16. Dallas: Spring Publications.

Levinson, Daniel J., C. N. Darrow, E. B. Klein, M. H. Levinson, and B. McKee. 1978. *The Seasons of a Man's Life.* New York: Knopf.

Maas, James. 1985. *Speaking of Friends: The Variety of Man-to-Man Friendships.* Berkeley: Shameless Hussy Press.

Mason, Herbert, trans. 1970. *Gilgamesh: A Verse Narrative.* New York: New American Library.

Messner, Michael. 1992. *Power at Play: Sports and the Problem of Masculinity.* Men and Masculinity. Boston: Beacon Press.

Miller, Stuart. 1983. *Men and Friendship.* Los Angeles: Tarcher.

Monette, Paul. 1988a. *Borrowed Time: An AIDS Memoir.* San Diego: Harcourt Brace Jovanovich.

———. 1988b. *Love Alone: Eighteen Elegies for Rog.* New York: St. Martin's Press.

Nardi, Peter M., ed. 1992. *Men's Friendships.* Research on Men and Masculinities, 2. Newbury Park, Calif.: Sage.

Pronger, Brian. 1990. *The Arena of Masculinity: Sports, Homosexuality, and the Meaning of Sex.* London: Gay Men's Press.

Rotundo, E. Anthony. 1993. *Manhood in America: Transformations in Masculinity from the Revolution to the Modern Era.* New York: HarperCollins.

Segal, Lynne. 1990. *Slow Motion: Changing Masculinities, Changing Men.* New Brunswick, N.J.: Rutgers University Press.

Sherrod, D. 1987. "The Bonds of Men: Problems and Possibilities in Close Male Relationships." In *The Making of Masculinities: The New Men's Studies,* ed. Harry Brod. Boston: Allen and Unwin.

Stein, P. J. 1989. "Men and Their Friendships." In *Men in Families,* ed. R. A. Lewis and R. E. Salt. Sage Focus Editions, 76. Beverly Hills: Sage.

Strathern, Marilyn. 1988. *The Gender of the Gift: Problems with Women and Problems with Society in Melanesia.* Stud. in Melanesian Anthropology, 6. Berkeley: University of California Press.

Whitman, Walt. 1949 [1860]. *Leaves of Grass and Selected Prose.* New York: Holt, Rinehart, and Winston.

Williams, Walter L. 1986. *The Spirit and the Flesh: Sexual Diversity in American Indian Culture.* Boston: Beacon.

———. 1992. "The Relationship between Male-Male Friendship and Male-Female Marriage: American Indian and Asian Comparisons." In *Men's Friendships,* ed. P. M. Nardi. Newbury Park Calif.: Sage.

Winkler, John J. 1990. *The Constraints of Desire: The Anthropology of Sex and Gender in Ancient Greece.* The New Ancient World. New York: Routledge.

Wright, F. A. 1949. "Athletics." In *The Oxford Classical Dictionary,* ed. M. Cary, et al. London: Clarendon.

PART V

Men's Bodies in Contemporary Culture and Religion

The Confines of Male Confessions: On Religion, Bodies, and Mirrors

BJÖRN KRONDORFER

Spiegel: noch nie hat man wissend beschrieben,
was ihr in euerem Wesen seid.
Ihr, wie mit lauter Löchern von Sieben
erfüllten Zwischenräumen der Zeit.

Mirrors: never yet has anyone described,
knowing what you are really like.
You, interstices of time
filled as it were with nothing but sieveholes.

—Rainer Maria Rilke,
Sonnets to Orpheus

When we confess, we have already lived a life that we are
now willing to abandon, and whose changes we are willing to share with
a public. To a certain degree, confessors have already detached themselves from a lived past. Confessions are a pouring out of personal
memories and thoughts, and may originate in a state of being confounded, of being disturbed by the way we have arranged ourselves with
our lives. Etymologically, the term *confusion* derives from the Latin *cum*
(together) and *fundere* (to pour), and carries the meaning of "pouring

out together," "mingling," of being "overwhelmed" and "perplexed."
In order to manage our confusion, we confess.

*When I set myself the task to write about religion and the body, I
thought I was prepared to address this issue. In my academic work,
I have been searching for pathways for studying the intersection of
body, identity, religion, and performance; and in my training in
experimental drama and dance I learned to use and to decipher the
body's creative vocabulary. I assumed that this background would
provide the methodological and emotional support necessary to
talk about the male body. Instead, I became wary about the subject, afraid of resuscitating old anxieties, memories, and inhibi-
tions.*

*I have ambivalent feelings about male confessions. Sometimes, I
like to read them (and often am tempted to write them); at other
times, I have no patience for this genre which inspires men to pour
out intimacies. Personally, I do not want to add to the extensive
literature of male confessions yet another lament about the difficulties of growing up male. I fear that such a beginning would turn
a private confusion into a public confession. But why would I not
allow myself this narcissistic pleasure?*

*In this essay, then, I will explore my ambivalent views on male
confessions: on the one hand my wish that men talk intimately
about their anatomical bodies and spiritual selves, and on the
other my frustration with the narcissistic longings of the male ego
exhibited in confessional writings.*

Confusion may compel us to confess but confessing is not the same as
confusing. Confessing is a recollecting of memories that emerge from
within us, although, as confessors, we assume a position that appears to
be outside and beyond the immediate moment. It imposes a new order
onto experienced chaos. A confession is always an interpretation of the
past, a revisioning of our lives, a reinvention of ourselves.

Confessions share many characteristics with autobiographical writings but the latter do not have to adopt the former's nostalgic perspective. Autobiographical statements can emerge from the immediate moment (a prisoner's diary written in the hope of his or her release) or from
an overtly political context (a memoir released in the hope of reelection).
These statements can also be written with the awareness that changing
the circumstances of one's life is either not desirable (because the author

enjoys a privileged position) or unfeasible because of political oppression, social dependency, or psychological impotence. In the confession, however, the confessor invites the public to become witness to the new meaning one has attached to one's life. The Latin *confessare*, a composite of *cum* (together, fully) and *frateri* (to acknowledge), conveys the public dimension of "acknowledging together," that is, to talk about one's life publicly. It also means to "fully acknowledge," the attempt to reveal oneself truthfully. In its best tradition, confessing is the result of a newly grasped awareness that is shared with others.

Does male confessional literature display such awareness? Many men have been successful in publicly sharing and communicating their religious, spiritual, political, or sexual conversions and transformations because patriarchal traditions have provided them with the means to do so, but they may have been less successful in being able to "fully acknowledge" their lives. The privileges men have enjoyed in Western cultures may have locked their confessions into a narcissistic meditation, blinding them to the fate of others.

As I ponder the challenge of writing about religion and the male body, two conflicting voices emerge from within me: the voice of a Lutheran minister, a career I once planned to pursue, advocating a Protestant work ethic and promising institutional authority and security; and the voice of a dancer and artist, calling for exuberance and playfulness and encouraging me to search for liminal spaces where I feel comfortable. In my adolescence, I sometimes fantasized leading a monastic life or becoming a millionaire. Asceticism versus debauchery, religion versus body, spiritual simplicity versus creative excess. I remember moments when these competing desires seemed to tear me apart. Is my academic interest in combining religion and the body the attempt at mediating these conflicting voices? Am I regressing as I write this piece? Have I lost perspective on myself?

Augustine and Leiris: Perspectivity and Redemption

In his *Confessions*, Augustine, despite the obsessive scrutinizing of his motivations and deeds, still has the privilege of perspective. It is the privilege of knowing oneself in relation and in opposition to the divine, a perspective that permits him to escape the danger of solipsism.

Augustine exuberantly praises God before he reveals any intimate details about himself. Only after he finishes glorifying God does he proceed to talk freely about his bodily needs and desires. "You are great, Lord, and highly to be praised. . . . Man, a little piece of your creation, desires to praise you, a human being bearing his mortality with him" (I.1). These opening lines frame Augustine's *Confessions:* the account of intimate details is placed into a proper cosmic order. Whatever intimacies the bishop of Hippo reveals about himself, they are ultimately a small thing compared to God's "immeasurable" power and wisdom.

Once the stage is set, a stage from which God has not yet been expelled (cf. Derrida 1978: 235), Augustine is ready to introduce the carnal necessities of his existence. "So I was welcomed by the consolation of human milk. . . . For at that time I knew nothing more than how to suck and to be quietened by bodily delights" (I.6). The privilege of a divine perspective enables him to portray the delights of human flesh.

I study and teach religion and, whenever possible, dance and perform. I enjoy moving in and out of these two spheres. But when religious people ask me about my dancing, or dancers about religion, I am uncomfortable and tongue-tied. To think publicly about the relation of expressive movements and the expression of faith continues to irritate me. A Christian world view that separates sensuality from spirituality still seems to exert its influence.

Augustine's sudden turn to physical intimacies may surprise us, since we are accustomed to characterize Christianity as a dualistic tradition that devalues the body and exalts the mind/spirit/soul. This hierarchization of values has led many to believe that the Christian culture does not talk about the body. This, however, is not true: it incessantly talks about it. Christian thinkers may not have pleasant things to say about the body. Yet, in their theological treatises, they often speak vividly about the delights, filth, rottenness, pleasures, temptation, sins, and punishments of the flesh. "And the beleaguered devil undertook one night to assume the form of a woman and to imitate her every gesture, solely in order that he might beguile Antony," wrote Athanasius about the fourth-century Egyptian ascetic. "[The devil] placed his confidence in the weapons *in the navel of his belly* [and] advanced against the youth. . . .

The one hurled foul thoughts and the other overturned them through his prayers; the former resorted to titillation, but the latter, seeming to blush, fortified the body with faith" (1980: 34). The intimate realities of the flesh must first be acknowledged before the body can be subjected to ascetic control.

In the past, I have rejected religious asceticism for its dualistic and disembodied attitudes. At the same time, I became intrigued by Artaud's and Grotowski's notion of the "holy actor" who does not "exhibit his body, but annihilates it, burns it, frees it from every resistance to any psychic impulse [and] sacrifices it" (Grotowski 1968: 34). The "holy actor" undergoes a rigorous training, in which he learns to transgress and transcend the social and physical limitations imposed on the body.

Today I wonder whether the holy actor differs that much from the Christian male ascetic. The early Christian ascetics renounced earthly desires and tried to discipline their flesh in order to uncover the spiritual possibilities of the body. The practical consequence of their idealism was a continuous struggle with and against their bodies. Likewise, the modern holy actor subjected his body to a discipline that countered social and aesthetic norms. He underwent ascetic-like training to explore the aesthetic possibilities of the body.

Perhaps, both the male ascetic and the holy actor live a more bodily existence than those men who do not problematize their bodies and merely employ them in pursuit of career, pleasure, and health.

Perhaps, ascetic discipline appeals to men not so much because it renounces the body but because it promises seclusion. Are men attracted to asceticism because it allows them to detach themselves from a community and live a solitary male existence?

When we compare Augustine's *Confessions* to Michel Leiris's *Manhood: A Journey from Childhood into the Fierce Order of Virility,* the wide gap between antiquity and modernity becomes evident. "I have just reached the age of thirty-four, life's mid-point," the French poet, anthropologist, and museum curator informs his readers in the opening paragraph. "Physically I am of average height, on the short side. I have auburn hair cut short to keep it from curling, and also to prevent the spread of an incipient baldness. . . . My eyes are brown, the edges of the lids habitually inflamed; my complexion is high; I am disconcerted by an irritating tendency to blush, and by a shiny skin" (1992: 3). Leiris, who broke with the surrealist movement when he began to work on *Manhood* in the 1930s, exposes the agonies of being and becoming a man. It is a modern version of male self-scrutinizing which places the body in the center. The male self is wrapped in physical self-consciousness.

The first thing the reader learns about Leiris's life concerns his physiognomy ("a straight nape" and "a broad, rather bulging forehead"), his habitual gestures ("sniff[ing] the back of my hand"), his chief activities ("literature"), his sex life ("sexually I am not, I believe, abnormal [but] have long tended to regard myself as virtually impotent"), and his "disgust of pregnant women." From the very beginning, *Manhood* is hopelessly entangled in a solipsistic perspective on the body. Leiris sings a hymn to the male body—to a body that is not beautiful, powerful, and sinful but homely, impotent, and mundane.

> *Writing about the male body is distressing. The male body is, after all, my body, and my body resists to be written about. It/I become very self-conscious precisely at the moment I want to write about my body. I feel the sensations in the tips of my fingers, the slight burning in my eyes, my tense shoulders. My body becomes almost an object outside of myself, an image disconnected from the person that is thinking and writing about it/me.*
>
> *What is the value of such solipsistic circling? How can I and other men escape it? Would a divine reality, as Augustine still assumes it, help men to transcend their self-centeredness?*

Leiris's accounting of his physical likes and dislikes takes up approximately the same space that Augustine needs to extol God in the opening paragraphs of the *Confessions*. Contrary to Augustine, who prepares the reader and himself to consider the physicality of a man's life by first establishing a divine perspective, Leiris's opening passage is tightly organized around the description of his body but concludes with a metaphysical allusion. "I should like to set down here, in a few lines, what vestiges I can gather of the *metaphysics of my childhood*" (1992: 6; italics in the original). His body does not only precede all metaphysics but the metaphysics Leiris has in mind never leaves the realm of the immature self. It is the metaphysics of childhood, of nostalgia. The point of departure is no longer God but the infantile past, not the superego but the id. Whereas Augustine's main task is to construe a theological position of omnipotence and eternity outside of himself, which enables him to talk freely about his mother's milk, Leiris construes his self around the aging male body, which has no perspective on itself except for its childhood. Leiris's body knows no redemption. He/it is subject to an inevitable process of disintegration.

On the far side of that abyss lies my early youth toward which, in recent years, I turn as the only happy period of my life, though already containing the elements of its own disintegration, and all the features which, gradually deepening into wrinkles and lines, give my portrait its likeness. (Leiris 1992: 6)

Voyeuristic Gazes and Male Intimacies

In the safety of my own bathroom, I can spend long times in front of a mirror, not just for cleaning and shaving my face but also for looking at it and trying to discover signs of aging. The more time I spend at home—to prepare for class, change my daughter's diapers, write, clean, read, or cook—the more often I check myself in the mirror. I do this to take a break, gather my thoughts, fight a feeling of emptiness, make sure I still exist. When my work takes me into the public arena, mirrors become less significant. The public, I assume, serves as a kind of social mirror. I feel confident in my existence if I see myself reflected in others. The public as an extension of the self.

When seeing photographs of myself, I am sometimes surprised to see a body that seems to be the other way round. I have noticed this phenomenon especially when my face shows a pimple. On the photograph, the pimple may be on my right cheek, though I imagined it to be on the left. My sensual memory remembers it on the left, and so does the memory of seeing my face in the mirror. What is the left side of my body is also the left in the mirror. This perception holds true, of course, only if "I" do the looking in front of the mirror. I can also project myself into my mirrored face, in which case "I" look back at me. Then, the left would be right, just as in the photograph. I am still perplexed by the tricks mirrors and memories can play.

Modern confessional statements function, perhaps, in a similar fashion. Once put into writing, the confession stares back at me. I no longer know whether it is me who does the looking or whether it is the written and remembered "I" that looks back. There was, for example, a large mirror in my grandmother's house. As a child, I would stand in front of it, slowly approach it with my eyes fixed on my body, and then quickly look behind the mirror in order to catch my image. Today, I am tempted to use this childish game as a paradigm for modern confessional writings: the vain effort of men to construct and hold on to an image of themselves.

Are confessions, which turn private thoughts into public property, an attempt at breaking out of the prison of solitude?

Michel Leiris may be correct in interpreting the world through his body and insisting on a metaphysics of childhood. A contemporary male confession would strike me as incomplete if no attention had been paid to the body and the wounds of childhood. Yet, both the search for childhood patterns that influence our adult lives and the scrutinizing of our carnal activities are signs of the modern affliction of self-gazing.

When Leiris begins *Manhood* with a description of his "auburn hair cut short to keep it from curling," we must assume that he wrote these lines in front of a mirror. How else would he have been able to present his physiognomy in such graphic detail? "Loathing his image in the mirror, [Leiris] sees thin, hairy hands, with distinct veins; inflamed eyelids; a bald head" (Porter 1991: 124). It takes courage to portray one's body with an authenticity that transgresses bourgeois expectations of decency. But Leiris is not the inventor of a new autobiographical style. "From Montaigne's *Essays* to Rousseau's *Confessions* through Stendhal's journals to the modern confessions of Gide, Jouhandeau, and Genet, the great writers of France have been concerned to a singular extent with the detached presentation of intimate feelings" (Sontag 1992: viii). Leiris does not present his male obsessions with passion but gazes at them coldly and detached.

I remember the discovery of my first pimple while standing in front of a mirror. I was fascinated by the growth on my skin, just beneath the nose. When I squeezed it and saw the white pus squirting out, I had a bodily sensation that is difficult to describe. I was awestruck. It felt like ejaculating though at the time I did not yet know what this was. I was not repulsed (only now am I a little embarrassed by the words I use to recollect this memory). I thought of an explosion, of something that had been contained and was now thrust forward. The image of a nuclear mushroom cloud crossed my mind. I experienced my still boyish and angelic looking face as undergoing a tremendous change. It/I was witnessing something aggressive, destructive, and liberating. I felt a step closer to adulthood.

Rousseau, the other grand confessor, avows in the opening paragraph of his *Confessions* "to display to my kind a portrait in every way true to nature, and the man I shall portray will be myself" (1953: 17). Rousseau no longer places himself within the universe of revealed religion, like Augustine, nor does he struggle with disciplining his body, like the ascetics. He articulates modernity's self-centeredness: *portrait, man, I, myself.*

Rousseau's casual style is surprisingly modern. He recalls various episodes not because they hold any special meaning but simply because they happened. "I do remember once having made water in one of our neighbour's cooking-pots while she was at church" (1953: 21). The image of young Rousseau peeing in a pot while the owner is at church conveys his mundane treatment of both the body and religion.

Northrop Frye called Rousseau's *Confessions* a "modern type" of Augustine's invented "confession form" (1957: 307). Yet, with respect to their perspectives on the world, the two confessions bear little semblance. Had Augustine reported the cooking-pot episode, he would have used it to explain to his readers how far he had gone astray from a righteous path. Not so Rousseau. For him, the body has its own trivial needs and worries. These can be exasperated in a religious environment but are spiritually insignificant.

When, for example, young Rousseau was accosted by a pederast in a religious convent, he reports this incident with indignation but does not raise any moral or doctrinal issues.

He resumed his caresses [and] tried to work up to the most revolting liberties and, by guiding my hand, to make me take the same liberties with him. I broke wildly away with a cry . . . for I had not the slightest idea what it was all about. . . . [A]s he gave up the struggle I saw something whitish and sticky shoot towards the fireplace and fall on the ground. (1953: 71)

Rousseau's body is no longer the battleground for the torments of sin
and the glory of repentance. The only lesson Rousseau learns is to guard
himself in the future "against the attentions of pederasts" (1953: 73).

> *As a boy, I was once cornered by a museum guard in front of a*
> *Greek statue in the Louvre, and another time harassed by a man*
> *in a train station in Paris. Like Rousseau, I had no idea what it was*
> *all about but enough sense to get away before being humiliated. I*
> *was more confused than ashamed. The incidents had no religious*
> *significance.*

Like Leiris, Rousseau wants to expose intimate details: "Since I have
undertaken to reveal myself absolutely to the public, nothing about me
must remain hidden or obscure" (1953: 65). But unlike Leiris, he seeks
the reader's empathy. Rousseau, who confesses because he feels misunderstood, supplies a chronology of dates, places, stories, explanations.
"I was born at Geneva in 1712, the son of Isaac Rousseau, a citizen of
that town, and Susanne Bernard, his wife" (17). Philippe Lejeune ridiculed such autobiographical prose as the misguided effort to fill out a
"questionnaire sent by a punctilious administration." The autobiographers are born, present "a family tree [and] one or more first memories;
next they go dutifully to school; they make the first discovery of everything they should, while drawing a spicy, compassionate, or incisive
picture of the family milieu; the crisis of adolescence comes along; and
so on" (1989: 235). Leiris counters such prose. He does not present a
chronology of his life but writes about a man (himself) who, out of a
sense of confusion, desires to confess without hiding things considered
to be repulsive and trivial. He confronts the reader with a self-loathing
mentality that speaks through his graphic descriptions of his body, his
sexual preferences, and his misogynist relations to women.

> *I can be disgusted by words depicting bodily activities even if the*
> *activities themselves do not repel me. For example, I may cringe a*
> *little at reading Leiris's description of his habitual gestures*
> *("scratch[ing] my anal region when I am alone"), though I perform*
> *similar gestures at home.*
>
> *Because reading remains a private act, my embarrassment is*
> *well contained. Would someone reveal such intimate obsessions in*
> *a conversation, I would blush. It is easier to write about pimples*
> *in a confessional mode than to speak about them publicly.*

Susan Sontag called *Manhood* an "exercise in shamelessness," a "sequence of self-exposures of a craven, morbid, and damaged temperament" (1992: ix). Roger J. Porter praised it as an "open wound" and a "courageous act" (1991: 125). Leiris himself is less concerned about issues of shame or courage and more intrigued by the arbitrariness of reconstructing one's life.

> Hence it occurred to me to write these pages, primarily a simple confession . . . with the goal of liquidating, by formulating them, certain obsessions, whose weight oppressed me. . . . [But] even as I write, the plan I had devised escapes me, and one might say that the more I look into myself the more confused everything I see becomes. (1992: 14, 83)

Leiris looks into himself and becomes confused. But does he really see his inner self, or is it merely the mirror image of his body that he sees?

> *I can relate to Leiris's struggle. The more I try to gain clarity about my body, the more it escapes me. Sometimes, neither looking into my past nor looking into a mirror solves the dilemma. Perhaps, modern men are cursed by the same dilemma that women in antiquity supposedly encountered: according to a misogynist belief reported by Aristotle, a mirror into which menstruating women gaze becomes spotted (cf. Rank 1971: 66). Mirrors play tricks: they always obscure the real presence of my body.*

Because *Manhood* remains arrested in negative narcissism it is also highly voyeuristic. Leiris does not only turn the reader into a voyeur but, above all, he himself gazes voyeuristically at himself. The entire perspective of *Manhood*, like the opening description of Leiris's mirrored body, is one in which the French poet looks at himself through the reflections of mythological figures, women, infantile wounds, dreams, and fantasies. Everything, including his body, is used as an object through which he can expose himself.

Gazing at the mirror image of one's body—searching for time lost, for signs of decay, for affirmation of the self—is an exercise in hermeticism. Mirrors confine. Susan Sontag perceptively remarked that Leiris wishes "to convince himself that this unsatisfactory body—and this unseemly character—really exist" (1992: xi). To the degree that mirrors make people conscious of their bodies, Leiris is body-conscious; but he is disrespectful of his embodied self. "This lack of esteem or respect for himself is obscene" (Sontag 1992: ix).

Leiris cannot embrace his carnality. "The autobiographer's lived experience of his body," Shirley Neuman writes about *Manhood,* "disap-
pears, yet again, into the metaphysics of the disembodied 'voice' of
masculine autobiography" (1991: 163). His embodied self is defined in
solipsistic rather than relational terms. *Manhood* deceives the reader
into believing that it is an autobiographical revelation of a male embodied self while, in fact, it is a disembodied gaze at a male body. Many
male confessions are infected by the same disease.

*When I dance, I can reveal myself without remaining imprisoned
by the disembodied gaze of male confessional writings. I especially
like contact improvisation, a modern dance form where people are
in physical contact with each other for most of the time. Contact
dancers explore the range of movement possibilities by always
conceiving themselves in relation to other bodies: giving and receiving weight, leading and being led, lifting and being lifted, full
contact and imagining contact in the space between bodies. Contact improvisation is intimate, at times erotic, but not sexual.*

*When I thus dance, I am fully in my body and responsible for
the other person's body. It is an embodied revelation in relation to
someone else that escapes the male self-gaze.*

*But how do I bring these experiences to bear upon the task of
writing religiously about the male body?*

Wounds and Vanity

Male theologians rarely identify themselves with their bodies. They talk
about the pain of the crucifixion, the joy of resurrection, the torment of
sin, and the glory of salvation. But they do not make their bodies the site
of God-talk. Tom F. Driver's "Tub Water and Holy Ground" is an
exception.

The theologian soaked in the bathtub. . . . Tired limbs and untoned muscle
spoke to him. "Wash us," they said. . . . It was not a prayer to God but an
instruction to himself. . . . Well, he had the gospel in his soul. . . . Where he
seemed not to have the gospel was in his body. (1977: 1–4)

Driver's bathtub theology, which challenges preconceived notions about
the production site of theology (the ivory tower, the altar, the desk, the
pulpit), runs the risk of being ridiculed. What good can come out of a

bathtub? Martin Luther's mental breakthrough at the *cloaca*, the toilet, serves as a reminder of the "explosive" significance of doing theology at profane places (Erikson 1962). Similarly, when Driver touches ignored parts of his body and explores theological possibilities, he seems to drag the glorious heights of theology to the trivial grounds of washing his thighs, but from his thighs rises again (though without phallic erection) a theological reflection of sin, forgiveness, salvation, touch, healing, God. His body is no longer a fountain of sin that requires divine salvation but a ground for therapeutic healing.

When I talk about my body, I usually like to have a reason: a physical pain, a political aim, a medical problem, a theological justification. I suspect that other men feel the same. We can talk about broken bones and war scars, abortion rights and AIDS-research, prostrate cancer, and sexual ethics. But talking or writing about our bodies without a "legitimate" reason is viewed as narcissistic, vain, obscene. What would be the point of describing the difficulties of my sexual awakening? Who would be interested in knowing that I did not masturbate until I was twenty years of age and only after I had had sexual intercourse with my first girlfriend? I can recall those old anxieties as if they happened yesterday, but I am not sure what their significance is today. I empathize with Leiris's admission that "the anecdotes I am telling here do not . . . represent anything crucial or exceptional for me; I offer them simply because they come to mind apropos of this idea of injury— a wound inflicted on a man with whom I identify myself " (1992: 77).

Driver locates his emotional woundedness in his thighs, and that discovery motivates him to do theology. Healing, for him, cannot be found in professing an otherworldly God but in recovering childhood wounds inscribed in his flesh. In this regard, Driver has more in common with Leiris than Augustine. "He felt that if his body's longing for salvation could not be answered then he did not have the gospel at all" (Driver 1977: 4). To still this longing, Driver focuses his attention on the thighs, which have, in the past, offended him. "Too soft and too white. Too much useless flesh" (7). What men often desire and fear in a woman's body (the soft, white, useless flesh), the theologian discovers hanging on his own legs.

Eventually, Driver finds salvation in the bathtub. After recalling Jacob's thigh, the thighs of girls riding on his shoulders at a high school swimming party, the unself-conscious kicking of his feet during angry outbursts, etc., "he lifted his left leg and stepped out onto the floor. Then the other leg, and reached for a towel. . . . He dried first his thighs, massaging the backs of them and feeling the muscle under the fat. His legs felt new. While there was plenty of fat and he had to stand with feet wide apart to dry the inner softness, still each thigh had more muscle than he had supposed" (1977: 27). Is the discovery of muscle Driver's redemption? Fat as the source of alienation, muscle as a promise of salvation? The imagery is peculiarly gendered. Finding muscle revitalizes his energy and, perhaps, renews his sense of masculinity. The bathtub episode comes to its conclusion. "His foot pressed the soil. His thigh pushed it there. . . . He was full of an energy that has no name" (28).

> *I locate my woundedness in my shoulders, chest, pelvis. Each part carries a different meaning: somebody watching over my shoulders, somebody sitting on my chest, something locking my pelvis. To free myself from inhibitions I had to leave the institutional realm of religion. In theater workshops and on stage I learned to relax my muscular tensions, dared to breathe and scream, and discovered the pelvis as the center of expressive movements. If spirituality denotes an experience of wholeness, then I have encountered them during movement improvisations, where I am fully in my body and fully aware of everyone and everything around me.*

I can appreciate Driver's bathtub theology for its risk-taking and honesty, but I wonder whether he could have conceived of writing about his body without legitimating it theologically. What would have happened had he described the cleaning and touching of his flesh without doing theology? As radical as his bathtub theology may strike us, the religious frame also protects against accusation of vanity. Is the theological perspective a distancing device that allows Driver, like Augustine, to relate to his body?

Driver does not preach the renunciation of carnality—in part, it seems, because he rebels against an American-puritan autobiographical style (cf. Couser 1979). By touching his thighs, Driver goes beyond the confines of a detached male self-gaze. When men, like Driver, touch themselves tenderly and consciously they may be on the right path to reach out to others and treat them with similar care and nurture.

> *Despite my frustrations with institutional religion, I remain fascinated by religious phenomena. Religion may actually be one of the few cultural systems that does not merely exploit the body for utilitarian ends but, almost despite itself, critically probes the body's possibilities and limitations. Early Christian communities, Brown suggests, differed from their pagan environments "in their estimate of the horizons of the possible for the body itself" (1988: 31). Even if one believes that the body is of no ultimate consequence for salvation, one still has to engage in an argument about the body and develop a practice that deliberately manipulates and disciplines the flesh. It seems to me that religions do not treat the body as devoid of meaning but as an entity dependent on cultural norms—and as such, the body can be socially de-constructed and then reconstructed for spiritual goals.*
>
> *Perhaps, it takes the perspective of a disobedient reader to fully grasp this paradox: in order to renounce the body one first has to become aware of it.*

The description of physical intimacies can easily be attacked for its vanity and inconsequentiality, and Augustine may have been among the first to renounce the modern exhibitionistic joy in body trivia. The (post-) modern arbitrariness is counter to what the fourth-century theologian would have wanted to convey—and that, perhaps, makes him once again attractive, yet inaccessible, to modern sensibilities. In his *Confessions*, Augustine talks about his body because he pursues a larger spiritual agenda. He acknowledges the reality of carnal pleasures and addictions which, however, do not produce happiness. True happiness lies in the surrender to God, beyond the body, beyond the self.

Augustine skillfully plays with the voyeuristic curiosity of the reader but at its peak switches to a dispassionate prose. He titillates the reader's imagination only to frustrate it a moment later. "Each time he evokes the 'torrent of pitch which boils and swells with the high tides of foul lust' (II.2), it is quickly followed by philosophical or theological reflection" (Miles 1992: 26). A moral lesson can be learned from each activity of the male body.

I am angry at Augustine because he stirs me in a direction where I begin to take my body seriously—only to be told that such a venture is pointless, if not outright foolish, for true happiness lies in a beyond-the-body relationship with God. But how can we be sure that "true happiness" is not a grand projection of the celibate male psyche?

I am also envious of men like Augustine because I no longer have the theological certainty of a perspective larger than myself.

Now that the Augustinian universe is no longer in place, what is it that men talk about when they talk about their bodies? The modern trend to reveal our innermost intimacies, as in Leiris's case, may have created a discourse in which intimacy becomes ultimately irrelevant. Why reveal myself if intimacy is no longer a value? How can Rousseau's peeing in a pot, Driver's thighs, or Leiris's sexual failures be of any interest to the public? Or, as one of my colleagues in religious studies told me in a conversation, "What do I do with my anus if it has no significance any more?"

Most confessors display some doubt about the relevance of their private revelations and are wary of being criticized for indulging in vanity. "Before I go further I must present my reader with an apology," Rousseau writes, "or rather a justification, for the petty details I have just been entering into, and for those I shall enter into later, none of which may appear interesting in his eyes" (1953: 65). Even Augustine is afraid of being laughed at. "Allow me to speak: for I am addressing your mercy, not a man who would laugh at me. Perhaps even you deride me but you will turn and have mercy on me" (I.6). The "you" in the text refers, of course, to God but also, figuratively speaking, to the reader. People may not have the patience to deal with Augustine's trivialities, but God (and the reader) hopefully will.

It is left to Leiris not to apologize for writing about trivial details. "I attach no excessive importance to these recollections from various stages of my childhood. . . . [There is] a certain arbitrariness in the choice of facts I am recording" (1992: 14,87). The real, and perhaps intended, scandal of *Manhood* is not the revelation of intimate details but its stubborn affirmation of the trivial. Leiris does not want the reader to attach meaning to the childhood memories of his injured body or to the loathing of his impotent adult body. The body simply is. The discomfort we may feel when reading *Manhood* may have less to do with the graphic depiction of his wounds and more with his professed disinterest in a larger order.

> *I am angry at Leiris for taking up my time with self-exposures that provide no vision beyond his own petty injuries. With Susan Sontag (1992: ix), I am tempted to say: "Who cares?"*
>
> *I am also envious of men like Leiris because I rarely allow myself the pleasure of publicly indulging in my injuries.*

The Pleasure of Danger, the Danger of Pleasure

How dangerous is it to engage in confessional writings? Are men afraid of trivia, of being laughed at, of losing their academic credibility and public honor? In confessional writings, men expose intimate memories of their woundedness. "After a year of work, tears and healing I began trying to write a book about what had been happening," John H. Lee writes in *The Flying Boy: Healing the Wounded Man* (1987: 79). Men generally regard the opening up of one's intimate self as a perilous activity; hence, they either despise the confessional work of their peers or praise it as an act of courage.

> *When I first invited responses to my "unedited" thoughts on the male body, I was nervous. I presented an unfinished draft of this essay to a working group on Images of Masculinity in Atlanta. "Why are you using two voices?" the participants wanted to know. "Who is your 'imaginary enemy'? Is there perhaps an unspoken third voice in your piece? What is it that you ultimately want to achieve?" The questions were inquisitive but not hostile.*
>
> *During the discussion I realized that my strategy of separating my essay into a critical and a personal voice protects me. I surround my self-revelations with academic discourse because, as author, I seek shelter from the public which I both fear and desire. I am skeptical about men talking about themselves but, at the same time, want to talk intimately about myself. The two voices help to maintain a dialogue between the tradition and myself—and I can hide somewhere in-between. "What I ultimately want is to improve the way we, as men, talk to each other—without ignoring our bodies and without remaining fixated on ourselves," I said.*

It later occurred to me that my strategy resembles Lejeune's vision for his scholarly work On Autobiography. *"I chose to work, academically, on autobiography," he wrote, "because in a parallel direction I wanted to work on my own autobiography. . . . As soon as I write . . . I share the desires and illusions of autobiographers, and I am surely not ready to renounce them" (1989: 132–33).*

"Let us grant once and for all," Leiris admonishes his readers, "that to write and publish an autobiography does not involve, for the man who undertakes such a thing . . . any danger of death" (1992: 159). Indeed, the ability to interpret and re-envision one's life is more of a privilege than a risk because it presupposes, among other things, socio-economic security, literacy, and poise. Furthermore, many men are well compensated for their fear of being ridiculed: their work frequently acquires canonical status.

If one of the aims of confessions is "to manage the body" (Neuman 1991: 138), then to write them offers men a safe means to make contact with their bodies. It is easier to *write* about one's carnal obsessions, fantasies, and dreams—even those which Mikhail Bakhtin (1984) attributed to the grotesque body—than to communicate them directly to a spouse, friend, companion, or colleague. Men seem to talk more freely about their bodies in confessional statements than in conversations with intimate others. Confessions are, therefore, not a private discourse (despite Neuman's claim that "confession, whether practised in the church or by means of one of its avatars in childrearing, tutoring, or medical consultation, remains an intimate and private discourse" [1991: 138]).

The act of writing functions as a buffer between private and public discourse. Confessions mediate intimacies. They transform inarticulate experiences into speech, body into voice. They are a safe way to acknowledge the woundedness which men may not otherwise admit. There is no immediate other to dispute the retrospective construction and interpretation of the male self. Such uninterrupted reconstruction must be regarded as pleasurable.

As I write this, I am flooded with memories: moments of sexual prowess and impotence, failed friendships with men, aborted affairs with women, my father, my eroticized passion of the Passion narrative, cross-dressing, masturbation, sensations of suffocation during worship, nurturing my child, my nipples, the feeling of

*constant flow when dancing, the pelvis as center of creativity and
anxiety, my voice that never seems to find the right pitch for
Christian hymns. . . .*

*My mind wanders off and I find it difficult to return to the task-
at-hand.*

*There are many issues I am tempted to address in this "confes-
sional" essay, though I would not share them directly with colleagues, friends, not even my spouse. These issues concern inci-
dents of social, emotional, and sexual embarrassment—moments
of shame where I felt powerless, vulnerable, exposed.*

*Am I beginning to do what I criticize in other men? Am I using
the confessional form as a distancing device in order to talk about
issues of male intimacy?*

When men write intimately about themselves, it is not uncommon
that they misrepresent the other gender. Women appear as a screen for
male fantasies, as mirrors in which men see themselves, or they completely disappear in the text (the latter is true especially for wives).
Leiris's contemptuous attitude toward his own body, for example, corresponds to his "whorish" relationships to women: "the eminently inaccessible actresses," "the girl who bit my lips," "the girl no longer young
but still pretty," "the whore encountered one night in an American bar,"
"the cold, arrogant American woman," "the submissive whore," "the
girl who had become the mistress of my accomplice"—each caricatured
portrait is followed by a short description of sexual activity, no less
flattering (1992: 96–97). Women as mirrors of the male pornographic
imagination!

In Augustine's *Confessions,* on the other hand, women disappear
almost entirely in the text. Augustine hardly ever mentions his female
lover and companion of thirteen years, though it is she with whom, we
assume, he has enjoyed most of his sexual life prior to his conversion.
Just as the pleasure of sexuality is always on the verge of vanishing in
the text, so are women. Augustine suppresses lust by banishing the
objects of his lust.

Augustine's mother Monica is the exception. Augustine portrays her
as the pious believer he wants to become. Upon her, Augustine projects
a spiritual desire that is to counter the lust he feels when associating
with other women. She is not the object of his sexual appetite but a

helpmate for stilling his spiritual hunger. When he finally takes the vows of celibacy, he exchanges the obsessively sexualized relationships with women for a spiritually intimate relationship with his mother. Mothers as mirrors of men's virginal desires!

What makes Augustine's portrait of his mother so unusual is not the spiritualization of Oedipal desires but the fact that he never blames his mother for his identity crisis. It may be for this reason that the modern reader is tempted to consider their relationship unhealthy. Blaming one's mother has become commonplace in modern writings. Especially the mythopoetic movement has turned mothers, archetypal or real, into negative mirrors, accusing them for inhibiting their sons' transition from boyhood into manhood. The son, according to Robert Bly, spent long months in the mother's body and "got well tuned to female frequencies." If he is not slowly "retuned" to the "older masculine body," the young man will suffer emotional starvation. "Women cannot, no matter how much they sympathize with their starving sons, replace that particular missing substance" (Bly 1990: 94).

"Sadly, I was my mother's mirror [but] my mother had not been the mirror I needed and longed for," remembers John Lee as he reflects on his dependency on his female lovers Kim and Laural. "Kim was [a mirror] whereas Laural only was to a degree. Kim showed me to me. . . . I looked into her face and saw my own" (1987: 9). When sons look into the faces of their mothers, and later lovers, they find the image of their own starving self. In Lee's search for his "feminine soul" and "negated masculinity," women are reduced to mirrors for his wounded, narcissistic self, mirrors that his mother did not provide. A truly Kafkaesque version of male blindness: every (female) face is man's own.

My relation to my mother turned particularly painful during adolescence. I remember my fury when she, on several occasions and behind my back, disinvited female friends I wanted to date. Her actions were part of a strategy to hold the family together as a closely knit union. Friends were welcome as long as they did not want to bond intimately with me or my siblings. The "intruder" would be emotionally shunned, sometimes made to leave. Her actions left me scarred at the time but, ultimately, she was left with the greater wound: after her children left home, she became increasingly depressed.

*Today, about two decades later and only after the birth of my
daughter, do I begin to fathom my mother's obsessive and desperate clinging to the image of a happy and intact family. When I look
at my daughter, still a toddler as I write these lines, I realize how
much she mimics me, and how much of myself I imagine to see in
her. I can already feel my heart ache at the thought of her leaving
the parental love and worries.*

In many male confessional writings, the female gender is viewed as
harmful to the development of the male identity. This is one of the great
downsides of men pouring out intimate thoughts. If men regard the
pleasure of writing intimately about themselves as dangerous, the danger
of such intimate pleasure is its ingrained misogyny. "The male psyche
is in continual danger of being inundated by the feminine sea [like]
sandy atolls in a monsoon-swept ocean," writes Sam Keen in *Fire in the
Belly*, a self-help book on male spirituality with numerous confessional
references. Keen detects a fragility of the male psyche that is "not
psychological, not neurotic [but] an ontological fact rooted in our being"
(1991: 15), a view which parallels Augustine's anthropological anxiety
around *concupiscentia*. Just as Augustine tried to contain the flood of
sexual lust in order to become a spiritually virile man, Keen wants
modern men, beleaguered by the "feminine sea," to become "fierce
gentlemen" who "discover a peaceful form of virility" (121). In Augustine's case, all women (except his mother) are dangerous; in Keen's
case, the peril stems from "ideological feminists" who continue "gen-
deral enmity and scapegoating" (195; cf. Bordo 1993: 710).
   The pleasure of writing intimately about the male self compels many
men to blame women for their woundedness, and it seems that they are
chronically unaware of this pattern.

Anus Mundi: A Different Kind of Mirror

I have argued so far that male confessions suffer from narcissistic fantasies, solipsistic gazing, patterns of blame and self-loathing, misrepresen-
tations of women, and other protective and deceptive devices to facilitate
a discourse on the male body. But why do men take recourse to such
defensive operations? What are they afraid of?
   A deep-seated male anxiety, I believe, is the fear of being shamed.

Talking about men's bodies, my body, touches on forbidden zones. Where the body is permeable, where it excretes and is open to intrusion, it is feared most. Whenever the discourse reaches these regions, men react with fury or withdraw in shame.

To contain these fears, men have construed their own bodies as closed, dry, and clean. The excreting body is not theirs but belongs to women: open, dirty, and dangerous. The church fathers feared woman's body as "the gateway for the devil," medieval theologians perceived the liquid body as morally debased, Victorian anxieties revolved around the *vagina dentata,* and archetypal psychology mythologized women as holes, darkness, void, water. Western culture, it seems, made a persistent effort to transfer male anxieties onto women, and turned the female anatomy into the antithesis of the male body. *They* are fluid, *we* are not; *they* are dirty, *we* are not. In reality, however, the male body, endowed with a mouth, ears, nose, skin, penis, and anus, is as permeable and liquid as a woman's body (except for menstruation, lactation, and the fluids of childbirth).

The most shamed and shunned area of the male body is the anus. Not surprisingly, there are only scant references to it in male confessions. The dread of feces: the anus is an opening that leads deeply into the male body, and from it primal "possessions" emerge (later, we learn to classify them as waste and dirt). There is also homophobic anxiety: the anus can be penetrated, that is, subjected to sexual pleasure and viola-tion. In a heterosexual culture, nothing seems farther removed from spiritual significance than this part of the male anatomy.

In his letter to the Corinthians, the apostle Paul called the body "a temple of the Holy Spirit." Yet, claiming the anus as part of God's sanctuary borders on blasphemy. Tom Driver "felt a bit dirty, perhaps subversive of worship" when he made the discovery "that to hit and sustain a high note while singing hymns in church, it helped if he relaxed the anus" (1977: 24). The Gnostic Valentinus went so far as to fancy Jesus' perfectly continent body as unable to defecate (Meeks 1993: 137). Even Martin Luther, whose bawdy language counters some of Christianity's repression, uses anal imagery predominantly as a weapon against the devil. "Note this down," he warned the devil, "I have shit in the pants, and you can hang them around your neck and wipe your mouth with it" (quoted in Erikson 1962: 244). Where a man's body "dirties" itself, it is profane, obscene, dangerous, and untouchable.

Many years ago, I came across C. G. Jung's boyhood fantasy of a defecating God. His story sparked my interest to start a card file with references to God and the anus in religious and literary works. The scattered notes include such names as Pasolini, Luther, Kundera, Artaud, and Native American trickster figures. I had once planned to use these notes to write a shit-ology, a theological reflection on the symbolic meaning of the body's rear-end. In my fantasy, I had already designed a title which, I then thought, would provoke a strong Cartesian reaction: "I shit, therefore I am." Needless to say, I never wrote the piece.

At the age of eleven years, C. G. Jung underwent psychological and mental torments before he allowed himself to envision God's anal processes and, as a result, experience "unutterable bliss." It started one day on his way back from school, when he was suddenly overwhelmed by the sight of the cathedral's roof glittering in the sun.

[He] thought: "The world is beautiful and the church is beautiful, and God made all this and sits above it far away in the blue sky on a golden throne and. . . . " Here came a great hole in my thoughts, and a choking sensation. . . . I kept repeating to myself: "Don't think of it, just don't think of it!" I reached home in a pretty worked-up state. My mother noticed that something was wrong . . . [and] I did have the thought that it might help me if I could confess to my mother the real reason for my turmoil. But to do so I would have to do the very thing that seemed impossible: think my thought right to the end. . . .

I gathered all my courage, as though I were about to leap forthwith into hellfire, and let the thought come. I saw before me the cathedral, the blue sky. God sits on His golden throne, high above the world—and from under the throne an enormous turd falls upon the sparkling new roof, shatters it, and breaks the walls of the cathedral asunder.

So that was it! I felt an enormous, an indescribable relief. Instead of the expected damnation, grace had come upon me. (1973: 36–39)

God's turd as a moment of grace? Is Jung's fantasy perhaps the seed that can grow into a spirituality that is based on embodied experience rather than transcendent principles?

Jung's story is, however, only a childish fantasy. Grace occurs at the climax of a boy's inner turmoil, and not as the result of a man's experience with his mature body. Adult, heterosexual men seem to have trouble relating to their anuses privately and publicly. (Today, the medical screening for prostrate cancer is one of the few occasions when "public access" is granted.)

In my card file, I find the report of a dream which a Catholic Korean student once related in a class I taught on religion and psychology. "A family type of dream: My sister was arguing with my wife, as usual. My sister said that my wife is not doing her best to me, as a husband. I was sitting on a toilet, not in the bathroom but inside a church. I could hear my mother praying to the cross, outside of the church. I felt strongly that I wanted to say or ask something to my sister. But I was very ashamed of being in the church with a naked body."

Women, mother, church, defecation, naked body, shame: the dream elements reveal a conflicted male identity and render the dreamer speechless. There is no relief. He is shamed to silence.

Why do anal processes either shame us into silence or become objects of "dirty" jokes? Children experience pleasure when noticing their first prized possessions. Why do adults not show the same awe? Is it because the anal pleasures of infants are pre-divine, that is, prior to experiencing God, and hence unworthy of mature theological consideration? Is shit too "human"? Milan Kundera may be correct when he writes, "I, a child, grasped the incompatibility of God and shit. . . . Either man was created in God's image—and God has intestines!—or God lacks intestines and man is not like Him" (1984: 245). The biblical conception of man being created in God's image has always spurred man's imagination, from Michelangelo's bearded Father-God to *God's Phallus,* the title of a recent book (Eilberg-Schwartz 1994). Why not, then, imagine a defecating God? "Shit is a more onerous theological problem than is evil," Kundera continues, because man can sometimes "accept the idea that He is not responsible for man's crimes. The responsibility for shit, however, rests entirely with Him, the Creator of man" (1984: 246; cf. Carrigan 1991).

Of course, to declare God responsible for shit, as Kundera suggests, assumes an overly naturalistic understanding of God's metaphoric possibilities. The crux, it seems to me, rather lies in the theological bracketing of feces. Shit is "matter," putrid matter, and as such the opposite of the *logos,* the word. As a bodily waste product it must be kept strictly separated from theology. Defecation cannot be permitted into consciousness because the closed and clean male body is believed to transcend matter. Shit destroys the illusion of the closed male body. What passes the anus smells of decay, of mortality, and that is exactly what confessional writings wish to overcome. Words are written for eternity, feces decompose quickly. Writing immortalizes, shitting does not. Are men afraid of becoming arrested in the anal phase when "thinking" about the spiritual possibilities of the rectum? Are they afraid of becoming identified with their most direct bodily product in which they see no redemption?

A couple of years ago, I listened to a radio interview of a California psychologist who had investigated the collective psyche of Germans and claimed to have found a particular anal fixation of the German character. As a German man living in the United States, I am therefore doubly careful to write about the anus, feces, defecation, and other such "queasy" issues.

James Broughton's *The Androgyne Journal* (1977) is the only confessional writing I have found that explores the compatibility of spiritual and anal experiences. It is a record of Broughton's erotic explorations of divine energies flowing through his androgynous body. Despite some occasional references to Christian symbolism and childhood memories, the bulk of the five-week long journal concerns Broughton's experiences with his mature body and pagan gods and goddesses. For example, on June 24, his first day in a woody old cabin near Mendocino, California, he is visited by a woman spirit at night who encourages him to pursue pleasure without shame. ("What is your name? I asked her. Are you Andromeda? Annabel Lee? Anima Mundi?" [10].) Step by step, Broughton discovers that to be ashamed of the shameful parts of the male body (nipples, phallus, anus) is wrong. On July 31, near the end of his stay in Mendocino, he sleeps with mother earth and reaches an orgiastic peak: "I dug the hole deep, and thrust my penis in. . . . I felt like some sacrificing hero of antiquity. I thought of Sky Father cohabiting Earth Mother to create the world" (67–68).

I admire Broughton's remarkable candidness. It is a genuine attempt at treating the male body not as a muscular, clean, iron entity but as an erotic, fluid, and vulnerable organism. His revelations touch areas of my own shame, and—though they embarrass, at times even repulse me—they make me aware of my own repressions.

However, the journal also irritates me. Reading it, I increasingly felt that I became witness to yet another male confession centered around the male, solitary ego. A man gazing at his body as he pleasures it/himself, cut off from any responsibilities to others.

The Androgyne Journal is the record of a solitary journey of a modern-day ascetic. The spiritual adventures of the early Christian desert fathers are replaced by the erotic explorations of a juicy hermaphrodite, the dry body replaced by an excreting body. What Broughton shares with the early ascetics, though, is solitude. He does not need the presence of other human beings for his erotic-spiritual quest because his androgynous body is self-sufficient: a pair of nipples and a functioning penis is all that is required.

I could feel the enticing Venus in me. . . . I could make love to her visible bloom till she squirmed and stretched in delight. Then I could be she loving the king in me . . . till he ripened and towered in desire. Finally, it was the royal pair in mutual adoring play, breast and phallus in equally passionate caress. (1977: 51)

"Shame is no longer possible [because] my sex is part of the divine whole," writes Broughton on the day he reconciles his genitals with spirituality (1977: 46). A few days later, he becomes aware of his "neglected backside." In a dream, he paints with "symbolic shit," then sets out to paint with real shit. He learns a new, universal truth: "When all colors are blended, the result is the color of shit. Is this what the spectrum of solar light ultimately boils down to? Is the color of Oneness, then, the color of shit?" As he further explores anal processes, he devotes a prayer to shit ("My Lord Sun, teach me how to accept this"); wonders whether he would have the courage to eat it ("a ritual act to acknowledge and experience the end as a beginning"); and, finally, observes and worships a "shit-colored gastropod worm" which he imagines to be a creation of his bowel movement and his earlier union with mother earth (1977: 53–55, 69–74).

Like Leiris, Broughton takes the risk of being ridiculed. He opens himself up to new bodily possibilities of spirituality. More than any other confessional writing I have come across, *The Androgyne Journal* removes the theological brackets around feces and puts excrements in the center of an embodied spirituality.

What is disturbing, though, is Broughton's masturbatory narcissism. The (male) androgynous body is nipple and phallus, male and female,

Hermes and Venus. Similarly, anal processes are beginning and end, creation and death. "Man, if he but knew himself, is the most sacred edifice on earth. For he contains all the gods and goddesses" (Broughton 1977: 57). The male body is a self-pleasurable unit, a self-contained cosmos.

The mature man faces its *faeces,* and sees nothing short of an entire universe. The male anus as *anus mundi,* a mirror of majestic proportions! Under the male gaze, even fecal matter turns into spirit.

Conclusion

Luther once wrote that God smiles at the father who "goes ahead and washes diapers or performs some other mean task for his child" (1962: 40). Although Luther used this example to emphasize the importance of faith rather than a father's duty to change diapers, the statement points to an issue that is missing in many male confessional writings: the value of relationality. Monad-like, the male self views itself as independent of the web of mutually dependent relations and sees itself mirrored in whatever direction it chooses to look. The male confessor gazes at his body, his lovers, his mother, his gods, and his feces and sees but a universe that is a reflection of himself.

The perception of the male body as a closed body is part of this solipsistic operation. The male body is closed anatomically (dry and clean) and relationally (not dependent on others). As a self-sufficient universe, the closed male body is not part of a network of relationships but remains arrested in narcissistic awe—hence, it is not responsible to others. A body that is perceived as not excreting and smelling cannot relate to other excreting and smelling bodies. It is no accident that almost all menial tasks that have to do with the cleaning of bodies are done by women: changing the diapers of babies, nursing the putrefying wounds of the sick, wiping the "bottom" of the old, cleaning toilets. The closed, male, heterosexual body does not consider as its primary task to nurture those bodies on a daily basis or to remove the smells of age, sickness, and death.

"Go to any landfill," Sam Keen suggests, "and see the mountain of disposable diapers . . . and it will be obvious that womankind is as compulsive a consumer as mankind" (1991: 197). A revealing statement, indeed! By laying the responsibility for soiled diapers and the blame for a spoiled environment into the lap of mothers, the male body remains clean and virtuous. It also remains an irresponsible and uncaring body. A closed body isolates and imprisons man, and dries him up spiritually.

I admit: until recently, the prospect of wiping, washing, and nursing other bodies on a daily basis would have frightened me, too. Only in dance did I experience my body as open and fluid and, at the same time, related to others. Occasionally, my dancing body— a body that was healthy and able to move in aesthetically pleasing ways—took me to spiritual peaks. But what about a body that cannot move, that spills its fluids uncontrollably and requires the care of others? Could I be spiritually enraptured by such physical processes?

The birth of my daughter was such an experience. Supporting my wife's back and shoulders, I watched the little head push its way out, blood and fluids gushing forth. Cutting the moist umbilical cord was scary; yet, I felt connected to something larger than myself—a muddled but ecstatic and deeply satisfying experience that I can only call spiritual. Today, when I change my daughter's diapers, I feel a similar physical and spiritual sensation of connectedness. Cleaning my daughter, I am neither disgusted nor ashamed, nor tempted to worship anal processes. Sometimes, I am impatient, at other times annoyed by the smell. But more than anything, I experience the cleaning as an intimate, humbling, and bonding act of love.

REFERENCES

Athanasius. 1980. *The Life of Antony and the Letter to Marcellus.* Trans. Robert C. Gregg. New York: Paulist Press.
Augustine. 1992. *Confessions.* Trans. Henry Chadwick. Oxford, England: Oxford University Press.
Bakhtin, Mikhail. 1984. *Rabelais and His World.* Trans. Helene Iswolsky. Bloomington: Indiana University Press.
Bly, Robert. 1990. *Iron John: A Book about Men.* Reading, Mass.: Addison-Wesley.
Bordo, Susan. 1993. "Reading the Male Body." *Michigan Quarterly Review* 32 (Fall): 696–737.

Broughton, James. 1977. *The Androgyne Journal.* Oakland: Scrimshaw Press.

Brown, Peter. 1988. *The Body and Society: Men, Women, and Sexual Renunciation in Early Christianity.* New York: Columbia University Press.

Carrigan, Henry. 1991. "Shit, God, and Kitsch: The Role of the Body in Milan Kundera's *The Unbearable Lightness of Being.*" Paper presented at the American Academy of Religion, Kansas City, November.

Couser, Thomas G. 1979. *American Autobiography.* Amherst: University of Massachusetts Press.

Derrida, Jacques. 1978. *Writing and Difference.* Trans. Alan Bass. Chicago: University of Chicago Press.

Driver, Tom F. 1977. *Patterns of Grace: Human Experience as Word of God.* San Francisco: Harper and Row.

Eilberg-Schwartz, Howard. 1994. *God's Phallus and Other Problems for Men and Monotheism.* Boston: Beacon Press.

Erikson, Erik. 1962. *Young Man Luther: A Study in Psychoanalysis and History.* New York: W. W. Norton.

Frye, Northrop. 1957. *Anatomy of Criticism.* Princeton, N.J.: Princeton University Press.

Grotowski, Jerzy. 1968. *Towards a Poor Theatre.* New York: Simon and Schuster.

Jung, C. G. 1973. *Memories, Dreams, Reflections.* Trans. Richard and Clara Winston. New York: Pantheon.

Keen, Sam. 1991. *Fire in the Belly: On Being a Man.* New York: Bantam.

Kundera, Milan. 1984. *The Unbearable Lightness of Being.* Trans. Michael Henry Heim. New York: Harper and Row.

Lee, John H. 1987. *The Flying Boy: Healing the Wounded Man.* Deerfield Beach, Fla.: Health Communications.

Leiris, Michel. 1992. *Manhood: A Journey from Childhood into the Fierce Order of Virility.* Trans. Richard Howard. Chicago: University of Chicago Press.

Lejeune, Philippe. 1989. *On Autobiography.* Ed. Paul John Eakin. Trans. Katherine Leary. Minneapolis: University of Minnesota Press.

Luther, Martin. 1962. *Luther's Works.* Vol. 55. Ed. Walther I. Brandt. General Ed. Helmut T. Lehmann. Philadelphia: Fortress Press.

Meeks, Wayne A. 1993. *The Origins of Christian Morality: The First Two Centuries.* New Haven: Yale University Press.

Miles, Margaret R. 1992. *Desire and Delight: A New Reading of Augustine's Confessions.* New York: Crossroad.

Neuman, Shirley. 1991. "Autobiography, Bodies, Manhood." In *Autobiography and Questions of Gender,* ed. Shirley Neuman. London: Frank Cass.

Porter, Roger J. 1991. "Figuration and Disfigurement: Herculine Barbin and the Autobiography of the Body." In *Autobiography and Questions of Gender,* ed. Shirley Neuman. London: Frank Cass.

Rank, Otto. 1971. *The Double: A Psychoanalytic Study.* Trans. Harry Tucker. Chapel Hill: University of North Carolina Press.

Rilke, Rainer Maria. 1962. *Sonnets to Orpheus.* Trans. M. D. Herter Norton. New York: W. W. Norton.

Rousseau, Jean-Jacques. 1953. *The Confessions.* Trans. J. M. Cohen. New York: Penguin.

Smith, Sidonie. 1993. *Subjectivity, Identity, and the Body.* Bloomington: Indiana University Press.

Sontag, Susan. 1992. "Foreword." In *Manhood* by Michel Leiris. Chicago: University of Chicago Press. First published: 1964. "Michel Leiris' *Manhood.*" In *Against Interpretation.* New York: Farrar, Straus & Giroux.

ELEVEN

Can Men Worship? Reflections on Male Bodies in Bad Faith and a Theology of Authenticity

LEWIS R. GORDON

The Greek expression from which we have gained the term "enthusiasm" is *entheos*. *Theos* is the Greek word for a god or God. *Entheos* literally means to be filled or entered by a god or God. To be enthused is to be imbued with a god, to be open, to be "entered" by a spirit. My purpose in beginning with this etymological exercise is to raise the following concern. If a man were to regard himself as a closed being, while enthusiasm, a possible precondition of worship (which from the old English *weorth* means also to value), requires an "open" body, a susceptible body, a vulnerable body, how would or could such a man stand before God?[1] If this man's posture is the posture of masculinity, we find ourselves abruptly facing a sticky problem: Can one worship God and remain masculine too? Can a male maintain his masculine identity and worship God in good faith?

Our questions have thrown us already into a specific area of philosophical concern: existential phenomenology. This is because our questions call for a form of anguish on the part of males over their identity. Existential phenomenology explores the implications and the possibility of studying the phenomenon of beings that are capable of questioning their ways of being. We have raised the question of the existential situation of a male figure who attempts to reach out to God, or perhaps more accurately, a male figure who faces the dilemma of losing himself insofar as the possibility of choosing to lose his identity as a closed identity, a closed being, is concerned. Is there something erotic, or perhaps homoerotic, about letting God "in"? The project of reaching God or letting God in may hold its own, frustrating existential features. The problem raises two existential concerns: the problem of bad faith and the problem of authenticity.

Jean-Paul Sartre has examined the concept of bad faith in contexts ranging from our attitudes toward our presented images[2] and emotions (Sartre 1948b), to our attitudes toward our neighbors and different races and creeds (Sartre 1948a, 1992). Bad faith is generally a lie to oneself that involves a flight from freedom and responsibility. The two forms of bad faith that will be of special interest to us are those which involve a flight from one's presence and the assumption of a thing-like existence or completeness in various situations. A situation is tentatively defined as a confrontation of freedoms, which for Sartre is identical to a confrontation of human significance. We will first look at a theory of the male body implicit in those two forms of bad faith. Then we will offer an interpretation of the male body as a theological figure in bad faith.

The Body

Consciousness, phenomenologically understood, is always consciousness of something. Put differently, a world without objects is also a world without consciousness.[3] A consequence of consciousness' requirement of an object is the reality of perspectivity. Consciousness always exists, that is, from somewhere; being other than consciousness, an object is always "there," whereas consciousness is always simultaneously "here." We shall call that somewhere in which consciousness seems to be located, or perhaps better, situated, a perspective, and we shall call such a perspective—the body. The body is one's perspective on the world.

The body can be understood in terms of three dimensions. The first we have already mentioned: the body as one's perspective on the world. The other two are the body as seen by others, and the body's (consciousness') realization of itself as seen by others.

A peculiar aspect of my perspective is that I cannot surpass it. It is, in effect, non-positional by me. Take away the perspective of my eyes, for instance, and I see nothing; my flesh, my nerves, I feel nothing. But these aspects of perspectivity can be extended. My ocular perspective can be extended by a telescope; my finger tips can be extended by a walking cane; my height, by high-heeled boots. These perspectives are not identical with me. They are artificial, but they enhance my perspective on the world.

Without a perspective, I will be an anonymous consciousness without a point of reference. I would be a view, literally, from nowhere (Nagel 1986).

Since my perspective cannot be surpassed by me, I, in effect, live my perspective. It is simultaneous with my choices. My movement and my perspective are one; my choices, my feelings, are the same. I can live myself freely—as, metaphorically, fluid—or I can live myself unfreely— as, again metaphorically speaking, congealed, slimy.

Think, first, of fluid movement. We can live our body as freedom. We stride, with such an attitude, with grace and a simultaneous sense of responsibility. We move because we *will* to do so. But suppose our sense of movement takes the form of self-denial. We do not walk. We are "pushed" on by either circumstances or an imaginary presence as though we were effect to an external cause. The more causally affected we move, the more we live and regard ourselves as linked to a chain of events that we may claim is beyond our control. I don't raise my hand; my hand is raised. I don't hesitate to get out of bed on a cold morning; my body is either asleep or immobilized by the chill. Bad faith in this context is the assumption of our body's being a thing in the world, a thing that is no different from wood floating on water. This form of bad faith is the assumption of presence (facticity) with a denial of absence (transcendence). Sartre discusses transcendence, however, in ambiguous ways. Transcendence can pertain to that which is other than consciousness, in which case it could be an object or a fact, which suggests that a transcendent object can also be factical. But it can also pertain to that which transcends or is constituted beyond facts or the present moment, in which case it can be (for Sartre) "nothingness," the future, possibility, or freedom. Our use is restricted to the second interpretation.

The body is a lived ambiguity. The body can be seen, heard, smelled, felt. In this regard, the body appears as a thing-in-itself. The body, living, breathing, acting, choosing, intending—that body, manifesting all those significations of the human being as a metastable, elusive intention— comes to the fore in the single advancement of the body as freedom. A

corpse, for instance, is not a body in the sense in which we are considering body. Such a thing is unsituated, since a situation is ultimately an
anguish-riddled confrontation with choice (Sartre 1956: 83, 409, 432).
Corpses, for rather obvious reasons, don't choose to do anything. Yet a
consequence of assuming or choosing the existence of a corpse is the
denial of the transcendent aspects of the body: the body appears, but it
appears also as the locus of possibilities in the world.[4]

The possibilities of a seen body are not physiologically holistic. In
semantic terms, the body has a variety of interpretations, although its
spatial-temporal coordinate is a single referent. The body signifies different meanings in different situations.[5]

The final dimension is that of awareness of objectification: the body
understood as an awareness of being seen by others. This last dimension
has a rich history in psychology and philosophy — think, for instance, of
the work of Simone de Beauvoir and Jacques Lacan (cf. Bergoffen 1992).
The consequence of this dimension is a sense of the self as an Other; the
face that we think of when we think of ourselves is an understanding of
ourselves from the outside. It is an estranged intimacy.

The Spirit of Seriousness

The spirit of seriousness is a twofold attitude. In one form, it is the view
that values are external, material features of the world. Values, from this
point of view, exist independently of human beings. Another form of the
spirit of seriousness is the notion of self-importance beyond the scope
of judgment. With this attitude, one's existence becomes "necessary,"
"justified." "It is not simply that I exit, but," such a serious man might
say, "I *must* exist; I *ought* to exist." We regard the spirit of seriousness
as a form of bad faith because it calls for the elimination of the anguish
of responsibility over values: objectified values negate the anguish of
being responsible for those values as lived. Do or die, we encounter good
in the world, under the serious attitude, but we are not responsible
for it.

The classic case of the serious spirit is the cosmogony and theodicy of
the Persian Mani, "the Apostle of God," from whose name we have
gained the term *Manichaeism.* Mani's system was based on a dualism of
material good and evil in the world (Wilson 1967: 149–50). Under such
a model, one can rid the world of evil as one can eliminate bacteria from

a glass of water by heating the water. In *The Respectful Prostitute* (1955), Sartre's misogynist/racist character Fred declares the Manichaean credo; looking at the bed in which he has just spent the night with the prostitute Lizzy, he announces that "It smells of sin." Why? The odors of semen, discharge, and sweat permeate the room. Sin literally invades his nostrils and violates his lungs. On blacks, he advances his ontology: "A nigger has always done something." Why? *Because* he is a "nigger."

Serious values needn't be limited to attitudes toward people. We regard some material things as food and others as not food, even though we can eat either. Instead of admitting that we make certain things food by desiring them, we treat their desirability as their intrinsic features. "For the spirit of seriousness," writes Sartre, "*bread* is desirable because it is *necessary* to live (a value written in an intelligible heaven) and because bread is nourishing" (Sartre 1956: 706). With such an attitude, we face "inedible" objects as though we don't play a role in their determination or, in phenomenological terms, "constitution" as food.[6] We act as though the anguish of whether to eat or not to eat certain things were not in our hands. There are many nourishing substances that we don't desire or consider to be food.

The ultimate figure of seriousness is Absolute Consciousness—one that has achieved itself as its object of desire: God. God serves as an external, objective impetus of all value. But if God were to shout, "Do X!" the reason *why* cannot be God.

Consider, for instance, the story of Adam and Eve. Until Yahweh posed the problem of eating from the Tree of Knowledge of Good and Evil, there was no existential situation posed. We can go farther: There were no human beings—in the sense of mature creatures of self-reflection. There was liberty without freedom.[7] At the moment of Yahweh's command, they were placed in anguish and were thrust into freedom. For Yahweh could only serve as his own justification at this point: whether it was right or wrong to obey Yahweh was posed to them as a problem for them to decide. It is in obeying Yahweh that they would have substantiated the command, *Thou shalt be obeyed!*, but it is also in disobeying Yahweh that they posed their own responsibility. The very possibility of disobeying Yahweh thrust them beyond Yahweh.[8] They were thrown into the negativity of their own freedom. Ironically, their freedom was established by the restriction of their liberty.

Yet, our problem goes deeper. For now we see that the very possibility of Yahweh is insufficient for the elimination of anguish. Anguish is a confrontation with the self; it is a confrontation with one's responsibility for making choices in one's situations. Even if there were God, we face the question of how to act toward "Him." If we disobey, we reduce the value of God's command to us. If we obey, we make it the same for us. Thus, if we claim that the commands were valuable by virtue of their source—God—we would be in bad faith. We would be lying to ourselves.

The Sartrean formulation is atheistic in a strangely religious way.

Manliness

We now consider a bad-faith situation of manhood. A human being, we say, defies identity. Sartre expresses man's existence as a defiance of identity, as man being what he is not and not being what he is. Only objects of consciousness—seemingly things-in-themselves—are properly beings whose identity is one-with-themselves, beings that are "solid" in their being. Yet a man qua his masculinity appears unequivocal. He is solid. *He* fills things. Nothing enters him. He is closed.

Let us imagine a figure who accepts such an identity, such an interpretation of himself. His "closedness" makes his perspective that of an emanation from the center of reference. As a being whom he regards as invulnerable to entry, he thrusts himself into the world as pure, closed flesh—a protrusion of being—the *modus operandi* of the phallus. Such a man lives himself as sealed, as a being without holes. His very movement through space has the sense of a spear in flight, or light jabbing its way through vacuous darkness.

Woman, in this scheme, becomes an absence—in old Jungian and Adlerian jargon, holes. Yet the fleshiness of woman—her breasts, her inclined stomach's fat lining, her buttocks—defies such an ascription. So we may add: whereas the male flesh protrudes, the female flesh, seen under this schema, lives as the threat of implosion; it is regarded from the standpoint of a masculinity of seriousness and power as flesh caving in, flesh "succumbing" to invasion.

We should note that this analysis is of a particular form of interpretation of gender identity—one that is premised upon bad faith. Men and women are reduced to binary existents of power and weakness. It is a form of bad-faith reduction for the obvious reason that it fails to admit the viability of alternative, lived interpretations of human beings. A hole needn't, for instance, be passive. It can also be inviting, swallowing, etc. As Freud remarked,

We are accustomed to say that every human being displays both male and female instinctual impulses, needs and attributes; but though anatomy, it is true, can point out the characteristic of maleness and femaleness, psychology cannot. For psychology the contrast between the sexes fades away into one between activity and passivity, in which we far too readily identify activity with maleness and passivity with femaleness, a view which is by no means universally confirmed in the animal kingdom. (Freud 1961: 58–59)

The masculine-feminine dynamic lives on the level of the symbolic. This masculine-feminine dichotomy also has racial form. Whiteness is regarded as presence, as being. Blackness is regarded as absence of being. Frantz Fanon has observed that there is a homoerotic dimension of antiblack racism (Fanon 1967). In the presence of a white man, a black man stands as a gaping, black hole in being to be filled by a white presence. Let us take this observation to another level—that the black man is positioned as a symbol of the feminine when confronted by the white man. The confrontation would not necessarily be homosexual, but would be misogynistic. This would mean that the black male or the male of color may be situated as woman or the symbol of the feminine in an antiblack world.

Consider an example. In the popular film *The Crying Game* (1992), a white Irish terrorist discovers that a black woman whom he has been seeing is a male. But is s/he? Throughout the film, dimensions of masculinity and femininity are preserved. The white protagonist's identity of being a man isn't threatened. The leitmotif is that any man can understand why the protagonist would maintain a relationship with this transvestite. The film drew great attention from "mainstream" audiences. Would the film have been popular and would the significance of the characters maintain its integrity if the transvestite were white?

At the end of the film, a white female Irish terrorist confronts the black English transvestite. It is clear in the scene that she is a "man" and he is a "woman"—although in the scene he is dressed in a white cricket outfit and she is dressed in black leather. Both hold black guns. Where, in this scene, stands the phallus? The phallus cuts through the confusion of decoy phalli. If both characters were stripped down to their ontological essentials—that is, their bodies—the matrix of power emerges in full bloom. The phallus appears to be white skin.

Gender identity is more complex, of course, than bodily presentations. It should be clear, for instance, that the hallmark of the phallus in *The Crying Game* example is power. But how could a white woman have power in such a way that makes her stand as a man before a black man?

Sartre is instructive here. In *Being and Nothingness,* he observes that it is the hallmark of power to be able to regard boundaries as fictions. From the standpoint of the bourgeoisie, for instance, the proletariat's assertion of a class struggle is misguided since there "are" supposedly no classes. But for the proletariat the reality of classes is confronted, is lived, every day. Thus, when the bourgeoisie deny that they in fact have more power than the proletariat and assert that there are no class distinctions, they make themselves bourgeois in their attitudes. For they can act upon their assertions, which reinforces their delusions. They don't have boundaries. They constitute them. They are who all must contend with and eventually surpass to live and to make a living in their society. That is what it means to have power. Similarly, a white woman may have fewer boundaries than a black man in an antiblack world. She stands before him as a presence when it comes to matters of recognition before the law. She knows that in the eyes of her society her life is more valuable than his. A similar phenomenon occurs among blacks. Middle-class blacks have more options than working- or so-called underclass blacks. In relation to other blacks, then, a middle-class black may say that race doesn't matter, but that is because he has the luxury of dealing with different racial dynamics than the link between race and poverty. He knows that his economic status makes him appear more valuable than lower-class blacks. Yet, he knows that in an antiblack society, class status doesn't tear down all boundaries. Cornel West's reflections in his preface to *Race Matters* are instructive here:

I waited and waited. After the ninth taxi refused me, my blood began to boil. The tenth taxi refused me and stopped for a kind, well-dressed smiling female fellow citizen of European descent. As she stepped in the cab, she said, "This is really ridiculous, is it not?" Ugly racial memories of the past flashed through my mind. Years ago, while driving from New York to teach at Williams College, I was stopped on fake charges of trafficking cocaine. When I told the police officer I was a professor of religion, he replied "Yeh, and I'm the Flying Nun. Let's go, nigger!" I was stopped three times in my first ten days in Princeton for driving too slowly on a residential street with a speed limit of twenty-five miles per hour. (West 1993: x)

In the context of race, gender significations betray their symbolic character. One is not simply a man or a woman.

A Serious Man's Worship

Imagine a man who regards his "manliness" to be a material feature of his being. He is the objective value—white, masculine. If he is objectively masculine—a white protrusion of flesh and power sticking itself out at the world—how does he stand in relation to God? If he permits God to "enter," so to speak, his identity could be lost. But if he penetrates God, then either God is black or woman or homosexual, or he regards himself as God. [9]

At this point we need to take a pause and contract the parameters of our discussion. I should like to say that I suspect that the relativism implicit in cultural anthropological approaches to the question of religious variation is fallacious. There is the false dilemma of an exclusive disjunction between a single religious *Weltanschauung* and a multiplicity of cultural monads each distinct and epistemologically problematic to the other. Those are not necessarily our alternatives. There is also the possibility that religions have both shared and different features—if not in their intrinsic structure, certainly so in virtue of the historical fact of cultural cross-fertilization. Thus, to translate another religious world view into one's own is not identical with either claiming it is one's own or claiming that it is a version of the other to begin with. It could be the discovery that it is neither one's own nor anothers' exclusively. Thus, my decision to restrict my discussion to the Judeo-Christian historical situation(s) is simply a function of the fact that I simply know more about it (or them). My restriction doesn't argue for its universality or particularity. Only this author's particularity.

Let us consider Genesis 1:1—5, where Yahweh is introduced as a *presenting* or *constituting* substance.

In the beginning God created the heaven and the earth.
And the earth was without form, and void; and darkness was upon the face of the deep. And the spirit of God moved upon the face of the waters.

And God said, Let there be light: and there was light. And God saw the light, that it was good; and God divided the light from the darkness.
And God called the light Day, and the darkness he called Night.
And the evening and the morning were the first day. (King James Version)

Whatever the author(s) may have meant in this passage, it is clear that a great deal of my discussion follows almost axiomatically from this cosmogony.

It is theologically problematic to claim that Yahweh "enters" anything. Yet in the Genesis story something is added that was previously absent. Yahweh is clearly a positive force, a force that sticks out (or in), protrudes, and enlightens. Yahweh is powerful. Yahweh is masculine. Yahweh is white.

There is obviously something problematic about engendering and racializing God. Although God "needs" neither skin nor penis, "He" certainly needs power. In fact, the orthodox interpretation is that he is potency (cf. Jones 1973). That the phallus is not necessarily a penis and that gender is not necessarily a function of genitalia (despite its etymological significance) enable us to deal with an obvious "Catch 22"; even if Yahweh had female genitals, "she" would still be a "he." And if God had black skin?

Yahweh is linked to the light. It doesn't help matters to retort here that this linkage is only symbolic, for our point is that gender, race, and power are symbolic realities as well. That one symbol can take on an identity relation with another in bad faith is conceded. That doesn't mean that the identity relation cannot be critically interpreted.

We now face a number of problems. We cannot question in the abstract, "Can men worship with enthusiasm?" This is because "men" has been revealed to be a complex, ambiguous concept. We must now ask, "Can whites worship with enthusiasm?" It is clear that white women are already constructed with a dual problematic situation in our analysis, for they are "men" into whom it is generally considered legitimate to enter. I say "generally" because there are complex rituals around legitimate entry of white women. In Christianity, for instance, the association of cleanliness with God's relation to Christ's mother has left a symbolic heritage of a master's/power's accessibility to all women and the relegation of some women to the trap of becoming sacred artifacts. They are the epitome of the object of violation. But note, it is generally legitimate to enter white women when their symbolic whiteness has been eliminated. A white woman "womanized" is symbolically an emasculated male. She is, at that point, "colored."

So we are left with the white man as our focus. How can such a figure receive God?

Perhaps we should discuss what is at stake if he is rendered incapable of receiving God. Let us consider the Christian notion of salvation. Salvation is more than the situation of being brought back to life by God. It is also the realization of both deserving to be in the Kingdom of God and being there. One needs first to commit an act of repentance. From the Sartrean standpoint, repentance is loaded with futility in a world in which, at least morally, losers win. Only the oppressed, it seems, can attain salvation. Each individual bourgeois cannot, for example, change the relationship between the bourgeoisie and the proletariat, yet he is nevertheless responsible for such a relationship. Should he choose to fight on behalf of social justice or working-class emancipation, his project appears bankrupt in virtue of the realization that revolution is not *for him*. The white faces a similar circumstance; in the end, there is the realization that racial justice is not for *whites*. And "men" and "women"? To be a black woman, it has been argued, is to be at the bottom of the racial/gender hierarchy. This means, argue some black women theologians, that they are the embodiment of Christ (see Grant 1989). To be a white man may ultimately mean, in this historical moment, to be theologically condemned.

The white man finds himself facing three possibilities, if he seeks salvation: (1) an identity relation with God, (2) recognition of an ambiguous human situation, or (3) rejection of the whole theological problematic. Sartre, as is well known, opts for the third, but he retains a great deal of religious baggage in his conception of what it means to be human: the desire to be God (cf. Boni 1982: 169–80). Sartre is thus in support of (3), but his philosophical conception of man stands firmly in (1). Since our focus is on religious salvation, (3) will not concern us except insofar as it relates to the Sartrean interpretation of (1).

If the white man opts for (1), he attempts not only to become God, but he also makes himself Man. The history of the white man as Man need not be spelled out here. Suffice it to say that it is, in the least, the history of antiblack racism. If the white man becomes God, then there is no need to let God "in." He, the white man interpreted as God, enters others. But the white man knows that he is not God. He knows this, from the Sartrean perspective, not only because he is in fact not God, but also because as a conscious being he is able to pose God as an object of his desire with which he is not identical. The argument is complex, but in brief form it is that in order to be conscious of an object, we must be able to "nihilate" the object. We must be able to put it at a distance from ourselves. Joseph S. Catalano summarizes Sartre's complex argument:

One of the most striking things about Sartre's notion of being is that he maintains that the principle of identity is synthetic. A is A; a tree is a tree. True, Sartre claims, but this identity is constituted by its relation to consciousness. Consciousness is consciousness. False, Sartre claims, for who or what could constitute its identity over time. Who or what could hold it in existence? God? Perhaps. If he existed; but, I believe that a proper Sartrian answer is that not even God could create a knowing being that would be a knowing being; it would always have to be at a distance from itself to be aware of itself. Without this lack of identity, knowledge would collapse into an in-itself of a mechanical force. (1990: 665–66)

To take the route of an identity relation to God is a form of self-deception. The white man may be white and hence powerful, and God may be powerful, but the white man is not God. Yet, if God is powerful, would not God then be white and therefore symbolically identical with the white man? If this is so, then how could a white man be deceiving himself if he declares himself God? Wouldn't he be recognizing the fact of whiteness as Fanon urged everyone to admit "the fact of blackness" (1967)? How can he be deceiving himself by recognizing the symbolic truth of himself?

We raise here an equivocation that pushes the white man into option (2), to stand before God in a way that enables him to recognize his incompleteness—that he is existentially nothing but socially situated as something. He is existential absence, but he is social presence. The antiblack world throws blacks/women into the non-realm of the existential. To bring God "in" therefore requires a recognition of his existential situation. His existential situation is that he cannot be saved as a white man.

If he cannot be saved as a white man, can he be saved as a human being? Here the problem takes on a different dimension. For the human being is an embodiment of presence-absence. If we interpret the body as presence, then we face the same stock of problems. The human body has to be regarded in different terms; it has to be capable of being entered—not in the sense of having a hole or being "possessed," but in the sense of being open in its embodiment. The human body has to be the embodiment of authentic living, of authentic "practice."

We are now compelled to reconsider some of our previous observations. Recall that it is a form of bad faith to deny one's embodiment. It is also a form of bad faith to deny one's transcendence. Consider also that bad faith is a chosen attitude; otherwise, we would not be responsible for our bad faith. If it is inauthentic to make oneself closed—because it is to live on the level of substantiation—and it is a form of inauthenticity to make oneself completely open (for the same reason), then the notion of the spirit of seriousness has to be revised (cf. Sartre 1992: 3–4). For the problem of inauthentic worship is raised—a problem that could not be raised if worship in-itself were inauthentic. But how could this be, since worshiping depends on the conception of the self as open—that is, as enthusiastic? We have already seen that, given the interpretations of masculinity and femininity, white and black, power and weakness, and presence and absence, the white male figure is mired in a situation of inauthentic worship. We have added that for him to be responsible for his situation requires the possibility of authentic worship. What would this be?

Inauthentic worship is the reduction of human reality to any one aspect of its mode of living. Thus not only is the presentation of the self as pure presence a form of bad faith; it is also a form of bad faith to present the self as pure absence. The striking conclusion, then, is that worship is inauthentic. But we seem to have come upon a paradox. We have argued that pure openness is an inhuman mode of being. If we were open without choices that constitute being open, then to be open to God would be a mode of being that is no different from water's being open to our plunging ourselves into it. A human mode of existence emerges where there is choice. Authentic worship must therefore be a form of presentation of one's responsibility for one's relation to the object of one's (presumed good) faith. One *lets* the spirit in.

Conclusion

The possibilities of male worship considered here are meant to raise some questions about religious practices that may have an impact on gender/race identity. They are not meant as any definitive statement on male religious ritual. What I hope the reader has begun to consider is the complexity of the problem of interpreting gender and racial roles in religious contexts. If the symbolic becomes ontological, then the array of rituals available may experience what Judith Butler describes as "trouble" (Butler 1990: preface). She uses the term in the Sartrean sense, where consciousness is "clogged" and lives itself as unfreedom. The body lives in many ways that betray such trouble. We see it in its posture, its motion, its intensity—flesh attempting to live on the level of an ideal that it is not. What the male subject, and particularly the white male subject, faces from this standpoint is the problematizing of his religious experience. Worship is for him, should he attempt to maintain his masculine identity in the process, a homoerotic ritual. He is a phallus who lets "in" a phallus. The psychoanalytical significance of this observation is obvious, but it is my hope that examination may follow beyond the realms of homophobia, misogyny, and racism. If the symbolic functions on a level that seems almost "ontological," it may be fruitful to consider the possibilities of a phenomenology of the worshiping body. I leave that for further study (see part 4 of Gordon 1995).

NOTES

I would like to thank Carrie Schaffer, Leonard Harris, Jacqueline Mariña, William McBride, Renée White, Patricia Huntington, Gary Schwartz, and Björn Krondorfer for their helpful criticisms and suggestions on previous versions of this paper. I would also like to thank the Women's Studies Program at Purdue University for providing me with a forum in which to present this paper during the Fall 1993 semester.

1. By "worship" I mean a practice or ritual the purpose of which is to encourage the presence of God or a similarly revered figure. I use the word "practice" in the spirit of John Rawls's instructive essay. He writes, "I use the word 'practice' throughout as a sort of technical term meaning any form of activity specified by a system of rules which defines offices, roles, moves, penalties, defenses, and so on, and which gives the activity its structure. As example one may think of games and rituals, trials and parliaments" (1980: 581).

2. The form of bad faith discussed in this text is the presentation of images in the mode of perceptions. Perceptions are effects; whereas images are presentations. One chooses or effects an image, whereas one suffers or is affected by a perception.

3. I leave aside here the metaphysical problem of what would constitute a world without objects. For wouldn't such a world be an object?

4. I leave aside here a discussion of mind-body dualism. Suffice it to say that from the standpoint of a Sartrean analysis, the dichotomy is between being situated and being unsituated. A corpse is a different kind of being from a body. For a phenomenological perspective, see Schrag 1969; for an analytical one, see chapter 3 in Nagel 1986.

5. This aspect of the body, the embodiment of meaning, is developed in the work of Merleau-Ponty (1962), especially part 1, chapter 6. Although most philosophers see great difference in the analyses of Merleau-Ponty and Sartre, it is the position of this author that at least on the level of the body as meaning, the difference may be a matter of emphasis; freedom, perspectivity, and meaning are different dimensions of the lived body.

6. A discussion of the phenomenological concept of constitution requires a separate study, but briefly the problem is whether consciousness encounters an object constituted as a meaningful object or constitutes the object as meaningful. One is a passive interpretation of consciousness and the other is active. Sartre takes up this problem in his classic polemic, *The Transcendence of the Ego* (1988). For an alternative discussion of the problem(s) of constitution, see Husserl's *Cartesian Meditations* (1960), especially the third and fourth meditations, and Solomon 1987, chapters 10, 13.

7. St. Augustine's efforts to clean up the dirty business of theodicy left behind by the Manichaeans took him into a serious quagmire here; see *City of God*, Book XIV:10–12. He argued that Adam and Eve sinned merely by desiring the fruit of knowledge. Our concern is with the "nature" of the sin. Since St. Augustine's argument depends on the *desire*-in-itself being sinful, we could categorize his position as a form of spirit of seriousness. Adam and Eve were caught in a "Catch-22": the problem of whether to obey or disobey God was a necessary condition for their freedom.

8. This is implicit in St. Augustine's argument, that Adam and Eve sinned by virtue of desiring the fruit of knowledge of good and evil. But his effort doesn't get rid of the existential problem. The serious man would formulate the problem thus: Where did such desire come from? Our point is that the desire is *ex post facto*. The problem—whether to eat of the fruit or not—prepared the ground for desire. Thus our case is stronger. The Fall was implicit in the problem of freedom posed by the injunction of not eating from the tree.

9. Leonard Harris, while reading a version of this chapter, has noted that this consideration works if and only if God is regarded, at least symbolically, as homo sapient. I here assume anthropomorphic imagery primarily because such is the symbolism of the Judeo-Christian heritage in which I am making these investigations.

REFERENCES

Saint Augustine. 1950. *The City of God.* Trans. Marcus Doas, with an Introduction by Thomas Merton. New York: Modern Library.
Bergoffen, Debra. 1992. "Casting Shadows: The Body in Descartes, Sartre, de

Beauvoir, and Lacan." *Bulletin de la Société Américaine de Philosophie de Langue Française* IV, nos. 2–3:232–43.

Boni, Sylvain. 1982. *The Self and Other in the Ontologies of Sartre and Buber.* Washington, D.C.: University Press of America.

Butler, Judith. 1990. *Gender Trouble: Feminism and the Subversion of Identity.* New York: Routledge.

Catalano, Joseph S. 1990. "Successfully Lying to Oneself: A Sartrian Perspective." *Philosophy and Phenomenological Research* L, no. 4 (June): 673–93.

Fanon, Frantz. 1967. *Black Skin, White Masks.* Trans. Charles Lamm Markmann. New York: Grove Press.

Freud, Sigmund. 1961. *Civilization and Its Discontents.* Trans. and ed. James Strachey. Standard Edition. New York: W. W. Norton.

Gordon, Lewis R. 1995. *Bad Faith and Antiblack Racism.* Atlantic Highlands, N.J.: Humanities Press.

Grant, Jacquelyn. 1989. *White Women's Christ and Black Women's Jesus.* Atlanta: Scholars Press.

Husserl, Edmund. 1960. *Cartesian Meditations: An Introduction to Phenomenology.* Trans. Dorion Cairns. Dordrecht, The Netherlands: Martinus Nijhoff.

Jones, William. 1973. *Is God a White Racist? A Preamble to Black Theology.* New York: Doubleday.

Merleau-Ponty, Maurice. 1962. *Phenomenology of Perception.* Trans. Colin Smith. Atlantic Highlands, N.J.: Humanities Press.

Nagel, Thomas. 1986. *The View from Nowhere.* New York: Oxford University Press.

Rawls, John. 1980. "Two Conceptions of Rules." In *Philosophy of Law.* 2d ed. Ed. Joel Feinberg and Hyman Gross. Belmont, Calif.: Wadsworth. Originally published in *Philosophical Review* 64 (1955): 3–13.

Sartre, Jean-Paul. 1948a. *Anti-Semite and Jew.* Trans. George Becker. New York: Schocken Books.

———. 1948b. *The Emotions: Outline of a Theory.* Trans. Bernard Frechtman. New York: Philosophical Library.

———. 1955. *No Exit and Three Other Plays.* New York: Vintage.

———. 1956. *Being and Nothingness: A Phenomenological Essay on Ontology.* Trans. and Intro. Hazel Barnes. New York: Washington Square Press.

———. 1988. *The Transcendence of the Ego: An Existentialist Theory of Consciousness.* Trans. and annotated with Intro. Forrest Williams and Robert Kirkpatrick. New York: Farrar, Straus and Giroux.

———. 1992. *Notebooks for an Ethics.* Trans. David Pellauer. Chicago: University of Chicago Press.

Schrag, Calvin. 1969. *Experience and Being: Prolegomena to a Future Ontology.* Evanston, Ill.: Northwestern University Press.

West, Cornel. 1993. *Race Matters.* Boston: Beacon Press.

Wilson, R. McL. 1967. "Mani and Manichaeism." In *The Encyclopedia of Philosophy,* vol. 5. Ed. Paul Edwards. New York: Macmillan.

The Masculinity of Jesus in Popular Religious Art

D A V I D   M O R G A N

Popular American piety from the second half of the nineteenth century to the first half of the twentieth explored different experiences of Jesus as a male ideal, constructing his ministry and life in
terms of his appeal to men. Some viewed Christ as a gentle, effeminate,
occasionally even homoerotic friend; others portrayed him as an ethe-
real, mystical ideal; and still others saw in him a rugged, violent revolutionary. Conceptions of what Jesus was like and how he might have
appeared constantly underwent redefinition and could even embrace the
same visual portrayal. In a recent study of popular response to the
imagery of Warner Sallman, I discerned a prominent tendency among
those who admired Sallman's work (largely women) to see in his pictures
of Jesus a visualization of a Christology of friendship; and among those
who disliked his images (primarily men and male clergy) a strong contempt for what they considered the imagery's effeminate and/or homosexual characteristics (cf. Morgan 1996). The latter often espoused what
I call a Christology of the sublime, a gendered theological discourse
which understands Jesus as unambiguously masculine and often best left
unvisualized. Each of these responses is an interpretation rooted in
American religious history and has made effective use of images to
promote its experience of Christian piety. This chapter will examine the

12.1. Warner Sallman, *Head of Christ*, 1940, oil on canvas. (By permission of Jessie C. Wilson Galleries, Anderson University).

visual conception of Jesus and the treatment of his masculinity by focusing on the reception of one image in particular, Warner Sallman's *Head of Christ* (1940; figure 12.1). I wish to demonstrate the ambiguities inherent in the appeal to images with regard to Christ's masculinity and to show how images have participated in popular theological discourse and piety.

Friendship with Jesus offers an intimacy and privacy that many Christians since the nineteenth century and the rise of Dwight Moody's gentler form of evangelism have found appealing (Butler 1991: 41–61). Informing any number of revivalist and evangelical hymns of the last century (e.g., "What a Friend We Have in Jesus," "Saviour, Like a Shepherd," and Ira Sankey's "I Am Praying for You") was the experience of Jesus as a tender savior, the comforting principle that mitigated the angry father deity of Calvinism and the older revivalism (see nos. 583, 589, 660 in Sankey, McGranaham, and Stebbins 1894). The experience of Jesus as friend could even include an intimacy that seems homoerotic. The popular hymn, "In the Garden," foregrounds a secret meeting between the soul and the "Son of God":

> I come to the garden alone
> While the dew is still on the roses;
> And the voice I hear,
> Falling on my ear;
> The Son of God discloses.
>
> And He walks with me,
> And He talks with me,
> And He tells me I am His own,
> And the joy we share as we tarry there,
> None other has ever known. (Rodeheaver 1939: 187)

In fact, the erotic character of certain instances of popular religious culture seems undeniable. In a book published in 1911, aptly titled *The Friendship of Jesus*, the dean of a Bible school in New York described the spirituality of friendship with Jesus as one of privacy and homoerotic intimacy. Speaking of his relationship with Jesus, Robert Wells Veach portrayed both Jesus and himself in terms of combined opposites, e.g., sweet and strong, brave and gentle, joined in a secluded quiet:

We walk and work together, for He is ever with me. Apart from His strong sweet spirit I can be neither brave nor gentle. Very often we seek a quiet place; it is a sacred tryst where love meets love with every passion purified. Again, in the wild rush of the busy world where He loves so much to meet with those who toil, we mark off a little circle and talk together. Friendship with Jesus is the true sanctuary of the spirit; here we touch God breast to breast and live anew in His love. (1911: 18)

12.2. Gustave Doré, *Jonathan and David*, engraving after painting, n.d. (From *Cobbin's Commentary on the Bible for Young and Old*, vol 1. (New York: Selmar Hess, 1876)).

In language that perhaps wishes to emulate the erotic mysticism of Teresa of Avila but comes closer to the fantasies of Emma Bovary, the author sought to portray friendship as erotic, but not sensual, as "love with every passion purified." But the image of touching God "breast to breast" does not seem entirely purged of the sensual.

Friendship with someone other than with Christ could be treated similarly. An engraving of the famous biblical friends, Jonathan and David, produced from a painting by Gustave Doré and used in the American publication of *Cobbin's Commentary on the Bible for Young and Old* (1876), is a case in point (figure 12.2). The story of the friendship began when David appeared before Saul, Jonathan's father, after killing Goliath. The smitten Jonathan, whose soul was immediately "knit to the soul of David [whom] he loved as his own soul[,] . . . stripped himself of the robe that was upon him, and gave it to David, and his armor, and even his sword and his bow and girdle" (1 Samuel 18:1, 4). The two "made a covenant" with one another on the basis of their love, which Jonathan consecrated by giving David his clothing. After it became clear to Saul that his son had allied himself with David, he publicly disgraced Jonathan with these words: "You son of a perverse, rebellious woman, do I not know that you have chosen the son of Jesse to your own shame, and to the shame of your mother's nakedness?" (1 Samuel 20:30). Jonathan then went to David's hiding place to warn his friend of Saul's wrath. Friendship inserts itself in the place of the angry father. The two friends "kissed one another, and wept with one another, until David recovered himself" (20:41). Doré pictured the two friends in a secluded garden-like space (not unlike the secret meeting of "In the Garden"), one friend comforting another with an intimate embrace (note Jonathan's hand beneath David's hair). One popular commentator wrote that Jonathan loved his friend "with the tenderness of a woman" (Pierson 1883: 453). The contrast between David's rustic clothing and Jonathan's finery, including the dagger at which their hands meet, recalls their first encounter, which the Reverend Cobbin's *Commentary* sought to explain as an attempt at making David, who had been dressed as a shepherd, "fit to appear among the people of [Saul's] court" (273).

Friendship with Jesus in nineteenth- and twentieth-century Protestant piety was likewise private, passionate, and situated within a quiet garden of picturesque beauty. In contrast to the Christology of the sublime,

12.3. Warner Sallman, *Christ Our Pilot*, 1950, oil on canvas. (By permission of Jessie C. Wilson Galleries, Anderson University).

which equated the masculinity of the Father with his lofty inaccessibility, the Christology of friendship, which so many find visualized in Sallman's imagery, provided access to the distant Father through the friendly Son. This is visualized in a number of pictures by Sallman, such as *Christ Our Pilot* (1950; figure 12.3) where a privileged relationship exists between older and younger males. Like the hymn it seems to illustrate ("Jesus, Savior, Pilot Me"), Sallman's picture envisions Christ piloting the faithful lad "over life's tempestuous sea." But Sallman made no reference to the maternal element in the hymn: "As a mother stills her child,/Thou canst hush the ocean wild;/Boistrous waves obey Thy will,/When Thou say'st to them, 'Be Still!' " (see no. 366, Sankey, McGranaham, and Stebbins 1894.) Instead, Sallman's picture stresses the masculine character of the relation: a male bonding between the monumental Jesus and the tight-shirted young sailor. Sallman and his appreciative public were probably concerned to find in this and other images talismans which addressed the problem of securing adolescent males within the community of faith by conducting them through crucial rites of passage. The task for the image to perform as a gift to a young man consisted of visualizing his proper relationship with God and to serve as a marker in the passage from youth to young adulthood. The image commemorated and therefore preserved the relationship between the gift giver and the young male, despite the transit from a lower age and social status to a superior one. In such images as *Christ Our Pilot,* Jesus befriends boys and young men in order to guide them or to teach them about his Father. Sallman never portrayed God the Father in his images, but consistently stressed the benevolent Son, everyone's Friend. The Christology of friendship represented Jesus as the focal point of a devotion that understood the believer's relationship to the distant or invisible Father as mediated through the intercessory Son. In effect, the friendship of Jesus and his visualization in Sallman's devotional images have accomplished for many Protestants what the Virgin and her votive images (as well as those of other saints, male and female) have done for Roman Catholics in America: mitigate the wrath of God and ensure the benevolent presence of God in one's daily life. Although Protestants have insisted on representing this intercessory relationship in the singular, male figure of Jesus, his softened, gentle, quiet features in many images— so offensive to those who insist on his masculinity—is likely an attempt to imbue a Protestant Savior with maternal, feminine characteristics regarded as suitable for a benevolent intercessor. When the categories of male and female are blurred, homophobic viewers associate the image with gay sexuality.

In fact, the *Head of Christ* has evoked a stark divergence of response. The same face has inspired diametrically opposed reactions among viewers. One writer, for instance, responded to a query about the image with a story told to him by a local clergyman who claimed that the image could not be placed in the church building because it was "too much of a come-on for the homos in the parish and the community." [1] By contrast, a tradition of reception among conservative Christians has seen the *Head of Christ* as a distinctly "manly" portrayal of Jesus. In 1943, the Methodist preacher T. Otto Nall quoted Sallman as stating his intention thus: "I wanted to make my crayons picture a virile Christ for these rough days" (1943: 6). Another writer speculated in the same year, when the image had already been distributed to millions of American G.I.s, that the picture had gained widespread acceptance because all of Sallman's depictions of Christ

are uniform in one respect—in emphasizing the "humanness" of the character.

As a Sallman devotee once said, "He makes Christ a He-Man—not soft and effeminate."

This factor, above all others, has contributed to the success of his work. (Baylor 1943: 26)

Here, the very humanness of Christ is identified as his virility. T. Otto Nall observed that

all types of people, many of them not professing Christians, have been attracted by the high brow, searching eyes, firm lips, forceful chin of the Sallman head. There is something in all of us that seeks out its strong manliness. (Nall 1943: 6)

The notion of an instinctive response to the manly authority of Jesus was formulated for a popular audience in a bestselling book of 1924, Bruce Barton's *The Man Nobody Knows*. Barton's book, in turn, reflected what had become in the first two decades of the twentieth century a concern among Protestant men to masculinize Christianity by reclaiming it from the undue influence of women during the Victorian age (cf. Douglas 1977; DeBerg 1990: 75–98; Bederman 1989: 432–65). Sallman recalled in the early 1940s, after the early success of the *Head of Christ*, that he had received initial encouragement for his vocation as a Christian artist and for his future project of depicting Jesus from a faculty member of Moody Bible Institute, E. O. Sellers. In a forthcoming biography of Sallman, Jack R. Lundbom dates the conversation with Sellers to 1914.[2] But the date remains unspecified in the frequently published and variant accounts which appeared from 1943 on (cf. Ellis 1944: 5–6; Nall 1943: 7). The fullest version was published in 1947 by a friend of Sallman's:

One Saturday afternoon [Sallman] was called into the dean's office where the conversation went something like this:

"I understand that you're an artist, Sallman, and I'm interested in knowing why you are attending the institute."

"Well, I'm here because I wanted to increase my knowledge of the Scriptures. I want to be an illustrator of biblical subjects."

"Fine! There is great need for Christian artists. Sometime I hope you give us your conception of Christ. And I hope it's a manly one. Most of our pictures today are too effeminate."

"You mean to say you think Jesus was a more rugged type? More of a man's man?"

"Yes, according to the way I read my Bible. We know he walked great distances and slept out under the stars; he was rugged and strong. He preached in the desert, so He must have been tanned. More than that, the Word says he set his face 'like a flint' to go down to Jerusalem, so he wasn't soft or flabby. We need a picture of that kind of Christ, Sallman, and I hope you will do it some day." (Peterson 1947: 11)[3]

Another version of the story added that Jesus was "the Man who drove the moneychangers from the Temple, and faced Calvary unafraid and triumphant" (Bevis 1965: 5).[4] The account suggests that Sallman's destiny was to respond to the need for an authentic depiction of Jesus who had suffered emasculation at the hands of artists. Although Sallman and those writing his story remember his conversation with Sellers as antedating the 1924 charcoal, and therefore serving as its warrant, the account resembles a treatment of Jesus that appeared in the same year in *The Man Nobody Knows*. Barton faulted artists for perverse, misleading images of the savior, whom Barton portrayed as the executive authority, magisterial salesman, accomplished advertiser, and manly personality par excellence. Barton saw in the founder of Christianity the charter for the modern American businessman. Barton's was a virile Christ who was meant to contrast markedly with the feminization of Jesus and Christian life. Although Barton did not begrudge Mary her importance, he saw a telling symptom in her fame and the long disregard for Joseph:

with the glorification of Mary, there has been an almost complete neglect of Joseph. The same theology which has painted the son as soft and gentle to the point of weakness, has exalted the feminine influence in its worship, and denied any large place to the masculine. (1925: 40–41)

Barton objected to what he considered the typical representation of Jesus as a delicate "lamb of God":

A physical weakling! Where did they get that idea? Jesus pushed a plane and swung an adze; he was a successful carpenter. He slept out doors and spent his days walking around his favorite lake. His muscles were so strong that when he drove the money-changers out, nobody dared to oppose him! (n.p.)

Barton repeatedly complained of the inadequacy of artistic depictions of Christ. Almost all painters, he stated, "have misled us" on the appearance of Jesus. "They have shown us a frail man, under-muscled, with a soft face—a woman's face covered by a beard—and a benign but baffled look" (42–43). Barton identified a problem which Sallman, whether he was familiar with Barton's book or not, came to consider his mission as a Christian artist to solve. The account of his conversation with Sellers at Moody served as warrant and call.[5]

Ironically, the popular discourse on the virility of Christ was eventually turned against Sallman's picture. While many have considered the virility of Sallman's Christ to be the measure of its authenticity, others have found the image unacceptably effeminate, what one Lutheran seminary professor, echoing Barton, denounced as "a pretty picture of a woman with a curling beard who has just come from the beauty parlor with a Halo shampoo . . . [not] the Lord who died and rose again!" (Roth 1958: 9). How shall we account for this dramatic change in Jesus—from He-Man to crossdresser? Historical analysis of the reception of Sallman's image during the 1940s and 1950s should compare the positive and negative responses to the picture with the conflicting conceptions of Jesus Christ as the historical figure and personal savior of evangelical Christianity. Disagreement centered on the masculinity of Jesus and indeed, in some instances, even his gender was called into question. On the other hand, many Christians embraced it because their personal savior, while necessarily masculine, was nevertheless a Jesus befriended in the personal relationship, indeed, in the private walk "in the garden" of one's faith-life, where "He walks with me, and He talks with me, and He tells me I am his own." The hardiness and virility which many have claimed to see in Sallman's Christ may be a psychological construction necessary to allow for a feminine, nurturing relationship with Jesus which conceives of salvation not in the angry terms of Calvinist atonement, but as the persistent and faithful love of a friend. This God offers guidance and friendship, not judgment and retribution as the motive for belief.[6] The principal appeal of this Jesus was consolation in an untrustworthy and brutal world, as the words by E. G. Taylor in a popular hymn by the evangelical composer George Stebbins suggest: "Closer yet, O Lord, my Rock, Refuge of My Soul;/Dread I not the tempest-shock, Tho' the billows roll./Wildest storm cannot alarm, For to me, can come no harm, Leaning on Thy loving arm;/Closer, Lord, to Thee" (see no. 277 in Sankey, McGranaham, and Stebbins 1894).

While some might define masculinity in terms of paternal gentleness and consider the determined look of the *Head of Christ* to signify the figure's divinity, most admirers of Sallman's picture seem to view it through an ideological filter which predisposes them to see what they want to see. Consider a 1948 article in *Christian Life* entitled "Did Christ Look Like This?" The author illustrated the article with Sallman's *Head of Christ* and a head of Jesus by Heinrich Hofmann (figure 12.4) that was often excerpted from Hofmann's larger painting, *Jesus and the Rich Young Man* (1889). "Hoffman [sic]," she wrote, "in another day portrayed Christ as an appealing, almost feminine character. In contrast, Warner Sallman, a contemporary, has drawn from the scripture 'He set his face like a flint to go down to Jerusalem' a firm, more masculine figure" (Lindberg 1948: 19). While it is true that use of Hofmann's image belonged to an earlier generation in the material culture of American piety, it is difficult to see the difference which this author discerns.[7] But she wrote within twentieth-century conservative Protestantism's discourse on Christ's virility, which derived from the earlier fundamentalist concern to secure Christianity from the dominance of women (cf. Bederman 1989). In this preoccupation with virility, visual evidence could take secondary importance. The article in *Christian Life* blissfully ignored the appearance of both pictures, indeed, their striking likeness to one another, because of the need to posit an other, a feminine opposite required to define the masculine. Since the visual evidence was lacking, the discourse moved to provide the appropriate polarity. The image conformed to its description rather than the reverse. The discourse about virility appropriates images to itself, assimilates them such that one sees what

12.4. Heinrich Hofmann, *Head of Christ*, detail from *Christ and the Rich Young Man*, 1889, oil on canvas. (By permission of Riverside Church, New York).

one is told to see, what is ideologically significant. Although the discourse may claim that its representation of reality is unadulterated, even authorized by divine revelation as in the case of a late night dream which Sallman reported was the source of his image, [8] such representation is of course ideologically engaged. Indeed, one wonders whether popular religious art is not generally premised on a discursive vision which precedes it and predisposes its reception. If this is true, then the likeness of Christ—his femininity or his masculinity—is defined discursively. Likeness as physical resemblance amounts to seeing what one presumes should be there. In other words, people believe an image looks like Jesus because they conform the image's features to their expectations about Jesus. Such popular religious art as Sallman's is received as reinforcing what people *already* believe, telling them what they *already* know. That is why they recognize the image, why it seems so like Jesus. [9]

In the end, believers see what they are taught to see and scorn what they are taught to fear. The map of a human world is drawn over a topography of need and fear. Within this ever shifting, constantly reconnoitered terrain, the body and its genders are politically contested and the identity of Jesus is as unstable as the history of the search for his identity. Those who embrace Sallman's images of Jesus attempt to naturalize the discourse that informs their fears and needs. The devout seek in his depictions an image of what they wish the world to be. The function of the devotional image for many Protestants is to resist change, to fix the protean character of experience by merging map and territory. But the attempt to privilege one code by inscribing it over the surface of experience is doomed to erasure. To shift metaphors, the attempt to secure an anchor against the storms that rage without is forever compromised by ambivalence within: believers need more than one Jesus and have found him, uneasily, in the same image, Warner Sallman's *Head of Christ.*

NOTES

1. Letter 331 of 531 letters received by the author from readers of popular religious magazines in which an ad was placed soliciting response concerning the role Sallman's images have played in devotional life. All the letters are now on file in the Sallman archives, Anderson University, Anderson, Indiana.

2. Jack R. Lundbom, *Masterpainter: Warner E. Sallman,* typescript, 26. The

biographical note on the back cover of *Religious Masterpieces,* published by Kriebel and Bates in 1956, states that Sallman attended Moody from 1912 to 1917. Bates material, Sallman archives, Anderson University.

3. Ernest O. Sellers was at Moody from 1908 to 1918, where he served first as an assistant in the Music Department and then, from 1913 until 1918, as director of Night Classes, and taught courses in pedagogy, child study, and Sunday School classes during the day (see George H. Crutcher's Introduction to Sellers's *Personal Evangelism* [1923]: vi-vii). Although Sellers was never dean, his position of director of Night Classes and the fact that he left Moody in 1918 to serve as a member of the Speaker's Bureau of the Y.M.C.A. in Europe dates his conversation with Sallman (who had enrolled in a Saturday evening Bible class—see Lundbom, *Masterpainter,* 26) to the war years.

4. Depictions of the violent Jesus cleansing the temple are as common in Sunday School illustration as they were in the academic religious art of the nineteenth century which inspired so much devotional and instructional imagery in the twentieth century. Heinrich Hofmann produced a drawing of the scene, see *The Hofmann Gallery of Original New Testament Illustrations* (Philadelphia: A. J. Holman & Co., 1891); Julius Schnorr von Carolsfeld also produced a well-known version of the theme in *Die Bibel in Bildern* (Leipzig: Georg Wigland Verlag, 187?).

5. I do not wish to overemphasize the similarity between the Sallman account and Barton's book or to argue for a direct influence. Barton's low Christology was certainly not acceptable to Sallman or evangelicals. Barton offered a psychological account of Christ's life, one that was meant to appeal to its readership by describing the motives and instincts that drive all "manly men." Christ's miracles were explained by the force of his magnetic personality, not as the supernatural events that Sallman and most conservative Christians would have insisted they were.

6. Sallman rarely depicted a crucified Christ and his audience did not want him to do so. When asked by a colleague while producing Sunday bulletin covers for the Methodist Publishing House in the 1930s, whether he had ever considered portraying Christ as the terrible judge of the Apocalypse as described in the first chapter of the Book of Revelation, Sallman is said to have replied: "there would be no appeal for such a version." See letter 8, Sallman archives, Anderson University.

7. Hofmann (1824–1911), a teacher at Dresden's important academy of art, produced *Jesus and the Rich Young Man* in 1889. Reproductions of the face of Jesus from this image circulated widely in the United States, appearing on all manner of devotional items in religious supply house catalogs. It is no exaggeration to say that Hofmann's image of Jesus represented Jesus from 1900 to World War II, when Sallman's image largely replaced it in popularity. Yet many Christians are still familiar with Hofmann's *Head of Christ.*

8. There are numerous versions of the dream and its inspiration. For a discussion of them, see Morgan (1996).

9. This is not to suggest that "high art" is free of discourse, but that its function may be more one of generating, extending or even negating rather than corroborating existing discourse. Yet Tom Wolfe's satirical *The Painted Word* (1975: 62 *et passim*) argues that mid-century American avant-garde art followed from critical discourse rather than vice-versa.

REFERENCES

Barton, Bruce. 1925. *The Man Nobody Knows*. Indianapolis: Bobbs-Merill.
Baylor, Bruce. 1943. "A Man's Artist." *Sunday School Promoter* 5/2 (May): 24–29.
Bederman, Gail. 1989. "The Women Have Had Charge of the Church Work Long Enough: The Men and Religion Forward Movement of 1911–1912 and the Masculinization of Middle-Class Protestantism." *American Quarterly* 41:432–65.
Bevis, Katharine. 1965. "He Painted a Religious Masterpiece." *Sunday School Messenger*, March 21, 5.
Butler, Jonathan M. 1991. *Softly and Tenderly Jesus Is Calling: Heaven and Hell in American Revivalism, 1870–1920*. New York: Carlson Publishing.
Cobbin, Ingram, Rev. 1876. *Cobbin's Commentary of the Bible for Young and Old*. Ed. E. J. Goodspeed. Vol. 1. New York: Selmar Hess.
DeBerg, Betty. 1990. *Ungodly Women: Gender and the First Wave of American Fundamentalism*. Minneapolis: Fortress Press.
Douglas, Ann. 1977. *The Feminization of American Culture*. New York: Knopf.
Ellis, Howard. 1944. *Story of Sallman's "Head of Christ"*. Indianapolis: Kriebel and Bates.
Lindberg, Beth. 1948. "Did Christ Look Like This?" *Christian Life*, December, 19.
Morgan, David. 1996. " 'Would Jesus Have Sat for a Portrait?': The Likeness of Christ in the Popular Reception of Sallman's Art." In *Icons of American Protestantism: The Art of Warner Sallman*, ed. David Morgan. New Haven: Yale University Press.
Nall, T. Otto. 1943. "He Preaches as He Paints." *Classmate* 50 (December): 6–7.
Peterson, Sylvia E. 1947. "The Ministry of Christian Art." *The Lutheran Companion* 55/14 (April 2): 10–12.
Pierson, A. T., Rev. 1883. "Saul-David-Jonathan." In *Half Hours with the Lessons of 1883*. Philadelphia: Presbyterian Board of Publication.
Rodeheaver, Homer, et al., eds. 1939. "In the Garden." In *Christian Service Songs*. Winona Lake, Ind.: Rodeheaver, Hall-Mack.
Roth, Robert Paul. 1958. "Christ and the Muses." *Christianity Today* 2/11 (March): 8–9.

Sankey, Ira D., James McGranaham, and George C. Stebbins. 1894. *Gospel Hymns*. Chicago: The Biglow & Main Co.

Sellers, E. O. 1923. *Personal Evangelism: Studies in Individual Efforts to Lead Souls into Right Relations to Christ*. New York: George H. Doran Co.

Veach, Robert Wells. 1911. *The Friendship of Jesus*. New York: Fleming H. Revell Co.

Wolfe, Tom. 1975. *The Painted Word*. New York: Farrar, Straus and Giroux.

THIRTEEN

Baring the Flesh: Aspects of Contemporary Male Iconography

WILLIAM G. DOTY

Why . . . has there been an extraordinary amount of work on "the body" in recent years? In one sense, it is logical that the body, once thought to be the metonym of nature, would follow upon the deconstruction of gender and sexuality, thereby removing another foundational concept. In another sense, however, "bodyology" parallels the complex obsession with the body in late capitalist societies, the anorexic/bulimic object that engages, at one and the same time, in a feeding frenzy and a relentless thinning, fasting, tightening, and sculpting. And from still another perspective, this fascination with the body coincides with the moment of its disappearance—the dying AIDS body most dramatically, but also the death of a "natural body," replaced by cosmetic and sex-change surgery, genetic engineering, scientifically produced wombs, and other "organs without bodies."   —Domna C. Stanton,
Discourses of Sexuality

In a heavily draped society [as in the late nineteenth century], even a partial disrobing was an act of self-disclosure.
—E. Anthony Rotundo,
American Manhood

The contemporary Western personality itself is preponderantly a visible self, its identity embodied in external performance. . . . [T]he self tends to be construed as a purely sensual phenomenon.
—Kenneth R. Dutton,
The Perfectible Body

One of the major elements . . . that needs work [done] on it, is the role of iconography of dress and setting, and especially performers, the male types that are used, porn stars' images and so on, all drenched in ideological meanings.   —Richard Dyer,
Now You See It

Ecological theorist Leslie White observes that the earliest scientists looked as far away from human experience as one might look, namely at the stars. However "eventually, as researchers learned more about things at a distance, and as the social sciences matured, scholarship turned to studies ever closer to the self and the essentials of human experience" (quoted in Burroughs and Ehrenreich 1993: 2). Among the attention to those "essentials," we may now note the recent proliferation of writings on the human body, and indeed several volumes on women's bodies have already appeared. Kenneth R. Dutton studies "the perfectible [male] body" in terms of what he calls "human social anatomy" (1994: 13).

Hence my attention to the male body has a context, as in Terence Turner's reference to the body as a social text: "the surface of the body, as the common frontier of society, the social self, and the psychobiological individual, becomes the symbolic stage upon which the drama of socialization is enacted, and bodily adornment (in all its culturally multifarious forms, from bodypainting to clothing and from feather headdresses to cosmetics) becomes the language through which it is expressed" (cited in Burroughs and Ehrenreich 1993: 15). Such a text becomes one that represents a particular social coding of the reaches of identity: "the presentation of the body in a particular and recognizable shape or pattern (whether of body decoration or of its sub-species, clothing) represents a kind of code, which is meant to be read and understood as an answer to the question: Who am I?" (Dutton 1994: 15). Indeed we may speak with Leo Bersani, in *The Freudian Body* (1986: 85), of "the mythologizing of the human" as an aspect of the social enforcement of ideal norms of citizen selfhood. In another publication Bersani notes the power of the media " 'to manufacture subjectivity itself,' and in so doing to dictate the shape of an identity. The 'general public' is at once an ideological construct and a moral prescription" (Bersani 1987: 19).[1]

This chapter explores some possible religio-mythical meanings of the many bare social bodies/texts that confront us in public media today. Following a quick overview indicating the scope and the restrictions under which I operate, I direct some remarks to the importance of learning to analyze more public, popular, iconography than is usual in academic disciplines (here I am in particular indebted to the methods of the New Historians[2] as well as to David Freedberg's *The Power of Images* 1989). Then I present a sort of catalogue of the contemporary male body, and the ways that body is idealized and normalized by a tyrannical model that is essentially anti-natural. Subsequently, I turn to the post-patriarchal situation in which men, no longer women, are the object of the "gaze," before certain religious elements are engaged.

While I have no firm answers, I'm curious about the implications of my observations: do they reflect a more positive or a more negative regard for the human body? Do they not substantiate widespread rejection of concepts of a transcendental/divine, in contrast with the human-bodily? To what extent is masculinity a function of social facts such as these iconographic issues? Is the new nudity an eschatological nudity, a stripping away of a patriarchal layer of the culture and returning to some pre-enculturated level, or a discovery of some significance inherent in the physical male body that Western culture has heretofore found only in women's bodies? (But of course teaching Humanities again, I keep returning to the idealized Greek *kouroi,* and so find that "what goes around, comes around" for yet another cycle.)

The Body as Social Text

As an important social text, the representation of the human body, specifically here the extent of its coverage or baring, will reflect underlying cultural values, including religious shapings of deities' models for humankind.[3] In such a context, the "baring" of the male body today cannot but impress any attentive cultural critic. What I call *gratuitous nudity,* because unmotivated by the needs of simple transfer of information about a product, surrounds us not just in men's publications, but across the range of the public languages of magazines and advertising (see figure 13.1).

13.1. "Gratuitous Nudity." (By permission of Gianni Versace, Milano. The photographer is Bruce Weber and the model is Jeff Munroe.)

Some examples: both the *New York Times* and *Details* (a new magazine aimed at style- and status-conscious young men) reviewed 1993
mens' fashion shows, wherein several models wore no shirts, just vests
or sweater vests, open down to the navel, well-developed pectorals
bursting forth. Twenty-nine pages of one issue of *Details* (June 1993,
165 pages in all) featured at-least-partly-nude young men, out of 132
pages that had illustrations—that's one in every four pages! And in a
feature on Parisian-style men's clothing, of six scenes where the male's
trousers were visible, five portrayed them unzipped, noticeably baring
the crotch area.[4] Elsewhere, the relationship of the partly-clothed male
icon in an advertisement, and a product, is often obscure, although the
partial nudity may add a sensuous quality, as in Energizer's advertising a
hard, cold flashlight battery by staging a muscular, mostly-nude African
American male hefting an (exaggerated mock) battery over his head.

Representations of the male in advertising and clothing magazines,
and more recently in the spate of men's exercise journals, seem to have
been selected less on the basis of consumer awareness or logic than of
feelings: these are almost-religious claims rather than appeals on the
basis of modern science. It is hard not to feel confronted by something
numinous when facing a recent Obsession cologne ad that consists of a
candid photograph of a male body, nude from just above the penis to
just below the chin, adorned only with the brand name and the words
"FOR MEN FOR THE BODY." Or staring back at the three members
of a rock band on the cover of an issue of *Rolling Stone*, totally unclothed, but with their hands decorously cupped over their non-musical
instruments, and the name of the group running—hardly accidentally—
in a banner just below their crotches: *Red Hot Chili Peppers.* Or when
confronted by musician Bobby Brown, in an advertisement for his al-
bum, *It's the Next Step,* his muscular bare back turned toward us,
framed by an outfit of black leather that apparently has sleeves and a
strip across the yoke to form a neck, that's all.

The extent of representations of the partly- or nearly-nude body, flesh
bared to the point that it shouts out an intrusive subtext to the product
or topic being illustrated, is striking. Surely advertisers and illustrators
are not just following a fad. Rather, such trends in body representation
may signify deep cultural change.[5] The discussion of "partial" texts/
bodies in this instance is paralleled in the texture of this paper—I raise

a number of issues that cannot be treated extensively, just as I ask many questions that cannot yet (if at all) be answered.

That there is a previously unsurpassed amount of male nudity in popular culture is evident from many such advertisements and from Peter Watrous's *New York Times* observations (1991) about male semi-nudity in MTV. It is amazing, actually, how we've naturalized such bareness, as in the living-room atmosphere of a Jockey underwear ad with six down-home, smiling men from various professions wearing absolutely nothing but undershorts, or the ads with the smirking boy model (Marky Mark) who queries, "Do you have Calvin Klein under-wear on?"—found not only in newspapers and in magazines, but stretched along the entire side of city bus placards. I could multiply examples—students and colleagues bring them to me all the time—but let me note another aspect of this male flesh now being bared all around us: the exercise magazines and several of the men's clothing companies must have very clever photographers, to get catalogue shots of so very much of the male physique without quite showing the genitals—al-though the outlines are often quite distinct (see figure 13.2).

For example, the International Male clothes company based in San Diego has a range of thongs—swimwear or underwear with nothing but a string or a strip of cloth forming the t-back—or exercise unitards whose side hiplines come up about as high as a man's navel. The most revealing type that isn't utterly transparent comes in either a jockstrap or a unitard that has straps from the bottom of the crotch pouch up around the butt to the waistline, the rear is reduced to a thong, the front to a strip of fabric that just covers the vitals, then gaps before the straps that go around to the thong in back. Holly Brubach observes that in the International Male catalogue, "anonymous male genitalia are shown about to burst from mesh thongs, from string bikinis, from black lace briefs, from red jockstraps. . . . Bikinis gathered into a seam at the center back exaggerate the buttocks' cleavage" (1993: 68).

I want here to explore some of the significance of these yards of exposed masculine skin and muscle, and to examine historical argu-ments, such as those of Leo Steinberg in his influential book *The Sexual-ity of Christ in Renaissance Art and in Modern Oblivion* (1983). Perhaps rather irreverently, I bring alongside analysis of popular culture materi-als, such as the photographs of totally nude Sly Stallone in *Vanity Fair* (November 1993), Peter Watrous's attention (1991) to the hard body

Photo: David Morgan

13.2. "Bursting from Thongs." (Greg Sovell and Mike Tawill, of Basic Resources, Inc., 2(x)ist Industries, Inc., New York City, were extremely cooperative in providing this illustration; the photographer is David Morgan.)

gym-culture of the 1980s, and the wide expanses of male flesh in soap operas and MTV, and Suzanna Andrews's article that notes that while women can now be represented in the nude in films, "when a man is uncovered . . . the reaction is that he is extremely *vulnerable*" (1992: 13, my emphasis). "On film, audiences have come to accept seeing women naked. They have also come to accept dreadful scenes of throats being cut, faces bashed in and bodies blown to pieces [whereas in] a movie culture in which almost everything else is shown, male nudity is still too scary" (14). The obscene has come to be equated, for all practical purposes, not with anti-human violence, but with the male genitals (Davis 1991: 7).

Pop Culture/Representations

In a collection entitled *Men, Masculinity, and the Media* (Craig 1992), Fred J. Fejes's review of empirical studies of mass communication research indicates that "in media studies, the topic of masculinity is only at the very earliest stages of emerging as a research area in its own right" (Fejes 1992: 9). It is clear, however, that most of the time men are still represented in very traditional patriarchal roles (12).[6] Similar research status has to be ascribed to practical semiotics and pragmatic iconography as well, and there have been a number of methodological advances in the work of art theorists as well as media analysts (cf. Schor's schematic and inclusive survey, 1988) that have interpretive promise. While I cannot develop here a comprehensive overview, I will indicate some of the aspects of this new scholarship that I rely upon in my analysis.

Clearly *images matter,* a picture being worth a thousand words, and so forth, and an idealized figure such as the muscular, well-developed body, as Dutton notes (1994: 191) "is as much a cultural and imaginative construct as it is a physical object." But against the significance of the pictured or iconographic comes the whole logocentric bias of our millenium, if we think of the iconoclastic fervor that was reflected in the great Christian schism between East and West around 1000 C.E., or reaching back yet another millenium, if one wants to date it from Aristotelian and anti-Platonic denigration of the incorporeal or spiritual as opposed to the material.[7] The person-on-the-street belief is that images are secondary, temporary, and one seldom responds to them directly. But against such an assumption, Freedberg's *The Power of Images* (1989) argues that if images were so meaningless, so un-affecting, pornography laws would be laughable, the iconoclastic controversy would never have happened, no nation would prosecute those who deface such public emblems as flags or currencies, and the comicbook industry and *Mad* magazine would go out of business overnight.

Nor can the issue be self-conscious versus unconscious attention: "just because some people pay no attention to images, walk straight past them, or are generally indifferent to them does not relieve us of the burden of harking to those who do: it was a fine thing if the analysis of response proceeded only from the states of mind of those who concentrate!" (107; Freedberg's subjective grammar). Hence we have to deal with what Mauss and Durkheim referred to as social rather than experimental facts: "we need not test whether images are exactly as efficacious as they are said or seen to be: *it is enough that they are believed or proven to work in their particular circumstances*" (280, Freedberg's emphasis).

At the same time, we need to remain aware of the historical setting: our cultural eyes see nudity differently after years of exposure to *Honcho* or *Hustler*. Manet's *Olympia* of 1863 is a different culture-fact for us than for its original viewing audience, which saw it as insufficiently respectful of Georgionni's or Titian's splayed-out, idealized, nude women. Contemporary viewers' "views" are differently oriented than were those a century ago: we are not particularly upset by the Calvin Klein ads in which young couples pull at the unbuttoned waists of their partners' jeans, but many people are upset by Robert Mapplethorpe's extremely phallic and often homoerotic images (doubtless the same people who have slept any number of nights under his elegant photographs of flowers that are replicated frequently in hotel rooms).

The clinical term for cloaking the effect upon us of artworks is *repression;* repression may become suppression when the subject encodes cultural taboos, such as male nudity traditionally has been in Christendom. How else did *National Geographic* fund its first decades than by providing the first fully sanctioned popular images of nudity, always, of course nudity in cultures other than those inhabiting the white middle-class American living room, and hardly ever frontal males? What was it about Mapplethorpe's photographs that aroused so much enmity in the 1990s if not his representations of male nudes, often erotically titillating male nudes?[8] Arousing, tickling (titillate is from the Latin for tickling, or "to excite [another] pleasurably, superficially or erotically"—*American Heritage Dictionary,* 3rd ed.), or stimulation to action. Not only to sexual action, be it noted, but morally, to war (see the strong propaganda images in Sam Keen's *Faces of the Enemy,* 1986), or to follow causes (the several collections of photographs by children in South American slums that invite the viewer to contribute financially to the children's welfare), or to make long journeys (in order to experience firsthand the healing properties of a particular spring or religious icon), and so forth.

Freedberg's genius is to deconstruct how we are accustomed to treating women, primitives, and other declasse categories as inferior because they treat images differently: how many times have we heard the old chestnut about how "a primitive" thought the camera would steal her or his soul? [9] Yet surely we ought to refer to a certain affective primitivism in what happens in a successful Nike Air ad, or a Calvin Klein perfume ad, or an advertisement for Request jeans. Marketing psychologists assure us that viewers believe that we will achieve the qualities modeled in the ad, or at least that some aspect of the model will become ours when we make the purchase of the imaged object.

John Berger's *Ways of Seeing* (1972), the cover text of which begins "Seeing comes before words," remains a crucial cultural text disclosing how the lure of the glamor advertisement works by selling us a future, perfected image of ourselves, assuming that we buy the product represented. Freedberg also notes how one fuses with the represented image: "When we see the resembling image, we elide it with the living prototype it represents, unless . . . aesthetic differentiation by way of attention and abstraction supravenes" (1989: 276)—he is referring to a very different set of icons, but his point transfers easily. "Fusion precedes analytic suspension" (277), which is one reason students who have been exposed to Berger's *Ways of Seeing* develop critical attitudes toward the surrounding culture that make them feel superior to their still-fused peers. I would say they become more effectively perceptive citizens, as well, and I consider semiotic-iconographic education at least as important as conveying which emperor or pope succeeded another in Western political or religious history. In this particular context, Dutton is correct in stating that "the de-coding of the muscular male body is one of the more problematic issues in the analysis of contemporary imagery, whether serious or popular" (1994: 337).

In short, *there is more going on in the recent public baring of male flesh than a resolutely logocentric culture might recognize* (see figure 13.3). "We" (the everyday public the advertiser can depend upon to see

13.3. "The Available Male Body." (Greg Sovell and Mike Tawill, of Basic Resources, Inc., 2(x)ist Industries, Inc., New York City, were extremely cooperative in providing this illustration; the photographer is David Morgan.)

the images) will not admit readily to having erotic responses to the bared male flesh even when we do—which is one reason why so much of what we are addressing can seem gay-oriented, while at the same time a straight, ordinary Joe can say that he's just getting off on the muscula-ture, the clothing, the styles, or whatever "safe" category comes to mind. Brian Pronger (1990) describes ways the male body is played up in advertising, and how aspects of gay life are attractive to straights. Simi-larly, Michael Moon and Eve Kosofsky Sedgwick (1990: 28) comment acerbically on gay male figures in cinema who model themselves for the straight male. Repeatedly one hears, "But not in the [presumably asex-ual] way I look at it"; but similar disaffirmations greeted Steinberg's *Sexuality of Christ* (1983; see Freedberg 1989: 13, 17). The usual as-sumption is that surely "religious art," at least, must be asexual.

New Historical and other recent critical approaches ask post-Freud-ian questions about derivation and the originary: for instance, is there a direct connection between the brain, perceiving or looking at porn, and erotic or sensual impulses? Why is it that sometimes a certain image or a certain passage one reads evokes an immediate physical response? Do certain materials activate different brainwave patterns? But I wonder what else is activated, and why it is that pornography works as well as it seems to work for some people at some times, as well as what other sorts of materials work in the same way. Are there, for instance, certain shapes that go back to the mother's breast, certain ways of experiencing one's environment that go back to the womb, and hence are inflexibly impressed in the formats of the psyche? The successful use of porno-graphic videotapes to stimulate non-copulating gorillas at a Japanese zoo (reported in *Details*, September 1993: 46–47) suggests that *Homo sapiens* is not the only species turned on by filmic representation. Like the issues posed by Skinner boxes or the movie *Clockwork Orange*, this is a question of social conditioning, but it also concerns psychosocial issues such as how deities are represented and gendered.

Of course, that question raises others about advertising language: Why does the yellow double-humped "M" of McDonalds sell hamburg-ers? Is that what sells hamburgers? In turn, these questions seem corre-lated with body-types theory in psychology. Why, in our society, does the smoothly muscled, "sculpted" mesomorph take on the significance that he does, whereas in other cultures it was the large body, or the medieval anorectic female body that seems to have been repeated again recently in the post-Twiggy thinness of the ideal American female body? And how is the sensual impulse related—Steinberg's writings force us to consider this question—to the religious, mystical experience?

There is something more than mere genital eroticism—perhaps something religious—in the expanse of male flesh now being revealed, so that one has to ask what deep human experience is being tapped. Hence questions such as: Does the situation show a trust in human abilities as one moves away from an establishment theocracy in place since the founding of the country, or is there something even more universal-archetypal about the square-shouldered and firm-muscled male? The pectorals or abdominals of such an ideal figure seldom reflect the normal state of development, as one realizes from the snapshots of men sent into the "readers' picks" section of male flesh magazines like *Playgirl*, nonprofessional models in contrast to those of men's clothing catalogues, or from direct observations of strongly muscled workers such as carpenters, roofers, or road crews that one is likely to see working with their shirts off. Such factors lead me to think about the female body and the parallels in the revealing of female flesh within my own lifetime: *Playboy* began shedding some of the taboos that *Penthouse* then removed totally, and subsequently other explicitly pornographic materials became legal and widespread. But again questions: Why this particular body shape? Which aspects of the body? Does the fact that the penis still remains covered in the West (in recent Calvin Klein cologne ads, a completely nude male *lies on his stomach*) indicate that it is metonymic to the (aniconic) divine? Or is the issue the conundrum that the anatomically small, uncontrollable penis is so unreliable a signifier for the almighty mythoform phallus? And are there identifiable subtypes beneath the body physiologies that work as innate releasing mechanisms, the way Joseph Campbell often referred to physiological bases of mythological materials?[10]

The Portrayal of the Ideal Male Body

What the power of images entails is well illustrated in contemporary male iconography: the concept of "model tyranny" that my colleague Stephen Karatheodoris developed (1993) for a critique of the image of women in the communications media, transfers easily to the present context. But the transference to men may not be immediately obvious, as Dutton suggests in a comment that appears on a page above a photographed row of six young Chippendale models with bow ties drawing attention to their nude, impeccably modeled pectorals and abdominals:

> The "aspirational" male image—tall, lean, tanned, and muscular—has a greater influence in defining men's views of themselves (and of other men) in Western societies than is acknowledged by those who believe that only women have fallen victim to the "beauty myth." (1994: 185)

The tyranny of a few isolated somatic features determines the parameters of the ideal bodies. For example, a magazine column by Paul Hochman (1993) reveals the role of Martin Sullivan, every one of whose body measurements "so closely matches the world's [!] statistical mean that design houses from Ralph Lauren to the Gap to Armani to J. Crew hire him as their fit model, the human mannequin who tries on samples." With "thirty-eight-inch hips, a thirty-three-inch inseam, a forty-inch chest," Martin sets the prototypes of clothing: medium is his body, and "about 80 percent of anything anybody buys in the United States has been on [him] at one point."

Male model tyranny is quite real in some quarters. Richard Stengel (1992: 77; see also Mishkind et al. 1987) notes that about sixty percent of cosmetic surgery at the Beverly Hills Institute of Body Sculpting is performed on males; he worries about the anxiety produced by the search for the svelte, muscular, youthful body displayed in the media, when such a physique is as unattainable for most males as the Madonna body is for most women.

Mythologies and religions idealize particular ways of being human—Eve is to remain subject to Adam, for instance—and of reflecting a society's physical models—appropriate gender display is clear in the countless representations of Adam, reflecting how Christian men were ideally to look during various periods. A brief catalogue of contemporary body codes/types (see Moon and Sedgwick 1990; Stanton 1992) that determine what top dogs look like would include most of the following:

1. *The body is hairless.* Poor William Holden! In 1955 he had to shave his chest repeatedly for the movie *Picnic,* because of the unwritten rule of the day for art photography, namely that the male body must be aestheticized by being made metonymic with marble (Cohan 1993: 222, illustrated on 202; see also the study of the aestheticizing of Rock

Hudson's body by Meyer 1991). I don't think it is just a hairy man's observation that remarkably enough, models in catalogues or gay magazines are almost always hairless (Mohr notes that hairiness is a specialty item in gay porn catalogues, along with bondage or watersports, 1992: 148).

It has been years since I was forced through the athletic regimen of the public schools and was made aware how my hairy body seemed the odd-one-out every time, but in subsequent experience, I learned that very few grownup men are as "clean," as the sex-ads put it, as the models. Nor for that matter do many people have tans that leave no pale areas whatsoever in the crotch—earlier representations of the painted or photographic male nude in the several retrospective collections now available disclose that the fully-tanned, hairless body is only a recent paradigm.

For the ancient Greeks who modeled much of Western masculine self-consciousness, the appearance of body hair marked the end of one phase of maleness—the period in which one might be adopted by a somewhat-senior man, who introduced the youth into society, and also enjoyed sexual access to his body—and the beginning of the second phase, that of being the senior male, who in turn adopted young men before turning primarily to women for sex. Some men were accused of shaving their faces very closely so as to continue to appear beardless, and hair appearing on the rear-end of a youth was particularly a sign of status change.[11]

2. What I imply by refering to classical antiquity is that the male body represented in a large section of our public imagery today is likewise *pre-hairy, pre-nubile, adolescent;* in short it idealizes the *neotenic body of the older child,* not that of the grownup. Are we afraid of being grownup? The question follows a long period of adulation of youth in our society, but I wonder if we've misinterpreted it in terms of avoiding old age, rather than in terms of wanting to return to the relatively less-demanding time of childhood when an apparently transcendent father looked out for us. Ideals work in curious ways to drive sectors of the economy, but it would be informative to see just how models of the retirement years have changed over the last fifty years, as well as how the childhood mystique has gained so much influence upon midlife existence—bodily images will doubtless change in parallel, in each case.

3. We might question the category of the "natural," after such refer-

ences, but then that issue was already raised: what would appear to be the norm for men, hirsuteness (Davis 1986), is in fact seldom idealized except when merchandizing the hunter or lumberjack look. Nor, we may suggest, is the *small svelte frame*—or the opposite in lifters, *massive over-articulated bodies*—particularly "natural." The developed muscular body that looks so spectacular in competitions and photographs gets that look only after weeks of no-fat, high-protein, and vegetable/fruit diets, along with huge daily doses of diuretics that drain the moisture from the flesh to the extent that just before competitions, a lifter's speech slurs, his walk slows to a shuffle, and his tongue sticks to his teeth. Simultaneous use of steroids can cost up to $100,000.00 a year, and increase testosterone levels by a factor of 2000.[12]

In many publications today, the flesh of the coverboy undergoes extensive treatment in the photographic studio, removing freckles and blemishes, and heightening muscle definitions. Obviously there is just as much model tyranny going on with respect to males as has been true of women for a long time. No wonder Robert Bly's Wildman seems appealing—it's the body most of us already have (well, give or take the muscles; sometimes I wouldn't mind being described, as Arnold Schwarzenegger has been, as looking like "a condom stuffed with walnuts," Hoberman 1991).

4. *The body is active.* Not much choice on this one—activity is identified repeatedly in any of the materials I've considered as an index of masculinity. It is "natural" no less than the idealized women's appearance, although in fact, images of handsome, muscular male bodies are achieved only as result of extremely hard work and subsequent photo-manipulation in the darkroom. However, as Dyer observes from the backgrounds utilized for male pinups and in flesh magazines, they must *appear* to be natural (1992: 116). Melody Davis notes (1991: 10–11) that in photography action is almost *de rigueur* for male, passivity for female nudes. She suggests (13) that in this context, homophobia can be understood as being a self-protection of insecure males against slipping back into a passive, acted-upon childhood stage. In a widely-cited essay, Leo Bersani suggests that one appropriate synonym for phallocentrism is the denial that passivity can ever be positive (1987: 217). No wonder local men's movements have needed frequently to begin with sessions on learning how passivity is not an hyperallergenic strain of masculinity!

5. The body is *large and hard:* sometimes, as Ernst van Alphen

suggests, it becomes a displacement for the limp penis that one cannot always control (1992: 179; similarly Fussell 1993: 580). Certainly there are analogies between bodybuilding and sexuality that would bear out such a point. Jonathan Goldberg's rather snide treatment of Schwarzenegger cites the parallels between the "pump," the feeling that comes when a muscle is full of blood and short on oxygen, and sexual orgasm: "it's as satisfying as coming," says Schwarzenegger (Goldberg 1992a: 175). Of course if all of the body has orgasmic potential, then the phallos-penis would be denied its power, doubtless one of the reasons for the many easy parodies of hypermasculinity (Goldberg: "as excessive coming, the pump disconnects phallus and penis," 1992a 176).

In bodybuilding, as Goldberg notes (176–77; likewise Dutton 1994: 177), there is an all-inclusive narcissism that extends the idea of human perfectibility to the dream of immortality; Dutton speaks of an "archetypal bodily configuration" desired by the lifter. Might such perfectionism not represent a sort of religio-materialist conservatism, preparing the body for its physical resurrection in the next life, or an atavistic recourse to the progenitor Adam (Fussell 1993: 593)? In a contemporary bodyology, other religious issues would have to be faced in discussing the perfectability of the body—such as doctrines of concupiscence or original sin, anthropology, human fallibility, creation, eschatology, and the nature of the godhead/s. The Adamic idealism may, as Dutton suggests (1994: 176, 178) represent less a religiously oriented model than an anti-contemporary reaction that harkens back nostalgically to a more active, pre-technological lifestyle.

6. At any rate, among the body-reshapings contemporary consumers are eager to purchase is the fulfillment of the dream of the *massive penis:* for a set fee of four thousand dollars, a surgeon in Beverly Hills offers penile augmentation procedures. These offer as much as fifty percent gain in size—but the operation has to be repeated or about half the gain will disappear, and the procedure relocates one's own body fat to the penis, so that the bodies presented by some lean young surfer customers lack extra fat to transfer. Another alternative, the penile implants chosen by thousands of males, allow a man to have intercourse with a fully-erect penis, but lacking all penile sensation (see Doty 1993: 39).

7. Finally, strangely enough, for all its beauty, the male body in mass media representations today never *looks very interested in anything, or happy.* Like Kierkegaard, I do not complain that the times are evil,

but that they are banal; hence another aspect of contemporary male iconography that intrigues me is the number of apparently bored visages who lift weights or contort themselves through Soloflex or Universal exercise machines, or who model unitards or teeshirts in clothing catalogues. Perhaps the height of the mien is that found in Guess! advertisements, where the cowboy or greaser always needs a shave and usually grimaces. [13]

Even males paid to get "blissed out" with a woman or another male in porn magazines seldom smile or display any facial characteristic that wouldn't be a possible byproduct of a designer drug, but hardly compares with usual expressions of pleasure. I'm reminded of an old *Playboy* joke where the director of a porn film instructs the couple just filmed *in flagrante delicto* to do a replay, "But this time, Sam, take the cigarette out of your mouth!"

I cannot but be reminded of the masked faces of both genders that sometimes confront me in the classroom until we get to know one another a bit, or students get irritated at me, or amused. I suspect a sort of self-protectiveness going on, and I am reminded of the Stoic quality of *ataraxia* by which one learned not to care too much in an urban world of constant change, not to put one's persona too much out in the open, but rather to retreat inwardly, to have a quiet center in oneself and find one's values within. Such a posture depended upon a worldview that saw a universal Logos permeating all flesh (see Goux 1992)—a reasonability quite beyond the apparent "postmodernist" chaos—and the expression of today seems anchored in much less self-aware or philosophical perspectives. [14]

Certainly I am not suggesting that we want more hyperagitated people; and we're already saturated with that American Smile that the department store clerk flashes as she debits one's credit card account. But I find something lacking, something curiously amiss, when all the healthy musculature doesn't lead to something more than faces devoid of expressiveness and personality, even after every tooth has been adjusted to the exact vertical, and every pimple cosmetically hidden. Gendering is one of the scenes in which we are instructed about playing the roles that sustain social interaction within gendering scenarios today. I am not encouraged by the fact that often the most splendidly developed Soloflex bodies are topped by mechanically blank, affectless faces.

Men as Objects of the Gaze

Having introduced the concept of mythic determination of the culture's gaze in a previous section of this chapter, it is not unfounded to cite the Dutch semiotician Mieke Bal on their equivalence: "The gaze is . . . the visual equivalent of myth. It is a reading attitude that fixes the object and builds on the illusion that the object exists outside of time, space, and the viewer's body" (1991: 148; see also Bal and Bryson 1991: 190, 199; and Karatheodoris and Doty 1995). "Outside of time, space, and the viewer's body" is the realm of "the natural" as we have confronted that illusion repeatedly here. As developed by Laura Mulvey (1989) and others, the Lacanian concept of the gaze has to do with ways cultures self-replicate, in particular with respect to their hermeneutical significations of gender displays. That concept is close to Freud's observation of how one can know and not know something at the same time, what he calls "that blindness of the seeing eye which is so astonishing in the attitude of mothers to their daughters, husbands to their wives, and rulers to their favorites" (1955 [1895]: 117n1).

In an earlier work with a colleague (Karatheodoris and Doty 1995), we trace the establishment of the objectifying gaze of "Man" back to Renaissance humanism, in the artistic perspectivism following Masaccio; humanist understandings of the production of meaning generated a sort of visual machine in the use of one-point linear perspectivism. It was a machine for producing spectators, and the subject position produced was markedly that of males, whose social actions duplicated the control of appearances in the political order. Indeed, perspectivism has provided a hegemonic narrative of consciousness, by teaching us how to see and what to look at. Later, Freud taught us how little of self-consciousness was implicated in the looking itself, how in spite of Enlightenment ideals of equality and fairness, narcissistic, erotic subtexts always replicated the viewing machinery, and how until the present those subtexts have primarily been monofocal in terms of looking from the male to the female as the object of desire. "To represent," postmodernist art critic Craig Owens sees clearly, "is to subjugate" (1992: xv).

While Owens sought to clarify just how much of our viewing-gazing is materially determined and culturally impressed, and hence our need for caution in treating "images that appear to be natural, inevitable, universal, immutable," the earlier and now classic analysis of "the gaze" in the arts was Laura Mulvey's "Visual Pleasure and Narrative Cinema."[15] Mulvey noted that "woman . . . stands in patriarchal culture as a signifier for the male other, bound by a symbolic order in which man can live out his fantasies and obsessions through linguistic command by imposing them on the silent image of woman still tied to her place as bearer, not maker, of meaning" (1989: 15). Hence the correlations male:active, woman:passive. But woman both represents a pleasure to see (scopophilia) and reminds males of the possibility of castration — since, from the phallos-bearing male hegemonic perspective, she seems to have been castrated (21).

In films, the initial target of Mulvey's attention, the absence of the male controlling gaze within the view on the screen is striking (22). The deadly work of that gaze is done by implication: "the power to subject another person to the will sadistically or to the gaze voyeuristically is turned onto the woman as the object of both" (23). "Going far beyond highlighting a woman's to-be-looked-at-ness, cinema builds the way she is to be looked at into the spectacle itself" (25), and "the camera becomes the mechanism for producing an illusion of Renaissance space, flowing movements compatible with the human eye, an ideology of representation that revolves around the perception of the subject; the camera's look is disavowed in order to create a convincing world in which the spectator's surrogate can perform with verisimilitude" (26). In other words, the spectator is simultaneously trapped — within his own voyeurism and projections, rather than reality.

Mulvey's initial essay opened critical perspectives previously unrealized, and in her reflections upon it ten years later, she reshaped some of her Freudian perspectives in the light of Lacanian thought, reconsidering the inside/outside dichotomy upon which so much of her earlier analysis had relied. Subsequently, other analysts have confirmed or qualified Mulvey's analysis. Owens, for instance, observed that "more than the other senses, the eye objectifies and masters. It sets at a distance, maintains the distance. In our culture, the predominance of the look over smell, taste, touch, hearing, has brought about an impoverishment of bodily relations. . . . The moment the look dominates, the body loses its materiality" (1992: 178).

Jonathan Goldberg (1992a) also has noted aspects of a gay gaze directed toward bodybuilders, yet this topic is seldom discussed within

13.4. "The Gaze Reversed." (The Liberto Jean Company has gone out of business. Several attempts were made—unsuccessfully, as it turned out—to contact agents of the company and their publicists in order to obtain formal permission for use of this illustration.)

literature about the sport (Dutton recognizes homoerotic aspects, but primarily traces the wider issues of erotic voyeurism, of the perfect body as a pleasure symbol, 1994: 8, 16, 344–45). The designer of the Liberto jean advertisement in which a female is shown photographing a young man's bare torso (see figure 13.4) simply cannot have been ignorant of the long history of feminist discourse about the gaze, which is here not transcended but merely reversed, according to our culture's tyrannizing gender dichotomization (critiqued in chapter 2 of Doty 1993).

Already distinguished by analyses of the film *The Son of the Sheik* and the male pinup, in *Only Entertainment* (1992), Richard Dyer captures something of the issue at hand, in terms of the "active viewer"/"passive viewed object" dichotomy: "The term 'sex object' implies a certain passivity, a person just 'there' for the viewer to gaze upon. Sex objects are pinned up, fixed, to be looked at. This submissiveness accords easily with the female sex role, which is so heavily defined in terms of passivity;

288 WILLIAM G. DOTY

but what happens when it is a man who is the sex object?" (99; Dutton qualifies Dyer's interpretation, 1994: 338–44).

According to *Esquire* magazine (Davis 1986), Bruce Weber, the photographer who "turned men into sex objects, and gave us one more thing to worry about," understands the new conditions of the gaze. Studying the famous Calvin Klein ad of a young man wearing only well-stuffed white undershorts, shot from below, a y-shaped white stuccoed building above him, echoing the upside down taping of the shorts—a photograph not only reproduced in hundreds of magazine and newspaper advertisements, but screened onto a massive billboard that loomed over Times Square for months[16]—Peter Davis comments:

The photograph for this advertisement, which ostensibly sold Calvin Klein underwear and is accused of selling a subversive version of male sexuality as well, was taken by Bruce Weber. Bruce Weber is the fashion photographer said to have taken man out of the gray flannel suit and to have put him in underpants, said to have done more to change the look of men than anyone since Adam, to have reversed in fact, the trend toward concealment begun by Adam. Someone even said that God created Adam, but it took Bruce Weber to give him a body. (1986: 340)

Esquire writer Davis remarks upon his own apperceptions of Weber's photographs of young male bodies:

how I felt was that Bruce Weber's photographs attracted and repelled me and the scary part finally was not the attraction but the repulsion. The flicker of uneasiness they caused as the flesh crawled—toward the pictures? away from them?—was the margin between gleam and threat. The pictures exposed not only those portrayed in them but also those who looked. A new view of self was involved here, one that women would recognize better than men, one with a political as well as a psychological meaning. Men had become objects now, now and forever.

The source of the threat is not our fear that Bruce Weber's men are more attractive to women than we are. The Marlboro man is more attractive to women than we are, but we are not jarred by him, and we do not look and look and look again at the Marlboro man. It is the difference between Zeus and Apollo. Zeus rules; Apollo appeals. The Calvin Klein model in the underpants is a divine creature and he beckons. Beckoning, he attacks a man's concept of his own sexuality, his own heterosexuality. (1986: 346)

Davis leaves us up in the air with respect to the "attack" he experienced, but Ernst van Alphen's perceptive study (1992) of the works of Francis Bacon suggests that the British painter worked precisely against the traditional stereotypical replication/idealization of the male body that is the flip-side of "the gaze." Bacon intended to reject (phallocentric) wholeness and to produce fragmentation. He states that "what I want to do is to distort the thing far beyond the appearance, but in the distortion to bring it back to a recording of the appearance" (van Alphen 1992: 166). Hence Bacon's frequent recourse to disfigured people—just what Melody Davis (1991) finds recurrent in the six photographers she studies, who do not believe that the male body need be "pretty." With respect to Bacon, van Alphen notes (1992: 168) that "all figures are fragmented as if they [were] dwarfs or paralytics. Every figure, deformed or not, is disfigured."

Important with respect to my current context is both that few other painters in the West have focused so extensively upon the male body, and that "the Western construction of masculinity is one of the major stereotypical discourses challenged by Bacon" (van Alphen 1992: 168). Challenged, deconstructed, reconsidered. Bacon challenges and at the same time reconceives the tradition by which the nude has been presented—that is to say "the female nude, that token of the masculine gaze, fetish of the Western eye, and most characteristic representation of objectification." Of course such a representation entails important economic ramifications, since "by the nineteenth century the female nude had supplanted the male nude in academic tradition. The female nude had by mid-century in Paris become the most profitable and state-sponsored subject for painters" (Davis 1991: 1), and therefore the most salable in the art market.

Similar real-world contours are no less evident today: "in 1976, Jacqueline Livingston, in a well-documented case, was dismissed from Cornell because she photographed her husband, father-in-law, and small son nude" (Davis 1991: 159–60). Davis notes that there has been such an absence of male nudes that when they have appeared, they have drawn about them a strong animus of taboo. Only since about 1978 "has the critical and curatorial silence surrounding the male body begun to dissipate" (Davis 1991: 3), while the frequent use of the more or less nude male model dates only to the late 1980s.

In the art world, that fact in itself is fascinating: Mira Schor notes that

a person who would seek to learn about the physionomy of male genitalia solely through the visual documentation of painting and sculpture (rather than that of pornography) would be sorely puzzled by the discrepancy between the evidently phallocentric world of culture, of political and sexual dominance by men, and the less than impressive appendage to representations of male nudes in art. (1988: 3)

In just such an ideologically pregnant context, Terry Eagleton observes that "it is in the significant *silences* of a text, in its gaps and absences that the presence of ideology can be most positively felt. It is these silences which the critic must make 'speak' " (1976: 34). Likewise Mieke Bal (1991) returns repeatedly to the gaps, the omissions, the ignorings of what has become established in canonical perspectives. Phallic "wholeness" as a masculo-phallocentric construct is called into question radically. What contemporary re/constructions of masculinity/religiosity might construe as re/constructive remain possibilities of the post-phallocentric gaze, perhaps the post-religious gaze as well, given the usual freighting of "religious."

Religious Elements/Aporia

Various meanings of "religious" prohibit masculo-/logo-centric clarity in my concluding section. No longer merely "traditionally patriotic," which is what *religio* seems to have meant in Roman culture, "religious" now usually indicates something having to do with the transcendent or divine. But, following the etymological evidence in the *American Heritage Dictionary* (3d ed., 1992), I remain a partisan of the derivation of religion from linguistic roots indicating *ligature* or (to insight a different, Sanskrit, root) *yoga*, namely a tying-together of significances. Hence, over against the recent history of usage, I prefer to emphasize the holistic acting that people do in the name of religion, including establishing hermeneutical systems that regulate and preserve a society's myths, rites, and symbols, including in this instance icons of masculinity (Doty 1993 exhibits my perspectives with regard to this framework).

Given that etymology, my "religious" elements/aporias need not involve gods or goddesses, but may indeed focus upon how people make meanings, and especially the significances of being human, as imaged within religious communities that accept common attributions of meanings. Such a position seems to make more sense than the opinion promulgated by Rosario Assunto in the *Encyclopedia of World Art*, namely that the more spiritualized a religion, the more aniconic it will be (vol.

7, 1963: col. 801, [mis-]cited by Freedberg 1989: 54, who notes that "nothing here is borne out by historical or ethnographic evidence").[17]

Except for my references to Steinberg's study of Renaissance Christ-imagery, this chapter has had few references to either the divine or the non-material transcendent, trafficking instead in the very material elements of masculine corporeality and their possible signification today. Consequently, if I may be allowed to let "religious" stand for a broadest-possible concept for articulating existential meaning, with or without "gods/goddesses" (or as I argued in Doty 1986: 33–35, "suprahuman" entities of whatever sort), it seems useful to identify several possible significations from the materials presented in this essay.

Polysemy rather than monotheism has been a personal as well as professional quirk for decades, and those who know my various publications will recognize once again the tricksterish, multivalent hermeneutics that has been a leitmotif. Eschewing the single normative answer, post-modernist, postfeminist readings ought to open outwards toward a plurality of meanings, within the various settings (no longer the assumed "we" of the past) of our lives. Hence the wide range of observations shared in the essay and the many questions posed cannot be brought to a reductive single focus; the questions are not resolved, but indeed even more are posed in this conclusion. Honoring such an attitude, I conclude by outlining a variety of ways to interpret the religious significance of what I have explored:[18]

1. I have referred to Leo Steinberg's *Sexuality of Christ* (1983) several times; in this iconographic study of the *ostentatio genitalium Christi*, the direction of one's gaze to the genitals of the infant Jesus, Steinberg noted that during a very long period of Christianity, the problem of religious belief was not, as it is today, the divine element in the Christic event, but the human. In such a context the genitals of the baby signified innocence, not shame, but above all the real flesh (hence the term Steinberg develops, "humanation"). Likewise, the erection evident on many portrayals of the dead Jesus signified not macho-eroticism but divine rule even over death.[19]

Today, however, except in some Latinate Catholic altars, the concept of a nude Christ, let alone a representation with genitals, is almost inconceivable. In fact, even the representation of Jesus as so truly human as to appreciate a good joke is most unusual: a 1993 mail order catalogue of *Playboy* lingerie and erotica offered prints of Fred Berger's

"The Laughing Christ." It is "so powerful," we are told, that "*Playboy* still gets requests for reproductions over twenty-two years after it was first published."

If for much of Christian history, Jesus is represented as "the Representative Man," what might it mean that so much nude male flesh now appears everywhere? Is this literal unveiling (*apokalypse* or *revelatio*) a sign of an (or the) apocalyptic era?[20] If, symbolically Christ's nakedness becomes an index of his humanity, does more nakedness today mean more belief in our humanity and less belief in some concept of deity? The question seems senseless except in the long tradition of the *imitatio Christi*: Margaret Walters notes (1978: 73–74) how painters modeled a beaten, torn, and stripped Christus, and even in something like the great Isenheim altar, a suppurating, morbid body that was commissioned from Grünewald by the

Anthonites, a hospital order specializing in the care of those ill with plague, with leprosy, and with the terrible new disease syphilis. When the sick arrived at Isenheim, they were taken to pray before an image of God in their own diseased shape, which perhaps helped them to objectify and accept their tragic condition. (1978: 73-74)

Such identification with the scourged Christ (75–76, illustrated, 92) led the artist Albrecht Dürer to detail his *Self-Portrait as the Man of Sorrows* of 1522 with the specific lineaments of his own body and visage.

In the framework of Steinberg's analysis, does the male flesh so readily displayed today indicate a newfound or rediscovered trust in the human condition, a new humanism, just when we hear in critical theory of "posthumanist discourse"? Does it mean that when we today approach the fleshly and even the genital no longer as tabooed, but as simply everyday, fully secular, we no longer believe in the importance of the physical/sexual? Or do we believe in it, but now in a hegemonic ranking above the spiritual, non-embodied? Or are we remanded merely to the auto-erotic, masturbatory (Fussell 1993: 581), to older traditional patriarchal control-fantasies? After all, the earlier nude Christus was as much the specifically intended object of the gaze as were women, later. Such a fantasmic reality about the body is quite awkward to integrate with the illusionary nature of another powerful masculine ideal, in that "the irony of the illusion is that at his most powerful, our superhero, the bodybuilder, is virtually powerless. Flexing on stage, at the height of his seeming virility, he's pumped so full of steroids that he's literally impotent" (Fussell 1993: 587). Hence several postmodern alternatives: What would it look like to have a Gold's Gym Christus on the cover of the Christmas-liturgy bulletin? Why would Sylvester Stallone's nude body seem appropriate for the cover of *Vanity Fair*, but not for that same bulletin cover? In what ways can the same phenomenon (increasing display of male flesh) betoken different iconographic valences in the Renaissance (the godhead was really human) and today (the human is really divine)?

2. Using the phallos as synecdoche for the whole representation of masculinity, Melody Davis suggests that it indicated "an unbreachable schism between ancients and Christians" (1991: 4; see also Goux 1992). Given that historical difference in attitudes toward the represented physical masculine, as well as the subsequent centuries in which Christianity and sexuality have had (to say the least) a long history of dialogue, where at this point is that religion's most representative teaching about the body, about gendering, about sexuality?—there are few such liberal treatments of sexuality as James Nelson's (1988, 1992). Is it not time to revision "Athens and Jerusalem" in terms of masculine sexuality, indeed of sexuality as such? What does it mean that the excluded "pagan," with all its glorification of the idealized *kouros* and *kore*, is now part of the mainstream representation of the human, in contrast to so many centuries of abnegation of physical beauty within Christianity?

3. Rather more difficult to sketch, but no less important for all that: does the very fleshiness of the materials we have scanned not indicate a contemporary trust in the fleshly, the concrete-bodily, that previous generations have not shared? Updike (qua Goldstein 1993: 506) speaks of bodybuilders' "power" as being something exempt from time, transcendent. Where are we vis-à-vis earlier body-admiring civilizations, classical Greece primary among them? Ought we turn to them for nurturance, or are they so far removed from us in cultural history that they are irrelevant referents? What will shape the new canons of ideal reference, particularly in a time of dismay with respect toward scripturally represented gendering that is now voiced by postfeminist scholars?

What might it mean to the shape of American religions to hear from their pulpits not anti-materialistic, but body-affirmative messages, sermons proactive toward the flesh instead of shunning it? Can we conceive "non-sexist men's bodies" whose non-hegemonic, non-sexist contours share the proleptic qualities heretofore imaged primarily within

294 WILLIAM G. DOTY

science fiction, yet whose possible realizations extend across great expanses of possibly enacted modes and models of human selfhood?

4. Given the enchantment in our society with the bulemic/skinny female body, ought one anticipate that a similar fascination will promote the skinny male body to the social ideal? The norm of a 38 inch waist, mentioned above, would argue otherwise, but "medium" in men's clothing usually indicates a 30–32 inch waist, so that Dutton's comment alongside a photograph of a slender young male, posed with his jeans unbuttoned to expose his underwear, is to the point: "The contemporary Western ideal is slimness, reflecting athletic competitiveness and youthful vigor within a social system geared to promoting these as ideals" (1994: 180).

Especially in light of suggestions that body weight/appearance is genetically determined, to what extent ought religio-ideological models instantiate ideals of slightness? If persons concerned to scour children's books for instances of racism or sexism have had a clear mandate, what would empower others now to legislate against "bodyism"?

Obviously "model tyranny" is not just a matter of men's clothing catalogues or flesh magazines. Moral care for the language, be it words or icons, ought to be clear. If Dyer (1992: 131) is correct in asserting that "porn has rather cornered the market on the representation of sexuality," and that "much that is happening is also seeking to break down the category 'sexuality,' understood as 'genital sexuality,' and replace it with a new understanding and experience of the body in human existence" (169), then what is left for the realm of the non-pornographic? How might the non-pornographic be represented in a postmodern, no-holds-barred situation where the boundaries of the transgressive are seldom sharply defined? Where within religious hegemonies might transgressive boundaries be appropriately established?

To be sure, issues of representation are deeply problematic in post-foundationalist cultures. For example, Leo Bersani (1987: 198) highlights the moral issues in treating gay men and persons with AIDS in terms of care for our public discourse and its consequences; he would speak of "a crisis of representation" when the incursion of HIV is treated as an unprecedented sexual threat, or when it is treated in terms of protecting straight people in the future rather than healing contemporary sufferers.[21] Perhaps it is not customary to refer to the roles of religions in disciplining the communal discourse and catalogue of representations, but precisely what characterizes the hermeneutical component of religions is the selection of root metaphors and their particular mythic and spiritual elaboration. In our immediate context, how might religious diction allow contemporary gender consciousness a role in double-checking theological formulations and ritual texts?

5. Is the contemporary fascination with the perfect male body (phallic? the word derives from L. *fascinum*, a phallic-shaped amulet) merely another indication of our culture's dedication to the cult of youth (see Dutton 1994: 170, 335–55), and how is it different from the idealizing of the svelte female body, if it is different? Emphasis upon youth today in terms of a large percentage of the population is not striking, although that argument would lead one to expect many more models over fifty years old, as well.

As I mentioned when coding the body-handsome above, the focus upon youth may represent merely a cultural immaturity, a refusal to face aging or the restrictions of what Asian Indian culture refers to as the householder stage (one of the sequential *ashramas*). Dieter Lenzen (1989) argues for a radical Christian root: the recent emphasis upon freeing the inner child and psychological anamnesis may be merely a replay of Christian admonitions to become as little children. Lenzen considers this emphasis upon youth to result from an apocalyptic process that essentially nullifies history.[22] Certainly, worshipping youth, a society may fail to plan for the future (urban planning) or indeed for the present moment (politics).

Lawrence Grossberg refers to the baby boomer generation that wouldn't and won't grow out of the values and experiences of its youth (1992: 184). More recently we hear about "thirteeners"— those who comprise the following generation, born between 1961 and 1981—who do not have the luxuries or the bright prospects of their predecessors, and who challenge our sterotype of carefree youthfulness. I am talking, in terms of religion, about disenfranchisement, which frequently in the history of the world's religions accompanies religious revivalism, if not revolution or cargo cult formation.[23] Presumably, then, the "fascination" is not just phallic-patriarchal dominant, but also revisionary, "share the goodies" redress-seeking aggression of the younger generation, who, after all, are the most likely to be able to develop the idealized body. In this case, muscles mean not admiring human development so much as sentiments of "in your face," "up yours!"

296 WILLIAM G. DOTY

6. How different from traditional patriarchal views ought a contemporary regard for the male body be? To what extent is the muscular body correlated with or differentiated from the caring, sensitive male persona? Where are the traditional religious organizations in this context? Ought one speak of a Presbyterian body, a Church of Christ body, a liberal-Jewish body, and so forth? How is such a point different from Barbara Myerhoff's important suggestion (1978: 257) that a religion is transmitted and maintained primarily through its cultural inflections? How is the body that lives out such cultural-religious inflections distinguished from the *kashrut* (Jewish dietary customs), for instance? Our traditional religious separations between flesh and idea may need significant reconsideration, as we take seriously the embodied, materialist incorporations of religious experiences. Less idealizing, rationalistic abstractions of what religions might be like; more materialistic, encorporated concretions of how mythico-religious perspectives are enacted: a fully postfeminist perspective will not be satisfied with rationalistic explanations of historical derivations, but will demand an accounting of lived-out experiential perspectives from within. Again, developments within gender studies drive advanced analyses beyond earlier parochial limits.

7. Certainly the machine has been a major "divinity" of the late-nineteenth and twentieth centuries, and it is not coincidental that the body as a machine is a recurrent theme today. In *Body Theology*, James Nelson notes that the male counterpart to the feminist-liberationist guide entitled *Our Bodies Our Selves* was entitled *Man's Body: An Owner's Manual*—"there it is: the body is like a car—something to own, use, and keep in good operating condition for maximum performance" (1992: 106–7).[24]

One danger of such a Cartesian model is its dualism: "too often we have been taught by culture, by religion, and by medicine that our bodies are something quite different from our real selves. We have learned that our real selves exist in our minds or our spirits, while our bodies are but intricate machines" (125). How might contemporary gender studies have an impact upon traditional dualistic worldviews, so that health (earlier: *wholth*) becomes once again a concept of integral harmony between the mind and the body?

Another danger is that the machine-like body comes to seem a sort of armoring; it will ensure that there's no slippage between body and soul, or outer and inner worlds. A useful work for comprehending male iconography, Anthony Easthope's *What a Man's Gotta Do: The Masculine Myth in Popular Culture* (1990: 55), traces the manner in which portrayals of national issues—his example is the 1982 Falklands episode—may represent an extension of just such a patriarchal mode of thinking. Accordingly, allegories are developed in which the inside (the nation) is threatened from the outside (the aggressor); meanwhile we (those inside) are stable, unified, and rational, but they (those outside) are considered dangerously labile and slippery, and so forth. Jonathan Goldberg (1992b) persues a similar line of thought on the "sodomizing" of Saddam in the Persian Gulf War: it is obvious that the language of masculine machinery translates easily into terms of subjection of an enemy.

Elsewhere, Goldberg analyzes images of Arnold Schwarzenegger in order to demonstrate the parallels between his cyborg movie roles and his bodybuilding roles. Neither is "natural," the way the ordinary human body is: "the cyborg body—the bodybuilder's body—is 'grown'. . . . If the body that surrounds the machine somehow 'humanizes' it . . . the 'human' that the cyborg represents is the product of quite other technologies—a human produced through and succeeding as simulation" (1992a: 186).

The sorts of de-armoring or re-naturing necessary for psychic and social health are clear in contemporary psychotherapy and in many aspects of the men's movements: learning how to share emotions, to express affection, and so forth, are focal activities in retreats and monthly drumming sessions; the armor of the machine may not be as deeply set as phallic patriarchy has intended. Personally, I would be suspicious of a religious organization that did not offer attention to some of the disciplines that can help disengage the machine-like carapace. It helps to be aware of historical contexts: in previous generations, it would have been unthinkable for a self-respecting male not to cry copiously at a funeral (see Rotundo 1993). The machine of our own day may segue into a sharply contrasting model as the end of the millennium approaches (Grunge rock?).

8. Will Roscoe provides yet another striking possibility as we draw together some ways of responding to the bared flesh of today:

is it not possible to see in the gay [only?] fascination with bodybuilding, costuming, tattooing, and piercing, and with the physical and psychological extreme of sadomasochism, in particular . . . a radical transformation of the body [similar to self-castration, as in the Attis myth] that *constructs a new identity,* the removal of a part in a metaphorical operation of self-birth? (1993: 119; my emphasis)

The mythic background is that of the divine child or the hermaphrodite; while Roscoe's suggestion of a reorienting interpretation of the modified male body needs to be elaborated considerably, his essay helpfully begins the work of developing a mythography that is not limited to the expectations of the Western dual-gender system, as that is explored helpfully by Howard Teich in the same volume, in an essay entitled "Homovision: The Solar/Lunar Twin-Ego" (1993).

9. What do the observations of this chapter have to do with traditional spirituality and the social role of religions? Are there ways in which male spirituality ought to be, or can be, or might be oriented toward more physical forms than one now finds? Should synagogues/ churches nationwide join hands with the Fellowship of Christian Athletes to model the Christian body as the physically well-developed body? In that case, hasn't the YMCA/YMHA movement been the real representative of Christianity and Judaism in the twentieth century?—note the functional importance of men's organizations in the late-nineteenth century, especially.[25] Where I live, Southern Baptist Church building complexes incorporate weightlifting rooms in their huge gymnasium structures.

10. Dutton suggests that the emphasis upon the muscled young body represents not only nostalgia for a more pristine past, a point noted above, but also the latest incarnation of epic heroism (1994: 345). Consequently, the youthful figures in Calvin Klein advertisements are analogous to the models of antiquity: "in many ways the modern heirs of the Greek vase athletes" (352). But further exploration of this interpretive option would necessarily entail revisionist views of the hero today, as well as the fact that the sculpted, muscled *woman* has also appeared as a recent counterpart to the male, and in fact in the *Terminator* movies, challenges the very notion of masculine supremacy (see the extensive overview, Aisenberg 1993).

11. Finally, anathemas against patriarchy are now traditional, but are there openings in the materials in this essay to what Kaja Silverman (1992) terms "non-phallic masculinities"? Isn't phallicism basically the *bigness* of the muscles/body transferred to everything men manipulate—guns, income, house, cars? Hence: everything males touch, not just the penis. Even, by transference, one's women (or at least their breasts) or

male lover or spouse, and beyond that, one's athletic children (to distinguish them from mother-pride, which seems more generalized)—all these have to seem larger than life, or at least larger than the possessions of others. Certainly, as Lawrence Grossberg notes (1992: 506), "if the body is all we have, having lost the soul hypothesized by old-time religion, then making a spectacle of abundant material possessions is our era's special form of dandyism and bourgeoise vanity alike." So is the masculine simply a byword for consumerism? Is consumerism essentially phallic?

The phallic is the totalizing/singularizing, that-which-can-dominate, oversee; the male gaze is that of the possessor. And the possessor is conservative, fetishizing, and concealing. Easthope stings with his comments about the "concealing," hiding aspects:

despite all that has been written over the past twenty years on femininity and feminism, masculinity has stayed pretty well concealed. This has always been its ruse in order to hold on to its power. Masculinity tries to stay invisible by passing itself off as normal and universal. Words such as "man" and "mankind," used to signify the human species, treat masculinity as if it covered everyone. (1990: 1)

When masculinity presents itself as normal, it automatically makes the feminine seem deviant and different.

With respect to the totalizing claim, as Davis notes (1991: 23), Robert Mapplethorpe's photographic work followed just such a conservative aesthetic: "the full body becomes a phallus that symbolizes the fantasy penis of power and strength" (69, cf. 75), and that image is represented as flawless and totalizing: "in the bodybuilder physiques of Mapplethorpe's ideal, there is not a sag or wrinkle, nothing to interrupt the surface beauty, seamless as studio paper" (72), stray body hair as unwelcome as excess flab.

What might it mean to bring such auto-erotic, masturbatory control fantasies into contrast with other imaginings of the contemporary male? I have in mind particularly those of painters Francis Bacon, Eric Fischl, Paul Cadmus, and Lucien Freud—all of them repeat images in which the male body is deconstructed, fragmented, and only agonizingly brought into relationships with other men. While it is dangerous to read artworks as narrative preachments (just what happened to Giacometti, whose sculptures were widely interpreted as visualizations of "existentialist man," yet who repeatedly insisted that he was only producing pure art), it is no less legitimate to ask about contemporary artists' representations of gender—even when as fragmented and blurred as in cubism—since visual and plastic artists often stand at the threshold of the new metaphoring and iconography by which we come to understand ourselves anew. But for now that project must await research time.

Leo Steinberg's important work that opened art history to new directions and that has been utilized here for a new masculinist[26] approach, was a decade old at the time of writing this essay. Something of the necessary humility of writing academic prose is inculcated in such an instance, in that Steinberg's concluding sentence is just as appropriate to the tentative reaches of this essay as it was to those of his:

The field I have tried to enter is unmapped, and unsafe, and more far-reaching than appears from my present vantage. Much of what I have said is conjectural and surely due for revision. . . . I have risked hypothetical interpretations chiefly to show that, whether one looks with the eye of faith or with a mythographer's cool, the full content of the icons discussed bears looking at without shying. And perhaps from one further motive: to remind the literate among us that there are moments, even in a wordy culture like ours, when images start from no preformed program to become primary texts. Treated as illustrations of what is aleady scripted, they withhold their secrets. (1983: 108)

NOTES

A very brief but illustrated version of this essay was presented at a combined meeting of the Gay Men's Issues in Religion Group and the Men's Studies in Religion Group of the American Academy of Religion, November 1993. The essay has benefited from critiques by Ute Winston and the editor of this volume.

1. Silverman 1992: 16 is excellent on showing how certain hegemonic ideas get to be part of the entire concept of the world as *vraisemblance*, a process that is crucial to understanding the long-entrenched equation of symbolic phallos and physical penis. She seeks to identify where in our own culture it breaks down, 2; and she suggests that ideology may have little to do with consciously held ideas, 17.

2. I have in mind primarily the turn to materials of pop culture previously overlooked, but as "body history," there are other aspects, as pointed out by Goldstein 1993: 505: "Like so much recent historiography that has focused on the private sphere, body history seeks to redirect attention away from leaders, policies, and institutions, and toward the daily physical life of ordinary people."

3. Lest my claim seem unfounded, here is Sam Fussell's description of "the early twentieth-century tradition of the muscular Christian, [now] turned inward" (1993: 594). Not toward Christian charity but toward deltoid definition:

The body may be the temple of the Lord, but the gym is the place of worship, and in this church for the secular, one may experience communion (let's lift together), exaltation (the pump), confirmation (the mirror), benediction (the trainer's nod), resurrection (the promise of a new, purer body), ablution (the post-workout shower), redemption (the expiation of sin and guilt through physical frenzy), and even divine selection (genetics—anointed by God). As in any religion, doubt and skepticism, the artist's assets, are the disciple's worst sins.

4. *Details*, October 1994, issue. A delicious sendup of *Details* will be found in the January 1994 issue of *The Spy* as a section entitled *Retails*, pp. 37–47.

5. Doty 1993: chapter 6, "Narcissus and the Narcotic of the Self-Body Image," is background to much of the discussion here. One image element I have not developed is the conditioning of our seeing by the various publications in the wake of *Playboy;* we will hardly see Manet's *Olympia* in its shocking contrast to the earlier, delicate, and denatured female nudes unless we can bracket the more recent explicitness of showing-forth of the suppressed.

Kent and Morreau 1985: 57–58 cite a contemporary parallel to *Olympia* in the derision and abuse that greeted the Women's Images of Men exhibits at the London Institute of Contemporary Arts in 1980. They note parallels between the Manet and the well-known painting by Sylvia Sleigh, *Philip Golub Reclining,* 1971, in that both models being painted stare back at the viewer (inappropriately, in the traditional genre of the nude), 95–96.

6. Fejes's (1992) research survey and, in the same volume, Strate's article (1992), are valuable in grounding such an analysis as this, which is largely impressionistic. Strate's work is excellent in demonstrating how "the myth of masculinity" of our culture answers questions about "How does a man act? What does he do?" While focused upon his advocacy of homosexual society, Mohr's " 'Knights, Young Men, Boys': Masculine Worlds and Democratic Values," chapter 6 in *Gay Ideas* (1992), is valuable in developing an iconography of the masculine. A volume of essays on masculine images in Hollywood cinema (Cohan and Hark 1993) looks useful, but it reached my desk only as I was correcting the final manuscript.

7. See Hillman 1979, an essay that is crucial to understanding the psychological significance of the great schism. More recently, Mieke Bal's work contributes enormously to the deconstruction of the bias of the verbal in our culture; see especially 1991.

8. Although there were various ways to explain the reactions against the Mapplethorpe exposing of the penis, often erect (and as a subtext, possessed by African American males), Brooks notes that "Mapplethorpe's photographs . . . do not overwhelm us with the tremendous presence of the phallus, but rather they offer for bemused, even amused, inspection the penis doing its thing. These photographs are ultimately demystifying, something that much of our culture apparently is not yet ready to accept" (1993: 279). The age-old problem is how to demystify any subject around which a society has set such careful guards

against seeing differently, i.e., according to a demystifying or depotentiating hermeneutics.

9. The fall 1990 issue of *Aperture* magazine (no. 121), entitled *The Body in Question,* is devoted to closer-to-home contemporary taboos about photography—see for instance Ginsberg and Richey (1990), on the right to photograph children in the nude. Revisionist essays in Bryson, Holly, and Moxey 1991 explicate ways in which the direction of the viewing gaze is inculcated.

10. Obviously this sort of iconography must be opened up in parallel to the types of materials considered—as the New History now examines personal or business records for details—and it must develop some of the semiotic sophistication advanced by Bal and Bryson 1991; Bal's emphasis upon reading for the missing representations, the gaps in the "text," in several of her works, is important. Likewise one must sometimes bear with some of the dreck that one tends to ignore; Steinberg, 1983: 85, notes: "there are several reasons why an art historian might want to look at bad art"—at poor early copies, for instance, of a great painting, even when the latter survives in near perfect condition. In an essay contemporary with this, I suggest that the later epistolary novel raises a whole series of useful interpretive questions about the Pauline epistles. Teachers within religious studies must then perforce intrude such matters as the physiological ramifications of participating in religious ritual or the ultimately biological shapings of images of God/dess the Father/Mother.

11. There are several examples of complaints of butt-hair in the collection known as The Greek Anthology. With respect to facial hair in antiquity, according to Calasso 1993: 86, the first two hairs were named Harmodius and Aristogiton.

12. See firsthand accounts of these conditions in Hedegaard 1993 and Fussell 1993. Fussell notes how the idealized lifter body falsifies the sought-after blue collar worker's body (590) to the extent of becoming what Fussell calls "a self-willed grotesque" (582), and details the extraordinary regimen involving diet, constant straining exercise, and use of drugs—all part of what he sees comprising one appeal of the bodybuilder subculture, namely its appeal as a sort of outlaw mentality (585). Dutton notes that "practically all top competitors for the last twenty years or more have been steroid-users—although most have publicly denied the fact" (1994: 280–81); now the bodies of "natural" bodybuilders look "unnatural" by comparison!

13. It took me a long time to realize that the Guess company sold jeans. I finally made the connection when I saw the logo on a pair that someone walking in front of me was wearing, certainly not from it being obvious in the ads. But then an ad for Italian socks recently featured a young man standing on one foot, wearing nothing but a jockstrap, so who's to say what explicit means?

14. It is developed not so much consciously (which is the case when a recent widow is complimented on her "stoicism": "She hardly showed a tear!" when her husband died) as unconsciously, perhaps as an ingrained trait of the bodies of those who watch so much television. A Memphis State study found that half a control group who rested had no drop in metabolic rate afterward, whereas

the other half, after watching a popular TV show for the same period, had a drop averaging minus fourteen percent (reported in *Eating Well: The Magazine of Food and Health,* 3/15/1993, 19). The pre-World War II promise of the expansion of consciousness that television would bring now seems ironically bitter, indeed.

15. Mulvey 1989: chapter 3, originally written in 1973, published in 1975, and augmented later in "Changes: Thoughts on Myth, Narrative and Historical Experience," chapter 14.

16. Peter Brooks notes that in such instances, "advertising has achieved what no artistic or literary genre could: making the private body a subject of everyday public discourse, especially visual discourse"; "advertising has created a highly coded public discourse of the private" (1993: 257–58). Furthermore, one accomplishment of contemporary advertising is the eroticization of male underwear, a process which had to contend with heavier layers of social repression and perhaps indifference. To fetishize the male anatomy through its underwear took some doing, and the subsequent creation of male-style underwear for women was an act of cute cultural transgression wholly characteristic of late twentieth-century sensibility.

17. But on the other hand I find too abstract and distancing Connor's more inclusive statement, 1992: 140:

> The irony is that the rejoining in aesthetic theory of spirit and sense, intellect and body, form and content, is simultaneously an authentic attempt to restore the immediacy of the human body from its brutal abstraction into exchange-value and an abstract idealization which is the very sign of the sundering that it attempts to heal; the aesthetic is here both wound and cure.

18. I am much taken by the development of Bakhtin's "heteroglossia," in line with Derrida's "dissemination," particularly as developed by Bal and Bryson, 1991: They develop a visual semiotics that is able to heed the multiple voices in an artwork and in viewers at various times. Such a perspective uses the fragmentation of the text, that was the first task of structuralist methodology, as a means of keeping ideological criticism from searching for "the" meaning and thereby falling back into a naive revanchism. Allowing for a variety of possible clotures here recognizes that there is no single masculinist "answer" any more than there is a single feminist answer, and invites the reader more fully to take up the debate.

19. Carolyn Walker Bynum (1991: see chapter 3, "The Body of Christ in the Later Middle Ages: A Reply to Leo Steinberg") feels that Steinberg reads too many contemporary ideas back into the medieval world, especially those touching sexuality, and hence misses alternative iconographic and theological matters. Certainly the immediate claims of the book strike the reader as excessive, but I find that this is true only until the large number of examples are canvassed seriously. A single work might be questionable, but not in the context of the

sheer mass of representations of the two key scenes, and of parallels in the theological and homiletical teaching that he cites.

I do not have the resources to follow up on Perniola's observation, 1989: 245, about the work of Georges Bataille: "Bataille worked within a tradition that assigns great spiritual value to undressing. After Saint Paul, this spiritual value found an important expression in Saint Jerome's proposition, *nudus nudum Christum sequi* (to follow the naked Christ naked), which became a highly developed idea in the Middle Ages."

20. In his postscript to Steinberg 1983: 202, John W. O'Malley caught a nearby resonance: "we might have a deliberate play on the idea of 'revelation.' *Velum* is a veil, while revelare means to unveil. . . . This God, in other words, is unveiled, revealed, in these scenes as truly and fully man."

21. Bersani's brave article is also a dense and convoluted one, and one has to read it several times before garnering all of its information, but it is one of the most effective discussions of the moral implications of representation, and of the power of media to manufacture meaning by labeling, shaping the social categories by which various groups self-identify (is "gay" something like an "ethnic identity"?) Also valuable with respect to the crisis of representation: Craig Owens's course bibliographies for Visualizing AIDS and Visual AIDS (1992: 355–65); and see the large-scale art project reported in Boffin and Gupta 1990.

22. I am grateful to Daniel C. Noel, whose privately circulated *Lyonesse Letter* no. 6, 11 August 1993: 4, drew my attention to Lenzen's work.

23. Grossberg's scathing denunciation of the past decade, 313, aptly summarizes some of the separating seams in the body politic: Relations of inequality, domination, and oppression, many of which were beginning to be dismantled, have become the taken-for-granted structure of social organization. Commanding political alliances have been fractured and assumed political allegiances have been shattered. The lines dividing the population have been redrawn, sometimes in new ways, but always with less flexibility and mobility. The most visible manifestation of these changes is the redistribution of income, which is now as dangerously skewed as that of many third-world economies.

On the Thirteeners, see Howe and Strauss 1993, although one longs for less observation and clever design, and more penetrating socio-moral design.

24. An extraordinary portrayal of the machine-like body—as promise and as threat—can be traced through the indices to both volumes of Theweleit 1987, 1989.

25. See Mangan and Walvin 1987, and Carnes 1989. Rotundo 1993: 221 notes how frequently physical strength and strength of character were equated in the many fraternal movements.

26. Yes, I think it is time to capture "masculinist" for our analyses, in parallel to "feminist." Previously I have used it in a negative way, more-or-less equated with "patriarchal."

REFERENCES

Aisenberg, Nadya. 1993. *Ordinary Heroines: Transforming the Male Myth.* New York: Continuum.

Alphen, Ernst van. 1992. *Francis Bacon and the Loss of Self.* Essays in Art and Culture. London: Reaktion.

Andrews, Suzanna. 1992. "She's Bare. He's Covered. Is There a Problem?" *The New York Times Magazine,* 1 November, 13–14.

Bal, Mieke. 1991. *Reading "Rembrandt": Beyond the Word-Image Opposition.* Cambridge New Art History and Criticism. New York: Cambridge University Press.

Bal, Mieke, and Norman Bryson. 1991. "Semiotics and Art History." *The Art Bulletin* 73/2:174–208.

Bersani, Leo. 1986. *The Freudian Body: Psychoanalysis and Art.* New York: Columbia University Press.

———. 1987. "Is the Rectum a Grave?" *October* 43:197–222.

Berger, John. 1972. *Ways of Seeing.* London: The British Broadcasting Corporation and Penguin Books.

Boffin, Tessa, and Sunil Gupta, eds. 1990. *Ecstatic Antibodies: Resisting the AIDS Mythology.* London: Rivers Oram.

Brooks, Peter. 1993. *Body Work: Objects of Desire in Modern Narrative.* Cambridge: Harvard University Press.

Brubach, Holly. 1993. "Mail-Order America." *The New York Times Magazine,* 21 November, 54–61, 68–69.

Bryson, Norman, Michael Ann Holly, and Keith Moxey, eds. 1991. *Visual Theory: Painting and Interpretation.* San Francisco: HarperCollins.

Burroughs, Catherine B., and Jeffrey David Ehrenreich, eds. 1993. *Reading the Social Body.* Iowa City: University of Iowa Press.

Bynum, Caroline Walker. 1991. *Fragmentation and Redemption: Essays on Gender and the Human Body in Medieval Religion.* New York: Zone Books.

Calasso, Roberto. 1993. *The Marriage of Cadmus and Harmony.* Trans. Tim Parks. New York: Dutton.

Carnes, Mark C. 1989. *Secret Ritual and Manhood in Victorian America.* New Haven: Yale University Press.

Cohan, Steven. 1993. "Masquerading as the American Male in the Fifties: *Picnic,* William Holden, and the Spectacle of Masculinity in Hollywood Film." In *Male Trouble,* ed. Constance Penley and Sharon Willis. Minneapolis: University of Minnesota Press.

Cohan, Steven, and Ina Rae Hark, eds. 1993. *Screening the Male: Exploring Masculinities in Hollywood Cinema.* New York: Routledge.

Connor, Steven. 1992. *Theory and Cultural Values.* Cambridge, Mass.: Blackwell.

Craig, Steve, ed. 1992. *Men, Masculinity, and the Media.* Research on Men and Masculinities, 1. Newbury Park, Calif.: Sage.

Davis, Melody. 1991. *The Male Nude in Contemporary Photography.* Philadelphia: Temple University Press.

Davis, Peter. 1986. "The Man Who Undressed Men." *Esquire* June, 338–45.

Doty, William G. 1986. *Mythography: The Study of Myths and Rituals.* Tuscaloosa: University of Alabama Press.

———. 1993. *Myths of Masculinity.* New York: Crossroad.

Dutton, Kenneth R. 1994. *The Perfectible Body: The Western Ideal of Physical Development.* London: Cassell.

Dyer, Richard. 1990. *Now You See It: Studies on Lesbian and Gay Film.* New York: Routledge.

———. 1992. *Only Entertainment.* New York: Routledge.

Eagleton, Terry. 1976. *Criticism and Ideology: A Study in Marxist Literary Theory.* London: Verso.

Easthope, Anthony. 1990 [1986]. *What a Man's Gotta Do: The Masculine Myth in Popular Culture.* 2d ed. Boston: Unwin Hyman.

Fejes, Fred J. 1992. "Masculinity as Fact: A Review of Empirical Mass Communication Research on Masculinity." In Craig 1992: 9–22.

Freedberg, David. 1989. *The Power of Images: Studies in the History and Theory of Response.* Chicago: University of Chicago Press.

Freud, Sigmund. 1955 [1895]. *Studies on Hysteria.* Standard Edition. Vol. 2. London: Hogarth.

Fussell, Sam. 1993. "Bodybuilder Americanus." *Michigan Quarterly Review* 32/4:577–96.

Ginsberg, Allen, and Joseph Richey. 1990. "The Right to Depict Children in the Nude." *Aperture* 121: 42–51.

Goldberg, Jonathan. 1992a. "Recalling Totalities: The Mirrored Stages of Arnold Schwarzenegger." *differences: A Journal of Feminist Cultural Studies* 4/1: 172–204.

———. 1992b. *Sodometries: Renaissance Texts, Modern Sexualities.* Stanford: Stanford University Press.

Goldstein, Laurence. 1993. "Introduction" to an issue on The Male Body, part 1. *Michigan Quarterly Review* 32/4:503–9.

Goux, Jean-Joseph. 1992. "The Phallus: Masculine Identity and the 'Exchange of Women'." *differences: A Journal of Feminist Cultural Studies* 4/1:40–75.

Grossberg, Lawrence. 1992. *We Gotta Get out of This Place: Popular Conservatism and Postmodern Culture.* New York: Routledge.

Hedegaard, Erik. 1993. "Making It Big." *Details,* October, 136–43, 192.

Hillman, James. 1979 [1976]. "Peaks and Vales: The Soul/Spirit Distinction as Basis for the Differences between Psychotherapy and Spiritual Discipline." In *Puer Papers,* Hillman, et al. Dallas: Spring Publications.

Hoberman, J. 1991. "The Self-Made Man: Arnold über Alles." *Village Voice* 36/7, 12 February: 53, 58, 62.

Hochman, Paul. 1993. "seventh avenue." *Details,* September 1993, n.p.

Howe, Neil, and Bill Strauss. 1993. *13th Gen: Abort, Retry, Fail?* New York: Random House/Vintage.

Karatheodoris, Stephen. 1993. "Male Desire in the Political Economy of Sexual Difference." Ed. William G. Doty. In *Gender, Race, and Identity*, ed. C. Barrow, K. Frank, J. Phillips, and R. Sanderlin. Chattanooga, Tenn.: Southern Humanities Press.

Karatheodoris, Stephen, and William G. Doty. 1995. "Humanism and the Birth of Perspective in Renaissance Painting: Toward a Sociology of the Gaze." In *Picturing Cultural Values in Postmodernist America*, ed. Doty.

Keen, Sam. 1986. *Faces of the Enemy: Reflections of the Hostile Imagination.* San Francisco: HarperCollins.

Kent, Sarah, and Jacqueline Morreau, eds. 1985. *Women's Images of Men.* London: Writers and Readers.

Lenzen, Dieter. 1989. "The Temporality of World-Views and Self-Images." Essay trans. Philip N. Hewitt. In *Looking Back on the End of the World*, Jean Baudrillard, et al. Ed. Dietmar Kamper and Christoph Wulf. Trans. David Antal. Semiotext(e) Foreign Agents. New York: Semiotext(e).

Mangan, J. A., and James Walvin, eds. 1987. *Manliness and Morality: Middle-Class Masculinity in Britain and America.* Manchester, England: Manchester University Press.

Meyer, Richard. 1991. "Rock Hudson's Body." In *Inside/Out: Lesbian Theories, Gay Theories*, ed. Diana Fuss. New York: Routledge.

Mishkind, Marc E., et al. 1987. "The Embodiment of Masculinity: Cultural, Psychological, and Behavioral Dimensions." In *Changing Men: New Directions in Research on Men and Masculinity*, ed. Michael S. Kimmel. Newbury Park Calif.: Sage.

Mohr, Richard D. 1992. *Gay Ideas: Outing and Other Controversies.* Boston: Beacon.

Moon, Michael, and Eve Kosofsky Sedgwick. 1990. "Divinity: A Dossier, A Performance Piece, A Little-Understood Emotion." *Discourse* 13/1:12–39. Reprinted in Sedgwick, *Tendencies,* 1993.

Mulvey, Laura. 1989. *Visual and Other Pleasures.* Bloomington: Indiana University Press.

Myerhoff, Barbara. 1978. *Number Our Days.* New York: Simon and Schuster.

Nelson, James B. 1988. *The Intimate Connection: Male Sexuality, Masculine Spirituality.* Louisville, Ky.: Westminster/John Knox.

———. 1992. *Body Theology.* Louisville, Ky.: Westminster/John Knox.

Owens, Craig. 1992. *Beyond Recognition: Representation, Power, and Culture.* Ed. S. Bryson, B. Kruger, L. Tillman, and J. Weinstock. Berkeley: University of California Press.

Perniola, Mario. 1989. "Between Clothing and Nudity." Trans. Roger Friedman. In *Zone 4, Fragments for a History of the Human Body*, Part Two, ed. Michel Feher, Romona Naddaff, and Nadia Tazi. New York: Urzone.

Pronger, Brian. 1990. *The Arena of Masculinity: Sports, Homosexuality, and the Meaning of Sex.* London: Gay Men's Press.

Roscoe, Will. 1991. *The Zuni Man-Woman.* Albuquerque: University of New Mexico Press.

Roscoe, Will. 1993. "Dreaming the Myth: An Introduction to Mythology for Gay Men." In *Same-Sex Love and the Path to Wholeness*, ed. Robert H. Hopcke, Karin Lofthus Carrington, and Scott Wirth. Boston: Shambhala.

Rotundo, E. Anthony. 1993. *American Manhood: Transformations in Masculinity from the Revolution to the Modern Era*. New York: HarperCollins/Basic Books.

Schor, Mira. 1988. "Representations of the Penis." *M/E/A/N/I/N/G: Contemporary Art Issues* 4:3–17.

Sedgwick, Eve Kosofsky. 1990. *Epistemology of the Closet*. Berkeley: University of California Press.

Silverman, Kaja. 1992. *Male Subjectivity at the Margins*. New York: Routledge.

Stanton, Domna C. 1992. "Introduction: The Subject of Sexuality." In *Discourses of Sexuality: From Aristotle to AIDS*, ed. Domna C. Stanton. Ratio: Institute for the Humanities. Ann Arbor: University Michigan Press.

Steinberg, Leo. 1983. *The Sexuality of Christ in Renaissance Art and in Modern Oblivion*. New York: Pantheon.

Stengel, Richard. 1992. "Men as Sex Objects." *M* [a magazine for men] 9/10: 72–79.

Strate, Lance. 1992. "Beer Commercials: A Manual on Masculinity." In Craig 1992: 78–92.

Teich, Howard. 1993. "Homovision: The Solar/Lunar Twin-Ego." In *Same-Sex Love and the Path to Wholeness*, ed. Robert H. Hopcke, Karin Lofthus Carrington, and Scott Wirth. Boston: Shambhala.

Theweleit, Klaus. 1987. *Male Fantasies*. Vol. 1: *Women, Floods, Bodies, History*. Trans. Stephen Conway. Theory and History of Literature, 22. Minneapolis: University of Minnesota Press.

———. 1989. *Male Fantasies*. Vol. 2: *Male Bodies: Psychoanalyzing the White Terror*. Trans. Erica Carter and Chris Turner. Theory and History of Literature, 23. Minneapolis: University of Minnesota Press.

Walters, Margaret. 1978. *The Nude Male: A New Perspective*. New York: Penguin.

Watrous, Peter. 1991. "Pop Turns the Tables—With Beefcake." *New York Times*, 10 February, Arts and Leisure section, 1, 27.

Concluding Overview

FOURTEEN

Epilogue

JAMES B. NELSON

The title of this volume is well-chosen. As the editor stated in the introduction, it is impossible to speak of men's relations to God without speaking at the same time of their own body perceptions. He reminded us that, in spite of the spirit-body split in classic dualism, the male body was not rendered insignificant by men. It remained an important spiritual battleground. Indeed, men's understandings of their bodies have been part of their claims for divinely-conferred preferential status. Men's gods are inseparable from their interpretations of their bodies.

Thus, this book attempts to do *body theology* (see Nelson 1992). But the task is not easy. We struggle with ways to conceptualize these things because our body perceptions live so deeply within us that they are difficult to reflect upon. Our interpretations simply seem to be us—the natural and given part of who we are. As a philosopher once said, "Be careful how you describe the world. It *is* that way!"

The task is difficult also because the enterprise of body theology itself is relatively new. Surely, as is amply illustrated in these essays, our forebears perceived the world and its ultimate meanings in significant ways through their bodies. Nevertheless, the *consciousness* of this process is relatively new. That is illustrated by the fact that through the centuries most Jewish and Christians writings about body and sexuality have been essentially one-directional. Those writings began with religious perceptions (scriptures, ecclesiastical pronouncements, or theological doctrines) and then moved to bodily applications. It was believed that religion's truth was received quite independently of our bodily-sexual experience, and that truth simply needed to be applied to the body.

This persisting failure to take body experience as part of the conscious theologizing process was significantly linked to the fact that male theologians largely shaped these religious traditions. They typically assumed that theology was fundamentally a matter of spirit and mind, not body. In Christianity, under the influence of the ancient classical world's body-denigrating dualism, this was particularly pronounced. Yet, it was somewhat true even in a Jewish tradition relatively free from the body-spirit split. Theologically, the net result has been a more deductive than inductive approach, a movement from the abstract to the concrete, from religious propositions to body applications.

What is relatively new (and amply illustrated in the foregoing pages) is that body experiences are important theological data. The movement of theological liberalism beginning in Germany early in the nineteenth century established human experience as a legitimate and important theological source. Including body understandings in the definition of experience, however, came much later. In the last third of the twentieth century the discipline of body psychology has established the fact that bodies, far from being only photographic-like receptors, are active sources of meanings and world views (see Fischer 1986). Even more significant for this enterprise has been the impact of the feminist and lesbian/gay liberation movements in recent decades. For understandable-if-regrettable reasons within a continuing patriarchy, men have generally been less conscious of these things. One of the costs of the patriarchal practice of taking the male experience as normative for human experience is that men have become invisible to themselves. We rarely measure the measuring stick itself. But now that male self-consciousness is dawning, and this book has become possible.

Body theology is dialogical. It must be an ongoing conversation between body experiences and meanings, on the one hand, and religious perceptions, on the other. We move not only from our bodies to our gods but also in the other direction as well. The conversation moves in both directions, for each reality affects the other.

Consider the meanings of our sexuality as a case in point. Without recourse to specifically religious insights, we can see that human sexuality always involves far more than genital sex. Sexuality embraces our ways being in the world as male-bodied and female-bodied persons. It includes the gender meanings that we learn for our biological sex. It includes the meanings we attach to our varied sexual orientations. It involves our bodily hungers, passions, and needs for connection. It involves the very sensuality of our bodily existence. While we can make such claims without grounding them in a particular religious perspective, we need not stop there. Some of us want also to bring specifically religious meanings to the body. As a liberal Protestant Christian and one very conscious of Christianity's rootedness in Judaism, I claim both a strong incarnationalism (the divine is revealed through human flesh) and a strong commitment to the radical goodness of creation, including bodies and their sexuality. From my religious perspective I see human sexuality expressing the divine mystery of our creation. I see sexuality as a fundamental dynamic in our longing for intimacy and in our destiny to communion. I see it basic to the divine-human connection and one of the great arenas for celebrating the source of life itself.

Thus, not only do men's bodies give shape to their perceptions of the ultimate, men's gods also shape and potentially transform their body understandings. That conviction is also amply illustrated in these essays—in some of them explicitly, in others more implicitly. While the accents vary, the writers commonly employ social constructionist perspectives that emphasize our active role as social beings in shaping our body meanings. Even the two contributors who are fairly indebted to the mythopoetic men's movement eschew the strong essentialism and assumptions of intrinsic body meanings that characterize much in that movement.

Social constructionism is a hopeful posture, and this is a hopeful volume. It is filled with a variety of claims that men's bodies do not have to be "that way." Men's bodies are not fated to be controlling, violent, radically individuated, preoccupied with phallic values, racist, armored, mechanistic, or disconnected from close male friendship. Men's bodies can, indeed, become more fulfilling and life-giving to themselves, to others, and to the planet. Not only can they be transformed, but also they must. I see this moral commitment flowing through these pages. The contributors write not as disinterested observers of the male scene, but rather with personal investment and passion for change.

But change toward what? One major theological issue that runs through all of these essays, I believe, is *the call for an erotic transformation of men's bodies.* That call appears in a variety of ways. Men's need of and hunger for the erotic is obvious in Robin Hawley Gorsline's homoerotic reflections on the crucified Christ and in Scott Haldeman's celebration of masturbation as good news for the body. Eros is both evident and problematic in the longing for male friendship that both Philip Culbertson and William G. Doty explore. It is there in Lewis R. Gordon's description of the male body's openness and vulnerability necessary for worship. It is present in Björn Krondorfer's struggles with vulnerability in male body autobiographies. Doty's second essay raises intriguing questions about the erotic physicality of male nakedness in current popular culture. So also, David Morgan's exploration of the popular religious art depicting Jesus is infused with issues of male homoeroticism, both in its attractiveness and in the fears that such eroticism engenders. Michael L. Stemmeler's liberating anger for an empowered gay religious identity is fueled by eros, as is Garth Baker-Fletcher's anger as he analyzes the distorted eros in white racist constructions of African American male identity. The two remaining contributors, Tom F. Driver and Seth Mirsky, identify particular issues surrounding eros on which I want to comment. Driver's autobiographical essay identifies the erotic distortions of male narcissism that have produced an image of a self-made God demanding our absolute allegiance and worship. As he faces his own mortality, Driver also movingly explores a man's erotic hunger for the incarnate hands of God. Mirsky writes a strong critique of reactionary essentialist masculinities whose politics preclude feminist agendas. His argument, as I read him, leads to the question, what are the erotics of gender justice? I shall attempt to connect these issues, for I believe they are germane to the erotic questions raised by all of the other contributors.

Since it seems evident to all these writers that we men have not been well-conditioned to embrace eros, a few background comments about men, eros, and the sacred are in order.[1] Embracing eros is, of course, significantly different from prizing the virility and genital sex that typically mark traditional masculinity. "Real men" prize sex, but find eros foreign. We learned our formative lessons about manhood by cutting the erotic mother bonds and identifying ourselves over against anything suggesting the feminine, including gayness. Hence, those aspiring to manhood learn to devalue eros—the dimension of love that knows hunger, need, desire, passion, sensuality, and the yearning for fulfilling connections. Instead, we learn self-sufficiency and the rational control of all things bodily, qualities deemed much more appropriate to Western masculine spirituality.

Eros makes men anxious about their deepest bodily feelings. It also makes religious men anxious because it raises fundamental questions about the theologies men have written and believed to be true. Our primal experience of identity through separation has buttressed the religious belief in God's absoluteness and otherness. In such a view, divine perfection means completeness. God is never needy. Through the centuries patriarchal theology largely imaged God as unilateral, non-relational power, glorified by the weakness and dependency of humanity, deficient in the erotic power of mutuality. That tendency, in turn, is directly related to the phallic focus of masculine identity and hence masculine spirituality. The phallus, the prized male erection, is taken as the quintessential symbol of manliness, and the idealized phallus is big, hard, and up. So we have accented those values in the divine. God, too, must be big, hard, and up: sovereign in power, righteous in judgment, the transcendent Other. We have lost the body revelation of the sacred that might come through our genital softness and vulnerability, experiences as male as the phallic.

But it is threatening to live with a God so imaged. Thus masculinized theology compensated by attributing to the divine a one-sided and unilateral love. Divine love, the model for proper human love, became sheer agape—sacrificial self-giving. While there is important truth here, half truth taken as the entire reality becomes distorted. So, our theologies cheapened, devalued, even vilified the erotic and relegated it to the pornographic. Eros was characterized as egocentrism, selfish, narcissistic, and regrettably self-loving. Hunger, desire, passion, and yearning for fulfillment were banished as inappropriate to spirituality.

The problem with such spirituality is not only that it disconnects us from our own bodies, it also disconnects us from the neighbor and from our passion for justice. If we cannot feel the power of our own bodily life, we cannot feel the bodily reality of social violence, racism, poverty, or environmental abuse. The power of our moral agency in the world is diminished.

Patriarchal religion's concern for controlling the body has thus been manifest in the control and suppression of eros. The dualistic split between spirit and body has become the split between agape and eros, and hence the split between person and society. In all of this a *complementarity gender theory* has played a major role.[2]

The complementarity theory is a major expression of sexual essentialism. It endorses an essential feminine nature and an essential masculine nature, two elements presumably needing each other for human completion and wholeness. In both Jewish and Christian traditions, such gender complementarity most often has been viewed as divinely ordained, given in the very nature of creation. Males and females are seen as incomplete without the other sex, and the resultant sexual ethic requires permanent, monogamous, heterosexual marriage with genital sex permissible only therein.

The connection with classic spirit-body dualism is evident. Males have identified themselves as more essentially rational and spiritual, hence capable of agape. Men have identified the female as more essentially bodily, hence erotic and in need of control. And when the complementarity assumption is combined with patriarchy, it inevitably devalues both women and all persons of homosexual orientation, establishing both sexism and heterosexism as normative. In consequence, it has the effect of eroticizing sexual control, domination, and violence by men. Emotional and often physical violence results when it is believed that romantic love is necessarily grounded in a male over female dominant/subordinate relationship, when control and power over the other are felt more pleasurable than mutuality and sharing.

The eroticism of men's control of women plays itself out in the assumption of a divinely ordained and hence compulsory heterosexuality. This, in turn eroticizes the oppression of gay, lesbian, and bisexual people. A lesbian women's very existence speaks a resounding *No* to the complementarity theory. Her existence is testimony to the fact that at least some women do not need men to complete them, and this might mean that none does. In a different way, the gay man challenges complementarity. Violating prescribed masculinity, he is identified with women ("the weaker sex") and is the appropriate object for other men's misogyny. Furthermore, the gay man is viewed as traitor. He does not invest his own eroticism in controlling the sexuality of women, hence has broken ranks with the men's cause.

The dynamics of homophobia are numerous and multi-faceted. But one thing seems sure: homophobia in straight-identified males (where it is typically strongest) is directly connected to the fear of losing the institution of compulsory heterosexuality and men's control of women. The threat, in short, is the loss not only of male power, but also—and importantly—of men's erotic pleasure.

Thus, the issue of erotic transformation is critical for men's bodies and men's gods. In one way or another the hope for that transformation seems evident throughout this book. And it is a hopeful book, for social constructionists know that our bodies are not fated. What is constructed can be reconstructed and transformed. In these comments I have discussed some connections I believe important for that process.

It is clear that men in our society typically experience erotic deprivation of a *certain* kind. The capacities both to feel and to feel the legitimacy of need, desire, sensuality, and yearning for mutuality and fulfillment are not our strong suit. Part of the explanation lies in the fact that our dominant social constructions of masculinity are founded on the experience of separation and breaking the erotic connection. Men's fashioning of a self-made God—big, hard, and up after the phallic pattern—reinforces the "normalcy" of our erotic condition. But such deity is difficult to live with, and so the attribution of a one-sided agapaic love to that sovereign power functions to reassure us.

The notion of a God who demands our submission further reinforces the eroticization of dominance and control in men. Thus, it is not that we are bereft of the erotic. More accurately, male eroticism has been largely shaped around the pleasures of dominance and control.

We need erotic transformations both in our bodies and in our notions of the sacred. It is difficult for me to see how one will come apart from the other. Part of the transformative work is theoretical—and this book contributes to that process. Our alliance with pioneering religious feminists and with creative gay and lesbian liberationists in recovering and re-imagining alternative images of the divine is critically important. But theory and praxis must go together. So, an inescapable part of the transformative process is hard political work for the sexual justice that will change religious and societal structures to nurture the hunger for life, not suppress it. The process may yet allow men's hands and men's bodies better to incarnate the hands and body of God. And that will be more erotic pleasure for us all.

NOTES

1. See my "On Doing Body Theology" (1995) for an elaboration of these themes. Also, Nelson 1988 (especially chapter 5). A different but suggestive approach is taken by Eilberg-Schwartz (1994).
2. Anne Bathurst Gilson, *Eros Breaking Free* (1995) is an excellent and thorough treatment of the problems involved in the complementary theory. I am indebted to her insights.

REFERENCES

Eilberg-Schwartz, Howard. 1994. *God's Phallus: And Other Problems for Men and Monotheism.* Boston: Beacon.
Fischer, Seymour. 1986. *Development and Structure of the Body Image.* Vol. 2. Hillsdale, N.J.: Lawrence Erlbaum.
Gilson, Anne Bathurst. 1995. *Eros Breaking Free: Interpreting Sexual Theo-Ethics.* Cleveland: Pilgrim Press.
Nelson, James. 1988. *The Intimate Connection: Male Sexuality and Masculine Spirituality.* Philadelphia: Westminster Press.
———. 1992. *Body Theology.* Louisville, Ky.: Westminster/John Knox Press.
———. 1995. "On Doing Body Theology." *Theology & Sexuality* 2 (Spring).

Index

ACT UP, 136
Adam and Eve, 239, 249 nn. 7, 8
Adiaphoria, 6
African American men, 18, 65–68, 75, 79, 83, 89–92, 133, 271, 301 n. 8; male body, 17, 65–68, 71, 73, 78–90. See also Black Christ; Black theology; Racism
Africentricity, 66, 89
Agape, 165–66, 176 n. 7, 316
AIDS, 16, 97, 100, 105, 135, 141, 188, 217, 294
Androcentric, 14
Androgynous, 5, 8–9; body, 229–30
Antony, Saint, 208
Anus, 220, 226–31
Anus mundi, 225, 231
Archetype, 14–17, 23, 76, 195; archetypal, 193, 224, 226
Aristotle, 154, 158, 215
Arnold, Patrick, 13–14, 192
Artaud, Antonin, 209
Asceticism, 6–8, 207–8, 230; ascetic practice, 6; ascetic control, 209
Ataraxia, 284
Augustine, 7, 21–22, 151, 154–55, 165,

207–11, 213, 217–20, 223–25, 249 nn. 7, 8
Azurara, Gomes Eannes de, 66–68

Bacon, Francis, 288–89, 299
Bal, Mieke, 285, 290
Baldwin, James, 143
Barstow, Anne, 57–60
Barton, Bruce, 258–60
Basil of Caesarea, 163. See also Gregory of Nazianzus
Beauvoir, Simone de, 27–28, 238
Bersani, Leo, 268, 282, 294
Bibb, Henry, 69–70
Bi-sexual, 95, 126, 136, 163, 316
Black body. See African American men
Black Christ, 132–34, 142. See also Suffering Servant
Black clown. See Sambo
Black theology, 134, 137, 142. See also Cone, James H.; Womanist
Bly, Robert, 14, 34–35, 192, 224, 282
Body: as container of soul, 67; excretes, 8, 11, 15, 226, 230–31; fluids, 8, 226; grotesque, 222; memory, 139–40, 142; politic, 68; as temple, 226. See also Christ,

Body (*Continued*)
  body of; Jesus, body of; Nudity; Semen;
  Sexuality
Bodybuilding (bodybuilder), 283, 287,
  292–93, 297, 299, 302 n. 12
Body-mind (-spirit/-soul) dualism, 6, 165,
  208, 249 n. 4, 296, 311–12, 316.
Body theology. *See* Theology
Boyd, Malcolm, 100
Breast, 8, 240, 255, 278, 298. *See also*
  Nipple
Broughton, James, 229–31
Butler, Judith, 31, 248

Calvin, 10
Cassian, John, 173–74
Castration, 7, 164, 286, 297
Çatal Hüyuk, 57–58
Celibacy, 6–7, 9–11, 14, 135, 224; celibate
  clergy, 8, 11; celibate male psyche, 220
Christ, 6, 77–78, 83, 86–87, 126, 138,
  174, 292; asexuality of, 8; body of, 7,
  19–20, 138; disembodied, 165; as friend,
  251; maleness/masculinity of, 5, 167,
  252, 263; nakedness of, 292, 304 n. 19;
  virility of, 258, 260–61. *See also* Black
  Christ; Friendship; *Imitatio Christi;*
  Jesus
Christ, Carol, 43, 57
Christian household, 6–8
Christology, 78, 126, 251, 255; of friend-
  ship, 251, 255
Cicero, 151–52
Clark, Michael, 101, 105
Coitus reservatus, 9, 11
Coleridge, Samuel Taylor, 166–67
Competitiveness (competition), 54–55,
  185–88, 294
Concupiscentia, 225
Cone, James H., 132–34. *See also* Black
  theology
Continence, 5, 8, 163. *See also* Celibacy
Copula sicca, 9
Corpse, as different from body, 238
Crucifixion, 126, 136–44, 216
Crying Game, 241–42

Daly, Mary, 29
Defecation (defecating), 15, 226–29

Desire, 7, 11–12, 48, 116–17, 122, 125–
  32, 134–35, 139, 142, 208–9, 217, 223–
  24, 239, 246, 285, 315, 317
Divorce, 59
Dollimore, Jonathan, 131–32
Driver, Tom, 117, 216–20, 226
Du Bois, Cora, 169
Dutton, Kenneth R., 268, 274, 280, 283,
  294, 298

Effeminacy (effeminate), 167, 176 n. 8,
  251, 258, 260
Ejaculation (ejaculate), 15, 115, 212
Emerson, Ralph Waldo, 155, 167
Emission (nocturnal), 7
Encratites, 5–6
Epicurus, 169
Erection, 118, 217, 291, 315. *See also* Pe-
  nis; Phallus
Erotic, 117, 119–22, 126, 130–31, 159,
  182, 188–89, 222, 229–30, 236, 253,
  255, 278, 285, 287, 314–18. *See also*
  Homoeroticism
Eroticism, 18, 53, 187, 279, 291, 316–17;
  sado-masochistic, 20, 128. *See also* Ho-
  moeroticism; Sensuality
Eucharist, 5
Eurocentric, 49, 67, 89

Fanon, Frantz, 241, 246
Farajajé-Jones, Elias, 137
Feminism, 13, 27–36, 47, 58–60, 171,
  197, 225; feminist(s), 3, 12–13, 16–17,
  57, 123 n. 2, 127, 183, 192, 287, 312,
  317
Feminist theologian, 36, 37 n. 8, 126. *See
  also* Womanist
Food, 6, 239; spiritual feeding, 8
Foster, Guy-Mark, 129
Foucault, Michel, 90
Freedberg, David, 269, 274–76
Freud, Sigmund, 74, 241, 285
Friendship, 20–22, 125, 142, 149–75,
  181–99, 255, 261, 313; between Achilles
  and Patroklos, 194; with Christ, 255; between Gilgamesh and Enkidu, 194; between Gregory of Nazianzus and Basil,
  154, 157–58, 173, 175; with Jesus, 253,
  255; between Jonathan and David, 150–

51, 162, 171, 225. *See also* Christ, as friend; Jesus, as friend; Theology, of friendship

Gay: gaze, 286; liberation, 189, 312; men (people), 94–106, 121, 126–36, 139–40, 278, 316–17; porn, 121, 281; religious identity, 18, 94–106; sexuality, 258. *See also* Homophobia; Homosexual; Homosexuality; Queer(ness)
Gay theology, 101, 131. *See also* Spirituality; Suffering Servant; Theology
Gender, 31, 116, 285, 287, 314, 316; difference, 33; as different from sex, 27, 29; discrimination, 89; equality, 5, 14, 120–23; formation, 50; identity, 31, 34, 240, 242, 248; ideology, 14, 29, 121; role, 174, 183, 248; theory, 316; transgressor, 3, 9; variance, 5, 8, 14. *See also* Transgender
Genital, 191, 279; act, 163–64, 314, 316; component, 189; sex, 136, 294; softness, 315; stimulation, 115
Genitalia (male) 4, 230, 244, 272, 274, 291–92. *See also* Penis; Phallus
Gerzon, Mark, 195–96
Gnostic(s), 5, 6, 19, 226
God, 63–64, 77–79, 84, 101, 104–5, 112, 117, 119, 122, 135, 141, 151, 155, 158, 163, 168, 172, 174, 208–11, 216–20, 226–28, 231, 235–36, 239–40, 243–47, 255, 257, 261, 311, 315–58; as male Father, 257; maleness of, 51–52, 55, 57–58, 244. *See also* Yahweh
Great Awakening, 69
Gregory of Nazianzus, 154, 157–58, 173, 175
Grotesque body. *See* Body
Grotowski, Jerzy, 209

Hay, Harry, 103–4
Henry, John (legend of), 18, 66, 76–79, 90
Heterosexism, 28, 32, 96, 99, 102–3, 129, 132, 316
Heterosexual, 20, 34, 59, 61, 96–97, 102, 104, 132, 150, 161, 164, 170, 226–27, 231, 241, 316; majority, 97–98, 100
Heterosexuality, 59–61, 188, 288, 316–17
Heyward, Carter, 98, 102, 105, 142

High John de Conquer, 18, 66, 79–83, 90–91
Hofmann, Heinrich, 261
"Holy actor", 209
Homoeroticism, 20, 22–23, 132; homoerotic, 22, 236, 241, 248, 251, 253, 275, 287, 314
Homophobia, 32, 54, 103, 116–17, 136, 160–61, 163, 188, 192, 248, 282, 317; homophobic, 3, 18, 20, 60, 101, 139, 226, 258
Homo religiosus, 3
Homosexual, 19, 97, 99, 139, 150–51, 160, 188, 194, 243, 251, 316. *See also* Gay; Queer(ness)
Homosexuality, 54, 116, 132, 162–64, 167, 171; as mortal sin, 164. *See also* Gay; Queer(ness); Same sex
Homosociality, 158–61, 168, 170
Hughes, Thomas, 167, 176 n. 9
Hurston, Zora Neale, 79–80, 82–83
Hypermasculinity, 283

Iconography, of male body, 267–300
Imitatio Christi, 7, 292
Intimacy, 20, 22, 119–20, 136, 157, 159, 161, 164, 169–71, 173–74, 185, 187–88, 208, 219–21, 238, 253, 313; discourse on, 15, 220, 222; male, 21, 150, 211–16, 223

Jesus, 51, 78, 80, 84, 125–26, 128–44, 251, 259, 260–61, 263, 291; body of, 125–27, 135–36, 142–43, 226, 257; feminization of, 259; as friend, 253; in Gospel of Thomas, 6; as lover, 20, 129, 131, 135; masculinity of, 8, 22, 51, 126, 135, 251–52, 257–58, 260; in popular art, 22, 251–63; queer, 135–38. *See also* Christ; Friendship; Suffering Servant
Jung, C. G., 227

Kaufman, Michael, 29, 34
Keen, Sam, 13–14, 225, 231, 276
Kundera, Milan, 228

Lee, John H., 221, 224
Leiris, Michel, 22, 209–12, 214–17, 220–23

Lejeune, Philippe, 214, 222
Lewis, C. S., 164, 171–72
Liberation, 87–88, 92, 100–102, 173, 192
Liberation theology, 20, 104, 123, 128, 132–36, 138, 142, 173
Linga, 9. *See also* Phallus
Lorde, Audre, 119, 126, 128
Luther, Martin, 10, 217, 226, 231

Machismo, 186
Malcolm X, 89, 92
Male-centered, 46, 53, 59
Male mystique, 48
Manichaeism, 238, 249 n. 7
Mapplethorpe, Robert, 299, 301n. 8
Marriage, 8, 10–11, 21, 59, 97, 158–59, 161, 164–65, 173–74, 184, 196, 316
Masculine (male) identity, 113–14, 235–36, 248
Masculinity, 12, 14, 16, 27–36, 45–56, 60, 84, 89, 91, 114, 161, 182–84, 190–95, 197, 218, 224, 235, 240–41, 247, 257, 261, 269, 274, 282, 289–90, 293, 299, 315–57; discourse on, 29; hegemonic, 28, 30; pro-feminist, 174
Masturbation, 16, 19, 111–23, 217, 222
Men's movement, 30, 33–34, 150, 161, 168–71, 183, 197, 282, 297; mythopoetic, 12–14, 17, 21, 34–35, 192, 224, 313. *See also* Radical Faery Movement
Miles, Margaret, 130–31, 138–39
Miller, Stuart, 184–85, 187–88, 190
Miller, Tim (performance artist), 128, 139
Millett, Kate, 58–59
Misogyny, 6, 120, 192, 225, 248, 316; misogynist, 4, 13, 214, 239, 241
Mulvey, Laura, 286
"Muscular Christianity", 21, 166–68, 300 n. 3
Myth(ology), 181–99, 280
Mythopoetic. *See* Men's movement

Narcissism, 56, 194, 283; divine, 52; male, 54, 56, 59; masturbatory, 230; negative, 215
Narcissistic, 47, 55, 206–7, 224–25, 231, 285, 315
Narcissus, 194

Nelson, James, 15, 19, 61, 113–14, 119, 293, 296
Nipple, 8, 222, 229–30. *See also* Breast
Nudity, 269, 275; eschatological, 269; gratuitous, 269; male, 272, 275

Orgasm, 111, 115, 118, 131, 283
Ostentatio genitalium, 4, 291
Owens, Craig, 285–86

Patriarchal: culture, 286; domination, 11, 142; family, 10; household, 6; image, 19, 122, 196; neo-, 14; norm, 121; post-, 269; power, 9, 13, 102; religion, 16, 316; society, 29, 103; tradition, 207
Patriarchy, 28, 47, 52, 58, 60, 140, 142, 183, 297–98, 312, 316
Pederast, 162, 213–14
Penis, 6–8, 11–12, 23, 73, 75, 115–58, 121, 136, 226, 229–30, 244, 271, 279, 283, 298–99; absent, 9. *See also* Genitalia
Phallic, 295, 297, 299, 313, 317; erection, 217; experience, 118; image, 275
Phallocentric, 6, 15, 282, 289–90; post-, 23, 290
Phallus, 7–8, 12, 15, 118, 229–30, 240–42, 244, 248, 279, 283, 293, 298, 301 n. 8, 315; God's, 228; as *mysterium tremendum,* 118; as weapon, 116. *See also* Linga
Phibionites, 19
Pitt-Rivers, Julian, 149–50
Plato, 48, 158
Pleasure, 10, 113, 115–17, 120, 122–23, 140–41, 208–9, 219, 221, 223, 225–28, 286, 317–18
Pornographic, 19, 279, 315; image, 12, 120–21, 131; imagination, 223
Pornography, 116, 120–22, 123 n. 2, 275, 278. *See also* Gay, porn
Post-modern(ism), 183, 198 n. 2, 219, 284–85, 291, 294
Prostitution, 164
Puritanism, 19

Queer(ness), 18, 97, 100, 128, 135–37, 139–42. *See also* Gay; Homosexuality; Radical Faery Movement
Queer theology. *See* Theology

Racism, 14, 22, 73, 76, 90, 127, 241–42, 245, 248, 294, 316
Radical Faery Movement, 104, 106, 128. *See also* Queer(ness)
Rape, 71, 116, 137
Redemption, 6, 86, 211, 218, 229, 301 n. 3. *See also* Salvation
Reformation, 10–11
Repression (sexual), 113, 117, 120, 122, 229, 275
Resurrection, 78–79, 118, 216, 301 n. 3
Ritual, 36, 230, 244, 248; of friendship, 190; masturbation as, 122; of self-love, 119
Rousseau, Jean-Jacques, 212–14, 220

Sallman, Warner, 8, 22, 51, 251–52, 257–61, 263
Salvation, 67, 138, 144, 216–19, 245, 261. *See also* Redemption
Sambo, 66, 71–76, 90
Same sex, 94–96, 163–64. *See also* Homosexuality
Sartre, Jean-Paul, 236–40, 242, 245–46
Scopophilia, 286. *See also* Voyeurism
Sedgwick, Eve Kosofsky, 130, 132, 159–60, 278
Seed (male), 9, 113. *See also* Semen
Segal, Lynne, 192
Semen, 6, 19, 239. *See also* Seed
Sensuality, 18, 278, 313, 315, 317. *See also* Eroticism
Sexism, 12, 14, 28, 44, 61, 294, 316
Sexuality, 6, 10, 46–47, 53, 59–61, 73, 75, 101, 104–5, 114–18, 120–21, 135, 171, 194, 217, 223, 258, 283, 288, 293–94, 312–13, 317; discourse on, 15; renunciation of, 7
Sexual orientation, 15, 94–95, 97, 106, 114, 313
Shame, 6, 113, 115, 117, 215, 223, 226, 228–30, 291
Slavery, 65–70, 74, 81–83, 87–89
Slaves, 65, 69–72, 80–88, 91
Sodomy law, 95
Solipsism, 208, 210, 216, 231. *See also* Narcissism
Sontag, Susan, 215, 221
Spirituality, 117–19, 208, 218, 230, 298,

315; based on bodily experience, 117; embodied, 18, 36, 227, 230; feminist, 36; friendship as, 173, 253; gay, 18, 20, 98–99, 100, 102–3, 106; male (masculine) 8, 12–15, 21, 28, 35–36, 192, 225, 298, 315; spiritual possibility of body, 209, 230
Starhawk, 37 n. 8
Steinberg, Leo, 4, 272, 278–79, 291–92, 300, 303 n. 19
Stoltenberg, John, 36 n. 2, 55, 121
Suffering Servant: black, 77–78, 133; gay people as, 10
Synesius of Cyrene, 166

Theological: construction of masculinity, 126; gendered discourse, 251; justification of enslavement, 66–67, 69; position of omnipotence, 211
Theology, 161–62, 315; of authenticity, 235; "bathtub", 216–18; body, 311–12; of friendship, 164; of heterosexuality, 59, 61; male-centered, 59; phallocentric, 15; queer, 20, 142; of relationship, 60. *See also* Black theology; Feminist theologian; Gay theology; Liberation theology; Womanist
Theopraxis, 101
Transcendence, 210, 237, 247, 293, 315
Transgender, 126–27, 133, 136
Transvestite, 241
Trickster, 73–74, 81
Turner, Nat, 18, 66, 83–88, 92
Twain, Mark, 112–13, 123

Valentinus, 226
Violence, 28, 92, 116, 126–27, 129, 137, 139–40, 142, 274, 316; against women, 36, 116, 121, 123. *See also* Rape
Virginity, 8, 71, 224
Virility (male), 7, 167, 225, 258, 260–61, 292, 314; of Christ, 258, 260–61
Voyeurism, 215, 286–87. See also *Scopophilia*

Wahba, Rachel, 99
West, Cornel, 242
Womanist, 93 n. 4, 126–27, (black women theologians), 245

Women: as body, 4; as commodity, 159; control of, 317; degradation of, 121; movement, 44; nature of, 8; oppression of, 28; ordination of, 5, 10–11. *See also* Violence

Wound (woundedness), 217–22, 224–25;

wounded healer, 100; wounded man, 13, 221; wounded nature, 106

Yahweh, 239–40, 243–44. *See also* God

Yeskel, Felice, 100